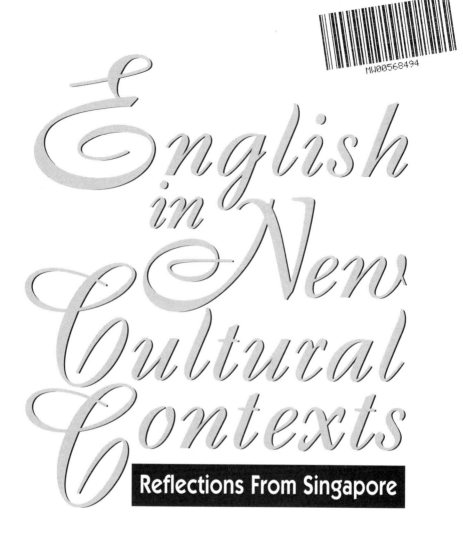

English in New Cultural Contexts

Reflections From Singapore

J. A. Foley • T. Kandiah • Bao Zhiming
A. F. Gupta • L. Alsagoff • Ho Chee Lick
L. Wee • I. S. Talib • W. Bokhorst-Heng

SINGAPORE
INSTITUTE OF
MANAGEMENT

OXFORD
UNIVERSITY
PRESS
SINGAPORE

Oxford University Press

Oxford   New York
Athens   Auckland   Bangkok   Bombay
Calcutta   Cape Town   Dar es Salaam   Delhi
Florence   Hong Kong   Istanbul   Karachi
Kuala Lumpur   Madras   Madrid   Melbourne
Mexico City   Nairobi   Paris   Singapore
Taipei   Tokyo   Toronto

and associated companies in
Berlin   Ibadan

Oxford is a trade mark of Oxford University Press

© Oxford University Press 1998
First published 1998

ISBN 0 19 588415 9

Printed by Kin Keong Printing Co. Pte. Ltd.,
Published by Oxford University Press Pte. Ltd.,
37 Jalan Pemimpin, #03-03 Union Industrial Building, Block A, Singapore 577177

A Note to the Reader

The Singapore Institute of Management (SIM) is an independent, not-for-profit professional organization founded in 1964, with the mission of helping to enhance managerial and organizational effectiveness in Singapore. Over its 34 years of development, SIM has expanded its role and scope beyond management development. Today, it is the leading private human resource developer in Singapore, providing training and education opportunities for working adults across a wide spectrum of industries.

The institute is widely credited for its experience in organizing part-time further education programmes for a broad cross-section of the working adult population. It is recognized for its strong affiliations with prestigious universities and institutions, and its close links with industry.

In 1992, the Ministry of Education appointed SIM to run the Open University Degree Programme (OUDP) for Singaporeans. Run in collaboration with the UK Open University (UKOU), this programme is aimed at giving working adults opportunities for tertiary education and self-development.

Most of the OUDP courses are designed and developed by the UKOU. In order to meet the specific needs of Singapore learners, a small number of courses — especially those in the area of English language — are designed and developed by experts in Singapore.

One of these courses is EZS399 *English in New Cultural Contexts*. The course materials consist of a study guide, a collection of articles bound in the form of a Reader, an audio-cassette and a coursebook. This coursebook, *English in New Cultural Contexts: Reflections from Singapore*, has been specifically written as a set text. However, it is organized in such a way that it can also be read independently of the course.

Writers

Associate Professor Joseph A. Foley
Deputy Head, Department of English Language and Literature
National University of Singapore

Dr Thiru Kandiah
Senior Lecturer, Department of English Language and Literature
National University of Singapore

Dr Bao Zhiming
Senior Lecturer, Department of English Language and Literature
National University of Singapore

Dr Anthea Fraser Gupta
Lecturer, School of English
University of Leeds, United Kingdom

Dr Lubna Alsagoff
Head of Research and Development
Educom Pte Ltd, Singapore

Dr Ho Chee Lick
Lecturer, Department of English Language and Literature
National University of Singapore

Dr Lionel Wee
Lecturer, Department of English Language and Literature
National University of Singapore

Dr Ismail S. Talib
Senior Lecturer, Department of English Language and Literature
National University of Singapore

Ms Wendy Bokhorst-Heng
Part-time Lecturer, Department of English Language and Literature
National University of Singapore

Contents

Introduction

Throughout the history of the development of English, the sociolinguistic context has been changing constantly and there is little doubt that these changes were accelerated during the post-colonial period. The legacy of colonial Englishes has resulted in the existence of several transplanted varieties of English having distinct linguistic ecologies. These non-native varieties have, in turn, brought about changes in the native varieties of English and have also led to numerous sociolinguistic, linguistic and literary questions being asked (Kachru,1986). This present volume has as its aim to try to answer some of these questions by first positing a theoretical basis for the New Englishes, and by using Singapore English as an example of one path of development.

According to a British Council report (1997), the number of 15- to 24-year-olds speaking English as a first language is forecast to rise by 30% by the year 2050, with the numbers of Chinese, Russian, French and German speakers falling. It also predicts that on present trends this age group will have 65 million English speakers compared with 51 million now. China's vast population will still leave Chinese on top of the global league table, but with a drop from 201 million to 166 million in the number of young people using it as a first language. However, this report also warns that the spread of English may be reversed by political and cultural fashions. That is to say, the world 'may' turn against the English language, associating it with industrialization, destruction of cultures, infringement of basic human rights, global cultural imperialism and growing social equality.

Obviously, one of the reasons for such a large number of the world's youth learning English is because English is the worldwide lingua franca of much of modern-day technology and this is likely to increase with the growth of the Internet. However, this should not mean that English is to be consigned to the level of a technical language stripped of expressive and aesthetic characteristics and denuded of any critical or self-conscious dimension. The argument put forward in this volume is that the new varieties of English are expanding, allowing experience and culture to be 'read' not from the traditional metropolitan centres but from the peripheries, according neither the privilege of 'objectivity' nor the encumbrance of 'subjectivity'. The question is knowing *how* to read and not detaching this from the issue of knowing *what* to read. Languages are not finished objects and they create not only their own precedents, but their successors. Because English came from the West, it acquired world dominance and westerners have assumed the integrity and inviolability of their cultural masterpieces, scholarship and worlds of discourse (Said, 1993). Contrapuntal views on these masterpieces and this scholarship are possible through a world of discourse which uses as its tool of expression varieties of English other than that of the metropolitan sources. This, of course, brings in the question of *how* different — one of the major questions addressed in this volume. Cheshire wrote in 1991:

> Only a few centuries ago, the English language consisted of a collection of dialects spoken mainly by monolinguals and only within the shores of a small island. Now it includes such typologically distinct varieties as pidgins and creoles, 'new' Englishes, and a range of different standard and nonstandard varieties that are spoken on a regular basis in more than 60 different countries around the world...
> (Cheshire, 1991: 1)

If you consult a descriptive grammar of English such as Quirk *et al.* (1972), you might get the impression that English is relatively fixed, something unified and discrete. The emphasis is on commonality and plays down differences and the different ways the language is used in different English-speaking countries. Such usages are frequently taken as models for teaching and learning. Cheshire and others (like the writers in this volume) look at society in a broader framework. The discussion is about how English is used and what it means to its speakers in different contexts; the emphasis is on the diversity of English rather than on seeking a 'common core' (Graddol *et al.*).

With the recognition of diversity in English has come the insistence from many people on the validity of distinctively different Englishes. Verma has argued that Indian English is a valid linguistic system, on a par with other varieties of the language:

> Indian English is a self-contained system and follows its own set of rules. This system is closely related to the core grammar of English English. The Englishness of this socioregional dialect lies in the fact that its basic linguistic systems are the same as those of English English. Its Indianness lies in the fact that, within the overall general framework of the systems of English English, it displays certain distinguishing phonological, lexico-semantic, and also syntactic features. In terms of linguistic efficiency, these patterns are as good

as any other. They are not corrupt, but rather different forms of the
same language.   (Verma, 1982: 180)

The argument is not purely a linguistic one. English in India is used 'as
a vehicle of Indian culture to express culturally determined networks of
activities that are typically Indian' (Verma, 1982: 178). Clyne (1992) has
suggested that English can be regarded as a 'pluricentric' language, that is,
a language with several interacting centres, each providing a national variety
with at least some of its own codified norms.

Set against this is a fear that the spread of English will lead to its
disintegration: that it will develop into several mutually unintelligible
languages. Even those who believe that the need for international
communication will act as a brake on disintegration, have sometimes
expressed concern about the growing acceptance of distinct non-native
varieties of English. Quirk, for example, argued that non-native speakers
are well catered-for by 'a single monochrome standard that looks as good on
paper as it sounds in speech (Quirk, 1985: 6).

There is little doubt that what is needed is a comprehensive survey of
the new varieties of English, but that would be a considerable undertaking.
In many countries no official information is published about how English is
taught and how many people speak or write it, and very little academic
research is available on the nature of local variations in English structure
and use. This is not to demean the valuable progress which has taken place,
but many of the studies published in journals or chapters in books conclude
by stressing their programmatic character and drawing attention to the need
for in-depth descriptive or experimental research (Crystal, 1996). This
present volume is no exception, but there has been a growing body of
knowledge on Singapore English since the publication of Platt and Weber
in 1980. One of the main reasons for this was the establishment of a
department of English Language and Literature (including Theatre and Film
Studies) at the National University of Singapore. This is now one of the
largest departments of English Language and Literature in the
Commonwealth. Noticeably, this excludes the teaching of English Language
proficiency which is often a major function of English departments in other
parts of the world. In the intervening years since the publication of Platt
and Weber, a lot of research has been undertaken by members of the
department, including the establishment of a corpus of Singapore and
Malaysian English. A dictionary of Singapore and Malaysian English has
already been published (*Times-Chambers Essential English Dictionary*, 1997)
and a grammar is due in the near future.

However, it is also interesting to study the commonality of characteristics
in the sociolinguistic settings where these new varieties of English have

developed. For example, the setting is always in a bilingual or multilingual society, and therefore any study must look at the background of other languages. The status of English is also something that is always being called into question and consequently needs to be studied in its historical context. English may have been or still be the national language, an official language or one of the semi-official languages. However, where language is concerned nothing is static. In some nations English is spreading at the expense of local languages; in others, a local language has become the national language and taken over the place once occupied by English. In yet others, English has been replaced even as a main official language, but because of increased educational opportunities, more children than ever are acquiring it as their second language and its status is increasing again.

Kachru (1985) proposed a way of modelling this situation by his notion of the 'Three Circles of English', to help solve the problem of distinctions such as native and non-native, or first, second and foreign language, because they were 'functionally and linguistically questionable' (Kachru, 1992: 3). The question is: How useful are these distinctions? It has been suggested that perhaps the notion of the 'Three Circles' may be misleading and, indeed, devalue the accounts of the new varieties of English. This is essentially the argument put forward in this volume by Kandiah in his contributions entitled *Why New Englishes?* and *The Emergence of New Englishes*. There seem to be two general features that all varieties of English outside its original homeland share. One, related to the reason for the movement of the language from this homeland to the new environments in which these varieties have developed; the other, related to the demands made on the language to respond to the new environments. However, in the sociohistorical development of the new varieties of English, there is one major difference that sets them apart. The older varieties which were transplanted into new environments were used by settlers who already commanded the forms and usage as found in the home country. This ensured a fundamental continuity in the progression in the new environment, which was further secured by the fact that the mode of its transmission remained normal, with outsiders (other immigrants) fitting themselves into patterns of language use, maintenance and change determined by the original settlers. On the other hand, the new varieties were developed by new users, who initially had no acquaintance with the language and were separated by sociopolitical status from those from whom they had to learn it. That is to say, a very salient feature of the evolution of the new varieties was a certain discontinuity with what had gone before. The break was not absolute, as the colonial rulers made their standard of the language accessible to these new users, particularly through formal education, but what it did do was assign to this standard a presiding role within the evolution of the new varieties.

Bao, in his chapter on the *Theories of Language Genesis*, looks at two influential theories of pidgin and creole languages: the substratist approach and the universalist approach. At first these two approaches look to be diagonally opposed. However, Bao suggests that the real nature of pidginization and creolization lies somewhere in between: that there is a role of the substrate languages in the emergence of pidgins, and subsequently of creoles; at the same time recognizing the fact that pidgins and creoles, like other languages, do not violate the universal principles of language.

Gupta discusses *The Situation of English in Singapore*. She traces the sociohistorical development of English from the early nineteenth century to the present: how English came to Singapore, who uses English to whom and in what circumstances and how the use of English relates to the use of other languages. It is only by understanding the historical developments that we can see the effect these have had on the use of English and the linguistic features of Singapore English.

Alsagoff and Ho look at the features of language that make up *The Grammar of Singapore English*. They stress the importance of distinguishing between grammaticality and notions of what is socially or pedagogically correct. They claim there is a need to recognize the difference between Colloquial Singapore English and Standard Singapore English. When looking at the literature on Singapore English, they note a preponderance of comparisons between Singapore English and Standard British English, as well as between Singapore English and background languages such as Chinese and Malay. Although such comparisons are very useful, especially in pedagogical terms, in showing how Singapore English is different from British English, they can also be misleading in that they may not show the full picture and therefore detract from seeing Singapore English as having diglossic variation.

Bao, in a chapter on *The Sounds of Singapore English*, discusses the problem of investigating the phonology of a New English as an autonomous system to be studied in its own right. Most studies have looked at it from the perspective of Standard British or American English. In the first approach, the main benefit is that innovative and important sound patterns which do not exist in the more traditional forms of English, and which may be left unnoticed or dismissed as uninteresting, are given full cognizance. On the other hand, the second approach has the benefits of emphasizing the historical relationship between Standard English and the New Englishes, thus giving a convenient starting-point to study the changes that have taken place in each of the New Englishes. What Bao discusses is how to reconcile these two opposing views.

Wee investigates *The Lexicon of Singapore English* where a significant part of the lexicon consists of words borrowed from non-English languages. The presence of these non-English words often raises concerns such as: Can these words be legitimately considered as part of English? and: Can such a presence affect the intelligibility of Singapore English? Even recognizable English words such as *send* or *fellow* can be problematic because these words have undergone a change in meaning from what might be found in other varieties of English. In dealing with such questions a number of points have to be taken into consideration, for example, the educationalist would be interested in ensuring that learners actually acquire a variety of English that is maximally intelligible to English speakers worldwide. On the other hand, there is the question of national identity and solidarity to consider and what makes the Singapore variety of English distinctive, without always having to compare it with other varieties in some sort of normative process.

Ho and Alsagoff, in their chapter on *English as the Common Language in Multicultural Singapore*, focus on two major issues. The first is the common language status of English and its economic and political rationalization and the belief that Singapore depends upon English as a language of wider communication to survive in the global economy. This issue concerns Standard Singapore English as being ethnically neutral, but the ability to use it is a clear class marker. The inequality involved may be interpreted in a way that substantiates the belief in the 'necessity' of English for economic and social survival, and hence its linguistic and social domination. The second is to do with multiculturalism and the role of English in nation-building. English is seen as crucial to nation-building as it facilitates the exchange and sharing of diverse cultural perspectives among all the participating ethnic communities; however, it can also be seen as detrimental to the maintenance of this variety of cultures.

Foley, in his contributions on *Language in the Home* and *Language in the School*, looks at the relationship between language as a vehicle for learning and as a vehicle for thinking. This is seen as involving the move from common-sense knowledge of the home which may be established (and often is) in more than one language, to educational knowledge which, within the context of Singapore, is dominantly conveyed through English. The variety of English used in the home is the colloquial form while the formal school system is modelled around not Standard Singapore English but Standard British English. The question therefore has to be posed as to whether Singapore English in its diglossic variation can act as an effective communicative tool for the child's expanding knowledge. Essentially, the argument put here is that the expansion of a child's meaning potential is not simply a matter of constantly adding new options to existing subsystems, but rather involves the constant reconstrual of the system in the light of new linguistic experiences.

Talib deals with the problems of a *Singaporean Literature in English*. Since the majority of immigrants were of Asian descent and did not have English as their mother tongue, the cultural use of English as in the writing of literature was not readily accepted. This was apart from the other problem of English being the language of the British colonial masters. However, an alternative view could be taken, considering the colonial heritage and the legacy of English Language education that was left, as a fortuitous historical accident, rather than something entirely negative. The question now is not whether English should be used for the writing of literary works but whether the values that one imbibes are the values of one's own society as opposed to some alien value system. The argument over the use of the colloquial variety and a more standard form of Singapore English is often brought to the forefront in the hybrid art forms emerging in Singapore. Television, cinema and the Internet are providing new avenues for works in a more widely defined conception of 'literature'. With an increasingly 'borderless' world, it will become increasingly difficult to define what Singapore literature is.

The final contribution to this volume written by Bokhorst-Heng is on *Language Planning and Management in Singapore.* In spite of the linguistic diversity and complexity of the Singapore scene, there is no official language-planning body. However, any study of language in Singapore would have to highlight the sociopolitical nature of language planning; which means that, essentially, language planning is time- and society-specific. While the spread of English in Singapore can be seen largely as a result of deliberate government planning and policy, it cannot be said that all of the effects of this spread were planned. So what we often have is the management of these effects in the form of direct language policy measures with respect to the 'colloquial (Singlish) variety and more formal variety' debate and the 'relations with the mother tongues' issue. Effectively and politically, this means the spread and use of Mandarin. In multilingual Singapore, language diversity has been seen as an obstacle to nation-building in that language loyalty could lead to interethnic conflict when the functional status or sentimental value of one's own ethnic language is at stake. The pragmatic approach has characterized society in Singapore in its attitude towards language policy and management. It has allowed for flexible responses to changing social, economic and political conditions, such that language planning in Singapore represents a case of centralized planning without a central language planning agency (Kuo and Jernuud, 1994).

This volume, then, has three strands: firstly, there is a concern with general theoretical considerations on new varieties of English which consequently focusses on a specific case: the development of English in Singapore. Secondly, this development is looked at from the point of view of the structure of the language: the phonology, grammar and semantics. Lastly, the use and users are considered: Singapore English in a multicultural society, its place in the home and in the school, its role in literature, and how governmental policies have indirectly planned the development of English, now and in the future.

Joseph A. Foley
Singapore, November 1997

Chapter 1

Why New Englishes?

Thiru Kandiah

ঞ The Spread of English

At the beginning of the seventeenth century, the English language, it has been estimated, was used by some 5 to 7 million people. Almost all of these people lived in the British Isles (Crystal, 1995: 92). The estimates of those who use English today vary considerably, but are still dramatically different. Crystal (1994: 108-109) puts the figures at 377 million 'first language' users (of whom 57 million are users of English-based creoles or creolized pidgins) and 98 million 'second language' users, making a total of 475 million users. He also mentions that about 2 billion people — or about one-third of the world's population — 'are in theory routinely exposed to English'. Fishman and Conrad (1977: 6) make the figures at their time of writing 600 million, 300 million of whom use English as a 'first language' and the rest as an 'additional language'. Kachru's estimates range from 'a conservative figure of 700 million to 800 million to a rather liberal figure of two billion people', all of whom have 'some competence in English' (1992: 3).

ঞ Reasons for the Spread

Colonization

What could explain this phenomenal change in the circumstances of the language? It appears that there were two main reasons for it. The first was the driving force of colonization or empire. This was associated generally with political, commercial and religious motivations. It moved English away from its 'birthplace' and original home, England, and settled it in new places (Leith, 1996). Indeed, the movement of English under this colonizing impulse had begun even before the seventeenth century. It may be said to have begun with the conquest of Ireland (by the Anglo-Norman-speaking Henry II) in the twelfth century and the formal annexation of Wales by England in 1284. But it was mainly in Tudor times in the sixteenth century when the dominance of English over Irish, Gaelic and Welsh was irretrievably established. Shortly after, English began to move right across the globe. This took place with the more resolute inauguration of the 'empire on which the sun never sets' in the early seventeenth century.

The 'Global Village' and the Place of English within it

The second reason is related to the first. As the British Empire established itself and grew, it began to reconstitute the globe and make it into something different from what it had been. It did this through the gradual establishment of unprecedented global infrastructures in virtually all spheres of activity — trade, commerce, industry, military matters, diplomacy, communications, transport and travel, health, knowledge, entertainment...whatever. These infrastructures became the bases for the emergence of the inextricably interconnected world we now know; a world which we use the cliché, 'the global village', to describe. As might be expected, Britain had a claim to a somewhat special place within these emerging infrastructures in earlier times. The reason is that its empire was the most powerful among the several other European empires that also arose around the globe at about the same time. Subsequently, however, around the early twentieth century, America, a former colony which became the far stronger English-using daughter of the British Empire, went on to take over these infrastructures and, through them, wield its power virtually unchallenged across the globe. The result was not just that the English language reached right across the world, but also that its pre-eminent position was very firmly secured.

❧ *The Emergence of Differentiated Varieties of English*

Even before these various things happened, English had already become a highly differentiated linguistic entity while still in its original home. It had evolved from the speech of the Germanic settler tribes of the fifth to the seventh century and it reflected, in the different areas of England, the dialect differences that existed among these tribes. However, the developments described in the preceding paragraphs caused it to become even more differentiated, for they carried the language into new and unfamiliar contexts. These were, in general, marked by specific ecological, cultural, linguistic and other characteristics that were radically different from those of England. In the process, these developments added to English large new dimensions of historical and social experience. They drew it into unprecedented paths of historical development and placed it within social situations which were totally unlike any associated with its establishment and previous existence in the home country. Inevitably, therefore, as the language came to be used under these novel circumstances, it began to evolve distinct new features. These were of a kind that enabled it to meet the unfamiliar demands of communication, expression, action, interaction and so on that now began to be made on it. The result was that new varieties of the language began to emerge.

We can hardly expect, of course, that the resulting varieties would all be alike. The contexts out of which they arose differed considerably in their characteristics. What the language encountered in America, for instance, was as different as could be from what it encountered in India. Moreover, as we shall see below, the ways in which the language arrived and, subsequently, went on to settle and grow within such contexts were by no means uniform. As a consequence, there arose across the world a whole wide range of different varieties of English, which were distinguishable from each other in many significant ways.

The Need to Classify the Varieties of English and Clarify the Bases of Classification

Since there exist so many differentiated varieties of English across the world, we may quite naturally expect that there have been some attempts to classify them in various ways. Indeed, there do exist a large proliferation of labelled classifications of them. Among these are: first/second/foreign language; complementary/additional/auxiliary/other language; international/world language; mother tongue; native/non-native/nativized language; inner/outer/expanding circle variety; pidgin/creole; butler/babu/chee chee/broken language; interference variety; koine; old/new/third world English(es); English for general/specific/academic/occupational purposes; and so on.

Our concern in this book is with just one set of the varieties of English that exist across the world. Borrowing from the literature, we name this set New Englishes. Even as we do so, we must not allow ourselves to forget that, in an obvious sense, *all* varieties of the English language outside its original home, England, may rightly be considered to be 'new' Englishes. Yet, we select just one set of them for treatment under this rubric. In doing so, we (and the literature from which we draw) are, in effect, making a very definite claim. This is that there are principled reasons for separating just the varieties selected from other existing varieties and treating them as a distinct class. If we make such a claim, then in the interests of scholarly responsibility we are obliged to justify it. This we can do by clarifying as rigorously as possible the criteria which might provide a basis for the claim.

Regrettably, much of the current literature — which may be taken to define 'received or conventional wisdom' — in the field seems not to have taken this responsibility seriously enough. We search in it in vain for a clear and satisfactory account of what marks the field out and separates the varieties it draws into itself from the varieties it excludes. What we find too often instead are lists of forms, words and structures of New Englishes, which are accompanied by informal observations on and descriptions of them, some of these very good in their own right. The hope appears to be that all of this will of itself open out insights into the varieties under study, help explain their distinctive nature and self-evidently validate their classification together as New Englishes. This is a tendency which reflects a certain implicit belief about what scholarship entails — that what scholars primarily have to do is to empirically observe, list and describe forms, features and processes of the phenomenon under study. From such activity, then, insightful accounts of this phenomenon will in *some* way be straightforwardly derived, and these will explain all that needs to be explained.

Global developments in the realms of thought during the last few decades, however, have led to the emergence of a form of critical awareness which calls a great deal of this into fundamental question. Such developments are associated, among other things, with the appearance of critical theory, post-modern theory, post-structuralist theory and post-colonial theory. They have led us to recognize that the observations and descriptions we offer, as well as the labels we use for them, derive very much from underlying assumptions of a theoretical sort that we implicitly or explicitly make. In the case of phenomena which are socially embedded, these assumptions are also recognized to be ideologically vested. They express the self-enhancing interests and preoccupations of the groups who make them. All of this, in turn, goes with the recognition that it is just these assumptions, not some pre-existing reality, that determine the way in which the phenomena under scrutiny are seen, understood, classified and labelled. As Kress and Hodge put it, '...there is no "pure" act of perception, no seeing without thinking. We all interpret the flux of experience through means of interpretative schemata, initial expectations about the world, and priorities of interest. What we actually see is limited by where we look and what we focus on' (1979: 5).

Structural language study awoke to such recognitions a long time ago. Robert Lees, for instance, talking of Noam Chomsky's contribution to linguistic study, observes, 'There can be no data without a theory, no observation without some preoccupation' (1965: 22). Socially-oriented studies of language (which most certainly include the study of New Englishes) seem, on the other hand, to have been much slower in moving towards this realization, in spite of the very many things in their arenas of interest which would appear to make it inescapable (Parakrama, 1995; Singh, 1997; Kandiah, 1995).

The study of New Englishes makes the issue as transparent as it is inescapable. All such Englishes have their existence in former colonies which are engaged in tasks of post-colonial rehabilitation and reconstruction. The tasks are of vital concern to the lives of the users of the varieties and, also, to those of the compatriots among whom they live. They entail, among other things, contestation of and resistance to the hegemonic impositions of their previous colonial condition. This in turn involves the critical interrogation and examination by post-colonial peoples of the perspectives and understandings of their experience and reality that the previously dominant (Euro-American) centres had projected during colonial times. These reflected the concerns and interests of those centres and, generally, distorted the experience and reality of the subject peoples in ways that marginalized them as the insignificant 'Other'. (The 'Other', we might note, are those who get pushed to the unimportant margins by virtue of their differences from those at the 'Centre'. The differences are negatively measured and evaluated by norms determined at the Centre.) Such perspectives and understandings now began to be questioned on the basis of the valued concerns of the peoples involved.

Let us seek out the relevance of all this for the study of New Englishes. The 'received or conventional wisdom' in the field has emerged from Euro-American academic centres, even at times at the hands of post-colonials settled there. It is not too surprising, therefore, that that wisdom would reflect concerns, interests and perspectives which are very palatable to those who are comfortably ensconced in those centres. It would be equally unsurprising that a book like this one, which issues immediately out of a post-colonial context, might recognize that fact and want to question that wisdom from the point of view of what matters most to its occupants. The questioning has to be all the more searching because of the global pre-eminence that the language has been remarked above to have. This does not mean that the book will not introduce its readers to the conventional wisdom, at least in its basic outlines. The scholarly need to be aware of the historical evolution of the field alone makes that impossible. But the presentation of its features will not be done as if they display an incontestable and sacrosanct 'objective' characterization of what IS, so that nothing can be understood except by reference to them. Rather, it will be done in full recognition of the nature of the particular perspectives that that 'wisdom' is committed to and their often devaluing potential from the point of view of the actual users of New Englishes.

Three Frameworks for the Classification of Varieties of English

It would follow from the argument just presented that almost all of the labelled classifications of varieties of English mentioned earlier would raise issues which are relevant to an understanding of varieties of English around the world. Several of these issues will surface at various points below. But for the purposes of discussion, we focus our attention on the issues raised by what appear to us to be the three most significant of the classifications that have been proposed or assumed in the literature.

The Three Circles of English

The first, proposed by Kachru (1985), is based on a view of the spread of English across the globe in terms of three concentric circles: the inner circle, the outer (or extended) circle and the expanding circle, represented, after Crystal (1995: 107), as follows:

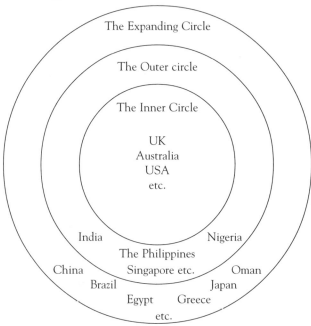

Figure 1. The Three Circles of English

The inner circle varieties of English are those used in countries which are 'the traditional bases of English — the regions where it is the primary language' (Kachru, 1985: 12) and which are 'dominated by the "mother tongue" varieties of the language' (Kachru, 1992: 3). Included here are the UK, the USA, Canada, Australia and New Zealand. The outer circle varieties are those used in regions which involve 'the earlier phases of the spread of English and its institutionalization in non-native contexts' (Kachru, 1985: 12) as 'an additional language' (Kachru, 1992: 3). Among the countries included here are India, Malaysia, Nigeria, Pakistan, the Philippines, Singapore and Sri Lanka. The varieties of English used in the expanding circle are termed 'performance varieties' (Kachru, 1985: 13). This circle comprises 'the rest of the world where English is used as the primary foreign language' (Kachru, 1992: 3), in 'recognition of the fact that English is an international language' (Kachru, 1985:13). It 'encompasses' the populations of such countries as China, Egypt, Greece, Indonesia, Israel, Japan, Korea, Saudi Arabia and Zimbabwe, among others (Kachru, 1985: 13).

The New Englishes that are the concern of this book are the varieties of English used in Kachru's outer or extended circle. However, we shall not in this chapter base ourselves on Kachru's concentric circles model. The reasons are, briefly, as follows. Kachru declares that he developed the model in an effort to escape from such distinctions as native/non-native, first/second/ foreign language and so on, which were 'functionally uninsightful and linguistically questionable' and lacked validity (1992: 3). But, as attested by the appearance of some of these very terms in the quotations from Kachru himself immediately above, he does not seem to have succeeded too well. And with the effective re-entry of such terms come in fact more than just uninsightfulness, but also misleading perspectives and unacceptable implications. As Kachru himself recognized in the words cited a moment ago, these lead to incorrect, and in the case of New Englishes, devaluing, accounts of the varieties.

There are other problems also with the scheme. It is not clear, for instance, that at the present moment in the history of the language in the world, much purpose can be served from the point of view of understanding global varieties of English by setting up an expanding circle. It is, in principle, conceivable that a case can be made for it, but then that case must be explicitly stated. Then there is the problem with the notion, 'traditional bases of English', when it is applied to such places as America, Australia, Canada, New Zealand and so on — in what way can these be considered 'traditional' bases? It only complicates the problem to define 'traditional' by equating it with the further notion, 'the regions where it is the primary language'.

Furthermore, there is the self-acknowledged inability of the scheme to handle English in South Africa and Jamaican English (Kachru, 1992: 3). In South Africa, this seems to be because the situation accommodates what is a New English *as well as* what we shall call below an Older (variety of) English. To complicate matters further, both of these are in competition with Afrikaans, a variety of another originally imperialist language in the same situation. In the case of Jamaican English, the difficulty seems to be partly because of the existence of what looks very like a highly complicated diglossic situation of sorts. In this situation, there is movement by the same users between what looks very much like a standard Older English for some purposes, and an indisputable creole for other purposes.

To turn to yet another problem, it is not entirely certain how English-based pidgins, creoles and decreolized varieties, such as Tok Pisin in Papua New Guinea, Krio in Sierra Leone, Hawaii English Creole and Black English Vernacular in the USA and Bislama in Vanuatu, may be accommodated within the scheme. This is an issue which those who apply the scheme never quite seem to address. In addition to these many problems, the scheme also appears to suffer from several other shortcomings, which might become clear as we go on.

We shall now present the framework we are going to adopt in this book. In doing so, we shall recognize that it is at present characterized very inexplicitly and that that creates certain problems, which we shall look at. We shall then move on to a characterization of it which, we hope, will put it on an acceptable basis.

New Englishes, Older Englishes and Pidgins/Creoles

The framework is one which in broad outline seems to be widely, if inexplicitly, subscribed to in the literature. In it, varieties of English across the world are seen as falling into three broadly distinct classes. Each class shares certain significant features even while accommodating considerable differences of various kinds among its members. We label the class which is the concern of this book 'New Englishes', simply because of the difficulty of finding a satisfactory term for them. We might recall that it includes all of those varieties which Kachru would include among his outer circle varieties.

We name the Englishes in the second class 'Older Englishes' by analogy with that term. In fact, though, some of them might even have shorter histories than certain of the New Englishes — for example, the Older English, Australian English 'got started' considerably after English arrived in India and began transforming itself into the New English, Indian English. For reasons that will become clear as we go on, 'English English', by which we mean the (highly variegated) English used in the original homeland, England, will be included among the Older Englishes. Alongside it will also be included, among others, the different forms of English that developed in adjacent territories (such as Wales, for instance) which England took control of in earlier times and incorporated politically to create the entity, Great Britain. The various forms of English used within this realm will all be taken to come under the more encompassing label, 'British English'. Included alongside English English among the Older Englishes is Scots, which survives in Scotland. This is because it had evolved from the language of one of the same groups of Germanic settlers from whose dialects English English evolved. These were the Angles, some of whom had, in the seventh century, moved from their original place of settlement in northern England to Scotland.

The third class comprises the various English-based pidgins, creoles and decreolized varieties mentioned earlier. It is necessary to observe that all of the labels given to the individual varieties listed within each class are labels of convenience. They must not be allowed to suggest that any of these varieties is a single, undifferentiated entity.

The following table sets down the classification we have described above, listing some of the more familiar varieties of English and also indicating the areas, and in some cases countries, of the world in which the varieties are based.

New Englishes	Older Englishes	(English-based) Pidgins, Creoles and Decreolized varieties

Africa
  Kenyan English
  Nigerian English
South Asia
  Indian English
  Lankan English
  Pakistani English
Southeast Asia
  Filipino English
  Malaysian English
  Singapore English
Etc.
	North America
	  American English
	  Canadian English
	Great Britain
	  English English
	  Scots
	Northern Ireland and
	the Republic of Ireland
	  Irish English
	Southern Indian and
	Pacific Oceans
	  Australian English
	  New Zealand English
	Etc.
		Africa
		  West African Pidgin
		Papua New Guinea
		  Tok Pisin
		Sierra Leone
		  Krio
		USA
		  Black English Vernacular
		  Hawaii English Creole
		Vanuatu
		  Bislama
		Etc.

Table 1. The Three Classes of Varieties of English

A More Traditional, Self-renewing Classification

The earliest responses to the new forms of English that were evolving across the globe would have found such a classification incomprehensible. They implicitly assumed a straightforward distinction between simply English as it was spoken in the 'home country', particularly in a standard form by those who mattered, and the rest of the emergent forms. The latter were seen as aberrant or 'broken' versions of the language which were most deplorably starting to develop outside of England. As time went on, and particularly as the twentieth century began to unfold, these responses began to give way to slightly more liberal ones. Even these, however, still maintained a version of the older two-way distinction. There was, on the one hand, English, which was now taken to include the varieties labelled 'Older Englishes' in the table; and then there were all those other, erroneous, 'broken' forms listed in the other two columns, which had no claim to be English. With broadening understandings of the realities of the world, this situation in turn began to change. The change was not a complete one, as shown by Prator's quite recent expression (1968) of the earlier approach, but it was enough to generate the classification represented in Table 1. Even here, though, as we shall see, the view that received expression in the earlier, two-way classification tends to smuggle itself back, albeit in a sophisticated, sanitized guise, to haunt the perceptions of scholars. Some of the discussion below, as well as in Chapter 3, will reveal how persistent this third classification is. It often makes a purportedly innocent reappearance in terms of a distinction between 'native' and 'non-native' English (see Kandiah, 1998, though).

ೋ *Searching for a Basis for the Classification Adopted: Current Characterizations*

As suggested earlier, the second classification, that represented by Table 1, seems to represent some kind of broad and often inexplicit consensus about varieties of English. That is the classification that we adopt in this book. The classification rests, of course, on the assumption that there are solid grounds for separating the varieties of English in the world into these three classes. Looking at this from the point of view of New Englishes, the unquestioning assumption seems to be as follows: the disparate varieties of English which we have elected to name 'New Englishes' do indeed collectively form a distinct class of linguistic objects; they are separated as a whole from other varieties of English on incontestable grounds and implicitly define a legitimate domain of academic inquiry in their own right.

The literature on New Englishes calls valuable attention to many considerations that are clearly salient to the classification. However, it has tended not to present them in the explicit, rigorous way that would allow us to derive from them convincing validation of the classification. Let us consider, for instance, Kachru's account of what he calls 'non-native' Englishes, as exemplified by Indian English and other South Asian varieties of English. Indian English, he states, is a 'nativized' variety of English, 'the result of the acculturation of a Western language in the linguistically and culturally pluralistic context of the sub-continent', which constitutes a 'new "unEnglish" linguistic and cultural setting' (1983: 1-2) in which it has been 'transplanted'.

Manifesting its acculturation in this alien context are the 'linguistic innovations' it shows. These represent 'deviations' from the norms of the language (1983: 2; 1982: 45). Such deviations are caused by the transfer of

Indian linguistic and cultural elements to English, which result in 'interference' with the language (1983: 100-102, 2, 66-67). Often, interference takes place because of interaction between the indigenous languages the users already command and the English language they acquire. In such a case it will be deemed to have taken place 'at the formal levels only' (1983: 66-67, 100-102).

Generally, though, there are functional motivations for this interference. These relate to the satisfaction of 'essential' 'pragmatic needs for appropriate language use in a new linguistic and cultural context' (1983: 2). There are four functions which call for particular mention: the *Instrumental* function (which 'implies the status given to English in the educational system'); the *Regulative* function (which 'entails the use of English in, for example, the legal system and administration'); the *Interpersonal* function (which 'provides a clue to how a non-native language is used as a *link* language...thus providing a code of communication for diverse linguistic and cultural groups'. 'In addition...English may also symbolize elitism, prestige and modernity'); and the *Imaginative/Innovative* function (which has resulted in the development of a large body of writing in English in different genres) (1981: 19-20).

The New Englishes that emerge in these ways are by no means homogeneous. They show variation corresponding with differences in geographical location, class membership, ethnolinguistic affiliation and so on (1983: 69-70). Nevertheless, they share several linguistic and other features in common. This suggests that they may perhaps all be brought together as a single class of structural objects. For instance, as far as grammar goes, African and South Asian varieties share the following features:

(a) There is tendency to use complex sentences.
(b) Selection restrictions are "violated" in *be-ing* constructions (e.g. use of *hear* and *see* in *I am hearing, I am seeing*).
(c) A "deviant" pattern appears in the use of articles.
(d) Reduplication is common (e.g. *small, small things, hot, hot tea*).
(e) Interrogatives are formed without changing the position of subject and auxiliary items (e.g. *What you would like to eat?*)

(Kachru, 1982: 46)

Presumably, it is such structural convergence among several New Englishes that leads Kachru to claim also that his outer circle (within which all New Englishes belong) 'forms a large speech community' (Kachru, 1985: 12).

There are several reasons why this account cannot provide the explicit and satisfactory basis for the classification of varieties that we are in search of. Crucial to the account is the alteration of the language in response to the functional demands made on it in the unfamiliar sociocultural contexts in which it had been transplanted. The problem is that not just New Englishes but *all* varieties of English outside of the home country had undergone similar processes of transportation, transplantation and adaptation. In the process, *all* of them had developed features and properties that rendered them adequate to the communicative, expressive and other needs of their users as they acted in and on their new contexts. Nevertheless, the term 'nativization' is applied only to New Englishes and not to Older Englishes outside of the home country. One consequence, as Singh (1994: 370) points out, is that 'One...talks about the Indianization or Africanization of English but generally not of its *"Americanization" or *"Canadianization" '. However, Kachru does recognize that the distinctness of even such Older Englishes 'developed for roughly the same reasons that are responsible for the nativization of other new varieties of English'. This allows him to talk of 'the processes of Americanization, Australianization, or Canadianization of the English language' as the settlers 'mould(ed)' the language to its new contexts (1983: 165, 166, 67). All of which raises a big question: if the processes of adaptation to new contexts are essentially shared by all varieties of English outside the home country, how can they become a basis for separating New Englishes from Older Englishes outside the home country?

There are further considerations of the same kind. Some of the discussion below will lead us to recognize that the descriptions above of the functions that New Englishes are called upon to perform are not very accurate or satisfactory. All languages anywhere in essence share the various functions and develop forms and so on as necessitated by them. This is not to say that a particular function will manifest itself in the same way everywhere. For instance, the regulative function might not in some contexts involve the use of the language in the legal and administrative spheres that Kachru talks of above. But that will not entail that the language does not perform some regulative function in those contexts. Similar comments may be made about the other functions. The conclusion is that no functional criteria can be found along these lines for separating New Englishes as a class from other varieties of English.

To complicate matters further, the notion of speech community which is invoked by the account to bring New Englishes together is a most unusual one, which it is difficult to give any substance to. This is a matter which will be further confirmed by the discussion of New English speech communities later in this book.

What appears to be the most promising of the differentiating factors mentioned in the account from the point of view of classification relates to the nature of the sociocultural settings in which English had been transplanted. Here, too, however, there are some difficulties. In all cases of English outside the home country, the settings in which it was transplanted were socioculturally different and unfamiliar. This raises the difficult issue of deciding where to draw the line in separating these settings into those which allowed the emergence of New Englishes and those which led to the emergence of new Older Englishes.

One crucial consideration here seems to relate to whether the settings were mono- or multi-linguistic/cultural. New Englishes arise typically in multilinguistic (and also multicultural) settings, within which English interacts with other indigenous languages (and the associated cultures) to emerge in its New English forms. As Kachru, talking just of the linguistic setting here, puts it (1985: 12), 'English is only one of two or more codes in the linguistic repertoire' of New English users. But this raises the question of whether the monolingual versus the bi-/multi-lingual nature of language users and their settings can validly be elevated to theoretical status in classifying varieties. Or, to put the question differently, can the language of monolinguals be distinguished from the language of bilinguals in a theoretically valid manner? The answer, from some of the things which will be said later in this chapter and in Chapter 2, appears to be 'no'.

There is a further related consideration. Almost all settings into which English moved from its original home country were initially significantly multi-linguistic/cultural. This means that if we are to explain how new Older Englishes emerged in some of these settings and New Englishes in others, it is not sufficient to talk simply of mono- or multi-linguistic/cultural settings. We need also to take into account significant differences in the patterns of sociohistorical development within the different areas of the colonized world. The reason is that it is presumably these which caused the areas to become differentiated from each other in ways that can explain the emergence of the two different kinds of English within them.

In spite of all such difficulties, there seems to be a firm assumption in the mainstream literature that the prolific catalogues of New English forms it supplies give us more than just examples of the adaptation of the language to its new contexts. It seems in addition to be assumed that these catalogues also, self-evidently, justify the separation of New Englishes from new Older Englishes. Since we are ourselves committed to the classification, we shall, in the rest of this chapter, explicitly draw out the considerations which appear to implicitly underlie the assumption, and examine whether, how and to what extent they provide principled support to the classification.

Three Approaches to the Search

The considerations themselves appear to reflect three fundamental dimensions of natural human languages, which involve three separate, if not unrelated, sets of issues: issues of language structure, issues of language genesis and issues relating to matters of context and sociohistorical development. We shall look at each of these in turn below, allowing the way they have actually been treated in the literature to determine some of the mechanics of the way we shall proceed. Thus, we shall discuss the structural issues mainly from the point of view of the attempt to distinguish New Englishes from Older Englishes, and the issues of language genesis mainly from the point of view of the attempt to distinguish New Englishes from pidgins/creoles. This does not, however, imply that we do not recognize that they are also salient to the class excluded in each case. The contextual and sociohistorical issues will, given the role assigned to them in the argument we are developing, involve all three classes.

A Structural Basis for the Classification?

Starting with the issues of structure, if Singh (1994; 1995) is correct, as we believe he essentially is, it would appear that they call into serious question the assumption on which Table 1 is based. Most of the literature on New Englishes does not, however, appear to recognize this. On the contrary, as mentioned above, it makes the assumption that the plentiful catalogues of New English linguistic features and properties it provides self-evidently play a major role in characterizing New Englishes as distinct *structural* entities. Thus it is entirely natural to expect our attention to be drawn to examples like (1), from Colloquial Singapore English (CSE). Such examples display structural characteristics which intuitively appear, because of their unfamiliarity to users of many other varieties of English, to be unique to the (sub-)varieties from which they come.

> (1) *Why so slow one? Wait, got no more, then you know.*
> 'Why are you taking so much time? If you delay any further, nothing will be left, and then you'll find out (the consequences).'

The words in this utterance function in certain distinctive, very literal, ways (the gloss, after all, metaphorically transforms the meaning directly expressed by the utterance). It shows other distinctive features too. Only one of its four underlying clauses specifies a subject noun phrase. There is no verb in the first clause which, moreover, ends with a distinctive element *one* (termed a 'nominalizer' in the literature). The weight of the whole second clause, a subordinate clause, is carried by a single verb *wait*. Mood and tense elements are not always explicitly specified. Such features and the particular ways in which they are packaged systematically together appear to uniquely define CSE. All varieties of any language show structural features and properties that mark them out in this way as distinct from other varieties of that language. Indeed, several of the chapters that follow in this book will examine further data of this kind that confirm that New Englishes are *individually* different from other varieties of English. That is, they are distinct varieties of the language defined by their own particular structural and other features and properties.

All of this is quite standard and unobjectionable. In practice in the study of New Englishes, however, such structural data are taken to define more than just varieties of the language that are individually different from other varieties of it. They are, in addition, implicitly deemed to define the varieties which they help establish in this manner *as New Englishes as such.* That is to say, they are regarded as, of their nature, providing a basis for taking New Englishes as a distinct class of structural objects. (See, for instance, the list of items (a) – (e) from Kachru 1982: 46, mentioned above.) This would only, of course, be possible on the basis of the following assumption: that structural features and properties of the kind that make up the data are of their nature qualitatively different from the structural features and properties of Older Englishes taken collectively, so that they uniquely define New Englishes. This in turn would make New Englishes qualitatively different structural objects from Older Englishes.

However, as Singh (1994; 1995), who first raised these issues, argues, there is something seriously wrong with this approach. As he points out, it is an empirical question whether the claims made for New Englishes and their features and properties in the preceding paragraph are correct or not. It is a question which, he goes on to say (1994: 294), can only be addressed by confronting with each other hypotheses of the following sort and structural data procured from all varieties of English:

1. There is no structural feature α such that all "non-native" varieties of English (= New Englishes) have α and no "native" variety (= Older English) does.
2. There is no structural feature β such that no "native" variety of English has β but some "non-native" varieties of English do.

Of the two hypotheses, the first is stronger, and if that turns out to be true it will also definitely be the case that the claims cannot be sustained. And, Singh points out, the evidence we presently have does appear to support it. The fact, surely, is that many of the structural features as well as associated rules and properties that are assumed by these claims to uniquely define New Englishes might also be found in at least some Older Englishes. An example he gives from his reading of the literature is the invariant tag feature which, far from being restricted to New Englishes like Indian English and Lankan English, is found also in the Older Englishes, American English and Canadian English. The only difference is the entirely unremarkable one that it is realized by means of different words or expressions in the four varieties, *isn't it* or *no* in Indian English and Lankan English, *OK* in American English and *eh* in Canadian English.

Other examples are forthcoming. Consider, for instance, the use of continuous aspectual forms rather than simple present or past tense forms which, for example, Indian English shows in sentences like:

(2) *I am thinking he is foolish.*

This is equally shared by, for instance, the Older English, Irish English. Similarly, the discharge of an entire clausal function by the verb in the second clause of the CSE utterance (1) is paralleled by both clauses in the sentence:

(3) *Waste not, want not*

used in many Englishes, New Englishes *and* Older Englishes. And, a structural analysis of (1) which goes beneath what we see on the surface will come out looking very much like an analysis of parallel utterances in many Englishes, New Englishes *and* Older Englishes, in several respects; for instance, in terms of the ability not to specify an overt subject noun phrase, the number of clauses involved, whether they are dependent or not, whether they relate to each other in a subordinative or coordinative fashion, and so on.

Note that the claim we are making is not that varieties of English are not structurally different from each other. This would make nonsense of the notion, 'varieties'. It is, rather, that there is no evidence at present that the structural differences among these varieties are of a *kind* that will allow New Englishes to be separated from the other classes listed in Table 1 as a distinct class of linguistic objects. This is not, of course, to deny that empirical research might just throw up some such evidence at some time. Nevertheless, in spite of the absence of such evidence at present, the literature persists in treating these differences as if they do lead to such a classification.

As Singh suggests, this is made possible only by the application to the structural data of a certain kind of procedure, one which judges the features of individual New Englishes by comparing them with the features of some Older English, generally a standard one. Having done so, it determines that what holds New Englishes together is that they all show features, however different these may be from each other, that are different from those of all Older Englishes. In other words, New Englishes form a separate class not because they share any specific defining structural features as such. Rather, it is because they are all structurally deviant forms of English, showing features that depart from the norms of what are presumed to be the true representatives of English, namely Older Englishes. This explains the surfeit of descriptions of New Englishes in terms of 'deviations' from or 'interference' with the norms of the Older Englishes, 'transfer' from outside the language, 'simplification', and so on (Görlach, 1988; Kachru, 1983; 1986; Kachru and Quirk, 1981; Platt and Weber, 1980; Thomason and Kaufman, 1988; Todd, 1984). Such descriptions provide some form of pseudostructural pretext for the near-uniform characterization of New Englishes as 'non-native' varieties, which are to be sharply distinguished from the 'native' varieties, namely the Older Englishes. It is only the latter that lend themselves to standard modes of linguistic description in which terms like 'deviation' and 'interference' have no place. Some of the literature describing these 'non-native' or 'interference' varieties (Kachru and Quirk, 1981: xv) use more transparent synonyms for such terms, namely 'errors' or 'mistakes' or 'aberrations' (Prator, 1968; Görlach, 1988: 194). These lay bare what such labelling and classification in fact represents: a reincarnation, in purportedly inoffensive guise, of the old two-way classification between (native) English and (non-native) non-English.

Chapter 3 will discuss the fundamental theoretical flaws in this entire approach. For the moment, we just need to note that, from a structural point of view, New Englishes are, essentially, linguistic entities of the same order as any other variety of English. In the process of their adaptation to their purposes within their contexts, they individually develop appropriate structural features and properties that will differentiate them from other varieties. Whatever differential structural features they thus develop, however, would be entirely comparable in *qualitative* terms to those that distinguish any two varieties of English or, for that matter, of any language. There simply do not appear to be any structural grounds for separating out the features that mark New Englishes for special and, as it happens, discriminatory treatment.

If, then, all the different varieties of English are entities of the same structural kind, the conclusion must be that there are no principled *structural* grounds in the present state of our knowledge for setting up a class known as New Englishes at all. And that is exactly what Singh (1995: 284) asserts when he says that all observable differences among Englishes 'lead only to the following picture':

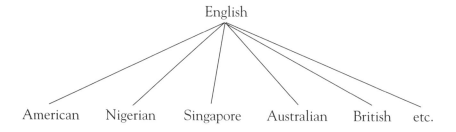

English — American, Nigerian, Singapore, Australian, British, etc.

and *not* to the following:

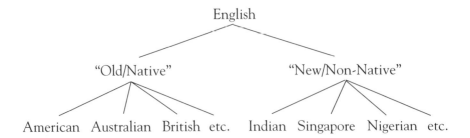

A Language Genesis Basis for the Classification?

Let us now turn to an examination of issues relating to language genesis. These make up the second major set of issues which we mentioned earlier as defining possible grounds for the classification of New Englishes as a separate class. As we shall see in a moment, our examination will lead to a very similar conclusion to the one we have just reached about a possible structural basis. This time round, though, we shall discuss the matter in relation to the presumed distinction between New Englishes and pidgins/ creoles. This is because it is that distinction that the usual discussions of issues of language genesis appear to make the most salient. For, in the study of varieties of English, it happens to be pidgins/creoles that have raised such issues most prominently. A lot of work on New Englishes seems, by its near total disregard of these issues, to take for granted that they are not very relevant to it. The assumption seems to be that New Englishes and pidgins/ creoles are clearly qualitatively different kinds of objects. That being so, processes that are relevant to the latter cannot be relevant to the former. But the fact, as Mufwene (1994: 25) argues, is that 'differences in kind among new Englishes' (including pidgins/creoles and New Englishes) 'do not suggest different kinds of linguistic change, restructuring, or adaptation, only different outcomes due to different values borne by variables of the same language contact equation' (1994: 26).

A proper appreciation of this point will require, among other things, a more specialized familiarity with the nature of language genesis issues than this chapter will be able to help develop. Here, we shall offer instead only a few general comments on these issues. We hope that they will be sufficient to show how much in fact the two classes share from the point of view of such issues.

The primary reason for this is that all the members of these classes are, alike, 'adaptations to new ecological ethnolinguistic conditions' (Mufwene, 1994: 25). As we saw earlier, this statement by itself is insufficient — *all* Englishes outside the original home country give evidence of this phenomenon. To fully understand the particular issues of language genesis involved, we need also to look at some of the specific significant features of the situations in which these adaptations take place, and recognize that the two classes under scrutiny share these features. Among such features are the following. (It must be mentioned that it is principally in the initial state of these situations that the features listed may be observed in just this form.) To start with, the situations invariably involve the phenomenon known as 'language contact'. The term is somewhat misleading, since it is not languages as such that are in contact but groups of people using different, unshared languages, who need, nevertheless, to do various things together in their shared situations. The situations themselves very often display a dimension of unequal social status among the groups of people involved. The next chapter will discuss some of the different responses that these people have made to the problems of communication and interaction raised within the situations. It will also indicate that these responses are by no means simple and that the explanations offered for them are ridden with controversy. But what these explanations do to some extent at least seem to agree on is that in such situations a new linguistic code emerges. The language of the dominant group in the situation assumes a certain privileged position relative to the new code, by defining some kind of target or basis or source for it. For this reason this language is called the *superstrate* language. The emerging code takes its vocabulary essentially from the superstrate language, earning for the latter the further label, the *lexifier* language.

In addition to vocabulary, the emerging code also develops new structure. Ignoring, in the interests of generality, some problems which pidgins, as distinct from creoles, raise from this point of view, we note that central to the emergence of the new code is the 'restructuring of the lexifier' (Mufwene, 1994: 25). This, Mufwene goes on, 'is the common element of all new Englishes.' The restructuring is guaranteed by another crucially important feature of the conditions under which the code emerges, namely 'interrupted transmission'. The term is best understood by looking at its opposite, 'normal transmission'. Normal transmission takes place when 'a language is passed from parent generation to child generation and/or via peer group from immediately older to immediately younger, *with relatively small degrees of change over the short run*, given a reasonably stable sociolinguistic context' (Thomason and Kaufman, 1988: 9-10; emphasis in original). It thus enables the 'transmission of an entire single set of interrelated lexical and structural features' (Thomason and Kaufman, 1988: 200).

The issue of the ways in which the emerging code develops its structural features under its conditions of interrupted transmission has been the subject of much controversy. The next chapter will discuss the controversy and outline in some detail two of the most important of the approaches that have been pursued with respect to the issue. These are the substratist approach and the universalist approach, the latter as exemplified by what is known as the Language bioprogramme hypothesis (Bickerton, 1981). Our description of these here will necessarily have to be very general. The substratist approach holds that the structure of the emerging code is provided essentially by the language(s) other than the superstrate or lexifier in use in the context. This earns for these languages the label *substrate languages*. The Language Bioprogramme Hypothesis, on the other hand, claims essentially that the structure of the emerging code derives largely from Universal Grammar — a genetically provided asset of the human mind which defines the principles, properties, features, kinds of rules and so on that all natural human languages must operate in terms of.

The chapter that follows discusses these competing claims and their strengths and shortcomings. It also provides evidence from both pidgins/creoles and New Englishes in support of Mufwene's claim (1986) that '(t)he universalist and substrate hypotheses complement each other'. The chapters below which analyse the structure and lexicon of Singapore English and other New Englishes will provide even more support for the claim. But what is most important from the point of view of the argument at this point is that the evidence in support of the claim comes from *both* New Englishes *and* pidgins/creoles. That is, New Englishes as much as pidgins/creoles show decisive evidence of substrate influence; *and* New Englishes as much as pidgins/creoles also show decisive evidence of features which have been claimed to come from Universal Grammar. Among such features are morphological 'simplification' (in spite of some of the substrate languages being richly inflected), zero copula, pro-drop, fronting of focussed elements and the absence of *syntactic* signalling of the difference between statements and questions.

All of this strongly suggests that 'the mechanics of their (pidgins/creoles' and New Englishes') development are not as different as they appear' (Mufwene, 1994: 27). This is hardly surprising, given that both sets evolve as language codes under conditions of broken transmission that are similar in many significant respects. Chapter 3 will endeavour to open out further dimensions of the process of the evolution of these codes that this account pays no attention to. For the moment, what we need to note is that our account so far indicates that any attempt to justify the separation of the New Englishes and pidgins/creoles into distinct classes on the grounds of differences of language genesis cannot be sustained. But we have still not seen the worst of it. The literature on language genesis includes, also, proposals according to which processes of creole genesis have taken place in the development of English English itself. Doubtless, the proposals are controversial, as Thomason and Kaufman's refutatory discussion of them

(1988: 123-126, 306-315) shows. But the fact that they could have been made at all, when taken together with the matters we have offered for contemplation above, appears to raise doubts in general about the possibility of justifying the classification in Table 1 on considerations of language genesis.

Issues of Context and Sociohistorical Dynamics: Three Patterns

By all of the three sets of criteria that we have discussed so far (three sets, if we include those reflected in what have been referred to above as current characterizations), then, there appears to be no firm support for the classification in Table 1. This raises the possibility that there are no certain reasons for treating what we have termed New Englishes as a legitimately demarcated class of linguistic objects. Yet our book does treat of New Englishes, which only reflects our conviction that they do exist as such a class.

The conviction reflects our recognition that there are other dimensions to the objects under study than are considered in the approaches to them discussed above. The current mainstream approach does, in fact, touch on several particular matters in the social contexts of the varieties that centrally exemplify these other dimensions. As seen from the discussion of it above, however, it does not subject them to the kind of treatment that would demonstrate how they might legitimately lead to the conclusion represented in Table 1.

The other two approaches are not oblivious of these other considerations. Both Singh and Mufwene, who, respectively, are primarily responsible for these approaches, underline their existence. They choose, however, not to focus on them. Rather, they direct their attention to the question of whether their objects of study may be characterized in terms of properties, features, processes and so on which may be taken to fundamentally define the very nature of natural human language itself. In doing so, they consider human language not in immediate contextual terms but in more abstract terms, as a unique biological endowment of the human species. In this way, they lead us to understandings of all varieties of English as equal representatives of the phenomenon of natural human language, which are not distinguished from each other in terms of their fundamental nature. Such understandings do more than simply enhance general or abstract theoretical inquiry. A specific value they have from the viewpoint of New Englishes and pidgins/creoles is that they expose the unsoundness of the unequal evaluations of these classes which often accompany their differentiation.

But in order to arrive at these understandings, the investigation needs to reduce the objects of study to the single dimension along which alone they might arrive at them. All those other dimensions of the reality of these objects which might distract from such understandings are, consequently, removed from scrutiny. The procedure is perfectly standard and legitimate. Anatomists and physiologists, for instance, lead us to valuable and necessary understandings of the essential anatomical or physiological oneness of humankind. They are able to do so only because they exclude from consideration all of those other aspects of humankind that *will* lead to valid classifications of them in other terms, for instance, race or class or culture or whatever.

It is much this kind of thing that is involved here. In their use in the real contexts in which the actual human users of the different varieties of English live their lives out, the differences between their varieties of the language and others have a significant qualitative dimension for them. This cannot simply be erased by the demonstration that all of these differences in any event stem from a shared abstract base of features, rules and properties. Part of what this dimension involves is a very general intuition that the differences among the varieties do invite a classification of them along the lines of Table 1. The evaluative responses that often accompany these classifications might vary considerably. Some of these responses have been remarked on earlier: New Englishes are different because they are deviant forms; they and pidgins/creoles may not, for negative reasons, even be regarded as English; and so on. We may agree or disagree with these evaluations. But the intuition itself remains intact and we can ignore it only at the cost of a failure to understand the nature of the objects we are seeking to understand. The reason is that the intuition itself is the result of the operation of definite forces and factors which enter into the constitution of the objects. An effort to probe it will, therefore, lead us to the recognition of significant dimensions of the objects which we might otherwise fail to note.

In this particular case, the effort will lead us to an engagement with more than just abstract properties, features, rules and so on. We find ourselves needing to pay attention also to the concrete, differentiated sociohistorical dynamics of the contexts out of which the members of these classes differently emerged at the hands of their human occupants. In other words, varieties of English are not only abstract structural and mental objects, they are also sociohistorical objects. We cannot properly understand them unless we recognize that fact.

For the purposes of the argument we are developing, we shall need to look at the sociohistorical dynamics of the Englishes which developed outside the original home country. Let us begin by reminding ourselves of two major features which, as mentioned earlier, they always seem to display. These are: one, that the language was carried outside its original home by colonization or empire, driven by political, economic and, often, religious motivations; and two, that it was called upon to adapt itself to new environmental conditions, marked by often unfamiliar ecological characteristics, flora, fauna and so on. In other important respects, however, the sociohistorical dynamics of the language were remarkably dissimilar in the different places it moved to. While the differences were of very complex and varied kinds, they may be seen as falling into three broadly distinct patterns. Each pattern is characterized by certain shared sociohistorical factors which led to the language developing in those places along certain lines rather than along others. It is here that we hope to find the basis of the classification in Table 1.

We shall now describe in the most general of ways the features of these patterns. In doing so, we shall confine ourselves to just the essential details. These help explain the differences among the three classes of varieties that emerged as well as the intuitions that they generated among the actual users of these varieties about these differences. Each of these patterns may be seen to bring several varieties of English together in a class. It must be emphasized, however, that the claim is not that the sociohistorical circumstances of all of the varieties included are identical. In fact, in this respect each of these varieties invariably shows features, some very significant, that are unique to it.

Pattern 1: Older Englishes (Outside the Home Country)

Bearing this caveat in mind, we shall outline the basic features of the characteristic pattern of development of Older Englishes (outside of the home country) through a discussion of the development of American English. (See Baugh and Cable, 1993, Chapter 11; and McCrum, Cran and MacNeil, 1986, for details which will fill in the outline given here.) A major stimulus to the kind of colonial enterprise which brought the English to America was its combination of mercantilist economic concerns and the Puritan ethic, both of which gave expression in their different spheres to the emerging capitalist spirit in Europe.

The 9.8 to 12.5 million native Indians who were occupying the land when the English speakers arrived had been there for some 25 000 years. They had developed, across the 600 or so 'nations' they had formed themselves into during that period and through the large numbers of indigenous languages that they spoke, a stable civilization based on the harmonious ordering of nature, economic needs and life. As Collier (1947: 102) puts it, 'These societies existed in perfect ecological balance with the forest, the plain, the desert, the waters and animal life'.

The English arrivals, however, were quite unable to recognize this as civilization at all. The standards by which they measured civilization were fundamentally determined by the emerging economic spirit. They expressed themselves by means of terms such as the following, which proliferate in the writings of the times: *comfort, commerce, commodity, enterprise, fortune, merchandise, plenty, profit, riches* and *wealth*. And these standards had the approval of God, for '...the whole earth is the Lord's garden, and he hath given it to the son of Adam to be tilled and improved by them' (John Winthrop, first Governor of Massachusetts Bay Colony, in 1629, quoted by Pearce, 1965: 21).

By these religio-economic standards, the Indian hunters, gatherers and subsistence agriculturalists were savages who, moreover, did not heed God's dictum to 'improve the land' (Winthrop again). All of this gave the arrivals economically and religiously sanctioned *carte blanche* to possess and settle the land, in the process expropriating the natives and, as far as possible, eliminating them. As Richard Hakluyt, the early seventeenth-century voyager, says, 'All the rich endowments of Virginia...are wages for all this worke: God in wisedome having enriched the Savage Countries, that those riches might be attractive for Christian suters, which there may sowe spirituals and reap temporals' (quoted by Pearce, 1965: 8).

From the point of view of the development of the English language in its new context, all of this ensured several very important things which determined how precisely it would evolve there. Most significantly it saw the emergence of what might be termed a 'reproduced language community' to sustain the language. This happened through the extensive settlement of English colonists in the new land, who then went on to take complete charge of it. The term 'reproduced language community' requires explanation. It is a community which, for all the huge differences between its circumstances and those of the home country, still reproduced enough of the linguistically relevant features of that country to ensure a fundamental continuity of development of the language between its original and its new home. This does not mean that the language did not adapt itself to its new circumstances. It did, developing vocabulary, structure, idiom and so on to ensure efficacy of use in its new context. At the same time, it continued to develop along lines that had already been essentially determined in the home country. It was passed on to succeeding generations by those who had brought it to its new context in various of its home country forms through a process of 'normal transmission', as explained above. The effects of such continuity were reinforced by the way in which the religio-economic developments discussed above ensured its comparative insulation from the pre-existing cultural realities of the context. Some words, phrases and so on were indeed borrowed from the native inhabitants. But the whole way in which the latter were treated guaranteed that the large potential which the new context offered for the language to develop on the basis of genuine, transforming multi-cultural/linguistic interaction was destroyed.

There were other sociohistorical factors which raised expectations that the language would develop in ways that would cause it to differentiate itself hugely from the language of the home country. But such developments in the language were also brought under the kind of control which ensured that they did not disrupt its essential continuity with the latter. To mention just a few of these difference-inducing factors, there were, for instance, the different forms of English that developed on the basis of different patterns of migration, settlement and so on. The best-known of the classifications these patterns were responsible for is that which separates the New England dialect, the Southern dialect and General American from each other (see Baugh and Cable, 1993, Chapter 11, for details). There was the forced immigration of the black slaves, whose creolized English had an impact, and not only in the south. There were the huge waves of immigrants from many countries of Europe who found their way from persecution, economic problems, misery and so on to this land of opportunity, as it was, and continues to be, widely seen. Their languages did have some kind of impact, if marginal, on English. There were a host of other things, too, all of which left their mark on the language as it grew in America: the emergence, alongside the opening out of parts of the country further west of the original settlements, of the colourful lifestyle along the Mississippi (immortally recaptured by Mark Twain in *Huckleberry Finn*); the institution of the cowboy; the Gold Rush; and many others.

The result of all this was that the language began to emerge looking somewhat different from English in the home country, for it reflected something of a wide-ranging diversity generated by the 'experience of struggle and difference' (Simpson, 1986: 9) out of which the nation itself emerged. However, none of this was permitted to disrupt the continuity between the two, in spite of not-infrequent linguistic declarations of independence. One of the best-known of such declarations is Noah Webster's, when he urged that: 'As an independent nation, our honor requires us to have a system of our own, in language as well as government' (*Dissertations on the English Language, with Notes Historical and Critical*). This was written in 1779, in the middle of the War of American Independence, through which America finally broke free from the mercantilist-type economic and political control of Britain.

After independence had been won and the external enemy put in its place, however, things changed. The diversity that was the hallmark of the American experience had from quite early times been perceived by the dominant groups in society as an internal threat to their economic and political aspirations. This perception was now allowed to develop further and consolidate. In spite of a public rhetoric of individual initiative, opportunity, pluralism and so on, a homogenizing image of unity and solidarity began to be pursued. For the purpose, 'certain interests had to be excluded or co-opted' (Simpson, 1986: 7) and difference contained by means of the 'melting pot'. Language was central to the entire endeavour, for, as they learned from philosophical apologists for the middle-class-dominated status quo in Britain like Thomas Hobbes, linguistic discord was closely related to social discord. Now more than ever before, therefore, the talk was all about a 'common language', with a focus on a standard language as a means of bringing the variety under control. And this standard language was based on the usage of the 'well-educated yeomanry' of New England, 'substantial independent freeholders, masters of their own persons and lords of their own soil' (Webster, *Dissertations*), who constituted a significant base of the propertied classes.

This, together with other factors, ensured that the standardizing impulse in America would be expressed around 'the central (British) tradition', which was retained far more 'than (it) is commonly supposed' to be (Krapp, 1925, quoted by Marckwardt, 1980: 7). Indeed, Webster himself declared that 'the body of the language is the same as in England and it is desirable to perpetuate that sameness', and retreated from his earlier independent position by withholding from his famous Dictionary American spellings like *bred, tuf, tung, thum* and so on which he had earlier advocated.

Such developments, affirming the decisive influence of the home language on American English, had always received support from the schooling system. When America began to be settled by the English, the modern schooling system was only just beginning to take shape. That system was a response to the development of emerging capitalist activity in Europe, which made education a social necessity. It began to appear under the initiative of institutions associated with both sides of the Reformation, which, as Max Weber has led us to recognize, had quite a close connection with such activity. From the very beginning, therefore, America had the benefits of the schoolroom. In the schoolroom, the standard language of the home country had pride of place, not least because of the paucity, for a considerable period of time, of teaching materials produced in America.

Against this background, it is not too difficult to see why commentator after commentator has spoken of the great similarities that exist between British English and American English in grammatical structure and syntax (Marckwardt, 1980), or of the 'extraordinary unanimity' which exists between them 'over the bulk of the language' (Quirk, 1972: 30).

It is such considerations that bring American English and English English, as well as British English, together in a single class — the Older Englishes. The other varieties we have included in the class might not have sociohistories identical with that of American English. Indeed, many of them, for example Australian English, have sociohistories which are very different in many respects from it. Yet all alike share the essentials of these considerations, which guaranteed a fundamental continuity between the emergent varieties and the original home language, thus providing the motivation for bringing them all together in a single class.

Pattern 2: New Englishes

New Englishes had a very different sociohistorical dynamics. We shall describe the pattern they illustrate on the basis of developments in Asia. This does not, however, signal a failure to recognize that the African situation was different in some significant respects from this or, for that matter, that the Asian experience too was by no means uniform.

The first trading station was established in India by the British East India Company under a charter from Elizabeth I as early as 1611. This was some ten years before the *Mayflower* arrived in America to give the first real start to American English. Nevertheless, the emergence of English in India was, in real terms, not part of the developments associated with the first British Empire, which created America. Rather, it was part of developments associated with the second British Empire, which replaced the first after the loss of America in the War of American Independence from 1775 to 1783. The loss taught Britain, among other things, something about the follies of the mercantilist imperialism which had created America. This was an imperialism which was driven by the conviction that a nation's strength was measured by the amount of wealth, specifically gold, accumulated within it. As a consequence, colonies had been considered to exist primarily for the purpose of enriching the home country. The second British Empire, on the other hand, gave expression to what was called the New Imperialism, which replaced mercantilist imperialism. The Agrarian and Industrial Revolutions had taken place in Britain in the late eighteenth century and the concern now was to service the rapidly growing industries of the burgeoning capitalist economy. There was a need to find new sources of raw materials, markets for the goods that the factories were producing in increasing quantities and places for profitable ventures in which surplus capital could be invested.

All of this made displacement of native populations and settlement less salient than they had been earlier. The concerns now were rather the establishment of trading posts in new territories, the control of sea routes, the subjugation of native populations and their rule, essentially by long distance, from the home country. Australia, South Africa and so on were exceptions. For reasons we need not go into here, both fell into versions of the American pattern, the former more clearly and the latter less so. The countries in which New Englishes developed, however, including the African countries, were taken into this new pattern of imperialist expansion.

Coinciding with these developments, somewhere around the turn of the eighteenth century, were the religious revival and the emergence of the spirit of liberalism in Britain. While these had strong internal relevance, their impact was also strongly felt in the colonies. The proselytizing Cross invariably accompanied the imperialist mast, and missionary activity was quite intense in these countries. The 13th Resolution of the House of Commons in 1813 expresses the combination of Christian and liberal sentiments that existed side by side with those of economic, political and military gain: 'It is the duty of this country to promote the interests and happiness of the native inhabitants of the British dominions in India and...measures ought to be introduced as may tend to the introduction among them of useful knowledge, and of religious and moral improvement'.

All of this meant that the indigenous cultures and languages of these countries remained essentially intact. This fact was crucial to the very different ways in which New Englishes developed in them when compared with the ways in which the Older Englishes developed in contexts like America. These countries were all multicultural and multilinguistic, home to many cultures and languages, several associated with Great Traditions. It had never been as easy for Europeans to deny the reality of these civilizations as it had been for them to deny the reality of Indian civilization in America. As Williamson puts it (1952: 166), ' "India" was a word of magic in those Tudor days...It stood along with "Cathay" for the whole vast mystery of Asia, the land of great cities, great emperors, and fabulous wealth, of silks, spices, perfumes, pearls and gems'.

Moreover, these civilizations showed strong evidence of their own nascent capital formations and so on. The evidence was found in the highly successful and profitable trading activities which many of them had developed and which the Europeans had long been trying to enter into. But Britain had superior military might, made possible by technological advances facilitated by the advances in scientific knowledge which attended upon industrial-capitalist development. She was, therefore, soon able to subjugate these countries. With that the estimate of these civilizations went down, as evidenced by, for instance, the British administrator, T. B. Macaulay's statement in the nineteenth century that 'I have never found one amongst (the orientalists) who could deny that a single shelf of a good European library was worth the whole native literature of India and Arabia'. Under the New Imperialist dispensation, however, displacement or eradication of the indigenous cultures and languages, accompanied by settlement, was not part of the agenda, and so the contexts retained their multicultural and multilinguistic character. Other things apart, this guaranteed that in making its new beginnings in these contexts, the English language would remain open to a complex multi-cultural/linguistic input from a pre-existing reality which was not erased. This is not to say, of course, that it was accorded equal treatment.

There were other salient matters, too, that ensured that English would develop very differently in these contexts from the way in which it did in countries like America. In America, the language arrived along with a population which settled in the place and subsequently went on to use and develop the language among themselves. There was no such population in these countries. Nevertheless they had to be ruled and run, and this was done by a comparative handful of English-using British administrators and others. From the beginning, therefore, there was a major utilitarian need for a knowledge of English among some at least of the native population in these countries. The reason was that, while government and the administration were in the hands of the British rulers, these rulers did not deign to learn the languages of their subjects. This raised the need for intermediate-level administrators with a knowledge of English among the natives. Their functions were to bridge the linguistic gap between the administration and the general populace, who knew no English, to maintain records, to help effectuate directives, implement decisions and so on (de Souza, 1960). Similar patterns repeated themselves in the important commercial establishments which the British set up. As De Souza, speaking of Singapore, says, 'the need was for people who could write English in a legible hand and who could understand invoices or comprehend directives' (1977).

Subsequently, a political motive was added on to this utilitarian one, namely the creation of 'an influential western-oriented intelligentsia as an aid to stabilizing colonial rule' (de Souza, 1960). The motive was to be pursued by forming 'a class of interpreters between us and the millions we govern — a class of persons, Indian in blood and colour, but English in taste, in opinions, in morals and intellect'. This was how Macaulay, talking particularly of India, put it in his famous minute of 1835. Similar motivations seem to have operated in Singapore too, as indicated by De Souza's comment on its founder, Stamford Raffles's (unsuccessful) proposal for the establishment of an elitist educational institution with four schools to cater to the sons of native Malay chiefs and the richer Chinese. Raffles's declared end was to give these pupils 'the lights of knowledge and improvement'. Contrariwise, De Souza suggests that it was probably 'the extension of social control through the education of the elite' (1977).

Implicit in all of this is a further matter which marks out the establishment and development of English in New English situations. This is that from the beginning a major role was played in the processes by the schooling system. In Sri Lanka (then Ceylon), for instance, the British East India Company inherited 163 schools from the Dutch, who had ruled much of the country for some 138 years before they were expelled by the British in 1796. Driven primarily by the profit motive, the Company allowed these schools to fall into neglect, with the endorsement of the colonial government, which shared the same motive. The result was a decline in the indigenous Christian population. This generated agitation by Christian revivalists back home for increased attention to be paid to schooling, resulting in the establishment of some 235 new schools by 1832. Attempts by the colonial government to produce more civil servants locally to save the cost of importing such officers from the home country (recommended as part of the Colebrook Reforms in 1933 in Ceylon) led to further encouragement of local English schools. All of this was supported, of course, by missionary efforts and by the liberal/political sentiments expressed by the Macaulay minute. Some additional support was provided by a certain recognition that expressed itself in Britain through the passage there of the Education Act of 1870, which made primary schooling compulsory. This recognition was that the industrial-capitalist system needed the dissemination of basic education among the general populace if it was to be kept going. However, it was mainly primary-level 'vernacular education' that benefitted from this in Ceylon.

By the middle of the nineteenth century, therefore, a sound formal system of English schooling had been established. The English schools provided both primary and secondary education, in some cases right up to pre-university level. While providing an emerging elite ready access to the language, these schools kept the superstrate standard consistently in the forefront of its use and development. It is important in this respect to note that 'English education' in a place like Ceylon meant 'not merely that the medium of instruction was English, but that the entire school curriculum and all books used were imported from British schools' (de Souza, 1960; see also Gooneratne, 1968). In India, too, a strong English-based education system was established, though with its own significant differences. One such difference was that English-medium education extended very early to the university level too, with universities being established in Bombay, Calcutta and Madras in 1857. In all these countries university education in England had been available to selected students, among other things through scholarships. Ceylon, however, had to wait until 1921, when a university college was established, for the beginning of its own system of university education. What is significant is that it was only in 1960 that the university system switched from the English medium to the indigenous language media. The significance of such matters to the way in which English developed in countries such as this can hardly be overestimated.

A further very important dimension of the development of the language in these countries, which distinguished it from its development in Older English countries like America, is that initially the mode of transmission was not 'normal' but 'broken'. The first generation of learners of the language obviously did not learn it from their parents in the home. Neither did they learn it through everyday interaction of the sort normal in a context in which it was a significant language of communication.

However, after the first generation, the situation began to alter. The alteration took place under the pressure of factors which bring up yet another significant dimension of the language in New English communities. It is a dimension which again distinguishes the language in these communities from the language in Older English communities like America. Very soon after the initial introduction of the language, a small bilingual elite emerged — the 'talented tenth', as they have been called (de Souza, 1960). This elite used English for official purposes and for communication with the rulers, and their own language for other more domestic purposes and for communication with the ordinary populace, who never learned English. There was, in other words, an interesting complementarity between English and the other languages in the environment. Therefore, as far as these people were concerned, neither their newly acquired English nor their indigenous language was an all-purpose language.

What we have mentioned here is only one facet of this complementarity, however. We see other facets if we look at the matter from the point of view not of individual users but of the wider social situation. This will show, quite obviously, that English was the language which was associated largely with all of those things which were introduced into the context from outside of it, while the indigenous languages tended to be associated more immediately with what was already there. That is to say, initially, the complementary relationship between the two languages in the repertoire of these bilingual individuals matched in some ways a similar relationship between them in the larger bilingual/bicultural society they belonged to.

The situation did not, however, remain static. Chapter 3 will go into the matter in more detail, but for the moment, let us recognize that, as far as individual bilingual people in this bilingual/bicultural setting were concerned, the distinct components of bilingualism/biculturalism did not simply remain separate or isolated from each other, but impinged on each other in important ways. This created for them a total experience, which Kandiah (1981a) describes as 'symbiotic', holding within itself in various interesting relationships to each other elements from both of its linguistic and cultural inputs. Nothing about this was simple or straightforward. For instance, English clearly remained to a considerable extent something on which the ordinary experience of the large mass of non-elite people did not leave too strong an impress. This was particularly so in imperial times, when the very presence of the rulers and the prestige and influence associated with them would have inhibited too much openness to the larger environment outside the privileged circles. Nevertheless, these English-using bilingual people did turn the language to account in the ways that made the most sense to them. They gradually extended its functions beyond just the formal and administrative and official, or the merely utilitarian.

Its prestige among them was very high, not just as the language of social and economic advancement, but as the language of the rulers whose cultural and intellectual superiority many members of the elite were more than happy to extol. We remember Raja Rammohan Roy's letter to Lord Amherst, Governor-General of India, on 11 December, 1823. It expressed disappointment at the colonial government's decision to establish a Sanskrit school in Calcutta instead of using the money for 'employing European gentlemen of talent to instruct the natives of India in mathematics, natural philosophy, chemistry, anatomy and other useful sciences, which the natives of Europe have carried to a degree of perfection that has raised them above the inhabitants of other parts of the world' (cited in Kachru, 1983: 60). The language soon, therefore, became the language of polite social intercourse among the elite and, also, the language of their homes. It became, in other words, a language which entered into their everyday social, emotional and imaginative lives.

This did not mean that it became for them an all-purpose language of the kind American English was for the Americans from the beginning. Neither did it mean that it kept itself tuned immediately to the everyday experience of the large mass of ordinary people in the wider environment (see Chapter 3). But it did cease to be simply a limited-purpose language, confined to a few comparatively undemanding utilitarian tasks or, for that matter, specialized academic matters. As a result, even though its bilingual users might not have used it for all of their purposes within their contexts, the code was not necessarily attenuated or impoverished. (See below, and Chapter 3, however, for some comments relevant to this matter.)

Some of these matters have implications for the issue of the mode of transmission of the language. Once the users moved beyond the first generation and their situation began to change in the manner just indicated, the mode of transmission also changed. The schoolroom never ceased to play a role in the process — the kind of role it discharged in many Older English situations. But processes of normal transmission became quite usual. Many members of the elite began to acquire the language, often alongside another language, from their parents and, also, through everyday exchanges with people in important spheres of their daily lives. There were, of course, others who belonged to non-English-using homes and came, therefore, to acquire it outside of their homes. But they, too, tended to 'pick it up', not just in the classroom but, in addition, in normal, everyday transactions. These included those which took place in school outside the classroom. Thus, their mode of acquisition of the language can hardly be described as 'broken' in any useful sense of the term.

Pattern 3: Pidgins/Creoles

Like New Englishes, pidgins/creoles also emerged from language contact situations created by the pursuit of the ends of colonization or empire. As pointed out earlier, these situations brought together groups of people who used mutually incomprehensible languages but who still needed to interact with each other. In pidgin/creole situations, however, the interaction tended to be confined to very restricted practical purposes, such as trade.

Generally, as in New English situations, the relations among the interacting groups were unequal. One group of them assumed a position of dominance relative to the others and exercised power over them. In the southern Pacific, for instance, pidgins/creoles emerged around the nineteenth century as a result of the extension of British colonial and commercial activity to the region. The commercial activity first involved the whaling industry. Later, just after the middle of the century when that industry began to decline, profitable plantations were established on the various islands of the area. Indentured migrant labourers using different languages were moved across the area in response to the exigencies of the enterprise.

The development of pidgins/creoles in the western Atlantic took place earlier, beginning around the second half of the sixteenth century, in association with the slave trade. The slave trade forcibly transported Africans from the West African coastal regions of today's Sierra Leone, Nigeria, Ghana, the Ivory Coast and so on. They were used as cheap labour for the developing agricultural industries (sugar, tobacco, cotton and so on) in the Caribbean and, soon, in America too. These slaves spoke several different mutually unintelligible languages (Hausa, Wolof, Bulu, Twi and so on). Pidgins/creoles arose out of their need to communicate with the crews of the ships which transported them and, subsequently, with their owners on the plantations they eventually ended up in, as well as among themselves in both these situations.

The specifics of the history of the emergence and development of pidgins/creoles among these people in these situations are not very certain. In the Pacific, for instance, it is known that the various pidgins/creoles bear relationships of various kinds to each other and also to pidgins/creoles outside of the area. However, it is not clear what these relationships are. Similarly, in the case of the Caribbean pidgins/creoles, there are reasons to believe that the Africans who were taken across to the plantations might already have been exposed to some prior (possibly Portuguese-associated) pidgin. The exposure might have been either in their own countries or through contact with their ships' crews. These crews were motley groups of people from both England and across the Mediterranean region, who might themselves have spoken an older pidgin as the most feasible means of communication among themselves and with the slaves. However all this might be, there are some generally accepted views about pidgins/creoles which we need to call attention to for the purposes of this discussion.

Pidgins are generally known as auxiliary or peripheral makeshift languages. They come into being as lingua francas among groups of people who have no common language but who still need to communicate with each other in pursuit of purposes that, as mentioned earlier, are quite practical and limited. They are generally considered to be based on the language of the dominant group, the superstrate language, from which they take most of their words. In fact, many pidgins have mixed lexicons, including words from more than the superstrate. The words themselves are generally limited in number. The grammar of pidgins, however, tends to come from the languages of the subordinate groups, the substrate languages. But it appears in a highly simplified form, so that it generally is reduced in structure and very rudimentary. Thus it does not use the copula verb *be*, prefers to replace affixes and other such indicators of relationships among words with independent full words, marks tense distinctions with similar separate words and so on. As, primarily, contact languages with highly restricted purposes, pidgins belong to no one and have no native users or speech communities to sustain them.

If the contact situations which give rise to pidgins are sustained for a certain period of time, the pidgins evolve into creoles. Children born to parents who have no common language and who, therefore, use the available pidgins to communicate among themselves and with their children, begin to acquire them as their mother tongues. They also begin to extend their functions within what begin to emerge as communities of native users of those tongues. This necessarily brings about an elaboration of their grammar, vocabulary, styles and so on, so that they will be able to meet the extended communicative demands that now begin to be made on them.

It is here that the controversies mentioned earlier about the genesis of these forms of language (these were expressed in terms of the universalist and the substratist hypotheses) become relevant. They concern the ways in which these creoles developed structure under conditions of, essentially, broken transmission. Details of this controversy, which in any event will be discussed in the following chapter, are not relevant to our argument at this point. One matter needs to be remarked on, however. This is that once communities of users to whom these creoles are very significant, if not primary, modes of communication come into being, the process of transmission too changes to normal, continuous transmission from generation to generation.

One final point which needs to be made about pidgins/creoles is that in very many cases they co-exist in the larger society alongside the standard

Older English. It is this that remains the language of prestige there and in many cases it has official status. This often triggers the process of decreolization, whereby the creole begins to modify itself in the direction of the standard at all levels, phonological, grammatical, lexical and so on. This results in what has come to be known as the post-creole continuum. The varying forms of the language that emerge as a consequence of different degrees of approximation to the targetted standard are seen as a continuum. The continuum is described in terms of a three-fold distinction: the basilect, which is the furthest away from the target, the acrolect, which is closest to it, and the mesolect, which is a transitional form between these two extremes. In some places in more recent times, for instance among black English-users in America, and among Jamaican immigrant settlers in London, sentiments of identity and self-assertion have led to the process of decreolization being curtailed. At times, it is even reversed, through what has been termed recreolization (Romaine, 1988: 188-203; Todd, 1984: 17).

⁄ Conclusion

What emerges from the discussion above is that there do not appear to be feasible grounds to support the classification in Table 1 on the basis of abstract issues of structure or of language genesis. Given claims about universals of language structure and genesis, there is nothing too surprising in this. The claims are that the properties of natural human languages and the principles which govern them derive from an innate biologically specified language mechanism. If they are essentially correct, it can hardly be expected that languages could differ in any crucial way in the respects considered.

However, the whole of our book rests on the classification. We, therefore, sought the distinctions which were essential to our project in the differing sociohistorical circumstances of these different varieties. Here, we found that there were two general features that all varieties of English outside its original homeland shared. One related to the movement of the language from this homeland to the new environments and the reason for this movement. The other related to the demands that were made on the language in all of these environments to adapt itself to its new realities and the responses to these demands.

There is, however, one set of major features of a sociohistorical kind which appear, even while bringing pidgins/creoles and New Englishes together, to separate them as a whole from the Older Englishes outside of the home country. In the case of these Older Englishes, the people who altered, developed and sustained the language in the new environments were settlers who already commanded it in the forms in which it was used in the home country. This ensured a fundamental continuity in the progression of the language in the new environment, since the mode of its transmission remained normal. Outsiders who might have subsequently come into the community (mainly through immigration) fitted themselves into patterns of language use, maintenance, change and so on determined by the people who were already there. In addition, the standard language of the home country retained a very powerful role in the midst of all the changes which were taking place in the language. Intuitively, therefore, all Older Englishes appear to retain a certain fundamental togetherness.

The case of New Englishes was, as we have seen, very different. They were developed by new users of the language who initially had no acquaintance with the language at all. Moreover, these new users were separated from those from whom they had to learn it by their subordinate sociopolitical status. That is to say, a very salient feature of the evolution of New Englishes was a certain discontinuity with what had gone before. However, the rulers made their standard immediately and significantly accessible to them, particularly through the classroom. In addition, their various motives for doing so assigned this standard a kind of presiding role within the evolution of New Englishes. The compliant attitude that the local elite users of the language generally adopted towards their rulers made it easy for them to accept this role of the standard.

Nevertheless, the standard Older English could not function in these contexts exactly as it did in the case of Older English contexts, for the very inauguration of New Englishes was through a process of broken transmission. Moreover, in spite of the presence and accessibility of this standard, the local users of the language, as also indicated earlier, did increasingly begin to take hold of it for themselves. Having done so, they went on to transform it to make it effective and viable in their environment, particularly in the spoken form. As it turns out, this is a process which has accelerated since the departure of the rulers (see Chapter 3). In transforming the language, the local users drew on their indigenous cultures and languages, which, even under the foreign rulers, had always maintained a large presence in the context. The potential of these languages and cultures as a source for such transformation was reinforced by their association with Great Traditions, however low the evaluation of these traditions might have been during colonial times. This again distinguished New Englishes from many of the Older Englishes outside the original home country, where indigenous traditions were not just denigrated but also virtually erased.

The processes of normal transmission which the transformed language now adopted for itself ensured continuity and viability for it in its new form. However, there were two factors which kept these developments under a certain kind of control, especially in the formal spoken and in the written registers. One was the presence of a local form of the standard which the never-absent classroom had ensured would always remain salient. The other was the recognition of the role the language needed to play for some of these users outside of their own immediate environment.

Yet basically, these developments altered the language in certain significant ways. Such alterations would not have come too naturally to varieties which maintained a fundamental and essential continuity with the original (home) community and culture. In New English contexts, however, they did take place quite naturally, leading New Englishes to look different from Older Englishes.

Of course, at the most abstract level of structure and genetic development there is no evidence of fundamental difference among any of the varieties of English, as we have recognized earlier. But even the hypotheses about universals of language which are related to this matter do recognize differences among varieties. They account for them by means of different choices these varieties make from among the possible features, elements and rules which Universal Grammar in any event specifies. These are tied to different settings of such features which the varieties make, details of which again Universal Grammar itself specifies. Presumably, such choices and settings would be determined by whether the context in which a variety is used makes them salient or not. The features of the new context in which it is now used awaken the language to universal possibilities which had always been available to it. Because it had not needed to draw on them in its previous contexts, it had remained oblivious of or unconcerned about them. The demands of the new context make various of these possibilities immediately salient, as well as available, to the language. The language, therefore, avails itself of them, and this causes it to be transformed along lines indicated by them. The result is a set of differences in the emergent varieties, which might not, however, show themselves at the most abstract levels of structure. Nevertheless, they would still remain, as qualitative differences which would be experientially recognized.

Taken as wholes, therefore, the new varieties do emerge looking qualitatively different from Older Englishes, though not in purely abstract terms. This seems to be strikingly attested in experienced terms every time we hear the multivaried voices that express themselves in English in the international media or read the new literatures in English. These, if anything, are eloquent testimony to the ways in which New Englishes have enrichingly extended the ranges of the language and enlarged its possibilities.

Pidgins/creoles do this as much as New Englishes, if somewhat differently. This is not surprising, for they share with New Englishes that discontinuity with Older Englishes that makes them qualitatively different in just the same way. As mentioned above, they emerged initially out of linguistic interaction among people who spoke different mutually incomprehensible languages. Moreover, one of the parties involved, that whose language assumed basal status with regard to the variety that emerged, generally assumed a superior position relative to all the others. When creolization took place, the users too, like New English users, took the language into their own hands and proceeded to develop it along lines that they found useful for their own purposes. This ensured that it would extend its ranges and possibilities in ways very comparable to those in which New Englishes did. In addition, they, too, moved the transformed language into the process of normal transmission, as soon as the initial stages of its formation were past.

For all this, there are differences between pidgins/creoles and New Englishes from a sociohistorical point of view which justify their separation into distinct classes, as in Table 1. At the initial stage of their evolution, pidgins/creoles began as makeshift languages, as mentioned earlier. This reflected the fact that the dominant group to whom the language exclusively belonged at that point in time did not, as it were, hand it over to its new users in any kind of complete form. In fact, this group themselves played a role in simplifying it along the lines indicated, something which did not generally happen in New English situations. This was possible because in pidgin/creole situations the initial intercommunicative purposes were very rudimentary, involving certain restricted practical everyday purposes.

In New English situations, too, at the very initial stages, the range of purposes was not comprehensive, being confined to utilitarian functions. But of their nature, these functions involved immediate access to the standard Older English, particularly for its property of intellectualization, as it has been called. This relates to the capacity of the language to handle abstract thought (Garvin and Mathiot, 1970), something which some of its utilitarian functions made necessary. Therefore, the standard Older English, particularly through the classroom, had from the beginning a significant presence as the New English developed. When, moreover, the political motive mentioned above for propagating the language was added, even more of the standard language was opened out to these people. Neither the classroom nor the standard Older English had anything like this kind of role in the evolution of pidgins/creoles.

When the standard Older English did begin to become salient to pidgins/creoles, it was in terms of the process of decreolization, which tried to alter these distinct varieties in the direction of that standard. The process of decreolization has, however, been irrelevant to New Englishes. They emerged throughout with direct access to the standard Older English, and in the process developed their own standard form, which still maintained close links with the original Older English standard. In fact, this indigenized standard form took over the function of norm-determination in the community. An occasional exception is in the realm of official policy, which even now in some places continues to subscribe in theory to the Older English standard. However this may be, the entire situation makes the whole notion of the post-creole continuum irrelevant to New Englishes, as Chapter 3 will also affirm. These factors also explain why the further process of recreolization is not relevant to New Englishes, as it is to some pidgins/creoles. These New Englishes simply continue to develop and alter as they always have, in both the colloquial and standard forms they have developed for themselves.

There are other such differences also to be noted. While indigenous languages and cultures clearly played a role in the evolution of both pidgins/creoles and New Englishes, the roles were not entirely comparable. This might possibly be because of a stronger presence of these cultures and languages in the environments of New Englishes. This is not a matter which it is easy to be too clear about. But the very fact that the Language Bioprogramme Hypothesis could have been proposed to account for the evolution of pidgins/creoles seems to confirm that the indigenous languages and cultures were not too prominent a presence in pidgin/creole contexts. Bickerton's claim after all, as Chapter 2 will remind us, was that creole genesis involved access to neither the superstrate nor the substrate languages. This suggests that the role of the indigenous languages and cultures was minimal.

A further difference relates to the mode of normal transmission into which, it was mentioned above, both pidgins/creoles and New Englishes moved quite early. It appears that this move was more thoroughgoing in the case of pidgins/creoles than in the case of New Englishes. This is because in the latter case, there were still people who entered the speech community in spite of their not having learned the language in their homes.

A final significant difference between the two classes relates to the following matters which were mentioned earlier: the complementary role of English and indigenous languages in New English contexts; the accessibility of the original Older English standard; and the attitudes of the indigenous New English-using elite towards those who introduced the language to them and towards themselves and their indigenous cultures. The differences between the circumstances of pidgins/creoles and New Englishes in these respects have led to the two classes generally showing different areas of 'fuller' development as far as functional resources go. (It must be noted, though, that both are presently in the process of compensating for their 'lacks', as altering historical conditions permit.) Thus, New Englishes tended quite early to show evidence of intellectualization, even developing a standard form of their own, however close it might have been in many respects to the standard Older English. But the larger presence of the standard Older English in these contexts did, perhaps, turn out to be somewhat restrictive, for it appears to have deprived them of access to certain wider resources of the language, relating to its spoken use for everyday living. In terms of their adaptation to the everyday life of their larger environment, therefore, they tended to be somewhat attenuated, remaining considerably what Gunatilleke (1954) calls 'language(s) without metaphor' (see above and Chapter 3).

Pidgins/creoles, on the other hand, did not develop elaborated standard forms of their own invested with the property of intellectualization. The arenas of life which required such a form were closed to their users. In any event, the Older English standard was in those arenas to perform the required functions, quite independently of them. But, pidgins/creoles did enter more completely into the everyday lives of their users in the fullness of their experience within the realities of their environment. As a consequence, they emerged as full-blooded codes, more immediately adapted to the imaginative, emotional and actional lives of their users. This, perhaps, explains their considerable richness and resourcefulness in dealing with these dimensions of experience, when compared with many New Englishes.

All of these considerations seem to support the classification of varieties of English along the lines proposed in Table 1. As the discussion above shows, each class raises particular kinds of questions and calls attention to particular kinds of issues which the other classes do not make salient. The other things mentioned above apart, this very fact indicates that each does legitimately define a unique domain of academic inquiry. Looked at from some other points of view, these three different classes might indeed all be brought together in ways that will equally illuminate other significant dimensions of all of them, as we have recognized. But if the argument presented above on the basis of sociohistorical considerations is valid, then we have good reason to recognize that New Englishes do define a separate class of sociolinguistic objects which warrant a book of this kind.

Chapter 2
Theories of Language Genesis

Bao Zhiming

~ Introduction

In communities which have a common language, verbal communication is hardly a problem. We may come from different regions with distinct dialectal features, or we may belong to different social classes with equally distinct accents, but by and large communication is often taken for granted. We grow up speaking our mother tongue in our daily interaction, and so readily accept it that we pay scant attention to it.

Human contact, and with it language contact, has happened throughout history. Language contact is an important external cause of language change. Such change is often evolutionary, and its effect can be seen more clearly with the passage of time. Modern English is a product of language contact. If we compare modern English with, say, Shakespearean English, we can see clearly the phonological, morphological and grammatical differences that time has wrought upon the language. Although the history of English is punctuated by periods of rapid change due to language contact brought about by foreign invasion, the continuity of the language among the general population has always been maintained (Jespersen, 1923).

The situation changes radically when groups of people with no common language come together. In Chapter 1, we discussed the linguistic consequences of colonization and massive human dislocation, namely, the emergence of pidgins and creoles and other new varieties of English. In places such as South and Southeast Asia and West Africa, where England imposed colonial rule without establishing a sizeable English settlement, a small, English-speaking elite emerged, but the general population continued to speak the local languages. In such multilingual societies, English enjoyed, and still enjoys, a prestigious status as a language of administration, education, commerce, law, science and technology. Quite often, as in Singapore, the local population is composed of different ethnic groups who speak different languages, and English functions as a neutral lingua franca for interethnic communication. Due to influences from local languages, the English language in such communities has evolved into new varieties which are quite different from British English, in pronunciation, vocabulary and grammar. Singapore

English, Indian English, Nigerian English and so on, are varieties of English which are transplanted in totally new cultural, social and linguistic environments. It is not surprising that they develop new pronunciations, new words, new structures and new meanings that uniquely serve their own communities.

Pidgins and creoles emerge in a somewhat different sociopolitical environment. *Pidgins* arise to fill a communication need in situations where no common language exists. One such situation is trade. Indeed, the popular belief is that the word 'pidgin' is derived from the way Cantonese-speaking Chinese traders pronounce the word 'business'. According to the Oxford English Dictionary, Pidgin English, which arises to fill the communication needs of the traders, consists of English words which are 'corrupted in pronunciation, and arranged according to Chinese idiom.'

Trade is not the only situation which necessitates the emergence of pidgins. Colonial rule and the slave trade created ample opportunities for the development of such new forms of language. According to commonsense understanding, a pidgin is a new language which takes its words from one language, called the *superstrate* or *lexifier language*, and the bulk of its grammatical structure from another, which is called the *substrate language*. This characterization is simplistic, and will be elaborated upon in due course. The way pidgins are formed is called *pidginization*. Collectively, the superstrate languages are known as the *superstratum*, and the substrate languages, the *substratum*.

In terms of social and political status, lexifier or superstrate languages are dominant over substrate languages. Not surprisingly, English, through active English participation in colonial expansion and the slave trade, lexifies most pidgins that we know today. The substratum, however, is quite diverse. Caribbean pidgins have an African substratum, reflecting the geographical origin of the slave population. The English-based pidgins spoken in Hawaii have a strong Asian substratum, due to the fact that many labourers were brought from China, Japan and the Philippines to the plantations on the Hawaiian islands. But these people did not speak the same language, so substrate influence on the pidgin is varied and difficult to isolate with certainty.

By definition, pidgins do not have native speakers. When a pidgin acquires native speakers, as is the case when children of pidgin speakers grow up speaking it, it becomes a *creole*. The process whereby a pidgin becomes a creole, with accompanying increase in grammatical complexity and lexical sophistication, is known as *creolization*. Pidgins and creoles are related in the way they are acquired, and creoles must have a pidgin as a predecessor. For this reason the two terms are often used together. Like their pidgin predecessors, creoles show superstrate and substrate influence, although this is often masked as their grammar develops and grows in complexity. Pidgin and creole grammars are never the sum of a superstrate vocabulary and a substrate syntax.

The exact nature of substrate and superstrate influence on the emergence of such new languages in general, and pidgins and creoles in particular, is a complicated matter that defies simple characterization. Students of new varieties of English, and of pidgins and creoles, never fail to be amazed by the linguistic diversity and innovation exhibited in such languages. Without doubt these Englishes are full-fledged systems of communication, with their own vocabularies and grammars. Despite the efforts of several generations of researchers, the question of how they arise and acquire linguistic structures remains as controversial as ever. The controversy comes under the rubric of *language genesis*, which focuses mainly on pidgins and creoles. The fundamental question is this: How do the structures of pidgins and creoles arise through language contact? Since we are only concerned with new varieties of English, we will restrict our attention to pidgins and creoles which have English as their lexifier language. The question before us is therefore narrower. We are concerned with the exact nature of the influence from the superstrate English and various substrate languages on the structure of English-based pidgins and creoles and, by extension, on the structure of other types of New Englishes whose genesis depends heavily on language contact, such as Colloquial Singapore English, or CSE.

Many theories have been proposed to explain the processes of pidginization and creolization. Two dominant theories are still being debated to this day. They are the *substratist theory*, whose advocates claim that the structure of pidgins and creoles derives from the substratum, and the *universalist theory*, whose proponents argue that pidgins and creoles reflect universal properties of human language. Neither theory is watertight, and perhaps some form of synthesis is needed to account for the diverse range of features of New Englishes. Before we examine the two approaches, let us familiarize ourselves with a few important notions associated with the study of pidgins and creoles.

Life Cycles and the Creole Continuum

It is customary to classify pidgins and creoles into four types: jargon, stable pidgin, expanded pidgin and creole (Romaine, 1988). Typically, *jargons* consist of utterances which are one- or two-words long; in addition, they are limited in function and exhibit a great deal of variability among individual speakers. *Stable pidgins* gain in grammatical complexity and stability among speakers, and their vocabulary increases to about two hundred words. *Expanded pidgins* have sophisticated grammatical construction, a large and stable vocabulary and varied social and political functions. A pidgin can become a creole at any stage, as long as it has acquired native speakers. Whatever its origin, in structure and function, a creole is much more complex than its pidgin predecessor. The development from a jargon to a creole is often called a *life cycle*, a notion due to the well-known creolist Robert Hall (Hall, 1962). Not all creoles have undergone the same life cycle. At least three types of life cycle have been established among creole languages (Mühlhäusler, 1986; Mühlhäusler uses 'stabilized' instead of 'stable'):

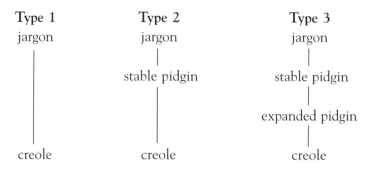

Type 1	Type 2	Type 3
jargon	jargon	jargon
	stable pidgin	stable pidgin
		expanded pidgin
creole	creole	creole

We can consider jargon, stable pidgin, expanded pidgin and creole as different phases of a creole's development. As the three life cycles indicate, a jargon may be creolized abruptly, skipping the middle two phases; or it may develop gradually, passing through all the phases before it is creolized. Scholars have identified Hawaiian Creole English as a Type 1 creole, Torres Straits Creole English as a Type 2 creole and Tok Pisin as a Type 3 creole.

It is often the case that a creole, its lexifier language and its substrate language(s) are spoken at the same time, so that the society is effectively multilingual. In English-based creole societies, Standard English continues to play an important role in commerce, education and other domains of life, and its influence on creoles cannot be overestimated. Linguists describe this mixture of creoles and standard languages as a *creole continuum*, or *post-creole continuum*. The idea is that people speak creoles with different degrees of sophistication in their referential meanings and grammatical soundness. At one end, the speech pattern resembles that of the standard language, i.e. the superstrate language; this pattern is labelled *acrolect*. At the other end, the *basilect*, the speech pattern is much more limited in vocabulary and grammatical complexity. In between we have *mesolects*, which are varieties of creoles with varying degrees of linguistic sophistication. There are other ways of characterizing the creole continuum. Romaine (1988), for example, identifies the creole as the basilect, the standard, superstrate language as the acrolect, and other varieties as mesolects. It must be pointed out that there are no sharp divisions along the continuum which define the boundaries of distinct varieties. To some extent, the continuum reflects the command of the creole language of various segments of the population. For obvious reasons the educated elite usually speak the acrolectal varieties, while the less educated tend to speak mesolectal or basilectal varieties. Creole continua make it difficult to describe the grammars of creole languages.

Associated with the notion of the creole continuum is *decreolization*. This is the situation when the grammar of the creole becomes indistinguishable from that of its superstrate language. In other words, the basilectal and the mesolectal speakers start adopting the acrolectal speech patterns and grammatical structure. This is found, in Bickerton's (1980) words, 'wherever a creole language is in direct contact with its associated superstrate language.' Although it is difficult to determine cases of decreolization, Romaine (1988) mentions a few creoles which have been decreolized. In North America, Black English started its life as a creole, and is now in the last stages of decreolization. What this means is that the grammar of Black English now resembles the grammar of Standard American English in more respects than it did previously. Other creoles that are in various stages of decreolization include those spoken in Jamaica, Guyana and Papua New Guinea — places where English, the prestigious superstrate language, continues to play an important role: a precondition for decreolization to occur.

The idea of a creole continuum is not without controversy. Some scholars reject the notion, and argue in favour of *diglossia* ('two languages'), with complementary communicative functions for the two languages. The term 'diglossia' can be used broadly to refer to two unrelated languages spoken in the same community, or narrowly to refer to two functionally distinct varieties of English (Ferguson, 1959). Typically, the 'high' variety, the socially more prestigious one, is used in formal situations such as education, media and government; the 'low' variety, which is the less prestigious of the two, is used in informal situations. In Singapore, English is one of the official languages, and is the language of government, education, law and commerce, due to the active participation of multinational companies in Singapore's economy. Through universal education, Singaporeans' linguistic repertoire includes Standard English (the 'high' variety), CSE, which some consider to be creole-like (Platt, 1975: a *creoloid*), and local languages — mainly Mandarin, several southern Chinese dialects, Malay and Tamil. As far as English is concerned, CSE is not a speech continuum, but the 'low' variety which is in diglossic co-existence with the 'high' variety, i.e. Standard English. The two varieties perform complementary communicative functions in Singapore.

The continuum-diglossia controversy is not going to go away easily. The core of the matter lies in the inherent difficulty of delimiting the boundary of a variety of language, whether it is a pidgin, creole, or 'normal' language.

ꙮ   *The Substratum*

In the preceding sections we described the distinction between pidgins and creoles, and some concepts associated with them. In this section and the next, we will examine the theoretical controversy surrounding the origin of pidgins and creoles. Among the theories which have been proposed by *creolists* (linguists who study pidgins and creoles), we will single out the substratist approach and the universalist approach. These two approaches are chosen because they have the widest acceptance, and the debate they have stimulated continues to this day. We will examine the substratist approach first.

As we mentioned earlier, pidgins are languages which arise in communities where there is no common language. They have a limited vocabulary from the superstrate, i.e. lexifier, language, and a simplified grammatical structure. It is generally accepted that the vocabulary of a pidgin comes from the superstrate language, which is the dominant language in the newly constituted communities where pidgins arise. The origin of the grammatical structure of a pidgin is less certain. The core idea of the substratist approach is that the grammatical structure of a pidgin is, to a large extent, determined by the grammatical structure of the substrate language or languages. The substratist approach was first proposed to account for the origin of pidgins. Later the idea was extended to the genesis of creoles as well. Here we examine the substratist ideas in light of the structures of pidgins and creoles, without making a conscious effort to keep them apart.

The evidence of a substratum in a pidgin or creole is not hard to come by. Researchers have demonstrated parallels in the structure of West African languages and the Atlantic English-based creoles, which originated in communities with a large African slave population (Holm, 1988; Romaine, 1988; Levebvre and Lumsden, 1989; Arends *et al.*, 1995; among many others). Structural similarities exist even among creoles which are lexified by different languages. On the structural affinities of English-based creoles spoken in the Americas and West Africa, Hancock (1971) says:

> [T]he grammatical structure of any one of these English-derived creoles is far closer to any one of the other creoles...whose words are not English-derived — such as the French- or Portuguese-derived creoles — than it is to English.

In the same spirit, Taylor (1971; 1977) examines some common grammatical features of French-based creoles, English-based creoles, Dutch-based creoles and Iberian-based creoles, and attributes these grammatical features to the creoles having the same or closely related substrate languages, principally the African language of Yoruba. We will not discuss Taylor's grammatical features, since some of them require specialized knowledge of linguistics. We will, however, discuss a few familiar grammatical features which substantiate substratist claims.

Bislama Pronouns

Jeff Siegel discusses the pronouns of Bislama, an English-based creole language spoken in Vanuatu. The pronouns are shown in the following chart (Siegel, 1996: 255).

	Singular	Dual	Trial	Plural
1st person inclusive		yumitu(fala)	yumitrifala	yumi
1st person exclusive	mi	mitufala	mitrifala	mifala
2nd person	yu	yutufala	yutrifala	yufala
3rd person	hem/em	tufala	trifala	olgeta

There is a four-way distinction in person in Bislama: singular, when the pronoun refers to one individual only; dual, to two individuals; trial, to three individuals; and plural, to more than three individuals. The distinction between 'inclusive' and 'exclusive' applies to the non-singular first person pronoun. When the pronoun refers to the speaker and the listener, it is inclusive; if it refers only to the speaker, and someone else, it is exclusive. One noticeable feature of the Bislama pronoun system is the lack of gender marking: the same pronoun, *hem* (or *em*), is used for feminine, masculine and neuter subjects (*she, he, it*). It is obvious that the words come from English, which is the lexifier language. We can easily segment the dual first person pronoun into 'you-me-two', and the trial into 'you-me-three-fellow'. But the four-way distinction of number, and the exclusive-inclusive distinction of person, do not come from English. Where do they come from?

The answer to the question can be found in the substratum of Bislama. The native tongues spoken in Vanuatu all belong to the Austronesian family of languages. One member of this family is Tangoan, spoken on an island not far from Vanuatu, which has the following pronoun system:

	Singular	Dual	Trial	Plural
1st person inclusive		enīarua	enīatolu	enīa
1st person exclusive	enau	kamamrua	kamamrua	kamamrua
2nd person	egko	kamimrua	kamimtolu	kamim
3rd person	enia	enrarua	enratolu	enra/enira

The actual pronouns are different: the first person exclusive dual is *mitufala* in Bislama, but *kamamrua* in Tangoan; similarly, the second person singular is *yu* in Bislama, but *egko* in Tangoan, and so on. In fact the Bislama pronouns are derived from English, for example, *mitufala* is derived from *me-two-fellow*, which explains why it is the first person exclusive dual pronoun; in contrast, the first person inclusive dual pronoun, *yumitufala*, is derived from *you-me-two-fellow*. The structure of the Bislama pronoun system, however, is exactly the same as that of Tangoan, in the sense that both systems maintain the singular-dual-trial-plural distinction and the first person inclusive and exclusive distinction. Siegel (1996: 256) writes:

> Thus it is clear that the forms of Bislama's pronoun system are derived from its lexifier language, English, but the grammatical distinctions are from its Oceanic substrate languages.

The Bislama pronoun system is a strong case of substrate influence.

Serial Verb Construction

Another area of substrate influence in the genesis of creoles is the serial verb construction, in which two or more verbs are used in series in the same sentence. This construction is found in Sino-Tibetan languages (Chinese and Tibetan are the two major languages of this family) and languages in West Africa, but not in English, or any other European languages. It is, interestingly, a general feature of creole languages. Arends *et al.* (1995) produce the following data from various languages:

(1) a. A tei goni suti di pingo   [Saramaccan]
         he take gun shoot the pig
         He shot the pig with a gun.

     b. Ode   adare   no twaa   nkromata   [Akan]
         he-take machete the cut-PAST branch
         He cut the branch with a machete.

(2) a. A waka go na   wowoyo   [Sranan]
         he walk go PREP market
         He went to the market.

     b. Oguang   koo   ahabang mu   [Akan]
         he-flee-PAST go-PAST bush   in
         He fled into the bush.

To which we can add the following from CSE [(3a) is taken from Ho, 1992]:

(3) a. I follow her go to market   [CSE]
         I went to the market with her.

     b. wo gen   ta qu shichang   [Chinese]
         I   follow her go market
         I went to the market with her.

     c. I walk go market   [CSE]
         I walked to the market.

     d. wo zou   qu shichang   [Chinese]
         I   walk go market
         I walked to the market.

Saramaccan and Sranan are two creole languages spoken in Surinam, for which Akan is one of the African substrate languages, and Chinese is a major language spoken in Singapore. The English lexical source is quite clear in the data. The serial verb construction of Saramaccan, Sranan and CSE, which does not exist in English, has parallels in the substrate languages. In (1), the first verb, *tei* in Saramaccam and *ode* in Akan, expresses an 'instrument' meaning; in (2), the second verb, *go* in Sranan and *koo* in Akan, expresses the 'destination' meaning. In English, these meanings are typically expressed with the help of prepositions, as indicated in the glosses. The CSE sentences are almost a word-for-word translation of the Chinese equivalent. The similarity in structure is striking. Although English is the source of the words, the grammatical structure comes out of the substrate languages, which happen to have the serial verb construction. As far as serialization of verbs is concerned, CSE, Saramaccan, Sranan, and other Atlantic creoles with African substrata, have more in common with each other than with English, their common lexifier language.

Already in Singapore English

The system of tense and aspect is another area of substrate influence. Here, we will consider the function of *already* in CSE. Many researchers have worked on the use of *already*, and shown that its functions are related to the Chinese *le* (Platt and Weber, 1980; Kwan-Terry, 1989; Ho, 1992; Bao, 1995). A note on the term 'Chinese' is in order. For all practical purposes we can consider 'Chinese' as a cover term for a group of mutually unintelligible languages. These languages are identified by the geographic locations in which they are spoken, and are often called Chinese dialects. Since the majority of the Chinese population in Singapore trace their origin to southern Fujian, the most common Chinese dialect is Hokkien (Fujian in *pinyin*).

Other major Chinese dialects which are represented in Singapore are Teochew, Cantonese, Hakka and Hainanese. Although their phonologies differ considerably, the dialects nevertheless share a core vocabulary and the basic syntactic structure. For this reason, we will use the term 'Chinese', and transcribe the data in *pinyin* in accordance with Mandarin pronunciation, whenever explicit reference to a particular dialect is not necessary. In Mandarin, *le* is etymologically the same as *liau* in Hokkien.

Already in CSE marks two aspects, the perfective and the inchoative. Aspects provide a perspective on the actions being reported, and the perfective and the inchoative have opposite aspectual meanings: the former means the completion of an action or state, and the latter means the beginning of an action or state. In English, the perfective aspect is typically expressed with the past tense — *Mei Mei cried* reports a completed event, and the inchoative aspect is expressed with the help of words like *start* or *begin* — *Mei Mei started to cry* reports an event that has just been initiated. In Hokkien, however, both aspectual meanings are expressed by *liau*: the expression *chat bun liau* — 'eat rice liau' — could have the perfective meaning of having eaten the meal, or the inchoative meaning of starting to eat the meal. Context of use will disambiguate the expression.

Now consider the CSE data below (Kwan-Terry, 1989):

(4)   a.   I cannot go inside *already*.

     b.   The tongue red *already*.
        The tongue has turned red.

Both sentences in (4) have the inchoative reading: in (4a), the speaker does not have the permission to go inside now, with the implication that he or she had the permission earlier — in other words, the speaker 'has started' to be in the new state. Similarly, in (4b), the tongue is now in the state of redness, which it was not previously. The sentences below are perfective (Kwan-Terry, 1989):

(5)   a.   I eat the cake *already*.
        I have already eaten the cake.

     b.   Close all the doors *already*.
        I have already closed all the doors.

From the sentences in (4) and (5), we can make the observation that *already* is inchoative when it is used with state predicates (such as *red*) or modal verbs (such as *can*), and perfective when it is used with event predicates (*eat, close*). This is evident in the following sentences (Kwan-Terry, 1989):

(6)   a.   Alice fell down in the hole *already*.   (perfective)

    b.   The red car go *already*.   (perfective)

    c.   Now my school is close *already*.   (inchoative)

    d.   I don't want it *already*.   (inchoative)

Since *already* occurs in the same syntactic position for both the perfective and inchoative interpretations, we would expect it to be ambiguous in some sentences. This is the case for the sentence below:

(7)   I eat durian *already*.
    i.   I have already eaten (the) durian.   (perfective)
    ii.   I now eat durians.   (inchoative)

The sentence is ambiguous between the perfective reading (7i) and the inchoative reading (7ii). Again, context of use provides cues to disambiguate the sentence.

    How does *already* acquire the two uses? To be sure, the two aspects are semantically compatible with the lexical meaning of *already* in English. But English expresses the perfective aspect with *have* and the verb's past participial form (*I have eaten durians*) and uses words like *start, begin* or *now* to express the inchoative aspect. *Already* does not perform any aspectual function directly. Therefore the source of CSE *already* cannot be found in English. We will show below that the aspectual function of *already* comes from the substrate language of Chinese.

    The Mandarin *le* can occur in two positions — after the verb, or at the end of the sentence. These are exemplified below:

(8)   a.   Zhangsan chi-*le*   pingguo.
        Zhangsan eat-LE apple.
        Zhangsan has eaten/ate the apple.

    b.   Zhangsan chi pingguo *le*.
        Zhangsan eat apple   LE.
        i.   Zhangsan starts to eat the apple.   (event)
        ii.   Zhangsan now eats apples.   (state)

When *le* is post-verbal, it expresses the perfective aspect, as shown in (8a). When it is used at the end of a sentence, as in (8b), it expresses the inchoative aspect: as a state, *chi pingguo le* means that Zhangsan now eats apples, implying that he did not eat apples before; as an event, the sentence means that Zhangsan starts to eat the apple. Note that the gloss of *pingguo* differs as well: in the event interpretation (8b-i), *pingguo/apples* refers to a specific apple or specific apples; in the state interpretation (8b-ii), it does not.

For state predicates such as *know*, *believe* and *red*, *le* expresses the beginning of the state, regardless of where it occurs in the sentence:

(9)   a.   Zhangsan zhidao zhe-jian shi   *le*.
              Zhangsan know   this   matter LE.
              Zhangsan knows the matter.

        b.   Zhangsan zhidao *le* zhe-jian shi.
              Zhangsan know   LE this   matter.
              Zhangsan knows the matter.

        c.   shitou hong *le*.   [cf. (4b)]
              tongue red   LE.
              The tongue is red/has turned red.

This is exactly the situation we saw with *already*.

From the above discussion it is clear that the aspectual function of *already* in CSE is derived from the Chinese *le*. We summarize the aspectual functions of the Mandarin *le*, and CSE *already* in the chart below:

	With Event Predicate	With State Predicate
le	perfective (verb-final) inchoative (sentence-final)	inchoative (verb-final) inchoative (sentence-final)
already	perfective inchoative	inchoative

Again, we see that the word *already* is derived from English, the superstrate language, but the aspectual functions are derived from Chinese, the major substrate language of CSE.

Substrate Influence in Phonology

Substrate influence in the pronunciation of a pidgin or creole hardly needs emphasizing. When we learn a foreign language, our pronunciation will most likely be influenced by the speech habits we have acquired in our native tongue. Foreign accents are not something new in our experience with language. In the formation of a creole, the phonological features of the substrate languages will show up here and there, and the features of the superstrate, particularly those which are not found in the substrate, will be dropped, or otherwise modified to facilitate pronunciation. Here we will consider how the distinction between long and short vowels in English fares in pidgins and creoles.

Tense vs. Lax Vowels

Hall (1966) describes the loss of contrast between 'tense' vowels and 'lax' vowels in pidgins and creoles. Tense vowels are pronounced with a noticeable degree of tension in the tongue muscles, whereas lax vowels are pronounced with relaxed tongue muscles. English maintains the distinction between /i/ *beat* and /ɪ/ *bit*; between /e/ *bait* and /ɛ/ *bet*; between /u/ *fluke* and /ʊ/ *book*; and between /o/ *coat* and /ɔ/ *caught*. In English, the tense vowels are typically lengthened or diphthongized; so /i, e, u, o/ are commonly transcribed as /iː, eɪ, uː, əʊ/. Some linguists transcribe the diphthongs /eɪ, əʊ/ as /ei, ou/, bringing out the common effect of the tongue's muscular tensing on the vowels. In Neo-Melanesian, a creole spoken in Papua New Guinea, the tense-lax distinction is lost, as shown in the following chart:

Words	English	Neo-Melanesian	Sound change
leg	lɛg	leg	ɪ > e
pussy	pʊsi	pusi	ʊ > u
forgive	fɔrgɪv	pogip	ɔ > o; ɪ > i

The tense-lax vowel pairs /e, ɛ/, /i, ɪ/, /u, ʊ/ and /o, ɔ/ become four vowels transcribed as /e, i, u, o/ respectively. Whatever the phonetic realizations of the phonemes /e, i, u, o/, the fact remains that the distinction between tenseness and laxness is no longer contrastive in Neo-Melanesian. In other words, due to substrate influence, the phonemic inventory no longer contains the tense-lax pairs of vowels. The loss of the tense-lax distinction is quite common across New Englishes.

Exactly the same sound changes happen in CSE. According to Tay (1982) and Hung (1996), CSE has five simple vowels, as shown below:

$$i \qquad u$$
$$\varepsilon \qquad ɔ$$
$$ɑ$$

plus the schwa /ə/. Among the vowels, there is no length contrast, nor is there tense-lax contrast. So, the following words are homophonous in CSE: *beat/bit* [bit], *bet/bat* [bɛt], *pool/pull* [pul], *caught/cot* [kɔt] and *lark/luck* [lɑk]. In Standard English, they are distinct.

The vowel system of CSE shows clear influence from the speech habits of its substratum, which includes the Austronesian language of Malay. Malay has the same number of vowels as CSE (Othman, 1990):

```
        i           u
        e           o
              a
```

plus the schwa /ə/. The vowel qualities differ slightly, notably for the mid vowels. In the articulation of Malay /e, o/, the tongue position is higher than that for English /ɛ, ɔ/. Nevertheless, the CSE vowel system is remarkably similar to that of Malay.

The CSE and Neo-Melanesian vowel systems are representative of the vowel systems of many New Englishes, including pidgins and creoles. Tok Pisin, a pidgin English spoken in Papua New Guinea, and Sranan, a creole English spoken in Surinam, have the same vowel contrasts, which are close to those of CSE:

Tok Pisin		Sranan	
i	u	i	u
e	o	e	o
ɑ		ɑ	
(Todd, 1984)		(Adamson and Smith, 1995)	

In addition to the five oral vowels, Sranan has five nasalized vowels, whereas Tok Pisin does not have nasalized vowels at all. It would seem mysterious why totally unrelated languages have exactly the same vowel contrasts. There are two plausible explanations for this. First, the five-vowel contrasts we see in CSE, Neo-Melanesian, Tok Pisin and Sranan are a direct result of simplification, i.e. the loss of the long-short and tense-lax distinctions in the vowels of Standard British or American English. Second, the substrate influence is similar, even though the New Englishes do not have the same substrate languages. For CSE, Neo-Melanesian and Tok Pisin, the main substrate languages are members of the Austronesian family; Sranan, on the other hand, has an African substratum. According to Holm (1988), African languages, such as Bantu, have the following vowel pattern:

	Front	Back
High	i	u
Mid	e	o
Mid	ɛ	ɔ
Low		a

Two mid vowel pairs, /e, ɛ/ and /o, ɔ/, are phonemic only in a few languages. For many African languages, then, there are only five vowel phonemes: two high vowels, two mid vowels and one low vowel. Such a vowel pattern is exactly that found in Sranan and other New Englishes with an Austronesian substratum. It is possible that the simplified vowel system of New Englishes results from simplification *and* substrate influence.

Pre-nasalized Vowels

There are two types of stop consonant which are found in some New Englishes, but not in Standard English: the co-articulated stops and pre-nasalized stops. Co-articulated stops are made at two places of articulation simultaneously. Two common stops of this type are /kp, gb/, which are produced at the velar region and the lips. These stops are found in many African languages and New Englishes with an African substratum, such as Krio and Nigerian Pidgin English. Typically, they occur in loan words from the substrate languages.

Pre-nasalized stops, symbolized as /^{m}b, ^{n}d, ^{ŋ}g/, are different from sequences of nasals and stops with the same place of articulation, such as *mb* in *bombard*. They are single phonemes, not sequences of distinct phonemes. Pre-nasalized stops are produced by lowering the soft palate to let airstream enter the nasal cavity before releasing the stop. They are found in Tok Pisin: *ta^{m}bu* 'taboo' and *em i ^{n}dai* 'he fainted' (Todd, 1984). It is not clear from Todd's description whether these stops are phonemic. Most likely, they are the phonetic realizations of voiced stops (/b, d, g/). They do occur as phonemes in some languages. In Saramaccan, a New English spoken in Surinam, pre-nasalized nasals have been analysed as distinct phonemes (Holm, 1988). Incidentally, they are phonemes in African languages, which are the substratum of Saramaccan.

Phonotactically Conditioned Sound Change

The combination of phonemes into syllables and words is subject to language-specific conditions known as *phonotactic conditions* or *constraints*. The phonotactic conditions determine the possible phonological shapes of words in a given language. Chinese, for example, does not allow consonant clusters at all, while English allows up to three consonants in word-initial position, e.g. *spring*. In Chinese, only nasals and voiceless plosives (in some dialects) can appear at the end of a word, but in English, we have a wider range, from nasals (*pen*), to plosives (*stop*), to fricatives (*leaf*). An English word can even end in more than one consonant (*six*). Thus, Chinese and English differ considerably in their phonotactic conditions.

In CSE, and many other New Englishes, we can observe two types of sound effect due to the phonotactics of the language. These constraints concern consonant clusters and the phonetic realization of stops in word-final position. We look at the cluster simplification first. To be sure, CSE allows roughly the same range of consonant clusters in word-initial position: C (*pay*), CC (*pray*) and CCC (*spray*). So there is no simplification there. However, in coda position, the final stop is deleted (for ease of comparison we use the same vowel and consonant symbols):

	Standard English	CSE
list	[lɪst]	[lɪs]
past	[pɑːst]	[pɑːs]
send	[sɛnd]	[sɛn]
friend	[frɛnd]	[frɛn]
mask	[mɑːsk]	[mɑːs]

The final consonant is not deleted when a vowel follows it:

listing	[lɪstɪŋ]
sending	[sɛndɪŋ]
masking	[mɑːskɪŋ]

So the best analysis is to assume that the phonemic representation of words like *list, send* and *mask* in CSE is the same as the Standard English input, and the word-final stops are deleted to simplify the coda clusters.

When a word-final stop is preceded by a vowel, it is unreleased, and the vowel comes to an abrupt stop. Since voiced stops devoice word-finally, the following RP minimal pairs are homophonous (the symbol ˺ means unreleased; only relevant phonetic details are shown):

tap	ta[p˺]	debt	de[t˺]	back	ba[k˺]
tab	ta[p˺]	dead	de[t˺]	bag	ba[k˺]

The devoicing of /b, d, g/ occurs as well.

The phenomena exemplified above have reflexes in the local languages. In both Malay and Chinese, consonants do not form clusters in word-final positions, and only voiceless stops appear in that position, and are realized as unreleased. So here are two cases of substrate influence.

However, the substrate influence is rather weak, since other types of cluster, such as [ks] in *six*, are attested in CSE, and onset clusters are the same as those in Standard English. The weakness of substrate influence in CSE is due to the strong influence of Standard English. In the development of the phonology of CSE, Standard English has won the tug of war over local languages.

Phonetic Realization

Substrate influence can be seen in phonetic realization of phonemes as well. In this connection, we will discuss three cases: aspiration, palatalization and devoicing. As is well-known, the voiceless stops in Standard English are realized as aspirated, except before /s/; compare *pan* [pʰan], *tan* [tʰan], *can* [kʰan] with *span* [span], *stan* [stan], *scan* [skan]. In New Englishes, however, the voiceless stops are typically realized as unaspirated regardless of what precedes them. CSE is typical in this respect; there is no difference in the phonetic realization of the voiceless stops in the two groups of words mentioned above. One may argue that this is due to substrate influence, since in Malay, an Austronesian language, voiceless stops are unaspirated. But there is a wrinkle in this argument. The majority of the population in Singapore is Chinese, speaking dialects of southern China which contain voiceless, aspirated stops. Whatever the explanation, it is a strong tendency for voiceless stops to be unaspirated in New Englishes.

Palatalization is a common phonological process which affects consonants, particularly alveolars and velars. In casual speech in English, /s/ becomes [ʃ] (*miss you*) and /t/ becomes /tʃ/ (*meet you*). Since /ʃ, tʃ/ are palato-alveolars, the change to [ʃ, tʃ], and other palatal sounds, is called palatalization. The English example is a typical case of palatalization: a sound becomes palato-alveolar or palatal when it precedes the high vowel /i:/ or the semi-vowel /j/. There is articulatory reason for this change: to pronounce /i:, j/, the body of the tongue has to be raised towards the palate, which will likely influence the pronunciation of the immediately preceding alveolars and velars. Palatalization is a very common sound change among the world's languages.

Among New Englishes, palatalization is responsible for the occurrence of a number of 'new' sounds, the most frequent of which is the palatal nasal /ɲ/. In CSE, this occurs before the high vowel /i/ and the semi-vowel /j/: *oni* [oɲi] 'only', *nonya* [noɲja] 'nonya'. Almost certainly in CSE [ɲ] is not a distinct phoneme, but an allophone of /n/. Its phonemic status in other New Englishes, such as Cameroon Pidgin English analysed in Todd (1984), is not clearly established. In Surinamese Creole Englishes, the velar stops /k, g/ are palatalized before front vowels: *gei* or *djei* 'to resemble'. Here, the palatal [dj] is not phonemic, but an allophone of /g/ (Holm, 1988).

Devoicing is a common process in New Englishes. Voiced consonants, especially the stops /b, d, g/ and the affricate /dʒ/, become voiceless at the end of a word. In Cameroon Pidgin English and Tok Pisin, /b, d, g/ are devoiced in *rub, bad, big*. In CSE, they are not only devoiced, but also unreleased. In the case of CSE, substrate influence can be established. In Malay and the southern dialects of Chinese, the word-final stops are all voiceless and unreleased.

Word Structure

Hall (1944) describes the grammar of Chinese Pidgin English in some detail. According to the author, this pidgin was in use since the eighteenth century in the treaty ports in central and southern China, 'as a medium of intercourse between Chinese and foreigners.' Apparently it was never creolized, since nobody acquired it as a native language. Two features in Hall's data show clear influence from Chinese. In Chinese Pidgin English, the word *side* is used as a suffix to indicate a location. Thus we find the following expressions: *Shanghai-side* 'at Shanghai', *office-side* 'at the office', and *you house-side* 'at your home'. Corresponding to these expressions, we have, in Chinese, *Shanghai na-bian* (Shanghai that-side), *bangongshi na-bian* (office that-side), and *ni jia na-bian* (you house that-side). In other words, the source of the locative use of *side* is *na-bian* 'that side' or *zhe-bian* 'this side'. The sentence *My go club-side* is a direct translation from Chinese: *wo qu julebu na-bian*.

CSE exhibits the same kind of substrate influence as well. One often hears expressions like *Clementi that side*, *Changi Village that side*, where *that side* has the same locative function as *-side* in Chinese Pidgin English. Both are translations of the Chinese *na-bian*.

Number in English is expressed through inflection. So we have *one book/ two books*. Chinese is not an inflectional language, and makes use of classifiers such as *ben* in counting (*yi-ben shu* 'one book'/*liang-ben shu* 'two books'). Not surprisingly, Chinese Pidgin English has forms like *two coolie, three rickshaw*. Interestingly, the word *piece* can used as a classifier in the above two expressions: *two piece coolie, three piece rickshaw*. The substrate influence is evident in the lack of number inflection and in the use of the classifier *piece*.

Some Problems with the Substratist Approach

In some ways the substratist approach is intuitively satisfying. Our common sense tells us that our native speech habits stay with us for a long time, and will not change easily in new linguistic environments. There are, however, problems with the substratist approach in the actual analysis of linguistic facts. Here we will mention three.

Hall (1962) argues that, unlike 'normal' languages which are transmitted from generation to generation, a pidgin has a life cycle. It begins its life as a 'minimum language' to fulfil the need for communication in communities where no common language is spoken. Therefore, its early, 'jargon' stage is simple in both vocabulary and grammar, and its functions are vastly reduced. At the phase of 'expanded pidgin', it has gained in vocabulary and grammatical complexity as well as communicative functions, particularly when it acquires native speakers, i.e. is creolized. If the superstrate language continues to be spoken in the community and commands the position of prestige, the speakers will have the sociopolitical, cultural and commercial incentive to adopt the speech standards of the superstrate language. The creole then experiences decreolization, until it becomes indistinguishable from the superstrate language, whereupon it has reached the end of its life. If pidginization reduces the vocabulary size and grammatical complexity of the superstrate and substrate languages, creolization is just the opposite: the vocabulary, grammatical structure and functions are expanded, sometimes vastly so. When we examine the features of various pidgins, we find that the substrate influence is the strongest in the jargon stage, and weakens towards the later stages. As the pidgin grows in grammatical complexity, the source of influence becomes difficult to isolate. Undoubtedly expanded pidgins contain grammatical constructions attributable to substrate influence, especially those which are inherited from early stages; substratists cannot account for the full complexity of creole structure.

Another problem with the substratist approach is the difficulty in identifying the substrate languages themselves. In some situations, it is possible to identify the source of substrate influence, as is the case with Tok Pisin, Bislama and CSE. In the Atlantic creoles developed out of the slave trade, slaves who were brought to the New World spoke entirely different languages. So the pidgin which arose in such a situation was not only used for communication between slaves and their owners, but for communication among slaves as well. This was the situation for Surinam creoles (Arends *et al.*, 1995). The lack of homogeneity in the substratum makes it all but impossible to attribute a grammatical structure to influence from a specific substrate language. And the passage of time also obscures the origin of grammatical features in a creole.

Finally, the substratist theories may fail to give a full account of a grammatical construction, even though the substrate source can be clearly identified. This is the situation with cluster simplification in CSE, which we have seen in an earlier section. While it is true that no more than one consonant can appear in word-final position in Chinese, the substrate account does not explain why cluster simplification applies only to word-final position, leaving word-initial clusters intact. This type of 'underexplanation' can also be found in substrate explanations of other grammatical constructions.

The Universalist Approach

While the substrate theorists are preoccupied with creole constructions which are traceable to substrate languages, the universalist theorists are impressed by the structural similarities among creoles with diverse substrata. The core process for the substratists is pidginization; for the universalists, it is creolization. There are many versions of the universalist approach to creole studies, which are discussed in such works as Todd (1984), Romaine (1988) and Arends *et al.* (1995); here we will introduce one such approach, the Language Bioprogramme Hypothesis, developed by the noted creolist Derek Bickerton.

The Language Bioprogramme Hypothesis is heavily influenced by generative linguistics developed in the 1960s by Noam Chomsky and his colleagues. So, before we examine the content of the Language Bioprogramme Hypothesis, let us outline Chomsky's view of language and language acquisition.

Chomsky and Universal Grammar

The theory of language that is associated with Noam Chomsky is mentalistic in philosophical orientation. Language is a mental faculty specific to the human species, and the job of linguists is to specify its structure in rigorous and formal terms. Chomsky expresses this idea in many of his writings (e.g. 1986). According to him, a child is born with the basic mechanism of acquiring language, which he calls the initial state. As a child acquires language, his mind 'matures' from the initial state to the final state, which is the fully formed adult grammar of the language. Between the two states there are various intermediate states, when the child's developing mental grammar is not exactly the same as the target grammar. Schematically we can represent the stages of child language acquisition as follows:

$$S_0 \rightarrow S_1 \rightarrow S_2 \rightarrow \dots \rightarrow S_n$$

where S_0 is the initial state, $S_{i, 0<i<n}$ are the intermediate states, and S_n is the final state. Although the states in the above schema are theoretical idealizations, we can imagine the one-word stage, the two-word stage, and so on, to be the products of the grammar in various states of the child's linguistic development. It must be emphasized that S represents a hypothetical mental state, which allows us to conceptualize the process of child language acquisition. The initial, innate state is also called Language Acquisition Device, or LAD. At the present time LAD has no biological reality, and remains a controversial concept of generative linguistics.

A related, and equally controversial, concept proposed by Chomsky is Universal Grammar. Universal Grammar is our genetically pre-programmed gift of the mind which will eventually 'grow' into the grammar of our languages. Since languages differ enormously, how does Universal Grammar account for the differences that exist among languages? In Chomsky's conception, Universal Grammar consists of two parts — principles and parameters. Principles are fixed, available to all languages. Parameters are like switches, which can be switched on or off. The differences among languages, big or small, result from specific settings of the parameters. The enterprise of generative linguistics is to discover the principles and enumerate the parameters that together determine the range of possible grammars of natural language. The relationship between Universal Grammar and grammars of particular languages is schematized below:

Universal Grammar

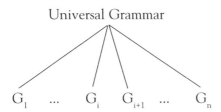

$$G_1 \quad ... \quad G_i \quad G_{i+1} \quad ... \quad G_n$$

Universal Grammar is the content of the initial state, S_0; it is a more explicitly articulated theoretical concept. Chomsky (1986: 146) summarizes the concept of Universal Grammar as follows:

> [We] may think of UG [Universal Grammar] as an intricately structured system, but one that is only partially "wired up." The system is associated with a finite set of switches, each of which has a finite number of positions (perhaps two). Experience is required to set the switches. When they are set, the system functions.

Switches are parameters, with either the 'on' or 'off' positions. The child's linguistic experience is obtained from the environment created by his or her caretakers, and this helps him or her decide whether to set a certain parameter in the 'on' or 'off' position.

To illustrate how the parameters of Universal Grammar work, we will discuss one common parameter: the so-called *pro-drop parameter*, which determines whether sentences of a language can have missing subjects. English sentences typically require a subject; where there is no plausible subject, a dummy is inserted to satisfy this requirement (Muysken and Veenstra, 1995):

(10) a. *He* eats   a'. *eats
      b. *It* seems that... b'. *seems that...

In (10b), *it* is the dummy subject, and '...' stands for any sentence. Spanish,

---

* Indicates unacceptable forms.

by contrast, allows null subjects. The two ungrammatical sentences in (10a')
and (10b') are grammatical in Spanish:

(10)   c.   Come   'eats'
        d.   Parece que ...   'seems that ...'

The grammaticality judgement is due to the setting of the pro-drop parameter:
English is [–pro-drop], Spanish is [+pro-drop]. It turns out that other
grammatical contrasts can be attributed to the same parameter. Consider
the following two contrasts:

(10)   e.   Spanish: Ha   venido Juan.
              English: *has come   John.
              John has come.

        f.   Spanish: Ha sido devorada la   oveja por el   lobo.
              English: *has been devoured the sheep by the wolf.
              The sheep has been devoured by the wolf.

In (10e), the subject *Juan/John* appears after the verb; in (10f), which is
passive, the original object (*la oveja/the sheep*) appears from the passivized
verb. The Spanish examples are grammatical, whereas their English
counterparts are not. The three syntactic features are all associated with the
parameter [pro-drop]. We summarize the effect of this parameter below:

	[+pro-drop]	[–pro-drop]
Missing subject	yes	yes
Post-verbal subject	yes	no
Post-verbal object in passive	yes	no

What appear to be unrelated grammatical features of English and Spanish
are united by a single parameter. The parametric study of language attempts
to derive grammatical features from a small set of parameters which are
universally available in the biologically endowed Universal Grammar.
Although we still do not have the full set of such parameters, the approach
nevertheless has its conceptual attractiveness.

Bickerton and the Language Bioprogramme Hypothesis

Bickerton is dissatisfied with the substrate account of creole genesis. The

---

* Indicates unacceptable forms.

basic observation is this: in a slave community, a pidgin arises to fill the basic communicative needs. It has a small vocabulary and a small repertoire of grammatical constructions, and performs a limited range of communicative functions. With little or no direct contact with either the superstrate or the substrate languages, children growing up in the community acquire the pidgin as their first language — in other words, the first-generation pidgin is rapidly nativized to become the mother tongue of the second generation. According to Bickerton (1981), this is the case with Hawaii Creole English, which evolved from a jargon to a creole in one generation, bypassing the stabilized pidgin and expanded pidgin stages. As has been observed by many students of creole languages, the vocabulary, structure and function of the creole are much richer than those of its pidgin predecessor. The question is, where does the additional structure in the creole come from? The extreme substratist would argue for a substrate source. This position is difficult to maintain in the case of Hawaii Creole English. Due to Hawaii's geographical isolation, children of slaves and labourers who had been brought to the plantations had limited access to other languages, whether English or the native languages of their parents. Nevertheless, they managed to acquire a creole which has a larger vocabulary and a richer repertoire of grammatical constructions. In relevant respects, creolization is language acquisition, except that a pidgin is being acquired as a native language of a speech community. Here the situation is quite severe: children with pidgin-speaking parents are not exposed to the same range of grammatical constructions as children of parents who speak 'normal' languages. The substratist approach fails to give an adequate account of the grammatical aspect of creolization. It is in this connection that Bickerton (1981; 1984) proposes his Language Bioprogramme Hypothesis as a theory of creole genesis. In the Introduction of his influential book, *Roots of Language*, Bickerton (1981: xii) says of his task:

> I shall examine the relationship between the variety of Creole English spoken in Hawaii and the pidgin which immediately preceded it, and I shall show how several elements of that creole could not have been derived from its antecedent pidgin, or from any of the other languages that were in contact at the time of creole formation, and that therefore these elements must have been, in some sense, "invented."...I shall discuss some...of the features which are shared by a wide range of creole languages and show some striking resemblance between the "inventions" of Hawaii and "inventions" of other regions which must have emerged quite independently;...

Inventions, or innovative grammatical features of creoles, particularly those which are shared across pidgins and creoles, are the tough nut for the substratists to crack.

Chomsky's influence in the formulation of the Language Bioprogramme Hypothesis is obvious. In Bickerton's words, 'the infrastructure of language is specified at least as narrowly as Chomsky has claimed' (Bickerton, 1984). If Chomsky's claim of a biologically endowed LAD is right, then child language acquisition is a process of parameter setting, which can be accomplished only through exposure to linguistic input. If a child hears *pro-drop* sentences, she 'sets' the *pro-drop* parameter as [+pro-drop]; if the language being acquired is not pro-drop, the child will be exposed to data where subjects are necessary for the well-formedness of sentences. Hence, the parameter will be set [–pro-drop]. The same process is repeated for other hypothesized parameters in Universal Grammar. When acquiring a 'normal' language such as English and Spanish, a child will have positive evidence for setting the parameters. Since a pidgin is simplified in structure, a child may have positive evidence for some parameters, but not for all of them. Bickerton hypothesizes that each Universal Grammar parameter has a default setting, which is activated in the absence of positive evidence in the linguistic environment. A child is born with Universal Grammar as part of her biological endowment. When she is exposed to English data, the parameters are set accordingly, and the child's Universal Grammar fleshes out to be the grammar of English; when she is exposed to other languages, the same process takes place, to create grammars of those languages. In a pidgin, she is exposed to limited data, and lacks positive evidence for some parameters. The grammar of the emerging creole will then contain structures from the pidgin, and new structures which result from the default settings of some of the parameters of Universal Grammar. This is, in a nutshell, the essence of Bickerton's Language Bioprogramme Hypothesis.

It is difficult to find relevant empirical facts to support the Language Bioprogramme Hypothesis, because of the lack of the right social conditions for creolization. Bickerton thinks that Hawaii, because of its relative isolation in the late nineteenth century and early twentieth century, provides just the right social environment for the study of creolization that bears on the Language Bioprogramme Hypothesis. In Bickerton (1981; 1984), Hawaii Pidgin English and Hawaii Creole English are compared, and five grammatical and semantic features are isolated. These features exist in Hawaii Creole English but not in the pidgin which preceded it — a case of grammatical innovation brought about by creolization. The five features are as follows (Bickerton, 1981: 17):

  a. movement rules
  b. articles
  c. verbal auxiliaries

    d.   *for-to* complementization
    e.   relativization and pronoun-copying

To better appreciate Bickerton's argument, we will take a look at three features, namely, articles, movement rules, and *for-to* complementization, in that order. All examples are quoted from Bickerton (1981).

Articles

In English, the referential capabilities of noun phrases are related to articles: the definite article *the* and the indefinite article *a/an*. In Standard English, the specific and non-specific distinction applies only to noun phrases, and is specified with the articles *the* and *a/an* respectively. *A/an* is used when the noun phrase does not refer to any particular object, e.g. *a man/an apple*. When we talk about specific things, we use *the*: *the man/the apple*. In Hawaii Pidgin English, the articles are used sporadically and unpredictably. There are two articles, the definite article *da* (*the*) and the indefinite article *wan* (*one*). The following examples illustrate:

(11)   a.   hi get *da* hawaian waif.
               He has a Hawaiian wife.

         b.   oni tek tu slais *da* bred.
               I only take two slices of bread.

Here, the use of the definite article *da* is unpredictable. In Standard English, one would use *a* in the first sentence, and no article at all in the second. In Hawaii Creole English, by contrast, *da* is used for noun phrases with specific reference only:

(11)   c.   æfta *da* boi, *da* wan wen jink dæt milk, awl *da* maut soa.
               Afterward, the mouth of the boy who had drunk that milk was all sore.

The indefinite article *wan* is used for first mention, where the NP reference is unknown to the listener:

(11)   d.   hi get *wan* blaek buk, daet buk no du eni gud.
               He has a black book. That book doesn't do any good.

The following noun phrases have no article:

(11)   e.   dag smat.
               The dog is smart.

f.   yang fela dei no du daet.
     Young fellows don't do that.

g.   mi ai get raesh.
     As for me, I get a rash.

The 'bare' noun phrase expresses meanings which call for different markings in English, as the glosses indicate. The generic use of the noun phrase in (11e) is marked with *the* in Standard English (*dag* vs. *the dog*), the plural use in (11f) with plural *-s* (*yang fela* vs. *young fellows*), and the indefinite use in (11g) with the indefinite article *a*. Bickerton terms all three uses non-specific. In Hawaii Creole English, the unmarked noun phrase groups together three categories which are kept distinct in Standard English. So, in referential possibilities, the noun phrase in Hawaii Creole English differs not only from its immediate predecessor, Hawaii Pidgin English, but also from the superstrate language, English. One might argue that the noun phrase is influenced by the substrate languages. But the substrate languages, among them Japanese, do not have articles at all. Bickerton concludes that the non-specific uses of unmarked noun phrases are an invention as Hawaii Pidgin English is turned into Hawaii Creole English.

Movement Rules

Word order in Hawaii Pidgin English and Hawaii Creole English is another invention which Bickerton thinks supports the Language Bioprogramme Hypothesis. The word order of a sentence is expressed in terms of the relative order of the subject (S), the verb (V) and the object (O). A typical English sentence has the order SVO (*John loves Mary*), and a typical Japanese sentence has the order SOV. A language can be characterized in terms of the word order of its typical sentences. So, English and Chinese are SVO languages; Japanese is an SOV language, and so on. The word order of Hawaii Pidgin English and Hawaii Creole English is summarized in Table 1 (adapted from Bickerton, 1981).

Word Order	Hawaii Pidgin English	Hawaii Creole English
SVO	yes	yes
SOV	yes	no
VS	yes	yes
VOS	no	yes
OSV	no	yes
OVS	no	yes

Table 1. Word Order in Hawaii Pidgin English and Hawaii Creole English

In both the pidgin and creole, the SVO order is the common and unmarked choice for all speakers. In Hawaii Pidgin English, word order preference sometimes signals ethnicity: Japanese labourers prefer SOV order and Filipino labourers prefer VS order. These orders are characteristic of the native languages of the speakers, betraying substrate influence in Hawaii Pidgin English. In Hawaii Creole English, however, word order is uniform for all speakers, and the SOV order is notably missing. All other orders are derived from the basic order SVO through movement rules which move either the object (O) or the predicate (V + O) to the beginning of the sentence. VOS is derived by moving the predicate to the front; OSV by moving the object; OVS by moving the predicate first, and then the object. VS occurs in both Hawaii Pidgin English and Creole English. But in Hawaii Pidgin English it is a result of the verb-first word order, possibly from Philippine languages. In Hawaii Creole English, it is the result of rules: O is deleted after VO is moved to the front to yield VOS. As for SOV, which does not exist in Hawaii Creole English despite the fact that it exists in its predecessor, the movement rules will not derive it from the basic SVO: there is no fronting of the object or predicate.

How does the word order of Hawaii Creole English arise? Japanese is a substrate language, and its word order is SOV. Yet SOV does not exist in Hawaii Creole English. Substrate influence may exist in Hawaii Pidgin English, but not in Hawaii Creole English which followed it. Bickerton (1981: 22) argues that substratists are unable to explain the distribution of word order shown in Table 1. He concludes:

> [I]t can hardly be accidental if that particular distribution turns out to be exactly what is generated if one assumes basic SVO order (which is virtually mandatory when you have no other means of marking the two major cases) plus a rule which moves either of the two major constituents, NP and VP, to sentence-initial position. We may therefore claim that the rules which move NPs and VPs cannot have been acquired inductively by the original [Hawaii Creole English] speakers, but must, in some sense of the term, have been "invented" by them *ab ovo*.

For-to Complementization

In English, embedded infinitive clauses may be introduced by *for*, as the following sentences show:

(12)   a.   Mary bought this for you to read.
       b.   Mary prefers (for) Bill to go.

c.   Mary prefers (*for) to go.

Whether *for* is obligatory or not depends on the matrix verb. In (12a), *for* is obligatory; it introduces the infinitive clause *you to read*. In (12b), *for* is optional, the infinitive clause *Bill to go* can appear without it. In infinitive clauses without an overt subject, as in (12c), *for* cannot be used at all. When a sentence or clause is used to complete the meaning of a predicate phrase, it is called a sentential complement, and the grammatical phenomenon is known as sentential complementization. Since the infinitive clauses in (12a) and (12b) are introduced with *for*, Bickerton calls the phenomenon *for-to* complementization.

In Hawaii Pidgin English, sentence-embedding of any kind is rare. Hawaii Creole English has sentential complements, marked by *fo* (from English *for*) and *go*. In Hawaii Pidgin English, *fo* is used as a preposition, and *go* is used as a main verb, as a marker of imperatives, and 'as a preverbal modifier of extremely indeterminate meaning and wildly fluctuating distribution' (Bickerton, 1981: 31). They are never used as complementizers, for the simple reason that Hawaii Pidgin English has no sentential complements. *Go* and *fo* as complementizers are illustrated below:

(13)   *go* as complementizer

a.   dei wen go ap dea erli in da mawning go plaen.
      They went up there early in the morning TO plant.

b.   so ai go daun kiapu go push.
      So I went down to Kiapu TO push (clear land with a bulldozer).

c.   ai gata go haia wan kapinta go fiks da fom.
      I had TO hire a carpenter TO fix the form.

(14)   *fo* as complementizer

a.   aen dei figa, get sambadi fo push dem.
      And they figured there'd be someone TO encourage them.

b.   mo beta a bin go hanalulu fo bai maiself.
      It would have been better if I'd gone to Honolulu TO buy it myself.

---

* Indicates unacceptable forms.

    c.   hau yu ekspek a gai fo mek pau hiz haus?
          How do you expect a guy TO finish his house?

Go and *fo* are used in places where English would use *to*. Syntactically, the two words have the same grammatical function of introducing embedded sentences; semantically, *go* is used to describe actions which have taken place, whereas *fo* is used to describe actions which are hypothetical. The realized-unrealized distinction is clearly indicated in the English glosses. Compared with its immediate predecessor, Hawaii Creole English exhibits three new grammatical and semantic features. First, sentential complementization has been invented; second, the preposition *fo* and the imperative marker *go* have acquired the new function of complementizer; third, the realized-unrealized distinction has been invented in sentential complementization. Bickerton argues that these new features could not have been inherited from Hawaii Pidgin English, since the latter does not have these features; nor from any of the contact languages. They were, therefore, invented *ab ovo*.

Summary

Inventions result from the intricate interplay of the universal principles and parameters of the language bioprogramme. In generative linguistics, the notion of constituency plays an important role. All linguistic processes, among them movement, apply to constituents, not random strings of words. The fact that the Hawaii Creole English movement rules move only constituents (objects O and predicates VO) to the beginning of the sentence is a result of universal principles. Exactly which principles and parameters are involved, Bickerton does not elaborate. The insight remains that the innovative aspects of creole grammar cannot simply be attributed to substrate languages, as staunch supporters of the substrate approach would argue. A plausible explanation of creolization lies in a thorough appreciation of linguistic universals. The innovative grammatical features conform to universal constraints which the human language bioprogramme imposes on the structure of language.

Some Problems with the Language Bioprogramme Hypothesis

The Language Bioprogramme Hypothesis has generated much excitement among students of pidgins and creoles, and it has been the subject of scholarly debate ever since Bickerton first proposed it. While it is attractive as a theory of creole genesis, it is nevertheless problematic in its conceptual underpinnings and empirical explanation. Conceptually, it is based on the view of language as a biologically determined mental faculty, but so far we have no biological evidence for this. Bickerton's language bioprogramme, just like Chomsky's LAD, remains a mentalistic construct. A theory of creole genesis based on such a construct is open to criticism from people with an empiricist philosophical persuasion. In addition, even if we accept the bioprogramme, we still do not know what constitutes a linguistic universal. And the features which Bickerton attributes to the bioprogramme can be interpreted in other ways. The specific vs. non-specific distinction in Hawaii Creole English is said to have arisen from the bioprogramme. But one can say, with equal plausibility, that the English definite article *the* is retained in Hawaii Creole English, and the indefinite article is replaced by *wan*. It does not bear on the bioprogramme at all, whether or not we accept the Language Bioprogramme Hypothesis as an adequate theory of creole genesis.

Empirically, it is difficult, if at all possible, to test the validity of the Language Bioprogramme Hypothesis in real-life situations. Although there are many pidgins in the world which have undergone creolization, not all of them can be used as evidence either to support or refute the Language Bioprogramme Hypothesis. Bickerton (1981) stipulates two conditions. A creole which is relevant for the Language Bioprogramme Hypothesis must be a language which:

1.   arose out of a prior pidgin which had not existed for more than a generation;

2.   arose in a population where not more than 20 percent were native speakers of the dominant language and where the remaining 80 percent was composed of diverse language groups.

The first criterion excludes cases like Tok Pisin, among others. The one-generation requirement minimizes the effect of prolonged contact with both the superstrate and substrate languages, which complicates the study of the language bioprogramme. The second criterion imposes on the creole community a sociological condition which is difficult to obtain, even in such an isolated place as the Hawaii islands at the turn of the century. In order to verify the claims of the Language Bioprogramme Hypothesis, one needs to examine creoles spoken in communities with little contact with the outside world, so that innovative grammatical features could be attributed to the language bioprogramme, rather than contact languages. Under such stringent requirements, most creoles do not qualify as relevant evidence. According to Bickerton, Hawaii Creole English is just about the only ideal creole for observing the language bioprogramme. Other researchers, among them Janson (1984) and Romaine (1988), disagree, arguing that the features of Hawaii Creole English which Bickerton discusses can in fact be interpreted in such a way that they do not bear on the language bioprogramme at all. Creolization is a case of language change. The development of Hawaii Creole English from Hawaii Pidgin English is therefore analogous to the development of Modern English from Middle English, and of Middle English from Old English. One need not invoke the hypothetical mental construct of the language bioprogramme.

The mentalist foundation of the Language bioprogramme hypothesis generates much debate of a philosophical nature. A universalist theory of creole genesis without the mentalist view of language is capable of accounting for the mechanisms of pidginization and creolization. Language universals are general tendencies found in the world's languages, and new languages are more likely to acquire features which would conform to the universals, not against them. For example, the bilabial nasal /m/ is found in all languages, and the inter-dental fricatives /θ, ð/ in only a few, among them, English. Not surprisingly, all New Englishes have the nasal /m/, and no New English has the fricatives /θ, ð/. By assuming that language is a biologically endowed mental organ we do not necessarily provide a better account of the emergence of language.

Despite its conceptual and empirical problems, the Language bioprogramme hypothesis is nevertheless an interesting theory which opens up a host of questions for future research in pidgins and creoles. The debate that has ensued has advanced our understanding of the structure and function of language in general, and pidgins and creoles in particular. The research it has inspired continues.

ೊ *Conclusion*

In this chapter we examined two influential theories of pidgin and creole languages, namely the substratist approach and the universalist approach. In their extremes the claims made by the two approaches are diagonally opposed. The former looks to the linguistic substratum for explanation, whereas the latter dismisses it as insignificant. From the perspective of the pidgin and creole data, the substratist approach gives a good account of pidginization, where substrate influence is the strongest; but it fails in accounting for creolization, particularly those constructions of creoles which come neither from pidgin predecessors nor contact languages. The universalist approach gives a good account of creolization, attributing it to the language bioprogramme. Creolization does not create structures that would violate universal constraints on possible human languages imposed by the bioprogramme. In their extreme forms the two theories are certainly not tenable. The real nature of pidginization and creolization perhaps lies somewhere between the two extreme positions. One must acknowledge the role of the substrate languages in the emergence of pidgins and subsequently of creoles, and at the same time recognize the fact that pidgins and creoles, like 'normal' languages, do not violate universal principles of language.

The two approaches need not be mutually exclusive, as Bickerton assumes. Mufwene (1986) says, 'most of the features of pidgins and creoles that the substrate hypothesis has been claimed to explain are not really accounted for unless some universal principles are accepted to apply at some stage of the formation of these languages.' Pidgins and creoles are human languages; as such they conform to universal principles which define human language in general. The grammatical features selected from substrate languages in the processes of pidginization and subsequent creolization are restructured in strict accordance with the universals of language, whether or not they constitute the bioprogramme.

It might be instructive to end this chapter with a quote from Bickerton (1986), which outlines the possibility of incorporating the linguistic substratum into a universalist theory.

> A universalist account by no means rules out substratum influences
> in principle; on the contrary, a universalist account...must assume
> that syntax includes a number of open options, where choices might
> indeed be determined by substratal influence.

Chapter 3

The Emergence of New Englishes

Thiru Kandiah

New Englishes and Theories of Language Genesis and Structure Formation

We saw in the two previous chapters that New Englishes arose under conditions of language contact created by historical developments. We also considered two different hypotheses about the processes of language genesis by which New Englishes emerged. According to one of these, the substratist hypothesis, the distinct structural forms of New Englishes were determined by the substrate language(s) that English encountered in the contact situation. The second, the Language Bioprogramme Hypothesis, claimed, on the other hand, that New Englishes emerged on the basis of Universal Grammar, the genetically supplied blueprint for natural language in the minds of human beings. In the literature, the two hypotheses generally tend to be framed in oppositional or mutually exclusive terms. However, the structural features of New Englishes that we have considered seem to provide evidence that sometimes supports one of them and sometimes the other. This indicates that it would be best to see them as complementing each other in explaining the birth of these varieties and their structures.

This is not a conclusion that ought to surprise us too much. For one thing, even in purely theoretical terms, the two hypotheses need not necessarily be seen as incompatible with each other. The claim of the Language Bioprogramme Hypothesis, for instance, is that the codes of New Englishes develop on the basis of Universal Grammar. But Universal Grammar itself is based on the assumption that *all* natural human languages are cut to the same biologically determined universal pattern. These would include the substrate languages too. In principle, therefore, accessibility to Universal Grammar is available either directly or through the substrate languages. For that matter, it is available even through the superstrate language, which itself would, according to these claims, be cut to the same underlying pattern. It follows that even when the emerging new codes draw on any available substrate language(s), they are still effectively accessing Universal Grammar. The one difference is that they do so in terms of the settings adopted by these substrate languages.

🌿 *The Role of Human Users in the Formation of Languages*

There are other considerations to be looked at, less theoretical but more immediately significant for our treatment of the emergence of New Englishes below. We mentioned in Chapter 1 that our approach to New Englishes in this book reflects the post-colonial context out of which they emerged. The perspectives it brings to bear on its objects of study will be driven by the concerns and understandings of the human subjects who, within the realities of their social, historical and linguistic contexts, actually created and now use the New English codes. As we mentioned earlier, in the language contact situations associated with the emergence of New Englishes, it is not languages as such which come into contact (this would suggest that they are actual concrete objects which have some kind of independent existence apart from the people who use them) but the very people themselves and the others whom they need to interact with there. These people are individual human beings, who find themselves in a situation in which they need to communicate and interact with other human beings who use a language different from their own. In response, they intuitively set about evolving out of that language a linguistic code which would enable them to do so effectively and self-empoweringly within the realities of their situation.

Among the various dimensions of their response are those that involve matters of language structure and language genesis. It is in an effort to better understand these that we examined the relevant theories of language structure and language genesis in the preceding two chapters. But that is just what they are, theories. That is to say, they are hypothetical constructs that have been proposed to explain in a principled way just those selected dimensions of what the human subjects are doing. So that they might better discharge their purpose, the constructs themselves were treated at a certain level of theoretical abstraction. This allowed them to be distanced somewhat from those other aspects of what was going on which would have distracted from an understanding of the dimensions under scrutiny. At this level, they were shown as operating primarily in terms of the interactions of codes as such, not of the actual people who used them. Moreover, they were explained by means of abstract principles, properties, rules and so on. These were hypothetically assumed to define the nature of human languages in general and, on that basis, to account for the genesis of new varieties of such languages and their codes.

As we recognized earlier, this represents perfectly standard practice in many fields of study. It is a practice which has undeniably helped advance understanding of the phenomena studied. If we might give an analogy for the purposes of indicating how it does so, consider the following. Let us look at the immediate experience of us human beings as we observe the sun in the sky. We perceive ourselves as remaining relatively immobile in our own place while the sun rises out of the eastern horizon, moves slowly across the sky and then vanishes downwards into the western horizon. Astronomers, of course, tell us that it is we who move, not the sun. By doing so, they have been able to lead us to our present very satisfying understandings of some crucial dimensions at least of our experience. That is precisely because they have detached themselves from those of its aspects that would have distracted and misled them. Instead, they have opted to formulate the abstract hypotheses which allow such understandings independently of those aspects. So it is with the hypotheses relating to the structure and genesis of New Englishes. These, Chapters 1 and 2 have tried to show, do lead us to better understandings of how New Englishes come into being along with the structural forms that mark them out as separate varieties.

To acknowledge this fact, however, is not to assume also that these hypotheses and abstract principles exhaust everything that needs to be said about the emergence of New Englishes. Indeed, they remain consciously detached from the human subjects centrally involved in the creation of New Englishes and from the doings of these human subjects. In doing so, they take attention away from certain other crucial dimensions of what is going on that demand treatment if we are to arrive at a fuller understanding. Specifically, they lead to a lowered appreciation of the ways in which these human users exercise their initiative in creating their new codes. In fact, if the claims made by the hypotheses are essentially correct, these users will not be able to act outside of the possibilities they define, for Universal Grammar defines the principles, properties and so on that define all natural human languages. It thus follows that New Englishes will not be able to simply set these various matters aside, for that would be contrary to the principles of Universal Grammar. It will not be possible, for instance, that a New English user could choose to make a question:

(1) *Along the man was running the road?*

corresponding with:

(2) *The man was running along the road.*

by simply moving the fifth word of the statement to the front.

However, this does not mean that the principles, properties and so on hypothetically posited by Universal Grammar apply in some deterministic,

---
* Indicates unacceptable forms.

mechanistic manner which takes all linguistic initiative away from the human developers of New English codes. They are not trapped in some choice-denying straitjacket. On the contrary, to the extent that these principles and so on are correct, they define a schema which characterizes the essential resources of language. These are freely available for human beings to make purposive use of in their pursuit of the language-assisted goals of effective and successful communication, interaction and action in the situations they find themselves in. Which is why Noam Chomsky, who originated the notion of Universal Grammar, would claim that it is a central source of the creativity of human beings, who are genetically endowed with it.

Against the background of such considerations, let us look at New Englishes from the perspective of the human users who actually created them. We see that they have emerged out of an unselfconsciously purposeful effort by these users to construct a fundamentally *enabling* code. Such a code would be one which would allow them to make meanings, interact and act within the realities of their sociohistorically constituted contexts in the most successful and effective ways possible. These are the ways that are of the greatest consequence to them.

There is something of a paradox here. From Chapters 1 and 2, we know something about the sociohistorical conditions which prevailed over a long period of time in these contexts. These were such as dispossessed these users and assigned to them a very unequal and disregarded position in terms of social status and power relative to that of the colonizers who initially brought the language to them. Indeed, their adoption of the language in these contexts when there were other languages of their own available was, in the first place, something that was imposed on them by the colonizers in pursuit of their hegemonic ends. Moreover, from the very beginning and right up to the time the colonizers left, it was the latter who claimed proprietorship of the language and the right to determine its norms of structure and use for its new users. It was a right which was exercised considerably, but not entirely, through the classroom, which, as mentioned earlier, played a significant role in the evolution of New Englishes. It needs perhaps to be observed in addition that these particular notions of proprietorship and rights did not always recede with the departure of the colonizers and the demise of empire. They are, in fact, still enshrined in the current official education policies of at least some erstwhile colonies. More significantly, they remain in the psychologies of many people who belong both in the former colonizing centres as well as in the former colonies.

What is remarkable, given the constraints that these sociohistorical realities could be expected to have imposed on them, is how the creators of New Englishes nevertheless set about constructing the enabling codes mentioned above. Even in such circumstances of disadvantage, they were codes which would satisfy the semantic, interactional and pragmatic needs of their creators. Interestingly, except at the very initial stages of the development of the codes, these needs were not determined simply by the exigencies of communication with the English-using colonizers. Very soon after the introduction of the language, these people were using the language, together with the other languages they already knew, to communicate and interact among themselves in various spheres of their lives. This played at least as large a role in the way they developed the code as their need to interact with their rulers, most likely in fact a larger one. However this might be, for their purposes they went to *all* of the varied resources available to them, whether these were provided by the superstrate language, the substrate language(s), Universal Grammar, their contexts, or whatever. These were resources which not even the disadvantages of their social position could deprive these people of. Some of them were there for the asking in the contexts. The rest of them were part of their innate, biologically endowed equipment. It should surprise nobody, therefore, that New Englishes provide clear evidence of input from all of these sources.

‘*Deviationist*’ Accounts of the Emergence of New Englishes

In a sense, our description in Chapter 1 of the sociohistorical circumstances under which New Englishes emerged has already gone some way towards recognizing the role of the human users involved in that emergence. Not least, this is by calling attention to the salient factors of the contexts within which these people lived their lives and made the relevant linguistic choices and decisions. However, the preoccupation of that description was with sociohistorical generalities. Therefore, even it does not go far enough to recognize adequately the ways in which these human subjects individually and collectively responded to the communicative and other linguistic tasks they were confronted with.

Once we turn our gaze fully on these human users, we begin in fact to see the emergence of New Englishes in somewhat different terms from those in which they are often seen in the literature. As suggested earlier, the most usual explanation of the emergence of New Englishes is in terms of ‘deviations’ from the Standard Older English(es) which constituted their original target. Associated with that term are several others of the same kind: ‘interference’ (with the target Older English by the indigenous languages in the contexts); ‘transfer’ (of items from these other languages and the associated cultural objects and practices into the target Older English and its mode of use); ‘simplification’ (of the target Older English); and so on (Görlach, 1988; Kachru, 1983; 1986; Kachru and Quirk, 1981; Platt and Weber, 1980; Thomason and Kaufman, 1988; Todd, 1984). All of these processes take place as a result of 'the acculturation of a Western language in the linguistically and culturally pluralistic context(s)' (Kachru, 1983: 1) in which the language has been 'transplanted' (Kachru, 1986: 130).

A lot of this appears to be consistent with the substratist hypothesis that we looked at earlier. There is one feature that strikes us about the account of New Englishes that is offered in the mainstream literature on the (implicit or explicit) basis of the hypothesis. This is the way in which codes, cultures, items and so on seem, as it were, to take on a life of their own. They appear to interact among themselves, almost independently of the human subjects who are crucially involved in everything that is going on but who nevertheless get pushed into the background. Recognition is thus diverted from the purposive initiatives of the human users involved. This makes it easier to treat the codes which these users play such an important role in bringing into being as emerging simply along the mechanical deviationist lines mentioned above. The forms developed by New English users begin to be seen entirely as code-determined departures from the targetted 'native' norms of 'English'. That is to say, they are, in effect, mistakes or errors committed by 'non-native' users who have been prevented by the deterministic intrusions of their substrate code(s) and associated cultures from taking proper control of the targetted norms.

It would appear that, within such an account, if the human subjects involved are to be brought back into the picture, they can be brought back mainly in terms that are consistent with the conservative treatment of varieties and users of English relative to each other, mentioned in Chapter 1. This would make these people perpetual 'non-native' users. The New Englishes they are responsible for developing, however much these might have been 'institutionalized' or 'nativized', would remain 'non-native' varieties (Kachru, 1986: Chapters 2 and 3). Clearly to be distinguished from them would be the 'native' users, with the language that *they* have developed and use being 'English'. It is not too difficult to see that all of this is very consistent with the treatment that New English users receive from Prator (1968), who sees in the codes they have developed evidence of 'imperfect' learning of the language.

Kachru (1982: 45) tries to retrieve the situation by bringing in a contextual consideration on the basis of which he attempts to separate 'mistakes' from acceptable 'deviations'. This is what he says:

> A 'mistake' may be unacceptable by a native speaker since it does not belong to the linguistic 'norm' of the English language; it cannot be justified with reference to the sociocultural context of a non-native variety: and it is not the result of the productive processes used in an institutionalized non-native variety of English. On the

other hand, a 'deviation' has the following characteristics: It is different from the norm in the sense that it is the result of the new 'un-English' linguistic and cultural setting in which the English language is used: it is the result of a productive process which marks the typical variety-specific features; and it is systemic within a variety, and not idiosyncratic... It can be shown that a large number of deviations 'deviate' only with reference to an idealized norm.

But that *is* the point. There *is*, according to this account, an idealized norm outside of New Englishes by reference to which their forms are seen. This norm happens to be the original standard superstrate target. As Kachru himself explicitly puts it (1983: 101), 'There are strong reasons for treating British English as the norm for I(ndian) E(nglish)'. But this immediately makes New Englishes simply collections of regular departures from the norm; that is, mistakes, which their users perpetrate. And the fact that they are regular and repeated or that they are the result of functional adaptations to a different setting does not turn them into anything else. Which is why it is so very easy for Görlach (1988: 194) to summarily dismiss what he describes as Kachru's efforts to 'make grammatical deviance from a foreign norm acceptable, i.e. turn the "mistakes" of a prescriptive tradition into permissible alternatives on the grounds that they are the consequences of necessary adaptation'.

The Cline of Bilingualism

Nowhere, perhaps, are such problems with this approach better exemplified than by Kachru's construct 'the cline of bilingualism' (Kachru, 1983: 129). It is a construct which assumes cornerstone significance in much of his work and also in the large tradition of study of New Englishes that derives from that work. An examination of the construct will more sharply reveal the nature of the problems we are looking at (see also Kandiah, 1987: Section III). In addition, it will also bring to light other significant problems with this approach. In doing all this, it will, we hope, point the way to a more useful approach to the study of New Englishes and their emergence.

Monolingual   Central   Ambilingual

Figure 1. The Cline of Bilingualism

The 'cline of bilingualism' is 'a scale of proficiency...to rank bilinguals in terms of their proficiency in English' (Kachru, 1983: 129). It is based on two assumptions: one, entirely justifiable, that very nearly all users of New

Englishes are bilingual, knowing English and at least one more indigenous language; and two, less justifiable, that these users invariably acquire English *after* they have acquired the indigenous language. On the basis of these assumptions, it attempts to formalize New English users' command of 'English' as follows. Monolingual users of indigenous languages who have no knowledge whatsoever of English are ranked at the 'zero point' on the scale. They have a 100% knowledge of the indigenous language and a 0% knowledge of 'English'. At the other end of the scale are the ambilinguals, who have a 100% knowledge of both the indigenous language and 'English'. To have such a knowledge of English is to be able to use the language like 'native' users of English, that is, users of OEs. Ambilingualism, however, is 'a rare, if not impossible, phenomenon'.

Users of Standard New Englishes (Kachru speaks throughout specifically in terms of Indian English, but his comments apply equally to all New Englishes) rank somewhere around the central point on the scale, though in later characterizations of the cline they are allowed to clamber up to a point 'somewhere between the *central* and *ambilingual* points' (Kachru, 1983: 99). These are people who have learned the Standard Older English target well enough to be able to use 'the language' effectively in various fields of activity and are, ideally, intelligible to native users of that target. But, even that, Kachru observes, 'does not imply that the user's command of English equals that of the native speaker' (1983: 129); for, while they have a 100% knowledge of their indigenous language, they have arrived at best at something like a 50% to 75% knowledge of 'English', having had their efforts to learn it interfered with by the other language(s) and culture(s) of their context. If we bear in mind that these people are, presumably, the 'best' users of New Englishes, it follows from all this that their varieties will not have 'a status equal to those varieties of English which are used as primary or first languages (= Older Englishes)' (Kachru, 1966: 256).

One obvious problem with the cline of bilingualism is that it includes even clearly non-proficient usage in its characterization of varieties, be it even at the lower end of the scale. This is indeed an unusual procedure. Of its nature any viable variety can only be characterized on the basis of the usage of its competent users. This is why Labov, for instance, when he carried out his famous New York study (1966), was careful to select for investigation only those whose usage would give him a basis for valid generalizations about his object of study. This is not to say that proficiency in the language is not a significant linguistic and educational problem in the bilingual countries in which New Englishes are used. It is, and very much so. The point, however, is that it needs to be recognized as a separate matter, which cannot be mixed up with the issue of characterizing the varieties as linguistic organisms.

A second significant problem with the cline of bilingualism is that it mixes up issues of the development of the varieties (issues of phylogeny) with issues of the acquisition of competence in them by their individual users (issues of ontogeny). Our own argument about the development of the varieties is that they have emerged from the efforts of the human subjects involved to develop an effective communicative and interactional code. For that purpose they have drawn on all available resources, including those made available to them by the superstrate and substrate language(s), negotiating across these resources as suits them.

This does not, however, imply that, in the process of acquiring the code, all New English users have to individually re-enact in their personal acquisitional histories the processes of negotiation across the feeder languages involved. Of course, they might subsequently contribute in similar ways to further changes in the code, but the code itself is not learned by them in that way. As mentioned in Chapter 1, from very early in the history of these varieties, they began to be acquired in most cases by processes of normal transmission. This means that most habitual users of these varieties 'picked them up' through natural interaction in them, at home and in community; and they picked them up in their 'arrived' form, without having to go through all the processes by which the codes arrived at that form. Gupta's account (1994) of the acquisition of CSE by young children in their homes, before they move on to the learning of Standard English, and even that not just in the classroom, provides persuasive evidence in support of this claim. The cline of bilingualism fails to recognize this. It makes the assumption that all individual users of New Englishes, as they acquire them, repeat all of those processes of interaction between languages that are assumed by it to have been involved in the evolution of the codes.

There are also other serious problems with the cline of bilingualism. The problems issue from its formal institutionalization, at the ambilingual end, of the norms of Standard Older Englishes for judging New Englishes. These are the norms which New English users will have to satisfy if they are to be considered to have achieved full control of the language. As recognized earlier, this guarantees the projection of New Englishes simply as sets of departures from those norms and, therefore, as lesser forms of *the* language.

This problem itself stems from a more fundamental theoretical misconception about the nature of the competence of the bilingual, which too much of the literature on bilingualism seems unfortunately to share. This is that the linguistic competence of the bilingual is to be looked at in simplistic additive terms, as the sum of the competencies of two monoglot users of the respective languages put together. This is a view that could perhaps come easy to those who operate out of profoundly monolingual and monocultural settings. However, this is as far as could be from the truth. Any discerning sensitivity to the actual experience of bilingualism within the realities of multicultural and multilinguistic contexts, and to the ways in which the human subjects involved in them in fact respond, would immediately awaken us to this realization. Like all human subjects, these bilinguals are driven by the need, mentioned earlier, to make meanings, interact and act in and on their contexts as effectively as possible and in the ways that make the most sense to them. In response to this need, they take hold of the linguistic codes which they have possession of and develop them in the ways that most allow them to achieve their ends, drawing for the purpose on *all* of the resources available to them.

The very nature of the complex multicultural and multilinguistic contexts they occupy guarantee that they do not do this in any monologic way. That is, they do not work simply within the restrictions imposed on them by monolingual users of either of their codes. This does not mean that they set these codes entirely aside, altogether disregarding how they have evolved at the hands of their monolingual users. Linguistic, historical and social realities do not make that a possibility. Yet neither do they concern themselves overmuch with using the codes exactly in the ways predetermined for them by these monolingual users in some other place than the one they, the bilinguals, actually occupy. The norms that monolinguals have determined cannot, therefore, assume the kind of salience for them that the cline of bilingualism assigns to them when it institutionalizes them at the ambilingual point. All of the codes of these bilinguals are, therefore, reconstituted by them into linguistic systems which meet their needs. In fact, while this is not our concern in this book, there is much research to show that not just English but also the indigenous languages used in these contexts have undergone considerable change under these imperatives. Kachru's term 'Englishization' (1994) expresses recognition of this fact. But, revealingly, it is mainly when *English* is altered in these ways that notions of 'deviation', 'interference' and so on and, together with them, doubts about levels of attainment and the status of the resulting codes, seem to raise themselves.

Fulguration

In fact, when we look at New Englishes from the perspective which we are here developing, we begin to see that such matters lead us away from an understanding of how they really emerge. That the creators of these new varieties have a firm eye on the superstrate and then draw into it features that seem to have obvious associations with the available substrate language(s) and culture(s) is indisputable. But the code that results from the process does not allow itself to be treated as simply the sum total of the two sets of features and elements that are brought into it. In such an account, these features and elements would be seen to be arranged in some static, coterminous manner relative to each other, such that one set is perceived as being unconformable (hence 'interfering') with the other. Nor can it be seen as simply some items of one set 'displacing' or distorting certain items of the other. On the contrary, what the users of these codes seem to do, presumably by calling upon the resources made available to them by Universal Grammar, is to fuse these various features into a new and different kind of organic, rule-governed, symbiotic system. Within this system, these features 'enter into all kinds of new relations with each other, relations which give them values, meanings, qualities, textures, whatever, that make it meaningless to try to interpret or judge them in terms of what they pristinely were, or what, presumably, they originally sought to be' (Kandiah, 1987: 37).

The following discussion of the semantics, grammar and use of the Lankan English word, *uncle*, reproduced from Kandiah, 1987: 37-39, will, we hope, clarify our point.

> L(ankan) E(nglish) speakers could use (the word *uncle*) to convey the meaning it would have to a speaker of Standard British or American English. In addition, without any sense of using a different word, they could use it to refer to or address various male relatives who, in the indigenous languages of Sri Lanka, are given at least three distinct names, depending on the nature of relationship they have (elder brother, younger brother, "cousin", and so on) to the parents of the speakers, and on whether the relationship is to their mother or to their father. What it is important to note is that they use the term indifferently for all these different kinds of relatives. In doing so, they are **not** invoking the meanings of the native terms, meanings that, in two of these cases, are transparently represented in the terms themselves.
>
> To complicate matters further, all adult males of equal social status tend, for reasons of respect and propriety, to be "uncles" to children, unless their relationship to them is defined in a specific way that requires some other specific term, like "sir", to a teacher. Perhaps as a result of this use, the syntactic behaviour of the word in L(ankan) E(nglish) is, too, very different from that of its homonym in British or American English, (for instance,) taking pre-nominal and post-nominal qualifiers with a freedom (which) that homonym lacks. (For example, sentences like the following are quite usual in L(ankan) E(nglish): *Give this to those two silly uncles wearing thick specs in the next room.*)
>
> Moreover, trading on this last-mentioned use of the word is a further, marginal use that is very Lankan. In this use, speakers simultaneously

express through it different attitudes that do not normally sit together. For instance, in a conversation about an adult male in a position of high authority, a speaker (often an adult male himself) who belongs well outside the sphere in which the object of his conversation operates, may, with slight humour, reassure his listeners with the words, *Not to worry, Uncle won't allow anything to go wrong.* The use of the word (here) simultaneously expresses the speaker's sense of his distance from the person referred to, his sense of confidence in that person and, also, a certain sense of affectionate identification with him.

....

Significantly, none of the words used in the local languages for the male relatives who are referred to by the word *uncle* in L(ankan) E(nglish) is used in quite these last few ways in those languages, so that these uses (and meanings) of the word derive directly neither from its original British English source nor from the native languages.

The conclusion to be drawn from all this is that the word demands to be described fully and properly as a systematic, synchronic element in its own right. Certainly, it cannot be accounted for in the manner that Kachru (1983: Chapter 6) proposes that the words of I(ndian) E(nglish) must be, by assigning "[+] or [-] Indian (semantic) features" to entries — that is, by adding to or subtracting from the (Older English) homonym. Neither can it be described satisfactorily in terms of a target that was originally aimed at but never achieved owing to "interference" from the native languages and environment. The reasons are as follows: first, as already mentioned, it can, when necessary, pick out exactly the individuals picked out by the British English homonym, and in exactly the same way; second, it picks out a whole set of other individuals who are not picked out in that way by words in either British English or the indigenous languages; and finally, even where the male relatives it picks out are just those who are picked out by the indigenous language terms, the word does not take on the **meaning** of these terms, and there is just no translatability between it and them.

What we see here, then, is a new systematic linguistic unit of Lankan English. It draws obviously on both the superstrate and the substrate languages. But it then transforms what it draws into a new entity which involves features and strategies which have prehistories in neither language, so that they cannot be traced back in a direct way to either of them. In spite of the considerable evidence the following chapters will provide of its ubiquity in New Englishes, this phenomenon has somehow escaped explicit formulation. It is labelled *fulguration* by Kandiah (1987: 39), who borrowed the term from T. L. Markey, who used it in a talk on 'The Typology of Majority/Minority Languages' at the National University of Singapore on 21 March, 1986.

If a further example is needed, consider the word *cheem*, meaning 'deep' or 'profound' (with an ironic judgemental texture), which Singapore English has borrowed from the substrate language, Hokkien. In terms of its syntactic behaviour, it is clearly an adjective. It observes the distributional rules of adjectives in the superstrate language, as shown by sentences (3) and (4) below.

(3) *Some very cheem books (can be) found there.*

Here, *cheem* is part of a subject noun phrase in which it immediately precedes and modifies the head noun. It is in turn premodified by the intensifier *very*. These are all distributional hallmarks of adjectives in the superstrate language.

(4) *Aiyah, lecture very cheem, what.*

Here, *cheem* is the head of an adjectival phrase functioning as subject complement in the sentence, again a syntactic hallmark of superstrate adjectives. In addition, it lends itself to morphological processes of the kind that superstrate adjectives can undergo. Thus, it allows itself to be inflected for the comparative and superlative forms, *cheemer* and *cheemest*, as monosyllabic superstrate adjectives do. It also permits a noun *cheemness* to be derived from it by the addition of the derivational suffix *-ness*, again just as superstrate adjectives might. Thus far, all we have noted about this Singapore English element is that it displays a set of features that have been derived directly from either the superstrate or the substrate language.

But then we begin to run into other characteristics which come from neither of them. In Hokkien, the substrate source of the word, it does not necessarily have the slightly ironic meaning that is always a part of the Singapore English word. Moreover, in that language, the word has both the literal and the metaphorical meaning of 'deep'. In Singapore English, however, it can have only the metaphorical meaning, so that:

(5) **The drain is very cheem.*

---

* Indicates unacceptable forms.

is ungrammatical. Clearly, this can have nothing to do with any influence from the superstrate language, so it must come from within the system of Singapore English itself.

Other such features that are unique to the Singapore English element may also be noted. For instance, for all the morphological behaviour it shares with the corresponding superstrate item, it detaches itself from it in its resistance to the derivation of an adverb from it. Thus:

(6) *The lecturer stated it cheemly.*

is not a possibility, although the superstrate allows:

(7) *He stated it deeply/profoundly.*

Moreover, Singapore English has derived a noun-like term *cheemology* (some prefer the form *cheeminology*) from the adjective. This appears to draw on a productive superstrate derivational suffix, but uses it in a way that is entirely impossible in the superstrate — there can be no superstrate terms *deepology, *richology,* and so on. And syntactically, too, this nominal term does not behave like any other superstrate term using the derivational suffix *-ology,* as in:

(8) * *He does not like cheem(in)ology.*

It is used almost invariably as a single word exclamatory comment on some particularly incomprehensible book, or lecture, or whatever.

🕮 *The Autonomous, Rule-governed Nature of NE Systems*

All such considerations illustrate the phenomenon of fulguration. One thing that this phenomenon indicates is that New English systems call for recognition as autonomous rule-governed systems in their own right. Certainly, what we are looking at are not collections of deviations or hodgepodges of idiosyncratic mistakes or failures to attain norms, caused by transfer or interference from intrusive substrate languages. The descriptions of the structural and other characteristics of the New English items discussed above, as well as the descriptions which the chapters that follow will provide of further such items, show this very clearly. The items display definite regularities of structure and behaviour. Moreover, these are shared by the users of the varieties, who agree on the grammaticality and other judgements

---

* Indicates unacceptable forms.

to be made about them. They definitely are, therefore, rule-governed. Doubtless, these regularities share features with both the superstrate and substrate languages. But they make use of them in ways that stand quite independent of these languages. It makes little sense, therefore, to try to describe them by reference to either of these languages. The systems of New Englishes have to be seen, in other words, as existing in their own right.

In spite of all this, our discussion here and elsewhere does fairly consistently elucidate the features and behaviour of New Englishes in terms of their differences from those of Older Englishes. This, however, is purely a matter of the logistics of argumentation, not a matter of theoretical commitment — most people are unfamiliar with the workings of New Englishes, and it is a useful discussion technique to clarify the point at issue against a reference point with which they are likely to be familiar.

Two Problems with the Autonomy Claim

Problem 1 — 'Shared' Features and their Differentiation by means of the Firthian Notion of System

Let us now look at two problems which the claim we made at the beginning of the last paragraph might run into. This is the claim that New Englishes emerge, through the various processes we have described, as systematic rule-governed entities in their own right. The first of these problems involves the autonomy claim. It relates to the fact that there are many features of New Englishes which appear superficially to be identical in all crucial respects with corresponding features of either the superstrate or the substrate language(s). In fact, Singh's argument in Chapter 1, which we accepted, is based very much on the claim that the very same features of New Englishes are, or could be, found in Older Englishes. At an abstract level, this certainly is not something we might want to dispute. This is particularly so if we subscribe to Universal Grammar, which specifies properties, features and so on which may, hypothetically, be found in any natural human language. However, when we begin to look more closely at the matter, distinctions of various kinds begin to surface. In order to see these, we need to bear in mind the intuitions about items that the human users of any given New English might have, as these intuitions are revealed by the different systematic, rule-governed ways in which they actually use them.

To illustrate from just the lexicon, consider, for instance, the verb *bring*. At first glance, Singapore English appears to share this word with Standard British English, not only in terms of its spelling and phonological structure, but also in terms of its basic semantic specifications. But we soon begin to realize that matters are not quite as they seem to be. This happens when we move from our initial response to a recognition of the fact that, for instance, a speaker of Singapore English, speaking to her child who is sick in bed in her Singapore home, could equally, depending on what she intends to convey, use the word in either of the ways illustrated by the following two sentences:

(9)   *You wait quietly in bed like a good boy when Mummy go shopping, and I'll bring you to England next year.*

(10) *You wait quietly in bed like a good boy when Mummy go shopping, and I bring you expensive toy, right?*

Clearly, the word is not quite the same in Singapore English and Standard British English. This seems to have something to do with the fact that for all that the word shares in the two systems involved, it does not occupy exactly the same 'place' within them. In the Singapore English system it contrasts with the word *take* in a way which it does not in the Standard British English system.

The notion of linguistic system we are invoking here draws on J. R. Firth's highly organic notion of system (1957). Let us phrase the notion in a way that transparently displays the support it provides to the point we are making. At an abstract level, elements which appear to call to be treated as the 'same' will not in fact be the same when they occur within two differently organized systems made up of inventories of items that are not identical. In each case, the element would derive its specific 'value' or 'texture' or 'quality' or even meaning, partly from its organic relationships, including contrastive relationships, with the other terms which accompany it in the particular system it belongs within. To give an illustration, the word *red* cannot mean the same thing when it is used in the following two systems for naming colours. One system has only the eight terms, *black, white, purple, blue, green, yellow, orange* and *red*. The other has the eleven terms *black, white, magenta, purple, blue, green, yellow, orange, red, scarlet, pink*. The real world colours that the term *red* will pick out will not be the same in the two systems. In the first, these will most likely include also the colours picked out by the words *scarlet* and *pink* in the second; possibly also the colour picked out by the word *magenta*. In the second, it will not do so. This is because it now contrasts with *all* of the other terms which the system contains, which would include these two (or three) additional terms which the other system does not have.

Doubtless, an attempt might be made to capture some differences of these kinds by means of abstract semantic features and so on, which are specified in universal terms. Indeed, the differences between the Standard British English and the Singapore English word, *bring*, as illustrated by sentences

(9) and (10) above, can, most likely, be captured in this way, through two different abstract semantic feature specifications for the word in the two varieties. In one, it would have, among others, feature specifications which would indicate movement towards the place of utterance; in the other, it would not. This might, of course, make it not one word but two different words. But it does not seem that all such differences among the large numbers of apparently identical elements in different varieties may be so simply captured. This is particularly so when one of the varieties in question happens to be a New English. The inventory of features of such a variety was drawn originally from both its superstrate and its substrate sources. It would, therefore, define a whole wide range of contrasts and relationships among features which will be very unlike anything that may be found in any Older English. Which is why, for instance, even though Yorkshire English can, apparently, use *bring* in both of the ways illustrated by sentences (9) and (10), *bring* in Singapore English will still most likely remain a different word from it.

Problem 2 — Transfer or Shared Propensities?

The second problem which our claim that New Englishes are autonomous systems might run into involves specifically the features and elements which these varieties appear to share with their substrate(s). Chapter 2 and the descriptive chapters later in this book look at many examples of this. Their presence in both the New Englishes and the substrate language(s) seems to lend support to a claim we have argued against when affirming the autonomy of New Englishes. This is the claim that these varieties are to be accounted for in terms simply of the mechanical transfer of items from the substrate code(s) to the superstrate code or in terms of interference by the former with the latter.

We would like to suggest that it might be more useful to look at these shared features in the following way, which recognizes the central role that the human users of the codes play in constituting them. If a New English and the corresponding substrate language(s) share certain characteristics, it is not because the latter has/have imposed on the former independently of the users. Rather, it is because there are certain preferred ways or modes in which the users want to make their meanings, and to act and interact linguistically. These are ways that their historical, social, cultural and other circumstances have led them to as the most salient and useful. We can expect, therefore, that *all* of their codes will have certain characteristics which will enable them to do these things in just these ways or modes. The one rider to this is that there might be several circumstances when they might not always want to make meanings and so on in exactly the same manner in all their different codes. That is to say, it is not the case that it is always the same meanings that they want to express in all their different codes, and through the same meaning-making modes. Otherwise, what would they need different codes for? In such cases, and there are very many, they *will* keep these codes distinct from each other.

Consider, for instance, the so-called deletion or ellipsis phenomenon illustrated by sentence (1) of Chapter 1, reproduced here as sentence (11).

> (11) *Why so slow one? Wait, got no more, then you know.*
> Why are you taking so much time? If you delay any further, nothing will be left, and then you'll find out (the consequences).

The gloss provides an idiomatic rendering of the message of the utterance. At the same time, it also clearly indicates that the utterance does not specify in explicit syntactic and lexical terms many of the things which it appears to convey. For instance, the whole of the second (conditional) clause is represented by a single word *wait*. There is a considerable literature, based largely on Standard Older English usage, which deals with this phenomenon of syntactic 'deletion' or 'ellipsis', as it has been called (for example, Halliday and Hasan, 1976; Morgan, 1973). In all of it, there is an assumption that underlying such incompletely specified utterances are fully specified syntactic-semantic structures which express their 'intended' meaning. The actual utterances we have, then, are the result of processes of deletion or ellipsis of items of these underlying structures. Most of the discussion of such utterances is directed towards finding out which items may be so deleted or elided and under what conditions. Part of the concern is also with the question of how all this might explain the ability of hearers to recover the intended meaning of these incomplete structures by retrieving the missing items. However, when we compare these so-called deletion phenomena in certain New Englishes with what is discussed in the literature, what strikes us most forcibly is that the items 'deleted' by New Englishes appear to defy all of the rules of deletion permitted in the literature. Moreover, they extend presumably quite unpredictably to many more features and items that its lists recognize.

Kandiah (1996), discussing the phenomenon in some New Englishes, argues that what is involved here is not 'deletion' but the operation of a hitherto unnoticed communicative strategy. It is one which does not require the users to overtly and unmistakably specify all elements of their message. What these users appear to do instead is merely to map out a 'broad set of syntactico-semantic protocols, as it were' (p. 118) and then leave it to the hearers to make the 'missing' part of their (the users') meaning for them, within a range of acceptable interpretations. This, Kandiah goes on to speculate, is possible because these New English users belong within cultures which are marked by two characteristics that distinguish them from Older English cultures. One is that they provide a significant place for other modes of knowing than the rationalist, empirical, positivistic ones which occupy so central a place in Older English cultures. Therefore, no particular premium is placed on explicitly and specifically articulating every single aspect of the message a person might want to communicate. The second is that these cultures are essentially communal. No particularly strong premium is placed on the individual and the inviolability of the individual's space. Therefore, there is no particular risk taken in handing over part of one's meaning to someone else to make.

As it turns out, where we find New Englishes which show evidence of the workings of this strategy, we find that the corresponding substrate languages also show evidence of it. This might well encourage the view that what is involved here is simply interference or transfer. But to try to account for this shared feature of 'deletion' in such terms would be difficult. The elements which are not overtly articulated in an utterance tend to be very unpredictable. Therefore, it will not be possible to specify a definite set of matching structures or structure-based operations across the languages in terms of which the transfer or interference can be characterized. To make sense of what is going on, we seem to need a different approach. In such an approach, it would first be recognized that certain cultures encourage or induce certain meaning-making propensities and tendencies in their members. It would then follow that any language which these people call upon to serve them in their communicative or interactional activities, whether a substrate language or a New English, could be expected to give expression to those same propensities and tendencies.

The Emergence of New English Speech Communities

Together with the emergence of New Englishes along the lines we have described above, there also came into being viable speech communities who sustain and are sustained by them. These are made up of people who, even as they helped develop the varieties, had transmitted or, in later generations, acquired them essentially through processes of normal transmission. Normal transmission has, of course, to be seen here as involving more than only transmission from parent to child, which does happen quite often (Gupta, 1994). It also involves transmission through ordinary social interaction. That is, users may 'pick up' their forms and rules through normal exchanges. However, as mentioned earlier, the classroom can also have some role to play in the process, as it often does in many speech communities. Like all speech communities, these New English speech communities also raise complex problems of description. For the moment, though, let us look at some of their essential features from the perspective of those within them who are the most habitual and regular users of the language and who command its full range of forms and registers. Such characteristics justify these people's being considered to be the main representatives of the communities and the major custodians of the language within them (see later, however, for some comments on the class-based nature of these people).

These people all alike show linguistic competence in their variety. This means that they share a rich body of intuitive knowledge about its formal workings. Thus they have a sound intuitive command of the grammatical rules of these varieties and are able to make all of those complex judgements about grammaticality, structural relationships, ambiguity and so on which mark out competent users of any variety of any language. This also means that they can produce appropriate instances of the language variety as necessary and interpret them when they encounter such instances.

New Englishes, Functional Versatility and Communicative Competence

It is not only linguistic competence in the variety that they share, but also communicative competence in it. This, again, is something they have acquired through the natural process of growing up within and getting socialized into the linguistic community. Thus, they control all of those principles or rules of use which allow them to make intuitive judgements and choices relating to which forms of the variety to use, when, where, to whom, for what purpose and so on. In doing so, they show sensitivity to the precise nature of a complex gamut of correlations between social variables and linguistic forms. Given such correlations, they also show intuitive understanding of the precise ways in which the forms may be drawn upon in specific situations, to make just the meanings that they need to in order to achieve their various goals. In other words, they remain in control of a complex repertoire of styles or registers that are well-adapted to a whole complex range of functions and purposes. Thus, most of the sentences cited above from Singapore English would be used in informal situations or domains. But, in a somewhat more formal setting, the same users could come out with versions of the sentences which observe a more 'standard' grammar. For instance, sentence (4) might very well be expressed as follows in such a setting:

(12) *That was a ridiculously deep lecture, right?*

Furthermore, the examples cited reflect a responsiveness not only to the formality/informality variable but also to other variables in the social situation. For instance, the sentence (11) cited earlier would generally be uttered among absolute equals who have fairly friendly relationships with each other or by a person who has greater authority to one who has less authority. In other words, the choice of that way of expressing that meaning shows sensitivity to the nature of the participants, their relationships to each other and so on. See, too, Gupta's discussion (1994) of the exchanges in her informants' homes for further evidence of the operation of such rules of use.

Complementarity and its Modifications

There are some points made in Chapter 1 which might suggest that, perhaps, some qualifications are in order. These relate to two claims: one, about the characteristically bilingual nature of New English contexts; and two, about the complementarity of New Englishes and the other indigenous codes available in these contexts. These claims indicate that there are some functions that will be discharged in these contexts by the indigenous codes rather than by New Englishes. If that is so, then would it not be the case that the range of uses of English in them would be considerably more restricted than the range of its uses in Older English contexts?

The question is very valid, but the answer to it is not so simple. When the colonizers were still around, particularly during the earlier years of their stay, the use of the language was indeed quite limited in certain ways. No doubt, it soon acquired functions beyond the merely utilitarian. But, even so, it did not penetrate much beyond the 'offices, drawing rooms and clubs' (de Souza, 1969) to the larger context occupied by the large mass of the people among whom its users lived. On the contrary, it remained largely confined to a comparatively small elite class, who tended to see the world considerably in the ways their rulers had taught them to. This guaranteed that it would not adapt itself to handling large segments of the experience which surrounded it in its contexts and which most immediately involved the large mass of people who never learned English. Thus, talking of Lankan English, de Souza (1969) points out that it lacked words and expressions to handle a great deal of the fauna, flora, cuisine and so on of its context. In like vein, Gunatilleke (1954) describes it as a 'language without metaphor', which remains 'derivative', 'at a second remove' from a lot of the experience of its users. It does not, therefore, enable 'the reconstruction of our own experiences in their actuality'. (See, too, Kandiah's discussion (1971) of the 'academic texture' of a great deal of Lankan creative writing until recent times. This reflected a preoccupation with standard superstrate norms, something which, he argues, interfered with the ability of the writing to recreate convincingly the indigenous experience it addressed.)

As time went on, however, things began to change. As already indicated above, the elite themselves began quite early to extend the use of the language to functions well beyond the utilitarian. They began gradually to bring it centrally into their personal, social, emotional and imaginative lives. Moreover, even well before these colonies began to approach independence, the language had begun to adapt itself to features of the environment which it had tended to disregard earlier. The process was considerably accelerated after independence, which restored respect and recognition to indigenous matters which had earlier been devalued and sidelined. Moreover, in all of these countries, language planning measures began to be taken which, among other things, brought far larger numbers of people into immediate contact with the language than ever before (see Chapter 12). The measures did not divest the language of its elite status. But they more fully opened the surrounding environment out to the language. As a result, more people entered the process of reconstructing the language than ever before, including many who came from backgrounds which until then had remained closed off from the language.

These developments went along with a certain more open climate of attitude. Together, they further guaranteed that the old complementarity between English and the indigenous languages would be modified in certain interesting ways. No doubt, there would still remain some functions which would fall within the province of one language rather than the other — for instance, communicating with monolingual users of an indigenous language, or participating in an indigenous or English cultural activity. But many crucial functions which were previously restricted to one or the other of the codes could now be discharged equally in either of the codes, or through a combination of them. An example is social interaction among members of the English-using elite, which was facilitated by the new-found respect for the indigenous code and indigenous ways of life. Neither of the codes was to simply take over domains primarily associated with the other. But, certainly, both codes began to develop a functional versatility that they had previously lacked. As far as New Englishes were concerned, all of this meant that they did begin to develop a wider range of styles and the kind of rule-governed, communicative, competence-related functional variability which any viable language would display.

‿ *Sociolinguistic Variability*

This is not, of course, the only kind of variability that the New Englishes showed. In addition, there were the other kinds of variability, associated with familiar societal variables in the speech community. The variables included such matters as class, educational level and ethnolinguistic differentiation. The last of these was, of course, entirely to be expected in such generally multicultural/multilinguistic environments.

These different kinds of variability have received considerable treatment in the literature, which reveals, on the basis of an examination of them, the sociolinguistically rule-governed nature of New Englishes. Such work lays bare the principled correlations between the different linguistic forms of New Englishes and the relevant social variables (class, ethnic language, education and so on). It demonstrates also how the variability reflects the communicative competence of the users and their control of the rules of use (see, for example, Agnihotri and Saghal, 1985; Gupta, 1994; Kachru, 1983; 1986; Pakir, 1991; Platt, 1980; Platt and Weber, 1980; Tay, 1979; 1986; and selected essays in Cheshire, 1991; Crewe, 1977; and Foley, 1988).

Variability and the Lectal Continuum

There is, however, one major dimension of variability in New Englishes which calls to be looked at again. The reason is that its treatment in the literature could inhibit a proper understanding of how these varieties emerged. This is a dimension which, particularly in the earlier Southeast Asian tradition of study of New Englishes, has been dealt with in terms of decreolization and the post-creole continuum. These are concepts that had been developed in the growing field of pidgin/creole studies in Europe and America. Thus a lot of the work on Singapore English sees in it a lectal range. The range extends from the basilect at one end, which shows many features of creoles, to the acrolect at the other, which approximates Standard (superstrate) English. The mesolect mediates transitionally between the former and the latter (Platt, 1977; Platt and Weber, 1980; Tay, 1979). The linguistic differences in the usage of socially and educationally differentiated groups of people are represented by the place this usage takes on the range. However, those people whose usage generally figures at the acrolectal end might also on occasion slide down to mesolectal or even basilectal usage. While most characterizations of the basilect recognize it as rule-governed (Platt, 1977), there lurks a feeling that it includes forms that are 'clearly unacceptable and must be called wrong' (Tongue, 1974: 12). The feeling receives some reinforcement from the frequent association of the basilect with minimally educated users. These users control only the basilect, so that they are unable to move up the continuum to mesolectal or acrolectal usage.

This approach assigns a central place to the superstrate standard. It thus reflects the more conservative, and quite tenacious, perspective revealed by the two-way classification of Englishes into native and non-native varieties discussed in Chapter 1. The whole situation is not too surprising. Most of the work that adopts this perspective is by scholars who come from the dominant Euro-American academic centres or who, for a variety of historical considerations, are very open to approaches which have been developed there. A growing sense of independent identity among New English countries in more recent times has, however, led to questions being asked about this approach. They were asked all the more searchingly, no doubt, because of exposure to work done elsewhere on New Englishes along other lines, including work done by Kachru (see, for example, Tay, 1985).

The problems with the lectal continuum approach from the point of view of the study of New Englishes stem precisely from the fact that it was developed in relation to the study of pidgins/creoles, the sociohistorical emergence of which, as we have seen, was different from that of New Englishes. New Englishes did not emerge from prior pidgins (neither, for that matter, did some creoles). The classroom played a significant part in their evolution, as it did not in the case of creoles. But once the initial period had been passed, processes of normal transmission and development came significantly into play, as in fact they did in the case of creoles, too. This caused them to emerge along the innovative lines discussed earlier. In emerging along these lines, New Englishes developed their own norms of structure and use.

All usage, including standard, colloquial and non-proficient usage, was to be judged by these norms. In this respect, we note two matters. One is that the lectal continuum, like the cline of bilingualism, does not always appear to clearly distinguish non-proficient from proficient New English usage. Thus in principle the continuum could well accommodate at the basilectal end of the range what might in fact be better treated as non-proficient usage. The assumption appears to be that such usage actually does have a role to play in characterizing the varieties. We have suggested earlier that the assumption is unsatisfactory.

The second matter is not unrelated to the first and is in fact the most serious shortcoming of the lectal continuum. It is that, like the cline of bilingualism, it institutes the standard superstrate as the norm aspired to by New Englishes. The literature on creoles seems to indicate that in the process of coming into being they move away for various reasons from superstrate norms. But then the continued presence of the prestigious superstrate standard in their contexts leads many of them to attempt to decreolize and to move back in the direction of the superstrate.

But, if our argument above is essentially correct, this does not appear to be a useful way in which to approach New Englishes. The superstrate standard had always been immediately available to New English users in the classroom. But the whole way in which they developed their codes involved the emergence of forms, along with the rules of structure and use which go with them, that all together defined new organically integrated variant systems of the language. These forms cannot validly be treated as falling into three separate ranges of usage, measured in terms of the extent of their departure from the superstrate norms that their users presumably aspire to.

Moreover, there is absolutely no principled way of demarcating the different ranges. At best, the literature merely provides arbitrary lists of so-called differentiating features, which is all it *can* do. No principled clarification of the linguistic grounds on which they are separated from each other is provided. Where precisely, for instance, does the mesolectal range begin, and where precisely does it end? And why? Also, in what comprehensible way can the mesolect be treated as representing some kind of transition from less standard to more standard forms? (Tay, 1979)

Making the case against the lectal continuum even stronger is a further consideration. This is that the standard form that intuitively presides over any New English situation, as the target which the speech community, in practice, aim at in their usage, is not in fact the superstrate standard. Rather, it is the standard form which the users of that New English have developed for themselves. It might share a great deal with the standard superstrate, as has often been observed (Tay, 1979; Gupta, 1994), but it is not identical with it. Other things apart, 'leakage' between the everyday colloquial form of that variety and the standard has caused it to emerge as something which still remains a distinct, organic New English form. This is not something that is often honestly recognized. Platt is one of the few exceptions, through his claim that 'a very distinct non-British acrolect is gradually emerging' in the case of Singapore English (1977: 84). This is not something that can be too easily denied. In fact, it is repeatedly confirmed by the actual responses and practice of editors of journals and similar people committed to the maintenance of Older English 'standards', when confronted with texts by New English users (Görlach, 1988; Kandiah, 1990: 131-134).

The rules of use that New English users control as part of their communicative competence govern their actual performance. The rules tell them when, where, to whom, under what conditions and so on to use their standard form rather than the colloquial form that is also available to them and *vice versa*. It is, thus, the factors in the context of use that will, for instance, tell Singapore English users whether to use sentence (11) or the standard equivalent that is provided as its gloss. Whichever form they use, they use it as a matter of choice. That is, they have alternative forms available to them which they are fully aware of. But in the circumstances they find themselves in, they reject one or the other as inappropriate. All of which means that they are not concerned about trying to make their usage in either of these cases conform to the superstrate standard, as the lectal continuum would lead us to assume. In other words, the entire phenomenon of decreolization which the lectal continuum is associated with seems to be quite irrelevant to them.

Platt (1975) recognizes some of these matters and acknowledges that they oblige him to see at least the everyday, spoken CSE as a different kind of linguistic entity from creoles. He tries to solve the problem this raises by renaming the subvariety a 'creoloid'. This, however, turns out to be largely a terminological concession which allows the conservative two-way classification of Englishes mentioned earlier to be maintained intact. Together with the classification goes the assumption of the central position of the superstrate standard in judging these Englishes. Our examination of the lectal continuum already implicitly expresses the alternative approach that we prefer to adopt instead to the variability under scrutiny. It is an approach which attempts to extricate the study of New Englishes entirely from that way of looking at them. It does so by projecting this variability in terms of socially patterned choices between the everyday colloquial form of the variety on the one hand and its standard form on the other. As this is stated, however, it makes the situation appear far simpler than it actually is. Therefore, we shall now look at some of the complexities that call attention to themselves.

New Englishes and Diglossia

The first point to note here is one that all of the linguistic data examined in this book will attest to. This is that the colloquial and standard forms of New Englishes differ in varying degrees from each other in their syntactic and morphological features and also, to a not negligible extent, in their lexicon and phonology. So much so, in fact, that in the case of any given New English, they appear to constitute separate subvarieties of it. These subvarieties, we have already seen, assume certain specialized functions and uses, and they are differently drawn upon by their users in ways that are socially patterned. The functions and uses which the standard subvariety is associated with make it more prestigious than the colloquial subvariety. Moreover, as we might expect, the classroom plays a kind of direct role in the acquisition of the standard form by these users that it does not play in the acquisition of the colloquial form. The features just described are associated with the phenomenon that has been called 'diglossia' in the literature. Here, a single language or variety is seen to have two separate subvarieties, a High subvariety and a Low subvariety (Ferguson, 1959). Therefore, researchers have been led to the view that what we see in, for instance, the Singapore English speech community is a form of diglossia, with SSE constituting High and CSE constituting Low (Richards, 1977; Gupta, 1994).

There is no doubt that this is a very useful way of looking at this dimension of the variability which New Englishes display as a result of their emergence along the lines described above. However, we need also to look at some of the additional complexities which New English situations introduce. One set of these relates to the differences between diglossia in New Englishes and Ferguson's more typical diglossia. Thus Low in Ferguson's scheme tends to have no orthography associated with it, whereas Low in New Englishes lays claim to the orthography associated with High. However, it comes to be actually written down in only a comparatively limited range of spheres, such as creative writing. The vocabulary, too, tends to be considerably shared by High and Low in New Englishes, whereas in typical diglossia, different words are often used for the same referent. However, the 'same' word may be treated differently, syntactically and semantically, in the two subvarieties. This is illustrated by the following example, which shows the noun *friend*, which High and Low share, being pressed into service as a verb in the latter. (Interestingly, Low shows also a way of making meaning which sees friendship as something to be purposively worked at and enacted rather than as just a static state.)

(13) *I won't friend you.*
  I will not be your friend (any longer).

The shared features of High and Low in New Englishes are probably to be accounted for by the fact that many people who use High also command Low (see below, however). In fact, this in turn seems to be associated with a further set of differences from typical diglossia. For, some users might even use both High and Low in the same domain, though for different purposes. Gupta's account of exchanges in Singapore English in the home domain, for instance, shows the mothers in question moving from predominantly High to predominantly Low and back in their exchanges, depending on changes in the operative variables there (1994). This being the case, it can also be expected that the acquisition of High is not confined to the school as it tends to be in typical diglossia. Gupta's evidence confirms this, by showing that the children in her study are already exposed to High in the home environment and begin to acquire it before formal schooling begins. It needs to be recognized, however, that some New English situations might differ somewhat from the Singapore English situation in this respect. In them, we might see considerably smaller proportions of users of the New Englishes being exposed to High in their homes before schooling than in Singapore. This would not mean, however, that normal transmission, in the redefined sense mentioned above, does not play a role in the acquisition of High even by the others.

Historically, too, the differentiation of High and Low does not take place in the same way in New Englishes as it does in typical diglossia. In the latter, there usually is some disruption in the natural social order and its evolution, which severs the immediate links between the elite and the rest of the populace. This leads the former to attempt to preserve the already existing (generally standard) form of the language while the latter continue to develop it under conditions of 'uncontrolled' growth. The eventual result is the differentiation of the language into the two subvarieties. New English situations also involved a disruption, namely the imposition of colonial rule. But it was a disruption which introduced English for the first time. It led to the emergence of a local elite who were defined on the basis of their possession of this new language. These then went on to develop among themselves for their distinct purposes systematic new varieties of it, which incorporated both standard and colloquial subvarieties. The subvarieties, moreover, continued to change and grow in interaction with changing sociohistorical conditions in a way that, for instance, the High of typical diglossia tends not to.

A further set of complexities in New English situations is brought up by the Singapore English case. It has often been noted that in Singapore English those who command High can slide down to Low, but that there are many people, mainly those from less educated and less privileged backgrounds, who are restricted to Low (Platt, 1977: 90). This observation clearly puts its finger on something important, but the way in which it is stated seems to miss what is actually involved. One reason is that it tends to confuse all non-standard everyday colloquial usage with a lack of proficiency. The argument above has already shown what is wrong with this. However, there is also another problem with the observation as stated — it does not look closely enough at what is meant by Low. It is, of course, correct that much of the colloquial usage in Singapore English does appear to share with creoles certain typical features. Among these are pro-drop, zero copula, syntactic 'deletion', morphological simplicity and so on. But this does not warrant the conclusion that there is but one Low subvariety in the speech community. As Pakir (1991) and Gupta (1994) recognize, the situation is not categorical but fluid and there are some important distinctions to be made.

All users of High will have some everyday, colloquial or spoken subvariety. But, in several cases, this subvariety will be much closer to the High than to what is generally regarded as Low. That is to say, even their everyday usage will remain fairly close to their standard usage. Others among them will indeed command an obviously Low subvariety, many examples of which will be discussed in the chapters which follow. But that does not mean that the features of their Low will define a uniform Low subvariety that will be shared by all users of Low right across the whole Singapore English community. The language planning measures that have been taken in Singapore since around independence have guaranteed a role for English across the whole of society which is very pronounced (see Chapter 12). This means that a whole wide spectrum of people in society, not just those who come from privileged or prestigious backgrounds, need to use English for at least some of their purposes. In many cases, they use it for straightforward, utilitarian transactional or service purposes. Those of them who come from less prestigious and privileged backgrounds and who, for that reason, might never acquire control of High, nevertheless develop a form of the language of their own. For all the creole features it shares with the Low of those who command High, it may still be different from it in certain significant respects. Thus, we hear examples like:

(14) *You want what? Tomorrow-eating banana or today-eating banana?*
Do you want (to buy) bananas which will be ready for you to eat tomorrow or today?

(15) *The mee you want hor, no more already.*
The (type of) noodles you asked for (is) are no longer available.

(16) *Angeline, my sister hor, she won the car.*
Angeline, who is my sister, won the car.

(I am grateful to Jeanette Ho for providing me with the last two examples.)

Such examples are not within the normal active range of usage of users who control High. They seem to be largely confined to people who come from less privileged or prestigious social backgrounds, for instance, hawkers, certain groups of sales persons, many taxi drivers and so on. (15) and (16) will also probably be confined to users whose ethnic language is Chinese.

This means, of course, that we cannot assume that there is only a single Low subvariety. This is not the only complication we need to recognize. It turns out that people who control only Low might also in other respects show a less than full command of English (Pakir, 1991: 174). The tendency has been to look at this usage simply as marking non-proficient usage in general. And indeed in domains outside of those in which they need to operate in English, these users do appear to display a lack of proficiency as such.

But, within the restricted spheres in which they need to operate in English, their usage is highly rule-governed, regular and productive. For that reason, it is also functionally effective. (14), for instance, shows a regular and productive use of a nominal pre-modifier (*today-eating* and *tomorrow-eating*). It may presumably be related to a post-modifying verb phrase (contained probably within a relative clause of the kind illustrated by the gloss in (14)) by perfectly conceivable formal means. Similarly, examples (15) and (16), according to Ho (1997), press a particle *hor,* borrowed from Hokkien, into service as an element which combines a focussing function with a relative clause marking function in a very rule-governed way. Such forms appear to be confined to less prestigious users of CSE. But those who use High have no difficulty at all in interpreting what is being expressed by them, so much so in fact that these users may be said to have a passive command of this usage. Doubtless, this passive command is something which might be facilitated by the fact that *their* Low might share at an abstract level some of the structural features of this other 'Low'.

All of this clearly also generates among all these different users of CSE a sense of belonging together in some special kind of way (see below). But this does not allow their two CSE subvarieties to be treated as if they are identical, as they tend at times to be in the literature. Indeed, there is also the further question whether it makes any sense to talk of the subvarieties in question as if they are only two in number. However that might be, there seems to be only one procedure by which such Low subvarieties can be brought together in this not quite legitimate way. This is by referring them to a High norm that is defined by the more prestigious classes alone, and then seeing all of these subvarieties alike as departing structurally from that norm in certain specific, though not necessarily entirely shared, creole-like ways. This is clearly unsatisfactory. Nevertheless, Low has tended persistently to be treated as a single undifferentiated colloquial variety, very likely on the basis of an inexplicit application of the procedure just described. And the fact that there has been no particular resistance to such treatment only demonstrates how difficult it is to escape the class basis of the language in New English settings and the perspectives it pre-defines — the standard defined by the more privileged *is* in practice taken as the norm for all the subvarieties. In Platt's time, the so-called Low subvarieties were brought together in this way on the basis of their shared departure from the norms of the superstrate, not the local, standard. The change in the point of reference today only reflects the difference in the location of the Centre.

NE Speech Communities and Issues of Proficiency

None of this renders the proficiency issue irrelevant. We need to recognize that there are some people in the wider social context who, while they may be *potential* members of the New English speech community, still remain outside of it. The reason is that they just do not have the knowledge of the linguistic and communicative rules which guarantees membership, even in very restricted spheres. That is to say, they simply are not proficient in the language in any reasonable sense of the term. As mentioned earlier, in spite of the general tendency in the literature to include the usage of these people in the characterization of New Englishes and New English speech communities, it has nothing to do with it in fact.

However, as mentioned earlier, there are some people who, while they might lack proficiency across the language as a whole as it is used in the community, are still able to use it with competence in a colloquial form in certain restricted spheres. For that reason, they have to be recognized as members of the speech community, even though they might not participate in it as fully as some others. Their situation is, of course, not very different from that of the many less privileged people in Older English speech communities who can handle well some regional or lower social dialect, but only that. They are nevertheless quite rightly seen to be part not only of the non-prestigious subspeech community they define but also in some significant way of the larger (British English or American English or whatever) speech community as a whole.

And then, there are those who command both a colloquial subvariety and also the prestigious (local) standard. For that reason they are generally taken to be the most representative members of the larger community. We might note that significantly involved here are non-linguistic matters such as prestige and privilege.

Even this very cursory description of the situation obliges us to recognize that it carries immense complexities which demand to be engaged with at considerable depth. This is something that we do not have the space to pursue here. But for the moment our description allows us as it is to make the point we are concerned with: that New English situations are characterized by the existence of viable speech communities. As a whole as well as through subspeech communities that they may include, these sustain the varieties and are sustained by them. The exact nature of the complexities involved might differ from one New English situation to another, but the Singapore English situation does open out valuable insights into the issues which all New English situations might be expected to raise in some measure in this respect.

New Englishes and the Native User

It should be evident that the account we have given of the emergence of New Englishes calls for a fundamental rethinking of the whole notion of the native user, as it is employed in almost all linguistic writing (see Kandiah, forthcoming a, for an examination of the notion in English from a post-colonial perspective). Drawing directly on a core meaning of the word *native*, the term *native user* invariably implies a proprietary right to a language. It gives expression to a naturally defined sense of inalienable ownership of the language, which confers on its human owners the right to determine through their usage and practice several important things about it. Among such things would be the following: What is grammatical or ungrammatical, acceptable or unacceptable, right or wrong in the way the language is used? Who is to be accepted into the speech community which it sustains and which sustains it and who is to be excluded from this speech community? How might users 'bend' the language or change it or enrich it or whatever, in order to make it express the meanings that they want it to, thereby allowing them, through its means, to act in and on their contexts so as to fashion out for themselves, and live, the kind of lives which make the most sense to them? And so on.

By these criteria, the account we have developed of the emergence of New Englishes makes their users native users of them. These users take hold of an originally alien code which, moreover, was imposed on them. But without disregarding entirely the nature of the rule-governed system they received from its original users, they still go on to reconstruct it to make it serve their semantic, actional and interactional purposes. In doing so, they operate in immediate interaction with the social, cultural, historical and other such particularities of their contexts. In addition, they operate within whatever constraints Universal Grammar might hypothetically place on their efforts. But they do it not just as helpless victims of abstract principles or codes, superstrate or substrate, but as interactive human subjects pursuing meaningful goals. The reconstructed codes emerge as new rule-governed systems which sustain and are sustained by the new speech communities which these people constitute themselves as.

The members of these communities display shared, rule-governed behaviour which uniquely defines them. They show full competence in the rules and principles of their new rule-governed systems and speech communities. Moreover, since it is they who have determined these rules and principles, they are able to control and apply them as no one from outside the communities can. Therefore, they are able to speak or write and otherwise use their New Englishes 'better' and more effectively than anyone else possibly can. Those among them who have been called upon by their realities to interact with users of other English-using communities have known how to invest their codes with the resources which enable them to do so. As a consequence, these codes give them the ability to handle both the immediate and extended realities of their contexts. Being almost invariably bilingual, they happen to control in this way more than just these codes and to belong to more than just these speech communities. But there is nothing which makes this fact an obstacle to the recognition of these people as native users of their varieties and, therefore, of the language — unless, of course, we have allowed the history of global hegemony over the last five centuries or so of Euro-American colonialism to persuade us that monoculturalism or monolingualism is the standard by which all such matters may be judged.

❧ *New Englishes and Identity*

The linguistic and discursive forms and practices which New English systems and communities develop help constitute and represent the lives and experience of the human subjects involved. They do it in ways that concretely realize these people's understandings of things, their particular existential and epistemological concerns and insights. These are, of their nature, symbiotic, holding together within themselves what they have drawn from their several, non-monotypical cultural and linguistic sources (Kandiah, 1981a; 1981b). These various inputs sometimes remain in creative tension with each other, at other times in resistance or oppositionality to each other, and at yet other times in harmonious complementarity or consonance with each other. This only reflects the complex linguistico-cultural personalities of these people. All of this means, of course, that New English systems will have particular self-identificational value for the human beings who constitute them and the speech communities which sustain and are sustained by them. They allow them to construct and project themselves as well as their distinctive views of reality, to give expression to their most immediate and significant concerns and to make their own distinctive voices heard in ways which have the greatest validity for them. In doing so, they also unmistakably compel recognition for what they separately and quintessentially are.

Quirk, Greenbaum, Leech and Svartvik (1972: 2), have claimed that English is 'the world's most important language' — which means that no country can escape using it for some at least of its valued purposes. There has also been a plentiful literature in recent times which has awoken us to an awareness of the hegemonic potential of the workings of languages. In the light of all these things, what we have just concluded is, perhaps, a very good thing indeed (Parakrama, 1995; Kandiah, 1994; 1995).

Chapter 4

The Situation of English in Singapore

Anthea Fraser Gupta

❧ Introduction

This unit focusses on how English is used in the ecology of multilingual Singapore. It traces the sociohistorical development of English in Singapore from the early nineteenth century to the present. It draws on concepts introduced in the first three chapters and provides a sociocultural and historical overview from which the following sets of units are to be understood: how English came to Singapore; who uses English, to whom, and in what circumstances; how the use of English relates to the use of other languages; how historical developments have affected the pattern of use of English; and (in general terms) the linguistic features of Singapore English.

❧ The Nineteenth Century

Politics

English did not, of course, arrive in Singapore with Thomas Stamford Raffles in February 1819. English speakers had visited the island of Singapore many times, trading and reconnoitring. But the treaty which Raffles and Major William Farquhar made with the Temenggong and the Sultan began a formal connection with Britain which was responsible for the prominence that English has in Singapore today.

The links of the British government with its East Indian possessions were at first mediated through the East India Company. As was often the case with British colonialism, commerce went first and rule later. Administratively, Singapore joined the other two settlements in the region which were under British control, Penang and Malacca. In 1826 the three trading centres were grouped together administratively, becoming known as the *Straits Settlements*, which were seen by the British authorities as the most Eastern Part of India. Their centre was at first the oldest of the settlements, Penang, which in turn was answerable to Calcutta, which in turn was answerable to London. Only six years later, Singapore had developed so much at the expense of Penang that it became the capital of the Straits Settlements.

Gradually the role of the British government became more explicit and more direct, with the gradual withdrawal of the dominance and mediation of the East India Company. By 1867 Singapore was a Crown Colony directly ruled from London. Over the course of the nineteenth century, more and more parts of the Malay peninsula and of Borneo were brought more or less under British control, but Singapore was always administratively distinct from them, being first of all one of the three Straits Settlements, and later a Crown Colony (the standard history of the region is Turnbull, 1980).

It is important to remember that the Straits Settlements were linked with each other and were a part of India. India now is a much smaller geographical area than it was in the nineteenth century, with several modern nations now composing the territory that once was India. When we write about historical periods we therefore need to use the place names that were used at that time.

The political history of British rule had impact in two areas that relate to the history of English in Singapore:
* movement of people
* development of educational policy

Incoming people

When we think of the history of colonialism we tend to think only in terms of people coming to Singapore from Britain. We may imagine the only English speakers to be people from the British Isles. We may even imagine that they all spoke late twentieth-century Received Pronunciation (RP). All these are wrong suppositions. The English speakers were from many places, both within and outside the British Isles. Even those from the British Isles did not predominantly speak RP — for example, many came from Ireland or Scotland. Furthermore, RP itself did not really emerge until the late nineteenth century and, as can easily be heard from archival recordings, has since undergone many changes.

The term 'native speaker of English' is a problematic one, used differently by different writers. In the discussion that follows, I use the term 'native speaker of English' to mean someone who grows up speaking English from infancy (some other interpretations are discussed in Tay, 1979; Singh *et al.*, 1995; Gupta, 1994). Native English speakers came to Singapore not only from the British Isles, but also from the USA (especially in connection with the Methodist Church — see Ho, 1964; Doraisamy, 1985/86) and people in turn came there from other parts of Europe (especially in connection with the Roman Catholic Church), some of whom did not know any English, and most of whom spoke it as a foreign language. These three categories were referred to as *Europeans* in the documents of the time. But most of all, the situation of Singapore in Greater India meant that people of a variety of kinds moved from the regional areas of longer-standing British control to the newer areas. The population of Singapore exploded in the early nineteenth century, with most of the rise being accounted for by non-European incomers. Singapore was the newest area of the Straits Settlements and was therefore a recipient of people from both Penang and Malacca but also from India and Ceylon. They encountered the other great movement of people into the Straits Settlements — from China.

Nineteenth-century Singapore was an ethnically segregated city. In Raffles's 1819 plan for Singapore he allocated sections of the city to the Europeans, the Malays and the Chinese (Buckley, 1902: 56f). Malays and Chinese living in the wrong zone were supposed to move. By 1822 he was allocating areas to 'Bugis settlers', 'Arabs', 'Amoy Chinese' and 'Chuliahs'. The *natives* (and that meant non-Europeans of all sorts) were set aside from the *European residents*. Buckley (1902: 450) quotes a contemporary account of the ceremonial presentation of a sword of honour to the Temenggong in 1846, which 'the natives seemed to consider...a holiday, and at an early hour Chinese, Malays, Javanese, Chuliahs, Hindoos, &c., &c., were seen swarming into the town from all quarters.'

However, there also came to Singapore, from the older British settlements, people who were ambiguous, neither really *natives* nor really *Europeans*. Some of them were *Eurasians*, people of mixed European and Asian ancestry — they came to Singapore from Malacca, India and Ceylon. While those of mixed ancestry from India and Ceylon usually spoke English (as well as other languages, often including Dutch in the case of those from Ceylon), the mixed people from Malacca usually spoke a Portuguese creole at home, and were unlikely to know English in the early years. Another important group to move to Singapore from Malacca were the Straits Chinese, a group that may also have been of mixed ancestry (Chinese and Malay), but which saw itself as ethnically and culturally Chinese, and used a variety of Malay in family life. Others were from minority groups that had operated in the British territories for generations — Armenians and Jews, most of whom came from Baghdad via India. Many of these ambiguous people came in roles that were of key importance in the transmission of English: as teachers, translators and clerical staff, and can be described as *brokers*. They had experienced British rule and many of them were familiar with English. They could be used by the Europeans to reach the natives in a way that was not possible for a European. These people had a tremendous impact on the way in which English developed in Singapore. We get a vivid picture of English-learning in the earlier years of the Straits Settlements in the account of Abdullah bin Abdul Kadir. Usually known as Munshi ('Teacher') Abdullah, he was a Malaccan of mixed Tamil, Arab and Malay background, who became a linguist and teacher of Malay to the British and

Americans in Singapore, and who wrote an autobiography that has become a classic of Malay literature. In 1823 he decided to learn English (he already knew Arabic, Tamil, Malay and Hindustani):

> I heard news that a newly arrived English padre was teaching children free, taking no fees or money even for his expenses. Everything was provided, even paper, ink and the like. When I heard this I was very pleased for I remembered the advice of Lord Minto and Mr Raffles who had said: 'If you learn English it will be very useful to you.' Ever since they had told me this their words had lived in my memory. At that time it was very difficult to learn English in Malacca for there were no schools. The sons of rich men had tried to learn, calling teachers to their houses and paying them high fees. They were not good teachers: neither were they proper Englishmen, the majority being Eurasians from Madras or the Dutch possessions who had learnt a little English. These were the people who became teachers in Malacca and asked exorbitant fees. Nobody of any other race in Malacca could read or speak English correctly, for there were none who learnt it.

(Abdullah, 1843; transl. A. H. Hill, in Hill (Ed.), 1969)

In his first encounter with the padre, a Eurasian child translated between the Englishman and Abdullah. Both that Eurasian child and Munshi Abdullah were acting as linguistic brokers.

In the nineteenth century very few Singapore residents spoke English. English was used among the European residents, and was beginning to be taught in English-medium schools. However, for most of the nineteenth century, the majority of those in English-medium schools came from backgrounds with some contact with English. Very few of the *natives* went to school at all, let alone English-medium schools (Gupta, 1994), nor did they learn English informally. There is no evidence that there was ever a pidgin English in the Straits Settlements. Well into the twentieth century, the predominant lingua franca was a Malay-based pidgin, usually known as *Bazaar Malay*. Bazaar Malay was widely known by people of all ethnic groups and was the language that European residents of the Straits Settlements expected to have to learn in order to communicate with *natives*.

Malay has played a large part in the formation of Colloquial Singapore English. However, the varieties of Malay that have been most important are Bazaar Malay and the kind of Malay spoken by the Straits Chinese (now usually known as *Baba Malay*). These two contact varieties of Malay had themselves been influenced by the southern variety of Chinese, Hokkien.

The lexical items in CSE which are not from English are overwhelmingly from Malay and Hokkien — contributed from these two varieties of Malay.

Education Policy

The educational impact of political developments was essentially a move from the private to the public. As the British government became increasingly directly involved in Singapore, an education policy began to develop (Bloom, 1986; Gupta, 1994). In the early years, education was largely in the hands of private organizations, churches and charitable bodies. The Annual Report on the Administration of the Straits Settlements has a brief section on education from the report of 1856–57 onwards, and this report gets more and more substantial as time goes on. Schools, both government and non-government, were increasingly supervised and compliance with policy had financial consequences as the century progressed.

In the early years, English-medium education was essentially for European and Eurasian boys and girls, and for the sons of those few *natives* willing and able to afford it (Gupta, 1996). Malays were encouraged to be educated in Malay and were especially discouraged from being educated in English — education in the medium of Malay was given financial support. Gradually the government gave more financial support to education in English and in other mediums, but policy underwent many changes of direction and financing (Bloom, 1986; Gupta, 1994).

It sometimes seems to be assumed that the early schools of the Straits Settlements taught British English with an RP accent. While some of the features of Singapore English did emerge in Singapore, we cannot assume that the starting-point was British English, let alone with an RP accent.

Let us look at the teachers in the English-medium schools in nineteenth-century Singapore. European teachers were largely restricted to senior posts. Indeed, 'Senior Teachers' were actually defined as those 'not educated or engaged locally' (Annual Report, 1915). An 1891 advertisement for Anglo-Chinese School (ACS) advertised 'Ten classes taught by the best trained European masters' (Ho, 1964: 32). Photographs of the teachers at ACS at the time, however, show the majority of teachers as still being non-European.

In 1901 another advertisement for ACS Singapore advertised itself as having '6 European and 12 native teachers' while Methodist Girls' School made a point that the kindergarten was 'under trained American teacher' (Ho, 1964: 139). In 1884 a list was given of the names and salaries of the teachers in the government schools. Using a combination of salary and name it is possible to determine the race of most of the teachers: the salaries fall into two sets, without overlap, one with a range of $240–$600 p.a. and one with a range of $960–$2520 p.a. Eight of the 31 teachers were on this higher scale, and all had European names (which could be Eurasian too, but probably were not, given the salary). Of those on the lower scale, 3 teachers had clearly Indian names, and 2 clearly Chinese. The remaining 18 were probably Eurasian, although of them, 7 had names of 'Portuguese' origin, like Gabriel, Pereira, De Rozario, Gomes, D'Souza and Oliveiro, which could be Eurasian or Indian. While we cannot retrieve exact figures from the nineteenth-century documents, it is evident from official returns and from advertisements that *European* teachers were in a small minority.

Furthermore, 'European' did not mean *British*, but *white*. The Methodist Church had a long-standing link with a group in Minnesota, and many of its early missionary teachers came from the US. They also had teachers from the UK and Australia, as well as from India and Ceylon. Meanwhile, the Catholic church was also drawing its European teachers from a variety of sources, including of course Ireland (English-speaking, and then a part of Britain), but also France and Belgium.

The input even of 'European' English was thus very mixed. Many of the colonialists were people who had led complicated lives. Buckley (1902: 133) reports how J. H. Moor, the first head of Raffles Institution, was an Irishman born in Macao — with a 'speech defect'!

In terms of pronunciation, RP would seem to have had little prominence in this rich dialectological soup. The single most important group in education in the earliest years were the Eurasians. Many of the early Reports of Education castigated the English of these Eurasian teachers (as did Munshi Abdullah). Their English should certainly be the starting-point in the analysis of Singapore English *pronunciation*. The teachers would have used Standard English. The term 'Standard English(es)' is used to refer to the varieties of English used throughout the English-using world in educational and formal contexts. These Standard Englishes are strikingly similar, differing from each other mainly in pronunciation and in a few lexical items (e.g. *flip flops/thongs/slippers*) with a handful of minor syntactic differences. The term Standard English can be used where it is not necessary to focus on these minor variations from one Standard English to another (see also Chapter 7). While the teachers did use Standard English, it was already as a 'New Variety' type of English, and it is likely to have had some input into the lexis and syntax of Singapore English. The impact is likely to be seen most in those few differences between SSE and British Standard English, and especially in those features shared by South Asian Standard Englishes and SSE, for example in the use of the invariable tag *is it*, and in the use of *will/would*.

Children in English-medium schools did not just learn English from their teachers, any more than they do today. They learnt also from other children, who in turn adjusted their speech to accommodate those around them.

It is often forgotten that many European families (not all of whom were

British) kept their children with them in Singapore, especially their daughters, and especially in the earlier years: as late as the 1970s the schools of the Tanglin group, the main schools attended by the British community in Singapore, had more female than male pupils (Veronica Goodban, former headmistress; personal communication). So in the early years (especially up to the 1920s) there were a lot of European children in the schools, including British children. The 1891 advertisement for ACS promised that: 'To English lads is offered a home, and to Chinese lads an opportunity to learn a correct accent and facility in expressing themselves in the English language.' Until the end of the nineteenth century, around half the pupils in English-medium schools were European or Eurasian. The composition was comparable to that of the International Schools of modern Singapore. In the girls' schools, the proportion of Europeans and Eurasians was even higher — other than these groups the main source of girls was from the Jewish and Armenian groups (both of which were officially classified as 'Indian' until 1915). Many of the non-European children in the nineteenth-century English-medium schools would have been exposed to English at home. The girls' schools were especially likely to have a majority of English-speaking children.

There were some similarities between the Eurasians, the Armenians and the Jews. Although the Jews were often Arabic-speaking Jews whose families were originally from Baghdad, many had come via India. Many of the Eurasians in Singapore were also of Indian or Ceylonese origin, and members of the Armenian community also had come from India. Other Eurasians came from Malacca. Another important group of children who attended English-medium schools in the nineteenth century were the Straits Chinese who usually spoke their own variety of Malay (and often Hokkien too). These four communities were all prone to using both Malay and, increasingly, English. As early as 1858 an Israeli traveller described the Singapore Jews as becoming westernized (Nathan, 1986: 3). The Straits Chinese came to be known as the *King's Chinese* in the early twentieth century. The Jews, Armenians and Eurasians were also likely to educate children of both sexes in English-medium schools. The Straits Chinese were the first Chinese group to place daughters in English-medium schools. These four small communities with vital brokering positions were crucial in the development of English, and their access to English and to contact varieties of Malay began the development of English in Singapore which moved it away from the Standard Indian/Eurasian English that had been the major input.

We see here why Malay has been so important in the formation of CSE. But not Malay Malay — rather, the *contact variety* of Malay which Eurasians, Europeans, Indians, Jews and Straits Chinese, all would to some extent be able to speak. Well-known features of CSE like *lah* and *ah* and lexical items like *kiasu* which have their origin in Chinese varieties, appear to have come into CSE via contact varieties of Malay.

Some areas of Singapore were English/Contact Malay-prone areas. In the nineteenth century this was especially the case for the Waterloo Street area on the eastern edge of the city — here Eurasians, Armenians, Jews and Straits Chinese lived side by side (Clarke, 1992). The major English-medium schools were also in this area. Until the 1900s, there was even an area nearby of European prostitutes, in whose houses English was used, though none of them were British. This was principally Malay Street, off Victoria Street and was of course conveniently located (Warren, 1993: 40f).

Later Katong, even further east of the city, became another English/Contact Malay-prone area — and to some extent still is. There was the same English-oriented mixture of Straits Chinese, Eurasians and a scattering of Jews.

Malay also had an important role in the English-medium schools, where the syllabus in 1874 consisted of arithmetic and geography (from Standard IV to VI), plus four measures associated with English skills. In these, pupils were assessed on reading aloud (and translating into Malay — English pupils were exempted from this) first words, then passages, of increasing difficulty; writing from dictation; parsing (from Standard IV) and writing a summary of a supplied text (from Standard V). This gave no practice in spoken language, or in free writing.

English Speakers in 1900

There were two ways in which you could be an English speaker in nineteenth-century Singapore:

- You could be from a family which used English, possibly because you were of European British or part-European British descent, or because your family had received an English-medium settlement in one of the older British settlements.
- You could have received some education in an English-medium school in Singapore.

We can group these English-speaking people as follows:

- European British (i.e. of British ancestry): nearly all native speakers of English, but of many varieties of British English; also American English.
- Other European: nearly all non-native speakers of English.
- English speakers of mixed ancestry (Eurasians) and non-Europeans with English-medium education outside Singapore: many native speakers of English and some non-native speakers of English.

- Non-Europeans with English-medium education within Singapore: non-native speakers of English.

The proportion of English speakers coming from these groups varied over time, with the last group increasing to become the largest numerically.

It is generally agreed that Singapore English had its origins in the English-medium schools of the Straits Settlements (Platt and Weber, 1980; Bloom, 1986) — there is no serious doubt about this. Although in this general sense I agree with the analysis of Platt and Weber in Chapter 2 of their 1980 book, there are several differences between my account of the history and theirs.

Analysis of the composition and growth of the English-medium schools of the Straits Settlements suggests that there were two distinct phases in the development of CSE: first, a stable period in which a high proportion of children in the English-medium schools were from English- and Malay-speaking homes; followed by a change in the first decade of the twentieth century which saw a sudden influx of Chinese-speaking children. The increase, in the same period, in English-medium education for females was also important in the establishment of an indigenous variety of English (Gupta, 1994).

The Twentieth Century

English on the Rise

When the Chinese children thronged into the English-medium schools in the first decade of the twentieth century, they entered a set-up that had been linguistically stable for twenty years. This was the moment when CSE came into real being, as the English-medium schools coped for the first time with a majority population of non-English speakers. Malay also receded in importance as fewer children came to school already able to use it. Apart from the Straits Chinese, the group of Chinese most enthusiastic about English-medium education was the Cantonese (Bloom, 1986), making Cantonese a possible source of influence on the English that emerged. The school photographs of this period begin to show the dominance of ethnic Chinese boys among the pupils.

After the influx of ethnic Chinese in the first decade of this century, they became the major group of English speakers in Singapore. As the Chinese were numerically dominant in the Straits Settlements, even though few of them were English-focussed, they quickly formed the largest group of English speakers. In the 1921 census, Nathan experimented with finding out the extent of knowledge of English. He expressed great doubts about the validity of the returns on this question, but it is worth looking at even so:

Ethnic group	No. of English speakers	% of community able to speak English	% of English speech community
European	5771	91	13.5
Eurasian	6090	78	14.3
Chinese	23361	6	54.7
Malay	1924	3	4.5
Indian	3939	8	9.2
Other	1588	23	3.7
TOTAL	42673	8	100

Table 1. Ability to Speak English in the Urban Areas of the Straits Settlements; 1921 Census (Nathan, 1922)

From this period on, English-medium education became more and more popular. In the 1920s Chinese and Indian girls began to enter English-medium schools in larger numbers, and these girls grew up to be able to speak English as one of the languages used in the home, giving rise to a new generation of native speakers of English. The change in the student body had its impact on the teaching population ten years later. In the early twentieth century the prominence of Eurasians in the teaching force diminished and the proportion of Chinese teachers increased. After the 1942–45 Japanese Occupation, Malay children in greater numbers began to experience English-medium education, and in the post-war years English-medium education gradually became the commonest form of education for both sexes and all ethnicities.

After independence in 1965, education was further extended to reach all children (in terms of class, gender and ethnicity). In modern Singapore education is neither free nor compulsory, but it can be described as universal. The trend during the British period had been for government to take more and more control of educational policy, and this was continued after independence. Education is now under tight government control, and the private sector is insignificant, being almost entirely restricted to foreigners. Gradually the use of English was extended after independence, so that it became first of all compulsory as either a medium or as a subject in all schools. The number of children electing to have education in a medium other than English dropped, and eventually (in 1987) all education under government control was required to be in the medium of English. In every generation a higher proportion of students would be second-generation English-educated, which would often mean that they spoke some English on arrival. The English-medium education of women was crucial for this step, allowing CSE to emerge as a native language. By the end of the twentieth century about half of all students will start education knowing English — in one sense, a return to the nineteenth-century picture.

Let us summarize the growth of English-medium education in the Straits Settlements. Four phases in the schools can be seen:

(1)   Nineteenth-century years: stable situation. High proportion of Europeans and Eurasians as pupils (even higher among girls). Relatively few Chinese and almost no Malays. Any Chinese pupils likely to be Straits Chinese. Teachers mostly Eurasian and from India/Ceylon with Europeans in senior positions. A high proportion of children would have spoken English and Malay on arrival in school. Some English taught through Malay.

(2)   Early twentieth-century expansion period: progressive reduction of both Malay speakers and English speakers in the school intake. Hokkien and especially Cantonese speakers formed an increasingly high proportion of English-medium school attenders, but school population still very diverse. Malay still used to teach English. Influx of Chinese teachers in English-medium schools. Few girls educated.

(3)   Mid-twentieth century: diversity of the school population due to multiplicity of dialects among the Chinese, and the arrival of more Malays in English-medium schools. More girls. Proportion of students being educated increased, and the proportion in English-medium education grew, though it did not exceed Chinese-medium until the 1950s (Bloom, 1986). Greater use of English as a normal means of communication.

(4)   Post-independence: English-medium education became universal. Rise in number of Chinese, Malay and Indian children having English as a native language.

Terminological Problems

Approaches to the study of Singapore English have varied greatly (see Chapter 5). Writers on Singapore English have ranged from those who see it as entirely 'error'-based, through those who see it primarily as a second language, to those who focus on the native speakers. Terms like *native language* can hold different definitions for different writers. *Singapore English* as used by some writers may cover the whole proficiency range (Platt and Weber) or may refer only to the English of native speakers (Gupta). It is clearly important to understand the population on whom a writer is drawing for data, and to read in the context of a writer's definitions.

Language is highly politicized in Singapore. The post-independence language and education policy has been a major factor in promoting the use of English in many domains. This politicization gives rise to two main elements to be considered in assessing the readings:

- terms acquire a particular definition within the sociopolitical system
- there is a clearly articulated language policy which has goals that are widely discussed and known by citizens

It is important to understand that everyone in Singapore has an official 'race' which generally reflects paternal ancestry and which may not reflect actual language knowledge and use (Gupta, 1994). The three official languages of Singapore other than English (Mandarin, Malay and Tamil) are defined as representing the three major 'races' of Singapore. These racial groups are subdivided into 'dialect groups' or 'ethnic groups'. As officially defined, the *mother tongue* is the superordinate language of one's official ethnic group. So the *mother tongue* of a 'Chinese' is deemed to be Mandarin, that of a 'Malay', Malay and that of a 'Tamil' or 'Malayalee', Tamil. The *first language* is the main medium of education (which is now always English) while the *second language* is the other language studied (usually the official 'mother tongue').

The term *mother tongue* in the Singapore political system therefore corresponds neither to the individual's childhood language(s), nor to the individual's ancestral language.

In Singapore one's officially allocated 'dialect group' normally corresponds to the paternal ancestral language, but does not necessarily correspond to anything in the individual's personal experience. Linguists usually use the terms *mother tongue, native language* and *first language* in the same sense. These terms usually refer to a language (which may be one of two or more) that a child learns before learning any other language, though some linguists use them to refer to an ancestral language that the child may or may not have been exposed to. The term *second language* as used by linguists normally refers to a language that is not an individual's native language, but which is used in daily life. Writings on language use in Singapore often use these terms without definition, with some using them in the same sense as the official definition, and others in the usual linguists' sense. Some readings slip between the definitions, and even seem to assume that the senses are identical. In all reading on Singapore it is crucial to contest the meaning of these terms, where they are not defined.

Sources of Data

It is extremely difficult to get accurate information on who uses English and in what circumstances. There have been some studies of the pattern of English use in Singapore, including census data. It is essential to assess this data. Asking people when and where they speak a given language is notoriously problematical. People simplify, misrepresent, forget and lie. The choice of a language (or a mixture of languages) from within one's personal repertoire is not an easy one, as where there is choice, that choice has social meaning. A question such as, 'If you needed to ask directions in the street, which language would you choose?' is impossible to answer. It depends on your own repertoire, obviously, but it also depends on your assessment of the interlocutor's repertoire (based on ethnicity, perceived social class, age and so on). Furthermore, people select who they ask directions of, and can therefore increase the likelihood of being able to use a preferred language. The census question, 'What language do you speak to your parents?' presumes that the same language is used to both parents, which is not of course necessarily the case. Questions of this type simplify, and force respondents into giving a straightforward answer where a hedged one would be more accurate. In all data of this kind it is important to examine the way the questions were asked and to predict the likely *direction of error*. To say that a survey or a decennial census has a likely direction of error is not to damn it. It is in fact extremely difficult, perhaps impossible, to improve the quality of information about language use that can be obtained from a large-scale survey, such as a census. Where enough information is given about the way in which questions are asked (as it is in the case of the census), the direction of error can be identified and caution applied where appropriate.

The contestation of terms and of facts in this area means that it is necessary to approach reports with an open mind, and to bring to them any knowledge of one's own about the language situation in Singapore. In all readings, for better understanding, it is essential to examine:

- the date of writing
- the date of data used
- the source of data
- the definition of terms

Those who are familiar with Singapore should compare data to their own personal experience of Singapore, either now or in the past. In a summary it is essential to simplify what is in reality great complexity, but the simplification should be one that is representative and that identifies larger patterns in a way that would be understandable to someone unfamiliar with the society. Those who are unfamiliar with Singapore face a harder task. They need to make assessments based on their experience of other societies, and will also find it useful to look for contradictions between one writer and another.

Who Uses English and When?

The pattern of language use in Singapore has always been complex, as in any multi-ethnic trading port. It has also changed substantially since the mid-twentieth century. The complexity and the rapid change together mean that:

- the relationship of English to Singaporeans varies considerably from one individual to another, so that the position of English in Singapore cannot be reduced to a single phrase such as *English as a second language*.
- descriptions of the status of English rapidly become outdated.

Descriptions of the role of English (or any other language in Singapore), including mine, must therefore be approached with extreme caution.

English exists in a linguistic ecology of several languages. A number of writers (such as Kuo, 1980; Platt and Weber, 1986; Gupta and Siew, 1995) have discussed the patterns of individuals' repertoires. There are expectations about the languages likely to be known by people of certain ages, social classes and ethnicities. And languages have niches or *domains* that tend (in a rather flexible way) to be associated with them. English has participated in this ecology since 1819, and can indeed be described as an exotic weed, which has become well-established and has flourished at the expense of some of the other languages.

The general position of English in Singapore in the second half of the twentieth century has been that the *knowledge of English*, and the *domestic use of English* have spread from a small elite to a wider population. It must be remembered that the population at any time includes people born over the previous ninety years. Thus a snapshot of the population preserves patterns of language use from an earlier period. A Singaporean born in the 1970s is almost certain to be able to communicate in and to read English. But only a minority of those born in the 1920s know English. In data such as census figures, it may be difficult to see anything but the snapshot.

In what follows I delineate the overall patterns of English use in Singapore. Reliable figures for this kind of information do not exist. There is census data, which I have discussed elsewhere (Gupta, 1994) and there are a number of smaller reports. But there is a great deal of opportunity for collecting data on language use in Singapore. (see, for example, Tay, 1979; Platt and Weber, 1980; Kuo, 1980; Gupta and Siew, 1995).

In the post-independence years, English-medium education became increasingly the norm. In earlier years education, and especially English-medium education, had not been evenly distributed across the population.

There had been some ethnic variation (with the Indians being most likely to receive it and the Malays least), but the major variation had been social. The higher the social class, the more likely a Singaporean was to know English. In post-independence Singapore the ethnic variation has been virtually removed (the majority Chinese are now slightly less likely to be literate in English than the other two major groups). To some extent the social differentiation remains.

Whatever measure of social class is taken, it is still the case that the higher the social class, the more likely it is that English is an important domestic language (this pattern can be seen in the 1990 census data, e.g. Table 2).

Monthly household income from all sources (S$)	% speaking English as main language to parents (in same household)
Below 1000	3
1000-1999	7
2000-2999	10
3000-3999	12
4000-4999	14
5000-5999	16
6000-6999	19
7000-7999	22
8000-8999	25
9000-9999	29
10 000 and over	35
ALL INCOME GROUPS	12

Table 2. English to Parents: Link with Income (Adapted from Lau, 1993: 87)

We need to consider the direction of error here. There are difficulties in questions whose effect is unpredictable (lying about income or about language use, making arbitrary decisions when one language is spoken to mother and one to father) but there are two areas where we can predict the effect of error. On the one hand, English is only recorded if it is the *main* language spoken to parents. This means that there are more people than this who speak English as a language to their parents. Secondly, these questions relate only to parents within the same household. The main effect of this would seem to be on age, as the younger people are more likely to be living with parents — partly because they have not yet set up independent households and partly because the older respondents are, the more likely it is that their parents will have died (not many 70-year-olds live with a parent). This will have the effect of increasing the number of English speakers, as the younger age groups are more likely to know English. None of these factors, however, affects the very clear direction of these figures — the richer you are, the more likely you are to speak English to your parents.

By the late twentieth century, unlike in the past, English is not *restricted* to the social elite. The main route of English in Singapore until the 1960s was, except for a tiny minority of people, almost entirely through education, and especially through English-medium education. Knowledge of English led to use of English, not only in transactions, but also in social and domestic settings. Once women knew English, it could become a native language for their children, as it was introduced, usually alongside other languages, into the home.

Within Singapore at the end of the twentieth century, then, there are adults:

- who know no English (very few people, mostly drawn from those born before the 1950s)
- for whom English is a foreign language they have little ability in and seldom speak (mostly older people, but also some less educated younger people)
- who learnt English at school and can use it but who have a dominant other language (many people, of all ages)
- who learnt English at school and for whom it has become the dominant language (many people, of all ages)
- who learnt English as a native language (sometimes a sole native language, but usually alongside other languages) and for whom English is still the dominant language (a minority at present, but an increasingly common pattern in younger age groups)

The rise of English in Singapore has, since the late 1970s, been paralleled by an equally dramatic rise in the use of Mandarin by members of the Chinese community. Benjamin (1976) identified Singapore's multiracialism as one which was based on encouraging ethnic identities, and in several areas this separatism has continued to develop (discussed in various recent books, including Chua, 1995). One effect has been the expansion in learning and domestic use of Mandarin.

The extension of Mandarin has been largely at the expense of other varieties of Chinese (the dialects) but there are some areas of social life where now Mandarin is to be heard where previously English was the norm. In multi-ethnic workplaces, in residents' committees, and at times in the media, Singaporeans who do not speak Mandarin are beginning to feel excluded. The Singapore school system requires that children study the language of their ethnic group, and since the 1980s it has become increasingly difficult for children to study other languages than the one that is officially theirs (Gupta, 1994; Chua, 1995). With insignificant exceptions, non-Chinese Singaporeans are excluded from the learning of Mandarin within the school system. As Mandarin has been promoted, and as the Chinese are increasingly seen by political dialogue as the mainstream, the minorities may feel excluded and marginalized. Members of ethnic minorities, and indeed some Chinese, thus promote English as the language of pan-Singaporean identity. The minority groups have a greater investment in English than the majority Chinese (Gupta, 1994).

English in Singapore can be identified as having a proficiency scale (see the discussion in Chapter 3). It is a traditional axiom of linguistics that all native speakers of a language are said to be equally proficient — any distinctions between the standard of English of its native speakers are based on political criteria that rate some native varieties as socially superior to others. However, non-native speakers of a language are traditionally ranged on a proficiency scale. This is not a distinction I feel entirely at home with when applied to highly proficient non-native speakers, but for those at the lower end of a learner continuum it is meaningful.

One area that gives rise to much confusion in understanding Singapore English is that a feature which some may see to be an *error* may in fact be a dialectal feature of Singapore English. If a speaker in formal settings marks the past tense, then does not mark the past tense in a domestic situation, there is no error — the speaker is merely using more than one kind of English. Chapter 5 discusses in more detail the *lectal continuum* and *diglossia* approaches to the study of English in Singapore, and Chapter 9 explains the importance of understanding what varieties of English a child is exposed to. At this stage I would like simply to emphasize that many Singaporean speakers of English move at will between Standard English and CSE. Skill in Standard English, as is the case in other English-using societies, is highly valued, and is often socially used to judge a person's social and linguistic status. In Singapore English, as in all or most languages, the way people speak gives information to other members of the community about their social position: their gender, age, social class and so on, and speakers often manipulate this information-giving either consciously or semi-consciously.

The areas in which English is used by Singaporeans vary considerably. Although linked to proficiency, it is not only proficiency in English which determines the areas in which language is used.

In Singapore, English *can* be used in all aspects of daily life. There are a few Singaporeans who seldom, if ever, need to use any other language; who perform all their work life, all their emotional life, and all their commercial transactions in English. However, most Singaporeans habitually use two or three or even four or more languages on a daily basis, and for most of them, one of those languages is English.

Language choice is usually referred to in terms of *domain*. In Singapore, English can be found in all domains (e.g. educational, business, domestic, religious) and is used by all ethnic groups. It can even be found in religious and cultural activities which are linked to particular ethnic groups. Most Muslims in Singapore are Malays, but English may be used in mosque-based activities. The mosque is a domain in which both Arabic and Malay have major functions. English can even (sometimes) be heard in exclusively Chinese activities such as religious auctions, where traditionally southern varieties of Chinese are used, and where Mandarin is also often heard. English is used domestically in many families of all ethnicities and (increasingly) all social classes. Although it *may* be used in all domains by just about anybody, that does not mean that it *is*. It is hard to pinpoint domains where English is *required*. The same predictivity applies to choices between Standard English and CSE. There are a number of contexts where an effort at Standard English is required — these are the formal and educational contexts which require Standard English around the English-using world. However, although there are some contexts where (given a choice of English) CSE is a likely choice (among close friends in a social setting; with family members), there are no contexts or domains where CSE is *required*.

There are some domains in Singapore, especially those involving contact with educational and governmental authorities, where English (and usually Standard English) will normally be the first language of choice if those involved in the situation are able to use it. If English is not available to both parties, there will be a process of negotiation to find a common language or a means of translation. For example, parents registering their child at a school will have a prior expectation of English as the preferred language of the transaction. However, other considerations may enter. If, for example, the school representative and the parents are both ethnic Malays, Malay is a possible choice, and ethnic solidarity may overcome the domain expectations.

This is true in all domains. The complexities of age, social class, ethnicity and language proficiency operate in all settings, so that it is not possible to simply specify the domains associated with particular languages. The asking of directions is an interesting example, because the asker has some choice in who to approach. Imagine you are an ethnic Chinese, whose English is excellent but whose Mandarin is weak. You are lost and want to ask directions. It may be that you have in the past been rebuked for not using Mandarin — 'Are you ashamed to be Chinese? Why do you speak to me in English?'. You may therefore choose to approach someone you can speak to in English without fear of rebuke — an ethnic Indian, for example.

When we study the domains and patterns of English use in a society, we look at general patterns and statistical trends. There are many aspects of language use which are not categorical. The domains in which different languages are used, the links between language and social class, between language repertoire and age, and so on, are all areas where there are many exceptions to the general behaviour and the general trend, and where individuals participate in complex choices.

❧ *The Effects of History on Form*

In Chapter 3 we saw how there are no features that distinguish all the New varieties from all the Old. This is true of all varieties. We cannot identify a single feature of *Singapore English* which is characteristic of only Singapore English. Nor is there any such feature of *British English*. Singapore English is a range of Englishes used by the people of Singapore, and can be defined only on that geographical basis, not on the basis of its features. So when we step from a geographical base into discussing the features, we are, once again, talking about the general or the dominant pattern, rather than about something which is unvarying and with no exceptions.

When you read about how Singapore English comes to be the way it is, or about the sources of features in CSE, you will see a good deal of speculation: e.g. does *lah* come from Malay? Hokkien? Cantonese? Could *ah* come from Tamil? And so on. Our answers to these questions must be plausible not only linguistically, but also historically. We need to assess which languages could have influenced Singapore English as we see it today (Chaudenson, 1979; Mufwene, 1990; Gupta, 1994). This is part of what is meant by *sociohistorical*.

The initial model of English in Singapore was Standard English, as used by the teachers in the early English-medium schools. However, only about a quarter of the teachers in the schools were Europeans of British ancestry. Most teachers (and especially those in contact with the youngest children) were Eurasian and many were from India and Ceylon. It was their variety of Standard English and, especially their pronunciation, which must be seen as the principal starting-point for the history of English in Singapore.

As larger numbers of non-English-speaking children underwent English-medium education, they adapted this initial model. It is an axiom of sociolinguistics that we speak like our peers, or that we try to speak like those we want to be seen as our peers (Le Page and Tabouret-Keller, 1985).

The role of children in developing the linguistic features of new settlements has often been discussed (e.g. Kerswill, 1996) — children soon set themselves aside in their pronunciation from children in other settlements and from adult incomers. This basic process was presumably in operation in the first two decades of this century in Singapore. *Imperfect learning* (see Chapter 3) was no doubt also a factor at this point, as most children experienced few years of education. The requirement in many schools that all communication be in English led to a communicative need for English. This resulted in the emergence of a kind of English that was almost a relexified (see Chapter 3) Bazaar Malay. It was this that was to become CSE. Only CSE has a substrate. We cannot speak of Standard Singapore English having a substrate.

The most important of the languages that were in contact in the turn-of-century period which saw the origin of CSE, then, seem to have been:

(1) **The superstrate**: Standard English. (Eurasian, Indian/Ceylon, British of various sorts, American.)
(2) **The principal substrate**: Baba Malay (the Malay of the Straits Chinese) and Bazaar Malay. Both these languages in turn had been influenced by Chinese (especially Hokkien) and possibly by Portuguese creole. The Portuguese creole may have had direct input too via the Malacca Eurasians.
(3) **The secondary substrate**: Assorted southern varieties of Chinese of which Hokkien/Teochew and Cantonese were likely to have been the most important. Hokkien was also a substrate to the two varieties of Malay which formed the principal substrate.

The individual learners of English brought to their learning of English their own language backgrounds, but they also heard the crystallizing variety of spoken English from their multiracial school mates.

Most of the languages which were in contact during the period of development of CSE are still in contact now (as an *adstrate*). The two contact varieties of Malay that were so important are in recession now, although both Baba Malay and Bazaar Malay can still occasionally be heard. Two other languages are in the adstrate which were not in the substrate. One is Malay (Standard Malay and other varieties of Malay spoken by ethnic Malays). This was not in the substrate because few Malays were given the opportunity of an English-medium education until after independence. It is important in the adstrate because knowledge and use of English (alongside Malay) is very widespread now among the Malays, and because of its regional prominence. Another part of the adstrate currently is Mandarin, which was not part of the substrate, because few in Singapore learnt it until the 1920s, and few spoke it regularly until the 1980s. Mandarin is now probably

Singapore's leading native language among the under-sevens (English is the runner-up), and has become a major language of everyday use in Singapore in the 80s and 90s. Although these adstrate languages are not part of the substrate of CSE, they are available to influence both CSE and SSE now.

The origins of features of Singapore English can be very complex. Elsewhere I have discussed the origin of the CSE *one* (Gupta, 1992), and in Chapter 7 there is a discussion of the origins of *what* and *ma*. Many of the lexical items of Hokkien and of Malay origin are used in CSE. They may have come into CSE from one of those two contact varieties of Malay or they may have come direct from Hokkien or Malay. We often cannot reach a firm conclusion about the route by which a feature reached CSE.

The same applies to features of pronunciation. The general absence of length distinction in Singapore English vowels (Chapter 6) could have come from influence from the substrate, but it could also have come from the Indian, Ceylonese and Eurasian teachers in the nineteenth-century schools, with contributions from the presence of Irish or American teachers. The same goes for the use of plosives where some other varieties of English have dental fricatives. This is common in many varieties of English, including the English of India, Ceylon and Ireland. The vowels of *go* and *take* are usually monophthongs in Singapore English, although they are diphthongs in RP. However, there is no evidence that the /o/ and /e/ of Singapore English are the result of monophthongization, as there is no evidence that diphthongal versions were the original model — there are similar monophthongs in many varieties of English.

Conversely, a common feature of most varieties of British (and American) English is variation between /n/ and /ŋ/ in unstressed syllables (*singin'* and *dancin'*). This variation is completely missing from Singapore English, which always has /ŋ/ (although in recent years a trendy /n/ has appeared due to the influence of the American media). This is all the more striking because in Singapore Mandarin /n/ and /ŋ/ are in variation (in words like *san* 'three', *shan*, 'mountain', *shang*, 'up'), and for most speakers do not contrast.

In English from England (and in RP in particular) the contrast between stressed and unstressed syllables is important and the high contrast results in many reduced vowels. In Singapore English (as in Irish, Scottish and Indian English, among others) there is less contrast between stressed and unstressed syllables, and fewer reduced vowels.

It is vital to examine the features of CSE in the context of its substrate, and to look at all varieties of Singapore English in the light of the other languages that may have influenced it. But this must be done in the context of a realistic assessment of the historical situation that Singapore English grew out of. Also, variation within Singapore English must never be forgotten.

Chapter 5

The Grammar of Singapore English

Lubna Alsagoff and
Ho Chee Lick

✒ *The Study of Singapore English Grammar*

Does Singapore English have a Grammar?

Before we examine the grammar of Singapore English, let us first explore the premise that New Englishes such as Singapore English have a grammar. It is necessary to do so in the light of the complaints commonly voiced by many in Singapore, especially in areas connected with pedagogy or the media, that Singapore English, or more precisely, Colloquial Singapore English (CSE) is 'bad' or 'broken' English. In such a view, it would be meaningless to speak of a grammar of Singapore English, since clearly the sentiment here is that Singapore English is haphazard, and has no consistent internal structure. To assess the validity of such views, it is clearly necessary to examine what we mean by the word *grammar*.

C. L. Ho (1995) explains that there are two ways in which the notion of *grammar* can be understood. From a prescriptive point of view, grammar is seen as a regulatory set of rules by which to judge the correctness or desirability of a language or its use. Such a perspective almost always views languages as being unequal in social status (see also Crystal, 1987). A new variety of English such as Singapore English is viewed as being socially less desirable than a more established variety like British English. Consequently, from a prescriptive point of view, Singapore English is seen as having bad grammar simply because its grammar is different from that of British English.

From a descriptive point of view, however, it is obvious that this statement cannot be correct. The term *grammar*, in its most basic sense, refers to the set of rules by which words of a language are strung together to form meaningful sentences or utterances. It is easy enough to demonstrate that Singapore English does indeed have a *grammar* in this sense. If we ask speakers of Singapore English, they are able, very clearly, to provide judgements in a consistent and systematic way as to whether an utterance qualifies as 'good' Singapore English, or 'bad' Singapore English. For example, take a sentence like *anything also can*. Many Singaporeans would 'condemn' this utterance, which means something to the effect that anything will do, as ungrammatical.

However, if it really were the case that this sentence was constructed in a haphazard manner, then we should be allowed to shuffle the words around without any consequence. This is clearly not the case — *Also anything can. *Can also anything. *Also can anything. are all not acceptable sentences to the Singapore English speaker. This small experiment shows that there is systematicity and organization in the ways words are arranged to form sentences in Singapore English. It is therefore clearly not true to say that Singapore English is haphazard, or has no grammar. It also cannot be correct to say that a language has no grammar because it does not conform to the grammar of the prevailing 'standard variety' (for a discussion of this term as well as Standard English, see Chapter 4). Saying that CSE is bad or broken English is perhaps more of an opinion about its low social status than its grammar. The point remains, however, that the social status of Singapore English should not be confused with the grammar of Singapore English.

While it is definitely true to say that CSE does not have the same rules of grammar as Standard English, it does not follow that because CSE users do not abide by the rules of Standard English, CSE has no grammar. If CSE is ungrammatical from the perspective of English, then a language like French might also be construed as ungrammatical from the perspective of English grammar. Thus CSE should not be referred to as 'ungrammatical' in the sense that it has no grammar or structure, no matter what our sociolinguistic stand on its desirability or undesirability is.

One question that arises from this discussion is why it is that a language like Singapore English should be called 'English' at all, since its grammar is so different. It is easy enough to understand that different languages should have different grammars, but why it is that different varieties of the same language should have such different grammars may not be so easy to accept. Here, we need to bear in mind that language issues are rarely made on the grounds of logic or structure. History clearly shows, as was discussed in the first chapter of this book, that decisions on issues relating to language are almost always determined on the grounds of economics, politics and power.

Stylistic Variation in Singapore English

When we speak of Singapore English having a very different grammar from British English, we need to be clear about the fact that like all languages, Singapore English exhibits variation. And in the variation, it is the informal variety that we see diverging most in form and structure from Standard English. The variety of Singapore English used in formal speech situations resembles very much the formal register of Englishes used in other parts of

---

* Indicates unacceptable forms.

the world. When lay people talk about Singapore English, they generally focus only on the informal or colloquial variety of Singapore English. This variety of English is, however, not the only one available to speakers of Singapore English. Consider the samples of Singapore English below. In the first excerpt, we see a sample of what we term Standard Singapore English (SSE). This is the English used by Singapore English speakers in educational and formal situations, in particular writing. Notice that this English is little different from the formal styles of British English, American English and Australian English (as was also mentioned in Chapter 4). In the second, we see an example of the informal variety of Singapore English, what we refer to as Colloquial Singapore English (CSE). This is the style that may be used by Singaporeans in informal contexts, such as talking to friends or family. The differences between SSE and CSE are stark. In addition to the non-English words used, there is also a great difference in the structure of the sentences.

SSE

You had better do this properly. If you don't, you may get told off. And since you are always asking her for favours, you should at least do this properly for her. You should! You cannot do it like this. Do it again. Come, let me help you.

Two people can finish this job very quickly. One person will not be able to do it as fast. You see, we're almost done. Wow, when she sees this, she'll be very happy. We will definitely get a very big present from her this New Year.

CSE

Eh, better do properly, lah. Anyhow do, wait kena scolding. And then, you always ask her for favour, and still don't want to do properly. Must lah. Like that do cannot. Do again. Come, I help you.

Two people do, very fast finish. One person do, not so fast. You see, almost finish. Wah, she see this, she will be very happy. Then we get big angpow for sure this New Year!

In the following section, we will look at the two major perspectives on the grammar of Singapore English, after which we will discuss the grammatical features of Singapore English. The description emphasizes the regularity and rule-governed nature of the structure of Singapore English.

❧ *Approaches To Singapore English*

There have been two main frameworks for the description and analysis of Singapore English: the lectal continuum model and the diglossia model. Platt and Weber (1980) represent the major work within the first approach, while Gupta (1994) represents perhaps the most important contribution to the latter paradigm. In what follows, we summarize the salient points of their descriptions of Singapore English.

The Lectal Continuum Approach

In the lectal continuum framework, variation within Singapore English is treated as dependent on the social status and level of education of the speaker. Descriptions of the features of the variation primarily use Standard British English as a yardstick of comparison, although Platt and Weber stress that this in no way implies that Singapore English is inferior or substandard:

> Unlike other varieties of English such as British English and the English spoken in U.S.A., Canada, Australia and New Zealand, where there are two dimensions, one on a scale of regional variation and one of social variation, the variation in Singapore English can be observed along one axis which is related to the educational level and the socio-economic background of the speaker...There is a considerable variation within spoken, and to some extent written, English from the more prestigious variety of Singapore English, the acrolect, through mesolects down the basilectal sub-variety, and speakers of Singapore English can be placed along a scale according to a range of linguistic features.
>
> (Platt and Weber, 1980: 46-7)

The lectal continuum approach emphasizes Singapore English as a non-native variety of English because the descriptions it offers of Singapore English are primarily in terms of how Singapore English differs from Standard British English. In addition, these descriptions do not emphasize the internal rule-governed system of Singapore English. Much of the work within the lectal continuum approach began in Singapore as early as the 1960s, when there was perhaps not such a large community of speakers who used English as their native language, or their principal language in thought and communication, along with the other indigenous languages. The statistics of Singapore show quite dramatically how this situation has changed, and continues to change (see Chapters 4 and 10). In particular, the second group of 'native speakers' is growing steadily in number, and it would be difficult to deny that Singapore English is a native variety of English.

The term *native speaker* is a problematic term, as has been pointed out in the previous chapter. We use here, basically, the same definition employed by Gupta, and say that a native speaker can be defined as any person that falls into any one of the following categories:

i.   Adults who have had their education in English from an early age up to a high level and who continue to use English in adulthood in all major domains to the extent that English is their dominant language (Tay and Gupta, 1983: 179).
ii. Persons who have acquired English in the home from birth, not subsequent to any other language. They may however have acquired more than one language at birth (Gupta, 1994: 14).

The lectal approach is still used widely, and is especially common when there is a need to emphasize the differences between Singapore English and Standard British English, which is useful and perhaps necessary to language teaching.

The Diglossia Approach

The diglossia approach, like the lectal continuum approach, acknowledges that there is variation within Singapore English, and that Singapore English can be viewed as a speech continuum. However, these two frameworks view this variation in very different ways, and emphasize different aspects of it. While the lectal continuum approach views Singapore English as primarily a non-native variety, the diglossia approach views Singapore English as a native variety. Gupta makes the point that Colloquial Singapore English should not be viewed as an interlanguage that is somehow an imperfect copy of some target language like British English:

> S(ingapore) C(olloquial) E(nglish) is still generally seen as imperfectly learned Standard English, both by scholars and the general public. Even Platt, in all his studies of Singapore English (e.g. Platt and Weber 1980) generally treats Singapore English as a non-native variety. This leads Valdman (1983:227), quoting Platt, and apparently not realizing that there are native speakers of Singapore English, to refer to it as a 'semi-pidgin'. However,...for many years something over a quarter of Singaporean children have had English (in nearly all cases SCE) as a principal native language. To refer to this contact variety as a...'semi-pidgin' is grossly misleading.
>
> (Gupta, 1994: 17)

The difference between Gupta (1994) and Platt and Weber (1980) might be seen as stemming from historical reasons: data collection by Platt and Weber in the 1970s may have yielded a different picture than in the late 1980s and 1990s when Gupta investigated Singapore English. It is significant to note that Gupta herself, along with other well-known researchers like Tay, subscribed to and wrote in the lectal framework, and only switched to the diglossia framework in the late 1980s.

An important consequence of viewing Singapore English differently in terms of whether it is native or not is that while the lectal continuum approach sees the variation as a cline of proficiency in a second language, the diglossia approach views this variation in terms of communicative choice and intent.

Thus Gupta writes:

> There is a High variety of English, which I call Standard English, which is much like Standard Englishes in the rest of the English-speaking world (Gupta 1986). ...This H-variety is the norm in formal circumstances, in education, and in all writing except some representations of dialogue.
>
> However, the Low variety of English in Singapore is sharply different from Standard English, especially in syntax and morphology. I refer to this variety as Singapore Colloquial English (SCE). SCE is the main kind of English used in the home and in casual situations. It is the normal variety to be used to small children, outside a pedagogical situation. Nearly all those children who have learnt English from birth will have SCE, rather than Standard English, as their native language.
>
> Singaporeans are conscious of these differences, which are also exploited in written texts. ...The use of SCE by those who have a command of both Standard English and SCE is not the result of error in using a language which may or may not be native, but a matter of choice based on context and affective message. Informal writing, comedy sketches, and songs exploit Standard English and SCE in ways which are meaningful in the community.
>
> (Gupta, 1994: 7-9)

Gupta gives a list of eight features for distinguishing between the H (SSE) and L (CSE) varieties (1994: 10-13). She claims that Singapore English utterances tend to contain a predominance of either H features or L features. She also makes a provision for intermediate varieties (between H and L) where particles and *be* deletion are used alongside Standard English verb and noun morphology.

CSE (L Variety)

i.   Use of pragmatic particles
ii. The presence of verb groups without subjects (PRO-drop)
iii. Conditional clauses without subordinating conjunction
iv. -*ing* as finite verb and verbless complements

SSE (H Variety)

i.   Aux + subject in interrogatives
ii. Presence of verbal inflexions
iii. Noun inflexions (genitive and plural)
iv. Certain complex verb groups

In recognizing Singapore English as a native variety, the diglossia model consequently describes Singapore English as having an autonomous grammar, i.e. one which can be described without reference to Standard British English, and which varies according to the context and the communicative intent of the speaker.

Why Comparison is Necessary

Having said all this, however, it is important to recognize that it is not an easy task to discuss grammars of New Englishes such as Singapore English autonomously. First, there has to be a great deal of work done before a grammar of Singapore English can be written that does not make reference to any exonormative standard. Second, because Englishes such as Singapore English are newly emerging languages, that have evolved out of contact with very different languages, it is of interest to see how they differ from their superstrate language – for Singapore English, it is British English; as well as their substrate languages – for Singapore English, these are Chinese and Malay. In this sense, a comparative approach is naturally required. This comparative approach is useful in the study of the evolution of language, which was discussed extensively in Chapter 2, where we saw how features of New Englishes, pidgins and creoles were argued to be a result of substrate influence, or counterargued to be the result of universal processes of language change.

That the comparative approach is somehow essential is seen in Gupta's own writing. Even while she advocates that the grammar of Singapore English should be described as an autonomous system, Gupta's own descriptions are not completely free of the comparative, non-autonomous approach. Consider for example what she writes about conditional and temporal clauses in CSE, and clause structure:

Certain conditional and temporal clauses do not require conjunctions. If translated into Standard English, the conjunction would usually be if, or when.

...-ing as Finite Verb and Verbless Complements. This has sometimes been referred to as BE-deletion. Standard English requires a verb BE in places where in SCE it is optional, such as between a subject and complement or as an auxiliary in a continuous verb group with an -ing verb.

(Gupta, 1994: 11)

In the first excerpt, the author talks about translation into Standard English, and in the second she makes a similar comparison of CSE to Standard English. She also assumes, without any argument or justification, that CSE distinguishes between finite and non-finite verbs (like English) when she speaks of -ing as a finite verb. In the next section of this chapter, we will discuss this briefly and give some indication that CSE may be like its substrate, Chinese, which does not divide its verbs on the basis of finiteness. We do note that Gupta's comparison is between CSE and SSE rather than Standard British English. However, since Gupta views SSE as similar to Standard British English, it is in some ways still a comparative rather than a purely autonomous approach that Gupta adopts. Thus, we see that although Gupta preaches an autonomous approach as an ideal, in practice, a comparative approach seems necessary, if not inevitable.

It is significant that Gupta compares CSE with SSE rather than with Standard British English. While we have acknowledged that the comparative approach is in some ways essential to the study of NEs, this comparison, however, should not be seen as one that measures Singapore English grammar against a superior superstrate grammar. In the past, researchers on Singapore English, in particular with respect to language education, have used a comparative approach in a way that emphasizes linguistic inequality – the superstrate was viewed as an exonormative standard by which to judge the status and 'quality' of Singapore English. A reaction to this was seen in the counterarguments that advocated an endonormative standard, where English language use is not judged using a non-local variety, but is instead measured against a local standard. More about this will be discussed in Chapter 10. For our purposes in discussing the grammar of Singapore English, this primarily emphasizes that whatever comparison is made, it should be one that treats the New English as being equal in status to its superstrate. To stress this point, we will talk about comparisons between CSE and Standard English, rather than between CSE and Standard British English, which makes the points that SSE is like Standard British English, and that the comparison should be viewed as a comparison of two linguistically equal varieties. Mention of British English in comparisons will only be made in those cases where SSE and Standard British English differ.

Dangers of Comparison

While comparisons can be extremely useful in elucidating the features of Singapore English, there is an inherent danger that investigating grammar comparatively can lead to important generalizations being lost (Mohanan, 1992). In this section, we will discuss one example of what this means.

M. L. Ho is one of many researchers who make the claim that some form of deletion of *be*, as well as a simplification of the verb morphology, takes place in sentences such as:

(1)   The book sell already.   CSE
       The book has been sold.   SSE

Ho (1995) would, in a comparative approach, interpret a sentence such as (1) as a passive, but where the main or lexical verb is not inflected, i.e. *sell* instead of the past participle form *sold*, and the auxiliaries *has* and *been* have not been used. In place of *have*, *already* is used to mark the perfective aspect (Bao, 1995). To determine if this is a correct analysis of the facts in (1), we need to take note of two other characteristics of Singapore English.
The first concerns the structural property known as pro-drop. Gupta (1994), as we saw above, notes that an important characteristic of CSE is that subjects tend not to be overtly expressed, i.e. pro-dropped (as indicated by Ø), in contexts where their identity is obvious to the hearer, e.g.:

(2)   a.   Ø Also can do.   CSE
             I can also do it.   SSE

       b.   Ø Want to buy this or not?   CSE
             Do you want to buy (this)?   SSE

The second concerns the topicalized or focussed sentence structures, where instead of a word order that is subject-verb-object, Singapore English can in many instances have an object-subject-verb word order. Basically the object (in bold) is fronted to highlight the information it refers to, e.g.:

(3)   a.   Certain **medicine** we don't stock in our dispensary.
       b.   One **subject** they pay for seven dollars.
       c.   This **kind** I find quite alright.

If we take a look at the examples in (1), given the information we have now, it is apparent that an analysis that simply compares Colloquial Singapore English and Standard British English cannot determine if the structure of (1) is that of a passive, or that of a topicalized sentence with a pro-dropped subject, i.e. it is unclear if (1) should be interpreted as (4a) or (4b):

(4)   a.   The book   sell   already.
              subject   passive
                              verb
       The book has been sold.

       b.   The book   Ø   sell   already.
              object   subject   active
                                             verb
       The book, I have sold.

What would be necessary if we wanted to determine which of these structures was correct would be an analysis of the properties of subjects and objects in Singapore English in order to ascertain the grammatical function of the noun phrase *the book* in the above sentence. Note that such a task would involve looking at the structure of Singapore English in an autonomous manner, without comparison to Standard British English.

⅍ *The Grammatical Features of Singapore English*

In the next section, we will examine some grammatical features of Singapore English. Most of the features that are discussed belong to CSE, rather than SSE, which we have said resembles Standard British English very closely. There will be comparisons made between Singapore English and Standard English on the one hand; and Singapore English and the substratal languages of Chinese and Malay on the other.

The approach in this section is largely comparative because the list of grammatical features discussed here focusses on those CSE structures that are different from Standard British and Singapore English, which we refer commonly to as Standard English (for ease of annotation of the examples in this section, I abbreviate this as StdE). The grammatical features discussed here represent those areas which have been researched to a considerable extent in the existing literature. However, because the approach taken here is comparative to a large extent, what is given is necessarily incomplete. At points, we mention areas where we feel that a comparative approach, primarily comparing Singapore English with British English, gives an incomplete or misleading picture of the grammar.

Features Connected with the Verb

Morphological Marking of the Verb

Many researchers such as Platt and Weber (1980) and Tay (1979) have pointed out that CSE verbs often appear in an uninflected form: the past tense is not morphologically marked, and neither is the singular present tense:

(5) a. She eat here yesterday.   CSE
(6) a. He always go market with his sister.   CSE

If we compare these CSE utterances with those of Standard English, we see immediately the difference:

(5) b. She ate here yesterday.   StdE
(6) b. He always goes to the market with his sister.   StdE

In CSE, the verbs appear in their uninflected form. The time or aspectual information that the verbal inflection in Standard English carries, is instead often borne by a time adverbial, e.g. *yesterday* in (5a). Platt and Weber, in looking at the class of strong verbs, give evidence that this lack of morphological marking cannot be a case of phonological reduction of consonant clusters: even with the subclass of strong verbs whose past tense forms have vowel changes , e.g. *go-went, see-saw*. There is no difference between the present tense and the past tense forms:

> My mum she come from China many years ago!
> Oh, I see him last week.
>   (Platt and Weber, 1980: 61)

For the third-person singular present tense marking, Platt and Weber (1980) imply that the non-differentiation in terms of morphology of agreement forms is primarily a result of substratal influence, because they observe that neither the Chinese dialects nor Malay have morphologically marked tense and agreement features (Platt and Weber, 1980: 61-62). They give examples such as the following to support their case:

> i chhut khi   [Chinese (Hokkien)]
> he out go
> He goes out.
>
> in chhut khi
> they out go
> They go out.

Dia pergi ke pasar   [Malay]
he go   to market
He is going to (the) market.

Mereka pergi ke pasar
they   go   to market
They are going to (the) market.

It is important to note, however, that while the grammars of Chinese and Malay have similar structures, we should not assume that this constitutes sufficient evidence to conclude that similar CSE features are due to substratal influence. Thomas (1996), for example, says:

> It may be, as John Platt (1991) has suggested that this is due to the influence of the local languages, Chinese and Malay, which do not mark verbs according to the subject. But this process occurs elsewhere when speakers of other languages learn English irrespective of whether these other languages themselves mark verbs according to subject.
>
> (Thomas, 1996: 227)

Thomas's point is clear if we look at what she documents about English dialects. She notes (1996: 227) that there are dialects of British English, such as East Anglian English, which do not mark, in a regular fashion, the third-person present tense, often omitting it in colloquial speech. This makes East Anglian English the same as Singapore English in respect to the non-morphological marking of agreement. However, it is clear that such similarities cannot be attributed to substratal influence because Singapore English and East Anglian English cannot possibly have the same substratum.

The Verb *Be*

In CSE, attributive or equative clauses, i.e. clauses that describe states, e.g. *Teck is very rich*, *She is a teacher*, *My sister is in the garden* do not require verbal predicates. Thus, while it is ungrammatical in British English to say *John very rich*, it is a preferred utterance in CSE. Copular verbs, although used in CSE, are not obligatory to the clause. The difference therefore is that British English requires all its clauses to have verbal predicates, while CSE distinguishes clauses that describe states from those that describe actions.

One important finding in Platt and Weber (1980) is that the non-realization of the morphological marking is not random or haphazard, but is structurally conditioned by what follows the verb. Their statistical findings show that this variation is very much dependent on the type of category of the complement that follows. For example, their study shows that the verb is used least of all when it precedes an adjective phrase, e.g.:

(7)   This coffee house __ very cheap.

and used most often when the following complement is either a noun phrase or a preposition phrase indicating location:

(8)   My sister ___ in the garden.
(9)   John   ___ my teacher.

Again, Platt and Weber attribute this non-realization or variant realization to the influence of the substratal languages. Thus they demonstrate, although here without statistical measure, that a comparison of Malay, Chinese and even Tamil yields a similar pattern.

Aspect

Aspect deals with the way in which an action or state is regarded, whether something has been completed, or is still ongoing. In CSE, the use of time adverbials is preferred over the morphological marking of aspect, e.g.:

(10)   a.   My father pass away already.   CSE
        b.   My father passed away already.   CSE
        c.   My father has passed away.   StdE

(11)   a.   She eat her lunch already.   CSE
        b.   She eaten her lunch already.   CSE
        c.   She has eaten her lunch.   StdE

The use of adverbials as aspectual markers is one reason why certain adverbials, e.g. *always, still, already* are more frequently used in Singapore English than in British English.

Morphological endings, however, are not completely absent, and do surface. However, even where they do, they are not accompanied by the auxiliaries. For example, instead of (10a), CSE also allows the main verb to appear in the perfective form, but does not have the perfective auxiliary *have* preceding it (10b). Similarly, in (11b), we see that the verb *eat* can appear as *eaten*, without the auxiliary.

Perfective Aspect: *Already*

The most common way to express the perfective aspect in CSE is to use the adverb *already*. Platt and Weber (1980) make the point that this use of *already* is very likely to be linked to the use of *liau* in Hokkien, which is used to mark completion. Bao (1995) extends this idea of substratal influence by demonstrating that the influence of Chinese may also be observed in the use of *already* as a marker of the inchoative aspect, in addition to the perfective aspect. The inchoative aspect, according to Bao, is to 'signal the beginning of an action which has not taken place before the time of utterance' (Bao, 1995: 183). This aspect is not associated with the use of *already* in British English. An example of the inchoative use of *already* is given in (12):

(12)   a.   My baby speak already.   CSE
        b.   My baby has started to speak.   StdE
                                         (Bao, 1995: 183)

In (12a), *already* indicates that at the time of utterance, the speaker's baby has just started to learn to talk. Bao argues that this inchoative use of *already* has no parallel in English, but clearly has one in Chinese. Using *le* from Mandarin (the equivalent of *liau* in Hokkien, and *leh* in Cantonese), Bao points out that these Chinese aspectual markers are used to mark both the perfective and the inchoative:

(13)   a.   wo chi le   liulian.
              I   eat LE   durian
              I ate durian.

        b.   wo chi   liulian   le.
              I   eat   durian   LE
              I now eat durian.
                                         (Bao, 1995: 184)

Bao (1995: 184) says that *le* used before the object indicates the perfective aspect while *le* when used sentence-finally, indicates the inchoative aspect. In the latter, a change of state is realized in the transition from not eating durian to eating durian. Thus, he argues that *already* is a calque of the Chinese *le*, and consequently displays syntactic patterns that are clearly indicative of substratal influence. In simple terms, a calque is a lexical borrowing that often has the guise of the superstrate word, but which has the structure and meaning of the substrate word for which it is a calque.

Progressive Aspect

Even though the present and past tense, as well as the perfective aspect, tend not to be marked, the progressive aspect is fairly commonly marked.

Thus, it is not uncommon to see the *-ing* morpheme being attached to verbs to indicate the progression of an ongoing event, e.g.

(14) a. She told you she going to the cinema with
us or not? CSE

b. Did she tell you whether she was going to the
cinema with us? StdE

The difference between CSE and Standard English is that the former does not use the progressive auxiliary *be*. The main verb, however, is marked with the *-ing* suffix. In addition, CSE often marks the progressive aspect with the adverb *still*, e.g.:

(15) a. Don't disturb them, they still studying. CSE

b. Don't disturb them, they are studying. StdE

Note that it is unacceptable, even in the most colloquial Singapore English to use the uninflected verb when the aspect marked is progressive. Hence, (15c) is not a well-formed utterance:

(15) c. * Don't disturb them, they still study. CSE

Gupta (1994: 11) makes this point rather obliquely by observing that *-ing* forms often appear as predicates of clauses. Note that she does not say the same of *-en*, i.e. perfective forms.

Irrealis Aspect

Platt and Weber (1980: 69) mention that CSE sees 'the use of *would* in structures where *will* normally occurs in Standard British English'. Such structures are those in which the irrealis aspect marks 'what is not actually so, but may be so'. What this means is made clearer by looking at the following examples:

(16) a. If I can induce anger in at least one reader, this article would have more than served its purpose.

b. It is strongly hoped that the reserved lanes would give priority to public buses.

(Crewe, 1977: 50-51)

---

* Indicates unacceptable forms.

In these two examples from Crewe, the use of *would* is used to point to events that have yet to happen, and that may or may not happen. The contrast between the use of *will* and *would* is very interestingly highlighted in the following sentence:

(17)   I will help you, but I am not sure if my brother would.

Here the speaker, in expressing what is within his control, i.e. his willingness to help, uses *will*, in contrast to his use of *would* which expresses the event he is unsure of: whether or not his brother will offer the same help.

This use of *would* to indicate the irrealis aspect is documented in earlier research on Singapore English such as Tongue (1979) and Crewe (1977). The origins of this use of *would*, Tongue writes (1979: 35), may have arisen from the understanding that Singapore English speakers have that *would* is 'more polite than *will*', which then logically extends to the use of *would* as a marker of tentativeness. This tentativeness is clearly related to the irrealis aspect, which basically marks what might but may not be so.

An example of the polite use of the modal *would* is given in (18):

(18)   I am sorry to tell you that I would have to turn down your loan
       application.

Would as a polite version of *will* is found also in British English, although such use is restricted to requests, e.g.:

(19)   Would you please shut the window for me?

The extension of this polite use of *would* to the use of *would* as a marker of tentativeness is also found in Standard British English:

(20)   I would like to make one suggestion about your dress.

However, British English does not carry this extension of meaning into the irrealis aspect.

The use of *would* as a polite form, a tentativeness marker, and as a marker of the irrealis aspect is found not only in CSE, but in SSE as well, as Crewe indicates in saying that his examples of the use of *would* as a marker of the irrealis aspect are found in written Singapore English, in newspapers and official notices.

Habitual Aspect

CSE frequently marks the habitual aspect with the use of the adverb *always*, which in Standard English is often marked by the use of the simple present tense:

(21)   a.   My brother always jog every morning.   CSE
       b.   My brother jogs every morning.   StdE

The Noun Phrase

Count vs Non-count

CSE tends to treat non-count nouns as count. Thus *furnitures, luggages* are possible forms in CSE. On the other hand, Platt and Weber note that the plural is often not marked in Singapore English. This is, however, a phenomena which is less and less common in attested corpora of Singapore English. It is worthwhile to note that Platt and Weber use students as their informants, in keeping with their view that Singapore English should be studied as a non-native variety. Thus they make little distinction between learner Singapore English and Colloquial Singapore English. The difference is important, however: the former represents an interlanguage, while the latter represents a conscious choice of an informal style. It is perhaps an error rather than a variation in style (and consequently not a true characteristic of CSE) that Platt and Weber document in this instance. Thus, CSE speakers would accept an utterance like (22a), but not (22b):

(22)   a.   Her brother very rich — got four cars!   CSE
       b.*   Her brother very rich — got four car!   CSE
       c.   Her brother is very rich and owns four cars.   StdE

Having said this, we would like to point out that there are many examples in which the plural inflection is absent in CSE, where Standard English requires one, e.g.:

(23)   a.   She queue up very long to buy ticket for us.   CSE
       b.   She queued up for a very long time to buy
            tickets for us.   StdE

Such instances, however, should not simply be analysed as a lack of the plural inflection. This sort of analysis wrongly presupposes that *ticket* in (23) is a count noun, and thus amenable to plural affixation. We would like to suggest here that it may in fact be used as a non-count or mass noun in such instances. Evidence for this postulation can be seen in the following

---

* Indicates unacceptable forms.

pattern: when *ticket* is used with a quantifier, e.g. *four*, *many*, it is always inflected; where it is uninflected, it always appears alone, without premodification. Most nouns that are, in Standard English, only classified and used as count, can in CSE be used both as count and non-count. This pattern is also found in the Chinese dialects and Malay:

(24) a. Ta   mai le che.   [Chinese (Mandarin)]
          He/she buy LE car.
          She bought a car/cars.

      b. Ta   mai le si   liang   che.
          He/she buy LE four CLASSIFIER car.
          She bought four cars.

(25) a. Dia   mempunyai kucing.   [Malay]
          He/she own   cat.
          She owns a cat/cats.

      b. Dia   mempunyai empat ekor   kucing.
          He/she own   four   CLASSIFIER cat.
          She owns four cats.

Articles

Most researchers working on Singapore English comment on the variation in the use of articles, in particular, the noticeable lack of the use of *a/an* with what appear to be, in Standard English, singular count nouns, e.g.:

(26) a. She got car or not?   CSE
          Does she have a car?   StdE

      b. She buy dress for what?   CSE
          Why is she buying a dress?   StdE

The lack of the indefinite article may perhaps be due to CSE treating such nouns as non-count, as we discussed in the previous section, which explains why they do not require articles. Note that a construction like (27), containing the noun *rice*, which in Standard English is non-count, is structurally similar to its Standard English counterpart in its lack of the use of the indefinite article:

(27) a. She buy rice for what?   CSE
          Why is she buying rice?   StdE

Therefore, in the use of articles, CSE is perhaps heavily influenced by its substrata in allowing a large number of what are just count nouns in Standard English to function as non-count nouns.

Relative Clauses

There has not been much work done on the structure of noun phrases. One important difference in this respect has been documented in Alsagoff (1995) and J. H. W. Ho (1997). These papers illustrate that the structure of noun phrases containing relative clauses cannot be characterized simply in terms of substratal influence, but must be described in terms of a careful amalgamation of structures of both the superstrate and susbstrate.

A relative clause, in its most basic sense, refers to a clausal modifier of a noun or noun phrase. For example, we can either say *the sad man*, or *the man who is sad*. In the first construction, an adjective *sad* modifies the noun *man*. In the second construction, a relative clause *who is sad* modifies the noun *man*. Languages differ in the way relative clauses are constructed, as is obvious from the following examples, modified from Alsagoff (1995):

(28)   a.   **That boy who pinched my sister** is very naughty.   StdE

       b.   **Budak itu yang mencubit kakak saya** sangat jahat. [Malay]
            Child the RP   pinch   sister my very naughty.
            That child who pinched my sister is very naughty.

       c.   **Nie   jie-jie de neige haizi** hen huaidan.   [Chinese]
            Pinch sister RP that   child very naughty.
            That child who pinched my sister is very naughty.

The phrases in bold are what we will refer to as *relative clause constructions*. These are noun phrases which contain a relative clause modifier. A simple analysis of relative clause constructions will reveal three basic components. For an easier understanding of the structure of a relative clause construction, let us look at Table 1.

Cross-linguistically, we can therefore generalize and say that a relative clause construction consists of three parts: a relative pronoun, a modifying clause (which together make up the relative clause) and a head.

However, while this generalization about the components of relative clause construction holds for English (Standard English and CSE), Chinese and Malay, to complete the picture, we need to state the actual ordering of the components. Therefore, although we can say that all languages have the above three components, we must next examine how languages differ

Relative Clause Construction		
Relative Clause		**Head**
Relative Pronoun (RP)	**Modifying Clause**	
StdE who	pinched my sister	that boy
Malay yang	mencubit kakak saya	budak itu
Chinese de	nie jie-jie	neige haizi

Table 1. The Structure of a Relative Clause Construction

in the way in which they order these components. In particular, we need to look at the relative position of the head with respect to the relative clause, as well as the position of the relative pronoun with respect to the modifying clause within the relative clause.

In an English relative clause construction, the order of the components can easily be summed up by the following statements:

(29) a. Head   *precedes*   Relative Clause
         b. Relative Pronoun   *precedes*   Modifying Clause

Similarly, in Chinese, the order of the components can be summed up as:

(30) a. Head   *follows*   Relative Clause
         b. Relative Pronoun   *follows*   Modifying Clause

We see therefore that the ordering of the constituents within the relative clause constructions of the two languages is very different. Let us see now how the differences in these structures show up in the CSE relative clause construction. In CSE, there are of course relative clauses that resemble Standard English ones, e.g. (31a). There are, however, relative clauses that look extremely different from Standard English ones, e.g. (31b).

(31) a. **That boy who pinch my sister** very naughty.
            That boy who pinched my sister is very naughty.

b. **That boy pinch my sister one** very naughty.
That boy who pinched my sister is very naughty.

The most apparent difference is in the use of *one* rather than *who* as the relative pronoun. In Alsagoff (1995), it is argued clearly that *one* should be treated as a relative pronoun, on grounds similar to why Li and Thompson (1981), for example, treat the Mandarin *de* as a relative pronoun. The other differences pertain to the ordering of the components. If we look at the statements in (32) which capture the basic pattern of the relative clause construction in CSE, we find that it is very much a case of amalgamating the English structure at one level (32a), and the Chinese at the other:

(32) a. Head   *precedes*   Relative Clause
(= English, cf. 29a)

b. Relative Pronoun   *follows*   Modifying Clause
(= Chinese, cf. 30b)

This demonstrates that while it is clearly the case that there is substratal influence on CSE, it is imperative that the influence be described in order to show there is a systematicity in its incorporation into the structure of CSE.

Sentence Structure

Pro-drop

Many researchers, including Gupta (1994), Platt and Weber (1980) and Tay (1979) have noted the pro-drop feature in CSE. What this means is that it is possible to have clauses in CSE where the subject and/or object is unexpressed. This is done when the identities of those pro-dropped elements are recoverable from the context of the utterance. It is common to hear utterances such as:

(34) a. Every year, $\emptyset_{subj}$ must buy $\emptyset_{obj}$ for Chinese
New Year.   CSE

b. Every year, we must buy pussy-willow for Chinese New Year.

In this CSE clause, neither the subject ($\emptyset_{subj}$) nor the object ($\emptyset_{obj}$) is present, at least not overtly. What they are is recoverable from the context of the utterance. Platt and Weber once again attribute this pro-drop feature of Singapore English to substratal influence from Chinese. They observe that Hokkien, for example, is a pro-drop language (Platt and Weber, 1980: 72).

Object-preposing

In CSE, and to a lesser extent SSE, it is common to prepose the object so that the canonical SVO word order of the sentence is altered to an OSV word order. The effect is to give discourse prominence to the object:

(34)   a.   Certain medicine we don't stock in our dispensary.
       b.   We don't stock certain medicine in our dispensary.

(Platt and Weber, 1980: 73)

Platt and Weber claim that such preposing serves to focus the element being fronted. However, they do not provide evidence to substantiate this claim. In fact, if we consider the discourse function of fronting in CSE, we find that CSE, like Chinese (Li and Thompson, 1981), fronts the topic. English, on the other hand, fronts the focus.

The difference between *topic* and *focus* is important. A *topic* is generally defined in the literature as old or established information on which the sentence is based or framed (Fries, 1983; Halliday, 1985). In contrast, a *focus* is defined as new information which has been introduced in the sentence, or an element that is being contrasted with members of a similar set (Chafe, 1976; Givon, 1983).

In CSE, the evidence clearly points towards the initial object being a topic. CSE in this sense displays influence of Chinese grammar over English structure.

Lack of Conjunction

In Platt and Weber (1980) and Gupta (1994), temporal or temporally related clauses, and conditional clauses in CSE are said to be conjoined without the use of an overt conjunction. E.g.:

(35)   a.   She never say hello. Walk in, sit down, talk to
            my sister. Always do like that.   CSE

       b.   She never says hello. She walks in, sits down,
            and then talks to my sister. She always does that. StdE

(36)   a.   You turn 21 can have big party.   CSE
       b.   When you turn 21, you can have a big party.   StdE

(37)   a.   You make like that can work or not?   CSE
       b.   If you make it like that, can it work?   StdE

Questions

Wh- Interrogative Constructions

In *wh-* interrogatives in CSE, it is commonly claimed that the interrogative pronoun (or the *wh-* pronoun) can remain *in situ* (Chow, 1995; Gupta, 1994; Tay, 1979), which makes it seem that substratal influence is at work. Chinese requires that the constituent questioned, i.e. the *wh-* element or word, remain *in situ*:

(38) a. ta   na   le   shen-me?   [Mandarin]
          he/she take LE   what?
          What did she take?

      b. *shen-me ta   na   le?   [Mandarin]
           what   he/she take   LE?

Moving the *wh-* element, *shen-me* 'what' in (38) results in an unacceptable utterance. English, on the other hand, requires that the *wh-* element be moved to the front of the sentence. Not fronting a *wh-* element is only possible if the question is not a 'real' one, but a rhetorical one, where the purpose is not to elicit information, but to express disbelief or surprise.

(39) a. What did she take?
      b. She took what?

CSE, therefore, combines features of both English and Chinese in allowing both types of structures. However, note that when the *wh-* element is an adverbial indicating reason, manner or place, i.e. questioned by *why, how* and *where* respectively, there is a strong tendency in CSE to front the *wh-* element.

The other property of interrogative structure that has been documented in past research on Singapore English is the variant inversion of subjects and auxiliaries. CSE has limited use of auxiliaries. Aspectual auxiliaries, *have* and *be*, and the passive auxiliary, *be*, as we have mentioned, are not commonly used in CSE. However, CSE does retain the use of certain modals, e.g. *can, must, should* and *would*.

Subject-auxiliary inversion is obligatory in Standard English, but not in CSE. It is accompanied by *wh*-fronting (40a). Where the *wh-* element appears *in situ* (40b), there is no subject-auxiliary inversion. In sentences where there is no auxiliary, CSE does not employ the use of a dummy operator *do*, as is done in Standard English to stand in place of the auxiliary.

---

* Indicates unacceptable forms.

(40) a. What can you buy at Tiong Bahru market ah?   CSE
      b. You can buy what at Tiong Bahru market ah?   CSE

Or Not

Yes/no questions in CSE often have the following structure:

(41) a. You can eat pork or not?   CSE
      b. Can you eat pork?   StdE

Instead of the subject-auxiliary inversion that we use in Standard English to mark a yes/no question, CSE employs a form of tag: *or not*. A commonly heard idiomatic question is:

(42) a. Can or not?   CSE
          Is this possible? / Are we allowed to do this?   StdE

which functions as a question that elicits basically the addressee's approval or opinion on the feasibility of what is being asked. The set answer to this, if positive, is *Can*, and if negative, is *Cannot*.

Tag Questions

In Standard English, the structure of tag questions varies according to the subject and the auxiliaries present in the clause to which they are attached, e.g.:

(43) a. She is teaching you how to swim, isn't she?
      b. She isn't teaching you how to swim, is she?

(44) a. They gave him a medal, didn't they?
      b. They didn't give him a medal, did they?

In CSE, the tag does not vary, and always takes the form *is it* or *isn't it*.

(45) a. She teach you how to swim, is it?
      b. She never teach you how to swim, is it?

(46) a. They give him a medal, is it?
      b. They never give him a medal, is it?

Is it is used where there is no expectation as to what the answer is. Notice that unlike Standard English, *is it* can be used even when the clause to which it is tagged is negated (with the use of *never* in CSE). *Isn't it* is used in those instances where the speaker assumes that the hearer is likely to disagree with him or her, or has indicated some unhappiness or disagreement about the expressed proposition:

(47)   a.   They give him a medal, isn't it?

(46a) and (47a) differ in one respect. While the tag in (46a) simply questions the proposition of whether a medal was given to him, the tag in (47a) indicates that the speaker believes that she is correct in assuming that the proposition is true, and anticipates the possible disagreement that the addressee might have with this. (47a) can therefore be roughly translated into:

(47)   b.   Am I not correct in thinking that they gave him a medal?

❧ *Conclusion*

In this chapter we examined issues concerning the grammar of English. We saw how it is important to distinguish between grammaticality and notions of what is socially or pedagogically correct. In judging whether Singapore English is grammatical or not, we also recognized the difference between Colloquial Singapore English and Standard Singapore English, whose features differ considerably. In examining the literature on Singapore English, we note that there are two different approaches to it, which emphasize different aspects of the language. Finally, in looking at the actual features of Singapore English, we note a preponderance of comparisons between Singapore English and Standard British English, as well as between Singapore English and the background languages such as Chinese and Malay, and discussed briefly why such approaches, although helpful in showing how Singapore English is a different language from British English, can be misleading in that they may not show us the full picture.

Chapter 6

The Sounds of Singapore English

Bao Zhiming

✺ *Introduction*

In this chapter we investigate the sound pattern of Colloquial Singapore English, or CSE. A methodological issue facing the student of New Englishes is the proper treatment of the relationship between New Englishes on the one hand, and British English on the other. There are two approaches to this issue. We can treat the phonology of a New English as an autonomous system to be studied in its own right, or we can approach it from the perspective of the phonology of Standard British English, which is commonly called Received Pronunciation (RP). To be sure, the two approaches serve different purposes, and neither is superior to the other. The first approach considers New Englishes on a par with 'mature' languages, paying scant attention to their historical connection to British English. This approach may lead us to discover intricate patterns of sound which are found in New Englishes, but not in RP. Most students of CSE have adopted the second approach, using RP as a frame of reference. Implicitly or explicitly, it treats the sound system of CSE as dependent upon that of Standard English. The drawback of this approach, as Mohanan (1992) points out, is that innovative and important sound patterns which do not exist in English may be left unnoticed or dismissed as uninteresting. Despite its potential problems, using Standard English as a frame of reference may prove to be a fruitful method in the study of New Englishes. By emphasizing the historical relationship between British English and New Englishes, it gives us a convenient starting-point to study the changes that have taken place in each New English.

In our investigation we will use RP as our frame of reference, and our focus will be on those aspects of CSE phonology which are not featured in RP. The use of RP as our frame of reference is methodologically expedient; we do not imply that the phonology of CSE is parasitic on the phonology of RP. On the contrary, many phonological processes which we will see are unique to CSE. The sound system of CSE is just as systematic as any other varieties of English. Expectedly, due to the historical connection between RP and CSE, the RP sound system has a decisive influence on the sound system of CSE, which we will see in due course. Although we may treat the

CSE sound system as independent and autonomous, we still need to appeal to RP in its analysis.

This chapter presumes some familiarity with articulatory phonetics and phonological analysis. There are many textbooks on phonetics and phonology; readers who feel unprepared to read beyond this point should consult the phonetics and phonology chapters of introductory linguistics textbooks, such as Fromkin and Rodman (1993) and Finegan (1994). For purely phonetics and phonology subjects, interested readers can consult Ladefoged (1993) and Roach (1991), among others.

Phonemic Inventory of Colloquial Singapore English

CSE has been studied quite extensively. The data discussed in this chapter are drawn from various sources, among them Tay (1979; 1982), Tongue (1979), Platt and Weber (1980), Tay and Gupta (1981), Brown (1988) and Hung (1996). The descriptions and analyses these authors have produced are not exactly the same. There are several reasons for this state of affairs. Firstly, the researchers do not adopt the same theoretical framework or the same research methodology. Secondly, they might have used different varieties of CSE as models of description and analysis. Thirdly, they use different phonetic symbols to transcribe the speech under analysis, which makes it difficult to compare their results. In order to provide a balanced picture of the phonology of CSE, to the extent possible, our description takes into account the research results of various scholars, as well as our own observations. To keep comparability with RP, we use the symbols from the International Phonetic Alphabet (IPA) to transcribe CSE. Although the IPA symbol set is widely used, it is by no means adopted by all linguists. In cases where different symbols are used for the same sound by the authors cited above, some modification is unavoidable; but the phonetic substance is essentially the same. Care will be taken in such modification, since the same symbol may be used for different segments, and the same segment may be transcribed with different phonetic symbols.

A brief note on citation. The data are cited from the sources mentioned above. In areas where the authors agree, we will not mention the specific sources. In areas where the authors disagree, the disagreement will be discussed and specific references will be given.

Consonants

At the phonemic level, CSE has the same set of consonants as RP. The consonant inventory is shown in Table 1.

	Labial	Interdental	Alveolar	Post-alveolar	Palatal	Velar	Glottal
Plosive	p b		t d			k g	
Affricate				tʃ dʒ			
Fricative	f v	(θ ð)	s z	ʃ ʒ			h
Nasal	m		n			ŋ	
Liquid			l r				
Glide					j	w	

Table 1. Consonants of CSE

Although the consonant inventory of CSE is not different from that of RP, the phonetic realization of these phonemes differs, sometimes considerably. The main difference is found in the articulation of plosives and affricates, particularly the voiceless ones /p, t, k, tʃ/, and /θ, ð/. The plosives in RP are aspirated, except when preceded by /s/: compare the plosives in these pairs of words: *pan/span, team/steam,* and *kin/skin.* In CSE, they are realized as unaspirated regardless of where they occur. As a result, the plosives in *pan/ team/kin* are realized in the same way as the plosives in *span/steam/skin.*

Unlike the voiceless plosives, the realization of the interdental fricatives /θ, ð/ in CSE depends on their environments, i.e. where they occur. Before vowels, they are realized as [t, d] respectively: *thin* [tin] and *this* [dis]. One might be tempted to say that /θ, ð/ are merged with /t, d/, so there are only twenty-two consonant phonemes in CSE, compared with the twenty-four in RP. The matter, however, is not so simple. At the end of a word, /θ, ð/ are realized as [f]: *breath* [brɛf], *breathe* [brif]. So we have the interesting alternation between *health* [hɛlf] and *healthy* [hɛltɪ]. Words which end in /t/ do not have this alternation: *guilt* [gɪlt] vs. *guilty* [gɪltɪ]. For this reason Hung (1996) concludes that /θ, ð/ are bona fide phonemes of CSE, even though they are never realized as interdental fricatives.

Vowels

The vowels in CSE show more variance from their RP counterparts than consonants. Nine simple vowels, i.e. monophthongs, are recognized by many scholars. They are shown in Table 2.

	Front	Central	Back
High	i		u
Mid	(e)	ə	(o)
	ɛ		ɔ
Low	(æ)		ɑ

Table 2. Vowels of CSE

(adapted from Tay, 1979; 1982; Brown, 1988; 1991; Hung, 1996)

Only six phonemes are consistently realized as monophthongs. The ones in parentheses may also be realized as diphthongs. In addition, CSE has five diphthongs /ai, ɔi, au, iə, uə/.

The vowels are exemplified below:

/i/	beat, bit	/ə/	bird, about	/u/	fool, full
/ɛ/	bet, bat			/ɔ/	caught, cot
				/ɑ/	lark, luck
/e/	day	/o/	toe		
/æ/	hair	/ai/	tie		
/ɔi/	toy	/au/	cow		
/iə/	beer	/uə/	poor		

The three vowels which appear in parentheses in Table 2 correspond to diphthongs in RP: /e/ to /eɪ/, /o/ to /ou /, and /æ/ to /ɛə/. These vowels may be realized as diphthongs as well in CSE, although the diphthong effect is not as strong as it is in RP. If we remove them from the vowel inventory, we have an inventory of six vowels:

	Front	Central	Back
High	i		u
Mid	ɛ	ə	ɔ
Low			ɑ

This vowel inventory is similar to the vowel inventory of Malay (Othman, 1990), which is one of the local languages spoken in Singapore. One might be tempted to speculate that the CSE vowel system exhibits strong substrate influence from Malay. Unfortunately, this is not the only possible explanation. In fact, most new varieties of English have a much reduced vowel inventory, similar to the one in CSE (Hall, 1966; Arends *et al.*, 1995). In other words, the substratum of New Englishes cannot be the sole cause of the reduced number of vowel contrasts. On the role of the substratum in the genesis of New Englishes, see discussions in Chapters 2 and 5.

Compared with RP, CSE has fewer vowel phonemes. These vowels have their characteristic features in terms of vowel quality and quantity. Some of the more salient features of CSE vowels are described below.

Vowel Length

One noticeable feature of CSE vowels is the lack of length contrast. RP has five long vowels, /iː, uː, ɔː, ɑː, ɜː/. For these vowels, length is a major phonetic feature which differentiates the vowels from their short counterparts, /ɪ, ʊ, ɒ, ʌ, ə/. In CSE, length is not distinctive, so the pairs /iː, ɪ/, /uː, ʊ/, /ɔː, ɒ/ and /ɑː,ʌ/ are merged into four vowels /i, u, ɔ, ɑ/. The RP minimal pairs *beat/ bit, pool/pull, caught/cot* and *staff/stuff* are no longer minimal pairs in CSE. (Minimal pairs are pairs of words which differ by one sound only.) In phonetic realization, the vowels /i, u, ɔ, ɑ/ may be as long as the long vowels in RP; but phonemically, they no longer contrast with short vowels. The RP mid, central vowels /ɜː, ə/ differ in length, but not in quality. Since the length distinction is lost in CSE, the two vowels merge into a single one /ə/. On vowel length, Brown (1991) writes:

> Most vowels are pronounced relatively short, except in open
> syllables (with no final consonant), and any length difference is at
> best produced sporadically.

The sporadic nature of vowel length is a clear indication that it is no longer distinctive in CSE, and people are not sensitive to the difference in vowel length as a clue to differentiating words, for example, *beat* from *bit*, *staff* from *stuff*, and so on.

The phonemic status of long vowels is by no means a settled issue. Hung (1996) is explicit in claiming that vowel length is no longer a distinctive feature among CSE vowels. His spectrographic analysis of one subject's speech shows no difference in either duration or formant frequencies, which in part determine the qualities of vowels. Although the data are collected from only one subject, the acoustic evidence furnishes support for this position.

Other researchers are less certain. Tay (1982) writes:

> At the phonemic level, length is one of the features used to
> distinguish the following pairs of vowels: /iː/ and /ɪ/, /ʌ/ and /ɑː/,
> /ɒ/ and /ɔː/, /ʊ/ and /uː/. In [CSE], length distinctions are consistently
> maintained at the phonemic level. At the allophonic level, however,
> length distinctions are not maintained in [CSE].

Tay's 'allophonic level' refers to the way a phoneme is realized. In other words, length is maintained phonemically, but not phonetically. Phonemically long vowels are realized in the same way as phonemically short vowels. Tay (1982) gives no evidence or argument to support this bi-level analysis of vowel length in CSE.

If length is never phonetically realized, what is the justification for postulating it as a distinctive feature at the phonemic level? While no reasonable justification can be found within CSE, we can appeal to RP. Since RP is the input to CSE, RP distinctive features must be available at the phonemic level. The difference between RP and CSE therefore is just a matter of phonetic realization. If so, the vowel chart in Table 2 needs to be expanded by including all RP long vowels. At the phonemic level, the vowel inventory is practically the same as RP; the difference emerges through phonetic realization of these phonemes.

In the same cautious tone, Brown (1988) correlates the pronunciation of vowels to the lectal divisions of the CSE continuum. Recall that according to some scholars, CSE is a speech continuum which consists of basilectal (low), mesolectal (medial) and acrolectal (high) varieties. Length distinction in acrolectal CSE is definitely maintained not only at the phonemic level, but in phonetic realization as well. Brown dismisses the basilectal speech patterns as too inconsistent for the purpose of systematic analysis. The focus, therefore, is on the mesolects. But there, considerable variation can be found as well. Brown (1988: 132-3) writes:

> However, considerable variation exists in mesolectal EMS [English in Malaysia and Singapore] speech, dependent on a variety of sociolinguistic factors, notably education and age. For example, there are EMS speakers who consistently distinguish RP's /iː, ɪ/. Others keep these vowels separate most of the time, but there is some overlap, while still others make no distinction, completely conflating the two RP vowels.

So, it is likely that the internal variability in the phonology of CSE is the reason behind the different views on vowel length. Until CSE reaches a stage where a generally accepted norm of pronunciation has emerged, uncertainty and indeterminacy will stay with us in our analysis of the phonology of CSE in general, and vowel length in particular.

Vowel Quality

In RP both front and back vowels can be characterized in terms of three phonetic features: high, mid and back. The difference between /iː, uː, ɔː/ and /ɪ, ʊ, ɒ/ lies not only in length, but in the position of the tongue as well. For the long vowels, the position of the tongue is higher than that for the short vowels. In addition, CSE does not have the front, low vowel /æ/, which is merged into /ɛ/: *bet* and *bat* are homophonous. The RP mid, central vowel /ʌ/ is merged into the low, back vowel /ɑ/, losing the length distinction at the same time.

Another significant vowel feature in RP is tenseness. In RP, /iː, uː, e, o/ are tense; they are pronounced with high muscular tension in the tongue. Tense vowels are typically lengthened, as shown in the first two vowels, or diphthongized. In RP, the two tense vowels /e, o/ are realized as diphthongs [eɪ, əʊ] (alternatively, [ei, ou]). In fact, many phoneticians treat them as simple, tense vowels, in contrast to the lax vowels /ɛ, ɔ/. In CSE, the two vowels /e, o/ are not realized as diphthongs. According to Tay and Gupta (1981), the tense and lax vowels tend to be 'equally tense'. In other words, tenseness is no longer a contrastive feature among vowels of CSE.

Diphthongs

By and large the five diphthongs in CSE, /ai, ɔi, au, iə, uə/, are quite similar to their RP counterparts /aɪ, ɔɪ, aʊ, ɪə, ʊə/. The transcriptional difference is not significant; it reflects the disappearance of /ɪ, ʊ/ in CSE. Three RP diphthongs, namely, /eɪ, əʊ , ɛə/, are in fact monophthongs, represented as long vowels /e:, o:, æ:/ in Tay (1982). Since length is not contrastive, Hung (1996) drops the length marker ':', and represents these phonemes as /e, o, æ/. The diphthongs /iə, uə/ contain the vowels /ɪ, ʊ/ in RP, but in CSE, they are realized as [jə] and [wə], respectively. In other words, the first vowels /ɪ, ʊ/ are realized as glides [j, w]. Since phonetically the vowels and their corresponding glides sound quite alike, the difference is a matter of phonetic realization which has no phonemic significance. So, phonemically we still recognize two diphthong phonemes /iə, uə/ for CSE.

For ease of reference, the vowels of the two varieties of English are presented in Table 3.

RP	CSE	Examples	RP	CSE	Examples
i:	i	beat	ʌ	ɑ	stuff
ɪ		bit	ɑ:		staff
ɛ	ɛ	bet	u:	u	boot
æ		bat	ʊ		book
ɜ:	ə	bird	ɔ:	ɔ	caught
ə		about	ɒ		cot
ei	e	bay	au	au	how
əʊ	o	boat	ɔi	ɔi	boy
ɛə	æ	bare	iə	iə	here
ai	ai	buy	uə	uə	poor

Table 3. Vowels of RP and CSE

❧ *Syllable Structure of CSE*

CSE syllable structure is remarkably close to that of RP. Given the fact that two main substrate languages, namely Malay and Chinese, have simple syllable structures, one might expect drastic simplification in the structure of CSE syllables. In fact, substrate influence in this aspect of CSE phonology is quite minimal. CSE syllable structure is quite complicated, and a complete description is beyond the scope of this chapter. Here, we will describe some of the more salient features of the CSE syllable.

Syllables are typically divided into two major constituents, the *onset* and the *rime* (or rhyme). The onset is made up of consonants, if any, up to the vowel, and the rime consists of the vowel and the following consonants, if any. In the syllable *pat*/pæt/, /p/ is the onset, /æt/ is the rime; in *blast* /blast/, /bl/ is the onset, /ast/ is the rime. The rime is further divided into the *nucleus*, which is the vowel, and the *coda*, which consists of the remaining consonants, if any. In the rime /æt/, /æ/ is the nucleus, /t/ is the coda; in the rime /ast/, /a/ is the nucleus, /st/ is the coda. The structure of the syllable can be shown clearly in a tree diagram (σ = syllable, O = onset, R = rime, Co = coda):

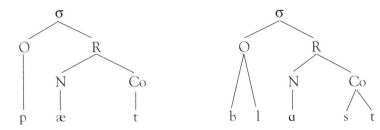

There are restrictions on the segmental composition of the onset, nucleus and coda. These restrictions are often called *phonotactic constraints*. Like their RP counterparts, onsets in CSE can have up to three consonants. In a two-consonant onset, the first consonant can be a stop or fricative, followed by /l, r, j, w/; in a three-consonant onset, the first consonant must be /s/, the second a voiceless stop, and the third /l, r, j, w/. Examples of onsets are shown in Table 4:

No onset	One-consonant	Two-consonant	Three-consonant
eight	pay	pray	spray
eye	say	tray	split
a	lay	gray	strain
in	ray	plea	scream
	bay	glean	
	man	spit	
	woman	flight	
		fright	
		sweet	

Table 4. Common Syllable Onsets in CSE

As can be seen from the table, nuclei are typically vowels, and onsets and codas are consonants, including liquids and glides.

Unlike onsets, most codas in RP and CSE contain one or two consonants: [t] in *lit* and [st] in *list*. In fact, word-internally, the vast majority of the syllables have no coda or one-consonant codas (*con-so-nant*). At the end of a word, a coda could contain two or more consonants, particularly when morphemes such as *-th* and *-s* are added. The syllable *six* [sɪks] has a two-consonant coda [ks]. When we attach *-th*, we get *sixth* [sɪksθ]; the coda now has three consonants [ksθ]. When *-s* is attached, we get *sixths* [sɪksθs], with a four-consonant coda [ksθs]. Complicated codas are typically the result of morpheme concatenations of this type, and occur at the end of a word.

Of the three constituents of the syllable in CSE and, for that matter, in all languages that we know today, only the nucleus is obligatory; the onset and coda are both optional. Using C for consonants and V for vowels (simple and diphthong), we summarize the major syllable types in Table 5:

Type	Example	Type	Example	Type	Example
V	a, eye	VC	at, eat	VCC	and, east
CV	key, too	CVC	sit, seat	CVCC	sand, yeast
CCV	play, free	CCVC	spit, sweat	CCVCC	stand, flint
CCCV	spray, stray	CCCVC	split, squid	CCCVCC	script, sprint

Table 5. Major Syllable Types of CSE

These syllable types are not exhaustive, but represent most syllables found in both RP and CSE.

We have seen that CSE does not differ much from RP in syllable structure; both varieties have the same range of consonant clusters in onset or coda positions. There are, however, a few areas where the two varieties diverge. We will investigate those areas in the next section.

Some Phonological Processes of Singapore English

When phonemes are combined into words, they might undergo change. Such change is called *phonological change*, or *phonological process*. Languages vary in the type or range of phonological change that takes place.

Syllabic Lateral and Nasals

In English, as in most languages, the nucleus of a syllable is typically a vowel. Sometimes, the lateral /l/ and the nasals /m, n, ŋ/ can occupy the nuclear position as well. When they do, they are called *syllabic*. In RP, /l, m, n, ŋ/ can be syllabic under two conditions. First, the syllable is not stressed; second, it must have a consonant in the onset. In polysyllabic words, such syllables are immediately preceded by a stressed syllable. These conditions are met in words such as *button* ['bʌtn], *mutton* ['mʌtn], *whistle* ['wɪsl], *bottle* ['bɒtl] and the monosyllabic *some* [sm]. In CSE, however, the lateral and nasals cannot be syllabic. Instead, the schwa /ə/ is inserted: *button* ['bʌtən], *mutton* ['mʌtən], *whistle* ['wɪsəl], *bottle* ['bɒtəl] and *some* [səm]. Tay and Gupta (1981) did a survey among forty-five undergraduate students, and found none of them had the syllabic lateral and nasals in their speech, while the consonant-lateral or consonant-nasal sequences were broken up by the insertion of the schwa /ə/. Although the study was done more than fifteen years ago, this feature can still be observed among speakers of CSE.

In RP, nasals cannot be syllabic in other environments. In CSE, however, syllabic nasals may occur in names which are borrowed from local languages. A common surname in Singapore is *Ng*, which is syllabic /ŋ/. See the later section on /ŋ/ and /n/ for further discussion of the nasals in CSE.

Devoicing

Voiced stops become voiceless, or *devoiced*, when they occur at the end of a word. This is illustrated in the following examples:

	RP	CSE
tab	[tæb]	[tɛp]
head	[hɛd]	[hɛt]
leg	[lɛg]	[lɛk]
judge	[dʒʌdʒ]	[dʒʌtʃ]
alive	[ə'laɪv]	[ə'laɪf]
news	[nju:z]	[njus]
beige	[beɪʒ]	[beɪtʃ] or [beɪʃ]

This, however, does not mean that voicing is no longer distinctive in CSE. On the contrary, in non-word-final position the voicing distinction is maintained: *to* [tu] vs. *do* [du], *writer* ['raitə] vs. *rider* ['raidə]. In RP, /t/ and /d/ differ not only in voicing, but in aspiration as well: the former is aspirated and voiceless; the latter is unaspirated and voiced. In CSE, they differ in voicing only; so the contrast is not as prominent as it is in RP.

As a consequence of devoicing, the plural marker *-s* and the possessive marker *-'s* are realized as voiceless [-s] in places where they are realized as voiced [-z] in RP. Examples follow:

	RP	CSE	
backs	[bæks]	[bɛks]	
bags	[bægz]	[bɛks]	(from [bɛgs])
beams	[biːmz]	[bims]	

The voiced velar plosive /g/ is devoiced as well, so *bags* sounds like *backs*.

Consonant Deletion

In CSE, a word-final plosive is deleted if it follows another consonant. This is illustrated by the following examples:

	RP	CSE
limp	[lɪmp]	[lim]
list	[lɪst]	[lis]
cent	[sɛnt]	[sɛn]
stand	[stænd]	[stɛn]
stink	[stɪŋk]	[stiŋ]
mask	[mɑːsk]	[mɑs]

Interestingly, word-final fricatives or affricates are not deleted when they are preceded by another consonant:

	RP	CSE
nymph	[nɪmf]	[nimf]
laps	[læps]	[lɛps]
lunch	[lʌntʃ]	[lɑntʃ]

Obviously, deletion applies only to plosives. As a result of deletion, CSE has fewer word-final consonant clusters than RP. In other words, the coda structure is a bit simplified, at least for codas at the end of words.

When the words are suffixed with a vowel-initial suffix, such as *-ing*, the plosives are not deleted:

	CSE	
limping	[limp-iŋ]	*[lim-iŋ]
listing	[list-iŋ]	*[lis-iŋ]
standing	[stɛnd-iŋ]	*[stɛn-iŋ]
stinking	[stiŋk-iŋ]	*[sti-iŋ]

The reason for the failure of plosive deletion is obvious. A plosive is deleted only when it occurs in a word-final coda with another consonant. When a

---

* Indicates unacceptable forms.

vowel-initial suffix is attached to the word, the plosive is no longer in the coda position. We can see the difference clearly in the syllable structures of the words *limp* and *limping*.

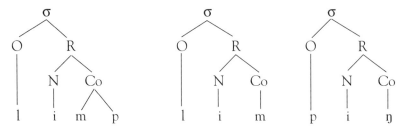

Other words in the above list have similar syllable structure. Clearly, codas in word-final position are simplified.

Plosive deletion affects the past tense marker *-ed* as well. In CSE, it is typically not pronounced when the verb ends in a consonant:

	RP	CSE
helped	[hɛlpt]	[hɛlp]
backed	[bækt]	[bɛk]
stabbed	[stæbd]	[stɛp]
bragged	[brægd]	[brɛk]
smiled	[smaɪld]	[smaɪl]
beamed	[biːmd]	[bim]

The CSE pronunciation of the verbs is straightforward, with the deletion of *-ed* [-t]. *Stabbed, bragged* need an additional step: /b, g/ become voiceless as well (see the earlier section on devoicing). The steps are shown below for clarity:

helped	/hɛlp-t/	→	[hɛlp]		
stabbed	/stɛb-d/	→	[stɛb]	→	[stɛp]

One consequence of this process is worth noting. Since *-ed* is seldom pronounced, the past tense is typically not signalled through verbal inflection in CSE. In casual conversation one often resorts to time expressions such as *yesterday, two years ago* to indicate temporal reference. The use of *-ed* is not consistent in speech and writing. A change in sound may eventually lead to change in the function of the suffix *-ed*.

Unreleased Plosives

The production of a plosive consists of three phases: the formation of obstruction in the mouth; the build-up of air pressure behind the point of obstruction; and the release of the obstruction. Let us use the voiceless bilabial stop /p/ as an example. It is articulated with the lips tightly closed, obstructing the airflow from the lungs; pressure builds up behind the lips, and when the lips come apart, the air rushes out, creating a bilabial plosive or stop. (The two terms are synonymous: 'stop' emphasizes the obstruction phase where airflow is stopped; 'plosive' emphasizes the release phase, where the trapped air rushes out.) In RP, word-final stops are typically pronounced, or released. In CSE, they are typically unreleased, accompanied by an abrupt closure of the glottis. (The glottis is the area formed by the vocal cords which controls the flow of air from the lungs.) In other words, unreleased stops often cause the preceding vowels to be glottalized. In the following example, the diacritic '˺' represents unreleased stops.

	RP	CSE
tap	[tæp]	[tɛp˺]
tab	[tæb]	[tɛp˺]
lit	[lɪt]	[lit˺]
lid	[lɪd]	[lit˺]
leak	[li:k]	[lik˺]
league	[li:g]	[lik˺]

As expected, word-final voiced stops are devoiced and unreleased. This phenomenon is clearly influenced by the phonology of substrate languages. In Malay and the Chinese dialects spoken in Singapore, word-final stops are not released, and the preceding vowels glottalized.

/ŋ/ and /n/

In CSE, the alveolar and velar nasals deserve a few words of comment. In RP, the distribution of the velar nasal is restricted: it can occur at the end of a word (*sing*), or in the middle of a word (*singing*). This is a strong phonotactic constraint in RP: not a single English word begins with the velar nasal /ŋ/. In CSE, this is certainly true: English words do not begin with the velar nasal. In words borrowed from local languages, particularly in names, the velar nasal occurs in word-initial position: *Ngee Ann* [ŋi ɑn], *Ngiam* [ŋjem], *ngo hiang* [ŋɔhjaŋ] 'a kind of spring roll'. (*Ngee Ann* is often pronounced as [ni ɑn], which conforms to the phonotactics of RP.) These examples lead us to conclude that CSE phonotactics is not point-by-point identical with that of RP, from which it is derived. Specifically, CSE lacks the RP phonotactic constraint which regulates the distribution of /ŋ/, at least among locally-derived words. Substrate influence is seen in phonemic inventory and phonetic realization. It is also at work in modifying the phonotactics of CSE.

Palatalization is a common phonological process which affects consonants, particularly alveolars and velars. In casual speech in RP, /s/ becomes [ʃ] (*miss you*), and /t/ becomes /tʃ/ (*meet you*). There is articulatory reason for this change: to pronounce /i, j/, the body of the tongue has to be raised towards the palate, which will likely influence the pronunciation of the immediately preceding alveolars and velars. Palatalization is a very common sound change among the world's languages. In CSE, /t, s/ are not palatalized, but the alveolar nasal /n/ is. The phoneme /n/ is realized as alveolar in most places: *name* [nem], *lean* [lin]; but before /j/ and /i/, it is realized as the palatal nasal [ɲ]: *nonya* [ɲoɲa], *Nee Soon* [ɲi sun]. The pronunciation of *only* /onli/ is interesting: /l/ is deleted when it is next to a nasal, and the nasal /n/ is palatalized: /onli/ → [oni] → [oɲi].

j-insertion

A few words show the insertion of the glide /j/. Three are listed below:

	RP	CSE
platinum	[ˈplætɪnəm]	[ˈplɛtɪɲjem]
villain	[ˈvɪlən]	[ˈviljen]
guidance	[ˈgaɪdəns]	[ˈgaidjens]

A close examination of the words in RP reveals three common properties. First, the immediately preceding consonant is alveolar /n, l, d/, which are palatalized to some extent in CSE. Second, the vowel in the preceding syllable is a high front vowel, /ɪ/ in RP and /i/ in CSE. Third, the syllable into which /j/ is inserted contains the schwa /ə/ in RP, but /ɛ/ in CSE. However, not all words which have the three properties exhibit *j*-insertion: *Dylan* RP [ˈdɪlən], CSE [ˈdilən]/*[ˈdiljen]; *silence* RP [ˈsaɪləns], CSE [ˈsailəns]/ *[ˈsailjens]. The phonological phenomenon of *j*-insertion in CSE is limited to only a few words.

Metathesis

Another phenomenon which is limited to a few words is *metathesis*, which means the switching of position between two segments. In metathesis, AB becomes BA. Many speakers of CSE switch the sequence *sp* into *ps*. This is shown in the following four words (Mohanan, 1992):

	RP	CSE
lisp	[lɪsp]	[lips]
crisp	[krɪsp]	[krips]
wasps	[wɑːsps]	[wɑps]
grasp	[grɑːsp]	[grɑps]

_____

* Indicates unacceptable forms.

Apparently the metathesis only affects the cluster *sp*. The clusters *-st, -sk* do not show metathesis; instead the stop is deleted from the cluster: *last* [las], *mask* [mas]; see the earlier section on devoicing.

Timing and Stress

In this section we will discuss two prosodic features of CSE, *timing* and *stress*. Prosodic features are features of sound which are found in words, phrases or sentences, rather than individual phonemes. Common prosodic features include tone, stress, intonation and timing. Like phonemes, they are part of the sound pattern of a language. The study of CSE phonology should include not only phonemic and phonetic properties, but prosodic properties as well.

Timing

Timing is the most frequently mentioned prosodic feature in the study of New Englishes, including CSE. It has been claimed that RP is a *stress-timed* language, where stressed syllables recur at regular intervals, interspersed with unstressed ones. In short words, the stress-timing effect is not obvious. In long words, however, the effect manifests itself quite clearly. Consider the following RP words:

Apalachicola   onomatopoeia
/ˈæ.pə.ˈlæ.tʃə.ˈˈkoʊ.lə/   /ˈɒ.nə.ˈmæ.tə.ˈˈpiː.ə/

Secondary stress is marked by a single "ˈ", and the main stress by a double "ˈˈ". One feature of English stress is that in words with multiple stresses, the main stress is on the last stressed syllable (Chomsky and Halle, 1968). As for secondary stress, it falls on every other syllable away from the main stress. The two words, ˈA.pa.ˈla.chi.ˈˈco.la, ˈo.no.ˈma.to.ˈˈpoei.a, are typical of the stress patterns of RP. Stress regulates the rhythm of speech at regular intervals. Stress-timed rhythm is also found in sentences. In the two sentences below, the interval between the stressed syllables *caught* and *mice/mouse* is roughly the same, despite the fact that *any* in (b) is disyllabic (adapted from Graddol *et al.*, 1996):

(a) No cat caught a mouse
(b) No cat caught any mice

By contrast, CSE is *syllable-timed*, where syllables, whether stressed or not, take up roughly the same amount of time. Incidentally, syllable-timing is not characteristic only of CSE, but of most new varieties of English. It is a feature of tone languages as well. Chinese is a syllable-timed tone language, and so are many African tone languages. Substrate influence can explain why many New Englishes are syllable-timed, since tone languages form the majority of the substrata of New Englishes.

On CSE rhythm, the view of Tay (1982) is representative:

> (CSE) is spoken mainly with a syllable-timed rhythm; this means that all syllables recur at approximately equal intervals of time, stressed or unstressed. This "machine-gun rhythm" is characteristic of all natural speech, even among highly-educated Singaporeans.

Syllable-timing does not preclude stress. Even though CSE is syllable-timed, it has an intricate stress pattern, to which we now turn.

Stress Patterns of CSE

Stress is best understood as a notion of relative prominence: stressed syllables are more prominent than unstressed syllables. However, syllable-timing obscures the difference in prominence between stressed and unstressed syllables. A casual listener may not hear the rhythm of stress in CSE. In RP, stress is typically realized in terms of pitch, loudness and length: stressed syllables are higher-pitched, louder and longer than unstressed ones. In CSE, in contrast, the main phonetic indicators are length and loudness (Tay, 1982). A complete description and analysis of the stress pattern of CSE is not possible at the present moment. By and large, the stress pattern of CSE closely resembles that of RP, with a few notable exceptions. Let us consider a few cases where the stress pattern of CSE deviates from that of RP.

Stress in Words

Consider the words below, where the underlined syllables are stressed:

	RP	CSE
Group (a)	con<u>tri</u>bute	contri<u>bute</u>
	<u>coll</u>eague	coll<u>eague</u>
	ass<u>ass</u>inate	ass<u>assi</u>nate
	<u>ex</u>ercise	exer<u>cise</u>
Group (b)	<u>comm</u>ent	comm<u>ent</u>
	<u>con</u>tent (noun)	con<u>tent</u>
Group (c)	<u>ca</u>lendar	ca<u>len</u>dar
	<u>Cl</u>ementi	Cl<u>emen</u>ti
	<u>cha</u>racter	cha<u>rac</u>ter

As a result of stress shift, the vowels may undergo change as well. For example, in RP, *contribute* is pronounced as [kə'trɪbjuːt]; in CSE, it is pronounced as ['kɒntri''bjuːt], with secondary stress on the first syllable. For the sake of clarity we ignore the distinction between primary and secondary stress, and possible differences in vowel qualities.

The examples given above substantiate the observation that unlike RP, stress in CSE tends to move towards the end of a word (Tongue, 1979; Platt and Weber, 1980; Tay, 1982). At first glance, the stress placement in CSE is random; in some words it is on the last syllable, in others it is on the penultimate, i.e. second from last, syllable. However, when we examine the RP pronunciation of these words, we see some pattern in the way stress in CSE deviates from RP. In Group (a) words, the last syllable contains a long vowel (/uː/ in *contribute*, /iː/ in *colleague*), or a diphthong (/eɪ/ in *assassinate*, /aɪ/ in *exercise*). In words like *purchase* and *bargain*, the last syllable is analysed in CSE as if it contains the diphthong /eɪ/: *purchase* RP ['pɜːtʃəs]/CSE [pə'tʃeɪs], *bargain* RP ['bɒːgən/CSE [bɒ'geɪn]. This is clearly due to the influence of spelling: *chase* and *gain* are regular words in English (Tongue, 1979). The stress pattern of these two words falls together with the words in Group (a).

In Group (b) words, the last syllable contains a simple vowel followed by two consonants (/ɛnt/ in *comment*). In Group (c) words, the penultimate syllable contains a simple vowel followed by one consonant (/ɛn/ in *calendar*, *Clementi*, *character*). If we use C for consonants, V for vowels, these syllables have the structures shown below (only the structure of the relevant syllable is shown):

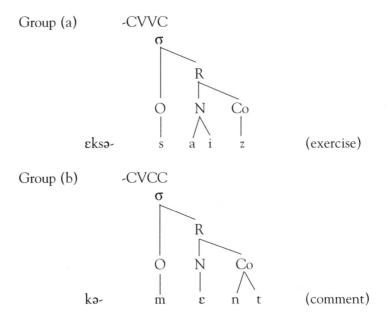

Group (a)   -CVVC

σ

R

O   N   Co

ɛksə-   s   a i   z   (exercise)

Group (b)   -CVCC

σ

R

O   N   Co

kə-   m   ɛ   n t   (comment)

Group (c)   -CVC

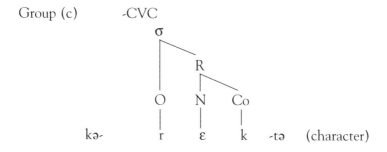

 kə-   r   ε   k   -tə   (character)

The syllables whose structures are shown above are called *heavy syllables*, in contrast to *light syllables*, which contain only one simple vowel and no coda. The exact mechanism with which stress is assigned in RP is very intricate, and requires too much phonological knowledge to appreciate. Suffice it to say that syllable structure plays a part in stress assignment. In many languages, RP included, heavy syllables are more likely to be stressed than light syllables. Given the present state of knowledge of the phonology of CSE, we are not yet in the position to formulate rules which will assign the correct stress pattern to each word based on the structure of the component syllables. We have said earlier that CSE does not contrast vowel length, so one might argue that the word *colleague* contains a long vowel in RP /kɒliːg/, but not in CSE /kəlig/. If all vowels in CSE are short phonemically, and stress is assigned on the basis of the phonemic representation of a word, we cannot use vowel length as a clue for stress assignment, and the stress pattern exhibited in the words cited above appears quite mysterious. But there is a way out of this dilemma. CSE takes its vocabulary from British English. We can use the RP pronunciation as the basis for assigning stress in CSE. In other words, we may adopt Tay's (1982) position that vowel length is distinctive phonemically in CSE, but nondistinctive phonetically. The phonemic representation of the words cited above is the same in both RP and CSE.

We can formulate three rules which assign stress to words in CSE:

Rule (i)   Heavy syllables are stressed.
Rule (ii)   Stress occurs on alternative syllables.
Rule (iii) If a word has more than one stressed syllable, the last stressed syllable carries the main stress.

To see the effect of the three observations clearly, consider the derivations of the CSE stress pattern in the words *assassinate* and *comment*:

Phonemic representation	ə.sæ.sə.neɪt	kɒ.mɛnt
Rule (i)	ə.sæ.sə.<u>neɪt</u>	kɒ.<u>mɛnt</u>

| Rule (ii) | ə.s<u>æ</u>.sə.<u><u>neɪt</u></u> | — |
| Rule (iii) | ə.s<u>æ</u>.sə.<u><u>neɪt</u></u> | — |

The dots break up the words into syllables. Rule (iii) says that the main stress is the last stressed syllable, indicated here by double-underlining. So, in *assassinate*, *-nate* has the primary stress, *-sa-* has the secondary stress. Since *comment* has two syllables only, *kɒ-* cannot be stressed. The vowel quality changes as a result of change in stress. In CSE, *comment* is pronounced as [kə'ment].

If a word contains no heavy syllable, stress in CSE tends to shift one syllable towards the end of the word: RP *<u>ve</u>hicle*, CSE *ve<u>hi</u>cle*; RP *<u>ca</u>tegory*, CSE *ca<u>te</u>gory*. We can see the shift clearly if we consider the syllable structure of the two words:

	vehicle	category
RP	[<u>vi</u>:.ɪ.kəl]	[<u>kæ</u>.tə.gə.rɪ]
CSE	[vi.<u>i</u>.kəl]	[kə.<u>tɛ</u>.gə.ri]

Rule (ii) says stress falls on alternate syllables. This is further exemplified by the following words:

	RP	CSE
monopoly	[mə<u>nɒ</u>pəlɪ]	[<u>mɔ</u>nɔpɔli]
monotonous	[mə<u>nɒ</u>tənəs]	[<u>mɔ</u>nɔt<u>ɔ</u>nəs]

These words may be more characteristic of basilectal speakers; nevertheless, this highlights the rhythm of stress captured in Rule (ii).

Stress and Parts of Speech

In RP, stress determines the parts of speech of many words. In CSE, it is hardly used for this purpose. Where an RP word has variable stress patterns, this retains only one of them in CSE. A few examples follow:

RP		CSE
noun	*verb*	*noun & verb*
<u>in</u>crease	in<u>crease</u>	in<u>crease</u>
<u>de</u>crease	de<u>crease</u>	de<u>crease</u>
<u>su</u>spect	su<u>spect</u>	su<u>spect</u>
<u>re</u>cord	re<u>cord</u>	re<u>cord</u>

In RP, stress is often accompanied by changes in the vowel quality, which can be observed in *suspect* and *record*. The stress patterns of these words in

CSE conform to the general rules discussed in the earlier section on stress in words, which assign stress to the last syllable, which is heavy in these words.

-logy and -ic

In RP, most suffixes are stressed as part of the word to which they are attached. While this is generally true in CSE, a few suffixes are stressed as if they are separate words. The typical example of this type is *-logy*, which has the stress pattern /-ˈlɔdʒi/, regardless of the word to which it is attached:

RP	CSE
tech.<u>no</u>.lo.gy	<u>tech</u>.no.<u>lo</u>.gy
tech.no.<u>lo</u>.gi.cal	<u>tech</u>.no.<u>lo</u>.gi.cal
bi.<u>o</u>.lo.gy	<u>bi</u>.o.<u>lo</u>.gy
bi.o.<u>lo</u>.gi.cal	<u>bi</u>.o.<u>lo</u>.gi.cal

In RP, stress is assigned to the syllable before *-logy*, whereas stress falls on the first syllable of the suffix in CSE. Again, you can observe the vowels change their qualities as stress shifts to a different syllable. In CSE, the stress pattern remains unchanged, and there is no corresponding change in vowel quality either. Note that the stress pattern of *-logy* words is consistent with the stress rules discussed earlier, particularly Rule (ii), which places stress on alternate syllables away from the syllable carrying the main stress, i.e. *-lo-*. Since *-logy* carries the main stress on *-lo-*, *tech-* is stressed, and *bi-* is stressed as well. This pattern is even extended to words derived from borrowings:

> <u>chee</u>.mo.<u>lo</u>.gy   (Chinese *cheem* 'deep' + *-ology*) = 'profound'

The suffix *-ic* is worth noting too. In RP, it attracts stress to the syllable immediately before it, but not in CSE:

RP	CSE
e.<u>co</u>.no.my	e.<u>co</u>.no.my
e.co.<u>no</u>.mic	e.<u>co</u>.no.mic
a.<u>ca</u>.de.my	a.<u>ca</u>.de.my
a.ca.<u>de</u>.mic	a.<u>ca</u>.de.mic

Stress does not shift at all in CSE, as evidenced by the words *economic*, *academic*.

Stress in Compounds

In English, a productive word formation rule is *compounding*: it combines two words to form a new word. Common compounds include *leather shoe, English Department, White House.* In RP, stress is on the first word of a compound: *leather shoe, English Department, White House.* But in CSE, stress falls on the second word: *leather shoe, English Department, White House.* More examples follow:

RP	CSE
stock broker	stock broker
sewing machine	sewing machine
table tennis	table tennis
Spring Festival	Spring Festival
bottle neck	bottle neck
hangover	hangover

The fact that stress falls on the second word of a compound reflects the general tendency of stress in CSE: the main stress typically falls towards the end of a word.

In RP, phrases do not have the same stress pattern as compounds. In phrases of two words, stress falls on the second word: *good book, slow walk.* In fact, stress is the only means of distinguishing a phrase from a compound made up of the same words. A few examples follow:

Phrase	Compound
white house	White House
black board	blackboard
English teacher	English teacher

Spelling is not a reliable way of distinguishing a phrase from a compound. Some compounds are spelled as one word, such as *hangover, downturn, blackboard.* Others are spelled as two, such as *White House, leather shoe.*

The meaning of a compound often differs from that of a phrase, even though they are composed of the same words. So, *an English teacher* is a teacher who comes from England, but *an English teacher* teaches English, and may come from any place, not necessarily England. Similarly, *a good question* is difficult to answer, but *a good question* is most likely a relevant one. In compounds, words often lose their usual meanings to some extent; in phrases, they retain their meanings. For example, *a blackboard* need not be black; in fact most blackboards nowadays are green. A *black board* must be black. For the same reason, *a green blackboard* sounds perfectly all right, but *a green black board* is odd. Since CSE does not rely on stress to distinguish a phrase from a compound, *a blackboard* could be interpreted either as a compound or a phrase. Only context of use provides clues to disambiguate such ambiguous expressions.

🔊 *Concluding Remarks*

In this chapter we surveyed the sounds of CSE. We found that CSE differs from RP in phonemic contrast and phonetic realization, and that there are phonological processes which are unique to CSE. Some of the phonological features of CSE, particularly in areas of phonetic realization, are due to substrate influence. However, it is obvious that substrate influence cannot explain all of them. In our description, we used RP as our frame of reference. This does not mean that the phonology of CSE is parasitic on the phonology of RP. On the contrary, we have seen that the phonology of CSE is a system in its own right, with its own set of phonemes, its own set of phonotactics, and its own set of phonological processes. Indeed, some of the processes will make sense only if we look at CSE as an autonomous language which is not parasitic on the phonology of Standard English.

The distinction between phonemic representation and phonetic representation is a useful one. It allows us to analyse the phonology of Singapore English at two different levels, and to make interesting comparisons with Standard English. But it creates analytical problems. Through our analysis, we found that differences in phonetic realization are unmistakable and easy to identify. Whether they are results of corresponding differences in phonemic representation is an entirely different question, one which does not allow an easy answer. Vowel length is a case in point. It is commonly observed that length distinction disappears in CSE: the long vowels are realized with the same length as the short vowels. But what is true of phonetic realization need not be true of phonemic representation. Here opinions diverge. Some scholars argue that since it is never phonetically distinctive, vowel length is not distinctive at the phonemic level. For other researchers, vowel length is phonemically distinctive, even though it is not distinctive phonetically. In our analysis of stress placement in CSE, we see that vowel length has an important role to play. But is vowel length a result of stress, or does it allow stress to be assigned in the first place? The question is not easy to answer within the domain of CSE. But if we look at the RP phonology, where vowel length is distinctive phonemically as well as phonetically, and use it as the input to the phonology of CSE, the stress pattern of CSE starts to make sense — RP long vowels are stressed in CSE. So it appears that phonemically, vowel length is distinctive in CSE. Since our analysis of the stress pattern of CSE is at a preliminary stage, the issue has yet to be resolved.

At the present moment, CSE is in a state of flux, as it has always been. Due to modern communication technology, it is constantly exposed to American English, Australian English and British English, and to the local languages such as Chinese, Malay and Tamil. Since the educational system emphasizes Standard English, with standards often defined in exonormative terms, the speech pattern of Standard English will filter into the speech pattern of Singapore English, whether consciously or not. The fact that the phonological features which we have examined are found only in the speech of some speakers could be the result of the complex linguistic and sociolinguistic factors at work in Singapore and Singapore English.

Chapter 7

The Lexicon of Singapore English

Lionel Wee

 Introduction

In previous chapters, we made a distinction between Colloquial Singapore English (CSE) and Standard Singapore English (SSE). In this chapter, we will be looking at words which are used in CSE as well as SSE.

The purpose of this chapter is to explore some of the issues that surround the lexicon of Singapore English. In Singapore English, a significant part of the lexicon consists of words that are borrowed from non-English languages. For example, in addition to containing recognizably English words like *send*, *fellow* and *car*, Singapore English also contains words like *ulu* (borrowed from Malay) and *kiasu* (borrowed from Chinese). The presence of these non-English words often raises concerns such as the following:

(i) Can these words be legitimately considered a part of English in the first place?

(ii) Does the presence of these words affect the intelligibility of Singapore English?

Even recognizably English words such as *send* or *fellow* are sometimes seen as problematic because of the observation that some of these words may have undergone a change in meaning so that they are used differently in Singapore English than in some other variety of English such as Standard British English. For example, in Singapore English, the word *fellow* can be used to describe a woman as well as a man (we will discuss how in Singapore English *send* differs from its Standard British English use later). The different use of *fellow* in Singapore English raises questions like the one below:

(iii) Is this an acceptable variation in the use of *fellow* or should the Standard British English use be considered the proper use, in which case the Singapore English variation would be considered an error?

These are important and complex questions, and it would be foolish to pretend that easy answers are available. In dealing with these questions, we will need to consider a variety of perspectives. For example, a teacher or educationist would be interested in ensuring that a Singaporean student learning English actually acquires a variety of English that is maximally intelligible to English speakers worldwide. To the extent that the Singapore English lexicon contains differences and variations that affect the ability of the learner to communicate effectively in English, the teacher or educationist might then have an interest in eliminating these differences and variations. On the other hand, there is also the question of national identity and solidarity to consider, in which case, it becomes important that Singaporeans speak a distinctively Singaporean variety of English rather than attempt to emulate a variety that reflects an identity associated with some other nationality. Finding a judicious balance between these differing concerns is no easy task.

In this chapter, we will also look at the meanings of Singapore English particles. These particles, such as *me*, *ma* and *what*, have often been held up as examples of linguistic innovations that are distinctively Singaporean. For our purposes, these particles are interesting because their meanings are much more related to the discourse context in which they are used, and they tend to express meanings that are more attitudinal in nature, indicating notions such as the speaker's attitude or intention. The chapter closes with a discussion of an attempt to 'control the vocabulary' of Singapore English by imposing a fairly detailed classification of its lexicon.

Semantic Analysis of New Englishes

Since Singapore English is a variety of New English, to better appreciate some of the issues mentioned above, it is useful to understand how the semantic analysis of New Englishes is generally conducted. The semantic analysis of words in New Englishes is not particularly different from the kind of semantic analysis conducted in any other language. The main difference, if it can be called one, is that there is often a very strong comparative orientation in the case of New Englishes. In other words, the meaning of a word in a variety of New English is usually compared with its meaning in some other, typically older and more established, variety of English. Of course, it is not necessary that this comparative orientation be present. It is entirely possible to merely focus on the meanings of various words in a particular variety of New English without making reference to any other variety.

But precisely because New Englishes are 'new', relatively speaking, we are in a position to observe a highly dynamic situation where a series of linguistic innovations and changes are being made as these Englishes struggle to define their space in their respective societies. The lexicon of a variety of New English does not necessarily consist only of English words. It also includes words that are borrowed from other languages indigenous to the area where the New English variety is developing. This means that most of the words in New Englishes are borrowed from two main sources: other varieties of English such as British English or American English, and background languages. We will refer to these as the *source languages*.

In Chapter Two, you read that in the case of pidgins, the words tend to be borrowed from the superstrate language, which is therefore often called the lexifier language. In our discussion of the lexicon of Singapore English, we will want to look at words that come from both the superstrate as well as the substrate languages. Therefore, we will use the term *source language* instead of *lexifier language* to refer to the language from which a particular word is borrowed. This is because, as noted, *lexifier language* tends to be equated with the superstrate language. We want to have a term which is more neutral as to whether a word is borrowed from the superstrate or substrate.

When a variety of New English comes about, it usually develops in a situation where it is influenced by other (already existing and developed) varieties of English, as well as indigenous or background languages. For example, in Singapore, the development of Singapore English is influenced by contact with British and American varieties of English, as well as background languages such as Malay, Chinese and Tamil.

The meanings of words in the developing variety of New English — in this case, Singapore English — then become interesting precisely because we want to compare how a word is used in the source language with how it is being used in Singapore English. Our interest lies in seeing whether the meaning has or has not changed when the word is borrowed from the source language into Singapore English. This is what makes the comparison issue particularly important when studying word meanings in Singapore English. The diagram below schematically characterizes the relationship between the words in Singapore English and the words in the source languages.

Source languages

Words from
background language(s)
                            borrowing
                          ──────────→   Words in Singapore English
Words from
other varieties of English

In general, most work on New Englishes has tended to pay more attention to other varieties of English as the source languages rather than the background languages. That is to say, relatively less attention has been focussed on what happens to the meaning of a word from a non-English language when it gets borrowed into a variety of New English.

There are two main reasons for this. One is that most researchers are interested in New Englishes as developing varieties of English. The interest lies in seeing how the developing varieties compare with established varieties of English. And it is much easier to develop a basis for comparison if English words are concentrated on. As an illustration, if we take a word like *fellow*, we can look at different varieties of English to see if the meaning of *fellow* changes from Standard British English to Singapore English to Nigerian English to Sri Lankan English. But suppose we take a word like *kiasu* instead. This is a word meaning 'afraid of losing out'; it is found in Singapore English as a result of borrowing from one of the background languages (the Chinese dialect Hokkien). There is little about *kiasu* that allows us to move from one variety of English to other varieties of English since outside of Singapore English (and possibly Malaysian English), no other variety of English is known to have *kiasu* as part of its vocabulary.

The second reason lies in the fact that, in order to see if there has been any change in meaning when a word is borrowed from one of the background languages into a variety of New English, it is necessary to be familiar with how that word is used in the background language in the first place. And unfortunately, research data on the background languages tend to not be as easily available as data on English. Consider the following situation in Singapore English. Singapore English uses the word *ulu* to indicate that a place is remote. The word is also commonly used to describe a person as being backward or unsophisticated. This word *ulu* is clearly borrowed from one of the background languages, in this case, Malay, which has the word *hulu* meaning 'the upper part of a river'. Tham (1990: 38) notes that traditionally, most Malay villages, where the common folk lived, were located in the upper reaches of rivers. In contrast, in the lower reaches were the town and royal palace. Thus, even within Malay cultural life, there was an association between the upper part of a river and notions of commonality and relative unsophistication.

This means that we cannot simply assume that the change in meaning from 'upper part of a river' to 'backward or unsophisticated' took place only when the word was borrowed into Singapore English. It is equally possible that the meaning change took place within Malay, and that Singapore English merely borrowed the various meanings already associated with *hulu*. This is an empirical issue, and can easily be resolved if there is access to sufficient data on the background language. But in general, semantic data on English words are much more easily available than semantic data on non-English words, which is why less attention has been paid to the changes in meaning that words from the background languages undergo as they get borrowed into New Englishes.

In this chapter, we will try to redress this imbalance and focus, where possible, on both words that are found in other varieties of English, as well as words borrowed from the background languages. However, given the nature of most available data, there may still be a tendency to focus on English words.

Comparison and Prescriptivism

As mentioned earlier, discussion of the meanings of words in Singapore English is often comparative in nature. Essentially, the meaning of a particular word (let us call it X for convenience) in some fairly standard and established variety of English (such as Standard British or Standard American English) is compared with the meaning of the same word, X, in Singapore English. The discussion then typically focusses on ways in which the meaning of X in Singapore English differs from its meaning in the other, more established, variety of English.

Let us assume that in Standard British English or Standard American English, the meaning of the word X is A. But when borrowed into Singapore English, the meaning of X changes somewhat; it becomes A'. Below is a schematic representation of the situation.

Standard British/Standard American English   Singapore English
meaning of X = A   meaning of X = A'

Given these circumstances, it is tempting to treat the change in meaning as being 'wrong' or 'unacceptable'. The meaning of X is whatever it happens to be in Standard British English or Standard American English. This is the 'right' meaning. The meaning of X in Singapore English is the 'wrong' meaning. This amounts to saying that the meaning of X should be A, not A', and that speakers of Singapore English simply do not know how to use X properly.

Of course, most linguists today reject such blatant prescriptivism. However, the temptation towards precriptivism is sometimes implicitly reinforced by the fact that Standard British English or Standard American English is often used as a basis for comparison, lending these varieties the (unintended) status of a reference. Precisely because of this, it is important to bear in mind that the choice of Standard British or Standard American English as a reference is merely a matter of convenience. It is equally possible to compare the meanings of X across two different New Englishes such as Indian English and Malaysian English.

And in fact, the comparison of word meanings does not always have to occur across varieties. Even internal to Standard British English, for example, the meanings of words change over time, so that it is possible to compare the meaning of a given word at different times in the history of the language. In many ways, then, the study of word meanings in New Englishes is essentially a study in historical or developmental semantics.

Of course, this does not mean that prescriptivism is necessarily undesirable. In fact, within a pedagogical context, it is arguably crucial to the language-learning process. However, to the extent that a language learner can be said to be striving towards a target language, then prescriptivism (on how to properly speak the target language) becomes possible only when there is already a reasonably detailed description of the target language in the first place. That is, proper prescription must be based on adequate description.

Organizing the Lexicon of Singapore English

As a general way of thinking about the lexicon of Singapore English, we can assume that it is organized into three main categories. The first category consists of non-English words, often borrowed from the background languages such as Chinese or Malay. The second category consists of English words which are used differently in Singapore English. And the final category consists of English words whose Singapore English usage is not observably different from the way they are used in other varieties of English.

There are two things which need to be noted about this way of organizing the Singapore English lexicon. First, with regard to the final category, precisely because there is little or no observable difference in how these words are used, this group of words has not been the focus of much discussion or interest. Likewise, we will have little to say about this group in the rest of the chapter. This leaves us with the other two categories to focus on.

Second, this is a fairly rudimentary way of organizing the Singapore English lexicon. The reason for this is deliberate. As we will see, when discussions of the Singapore English lexicon become part of a specific agenda (as in a pedagogical context, or as part of a larger attempt to delineate a Singaporean identity), it may be necessary to provide a finer-grained organization of the lexicon. In other words, more complex ways of looking at the lexicon are always possible. And the specific details involved will, to a large extent, depend on the kinds of purposes that particular individuals have in mind. In fact, in a later section, we will have the opportunity to examine an attempt to provide a more complicated organization of the Singapore English lexicon. However, it is important to realize that outside of any specific agenda or purpose, the Singapore English lexicon minimally requires a tripartite division of the kind provided here.

✑ *Inside the Lexicon of Singapore English*

Basically, as mentioned in the previous section, we will focus on two main groups within the Singapore English lexicon. The first group consists of words which are found in Singapore English, but not in other Englishes such as Standard British English or Standard American English. Some examples of such words are shown here:

(1)   a.   Ali is a very *kiasu* person.
      b.   The boss likes him because he knows how to *angkat*.

As we saw earlier, *kiasu* is borrowed from the Chinese dialect Hokkien, and is used to describe a person who is afraid of losing out. In (1b), the word *angkat* is borrowed from Malay where it means 'to raise or lift'. In Singapore English, *angkat* means 'to curry favour'.

Further examples of words belonging to this group are given below.

From Chinese

samseng	'a ruffian or gangster'
ang moh	'a Caucasian'
hongbao	'a small red packet, usually containing money, that is given out as part of the Chinese New Year celebrations'
cheem	'difficult to understand or profound'

From Malay

kampong	'a Malay village, usually of wooden houses on stilts'
hantam	'to make a wild guess'
bedek	'to bluff'
tahan	'to endure'

The second group consists of words which are found in other Englishes, but which are used differently in Singapore English. Examples of words in this second group are:

(2)   a.   I am *staying* in a house in the East Coast.
      b.   I'm going to *keep* these photos in that drawer.

In (2a), the verb *stay* is used to indicate permanent or long-term residence. This use of *stay* in Singapore English differs from its use in Standard British English where permanent or long-term residence requires the verb *live*, and *stay* only indicates temporary or short-term residence.

In (2b), the verb *keep* is used in Singapore English to describe an activity. In contrast, Standard British English tends to use *keep* to describe a state, for example, *The tools are kept in the shed*.

In addition to using English words with slightly different meanings, the words in the second group also include a number of coinages which reflect cultural or social aspects of Singapore society. Some examples are shown in (3):

(3)   a.   I've run out of *parking coupons*.
       b.   You seem to buy a lot of *branded goods*.

In Singapore English, a parking coupon is a coupon which a motorist has to display on the dashboard of his/her vehicle, in certain public car parks, in order for that vehicle to be legally parked. And branded goods do not merely refer to items with brands, but specifically to items which come from well-known and exclusive international fashion houses.

There are many ways in which the meanings of Singapore English lexical items can vary, when compared with how they are used in their source languages. In this chapter we will focus mainly on two general ways in which the meaning of a lexical item can change: its meaning can broaden or it can narrow.

Broadening and Narrowing of Meanings

Often, when we talk about the meaning of a word, we tend to assume that its meaning is unchanging, or at least that it is not undergoing any change while we are analysing the word. Our goal then is to state, as precisely as we can, what meaning that word has. This is a very static view of meaning which allows us to conveniently ignore the fact that languages are continually changing.

When we look into the history of a given language, we sometimes find that a particular word had a meaning that was quite different from its current one. For example, the word *pen* used to mean 'a feathered writing instrument where ink is used'. But nowadays, *pen* has a much more general meaning; it is simply a kind of writing instrument where ink is used. Feathers no longer need to be present. The meaning of *pen* has therefore undergone some change. This problem of meaning change is essentially a comparative one: we take a word, and compare how its meaning has (or has not) changed over time.

Specifically, the case of *pen* involves a particular kind of change where the meaning of a word has become more general or *broadened*. The word *pen* can now be used to describe a wider range of writing instruments than before; it can describe writing instruments with or without feathers.

In the case of *narrowing*, the meaning of a word becomes more restricted so that it is used to describe a smaller range of things than before. For example, the word *hound* in Old English actually had a very general meaning; it simply meant a dog of any kind. But nowadays, *hound* has a much more restricted meaning where it describes 'a dog used for hunting, especially one able to track by scent' (*Oxford Modern English Dictionary*). We call this a narrowing of the meaning of *hound* because the word has become much more specialized in its meaning.

An important point to bear in mind is that when the meaning of a word broadens or narrows, it is not necessarily the case that the original meaning is lost. In quite a number of cases, the original meaning continues to co-exist with the broadened or narrowed meaning so that the word is essentially polysemous, that is, it is associated with distinct but related meanings.

ᕈ᧞ *Broadening and Narrowing in Singapore English*

As mentioned, the narrowing of the meaning of a word results in that word's meaning becoming more specific or restricted. When we look at the lexicon of Singapore English, we find that examples of narrowing seem to be relatively rare, while examples of broadening appear to be much more common. We will speculate on the reasons for this later.

One example of narrowing in Singapore English involves the word *hawker*. In other varieties of English, such as Standard British English, a hawker is typically a person who runs a stall selling food or other goods (Platt and Weber, 1980: 88). In Singapore English, however, hawkers typically sell food. A person selling other goods such as shoes or magazines would not be considered a hawker by Singapore English speakers. This indicates that the sense of *hawker* has been narrowed or restricted in Singapore English.

Another example of narrowing involves the word *batch*. In British English, *batch* is used for either objects or humans. Thus, the *Oxford Modern English Dictionary* defines *batch* as 'a number of things or persons forming a group or dealt with together'. But Platt and Weber (1980: 86) note that in Singapore English, *batch* tends to be used mainly for humans. They give example sentences such as the following:

(4)   a.   We have a batch of girls promoting this product.
       b.   We've just had a new batch of students.

This suggests that there is a restriction or narrowing of the sense of *batch* in Singapore English so that it is used mainly for humans. The Standard British English *batch* lacks this narrowing, which is why it is not restricted to humans, but can be used just as easily with objects as well.

The above are some examples of narrowing that can be found in Singapore English. We now go on to discuss some cases of broadening, and we will find that such cases are much more common. Our first example of broadening in Singapore English comes from the word *fellow*. Platt and Weber (1980: 87) observe that in Standard British English, *fellow* can only be applied to males. But in Singapore English, the word can be used to describe both males as well as females. Thus, the following sentence (also taken from Platt and Weber), which would be odd in Standard British English, is actually quite common in Singapore English.

(5)   She's a nice fellow.

This broadening of the meaning of *fellow* to include females is not restricted to Singapore English. For example, Platt and Weber, citing Bamgbose (1971), note that in Nigerian English, *fellow* is also applicable to females as well as males.

Our next example of broadening in Singapore English involves the verb *send* (Platt and Weber, 1980: 95). In both Standard British English and Standard American English, *send* essentially requires that the entity being sent moves away from the sender. This means that the sender does not accompany the entity being sent. This is exemplified by the sentences below, where it is understood that there is no accompaniment:

(6)   a.   I'll send you out of the room.
       b.   I'll send you the documents.

In (6a), the speaker does not follow the person who is being sent out of the room. In (6b), the documents are understood to reach the addressee without being accompanied by the sender.

But in Singapore English, the sender can sometimes accompany the entity that is being sent, as the following sentences indicate:

(7)   a.   I'll send you home. (= I'll give you a ride home)
       b.   I'll send you to the airport. (= I'll give you a lift to the airport)

It is crucial to realize that Singapore English allows, but does not require, the sender to accompany the entity sent. Evidence for this comes from the fact that the sentences in (6) are also acceptable in Singapore English.

Our third example of broadening comes from the word *stay*. Platt and Weber (1980: 92) give the following example sentences of *stay* in Singapore English:

(8)   a.   We stay upstairs.
          b.   My wife's sister is staying in Jurong.
          c.   I am staying with my mum.
          d.   In Australia what place would you stay?

Platt and Weber state that, where Standard British English is concerned, the word *live* would be used instead of *stay* in the above sentences. This is because, in these sentences, the situations involve someone 'permanently residing at a particular place, not just temporarily (1980: 92).' In Singapore English, however, *stay* is not restricted to temporary residence, and can be used even when the residence is permanent.

In both Standard British English and Singapore English, though, *live* appears to have the same meaning. That is, in both varieties of English, *live* is used to describe permanent residence. And in cases where *stay* is used to describe permanent residence, its meaning then overlaps with the meaning of *live*. This is why in Singapore English, *stay* and *live* are sometimes used interchangeably. But notice that because in Standard British English, *stay* and *live* have different meanings which do not overlap, the two words cannot be used interchangeably.

A final example of broadening can be seen in the case of the word *amah*. According to Platt and Weber (1980: 83), this word is borrowed from the Portuguese *ama*, and when used in Singapore English, was originally used mainly to describe a Chinese nurse or domestic servant.

(9)   I always speak Cantonese to my amah.

But Platt and Weber note that, nowadays, the word also tends to be used for women of other ethnic backgrounds, not only Chinese. This results in the meaning of *amah* becoming more general so that it can be used to describe non-Chinese women as well.

In this section, we have seen cases of broadening and narrowing of meanings. We have found that broadening is much more common than narrowing. The next section discusses some possible reasons why this should be so.

Some Possible Reasons Why Broadening is More Common than Narrowing in Singapore English

One possible reason why broadening is more common than narrowing comes from a combination of two facts:

   (i) that Singapore is a multi-ethnic society, and

(ii) that Singapore English is the lingua franca.

Because of its role as the lingua franca, Singapore English, by definition, is used by members of various ethnicities. Therefore, any linguistic innovation initiated by members of a particular ethnic group, if it is to be accepted as a part of Singapore English, will most likely begin to spread beyond the initiating ethnic group to find a wider usage. A probable, though by no means necessary, consequence of this spread is that the linguistic innovation becomes applicable to members of different ethnicities, resulting in a broadening of the meaning of the linguistic innovation. We saw one such example in the case of *amah* where, over time, the term became applicable to women of various ethnicities, not just Chinese.

Other similar examples of broadening where meanings become applicable to other ethnicities include the words *towkay* and *samseng*. While for some Singapore English speakers *towkay* still means 'a Chinese wealthy businessman' (Platt and Weber, 1980: 85), for a number of other speakers, the word is losing its ethnic restriction so that even Indian or Malay businessmen can be called *towkays*. In the case of *samseng*, it is typically used to mean 'a Chinese hooligan, gangster, or ruffian'. But more and more Singapore English speakers are using it to describe hooligans, gangsters and ruffians of various ethnicities.

This kind of broadening, then, is motivated by the use of Singapore English by members of different ethnic communities. When this happens, there is little or no reason why a given word should be restricted to individuals belonging to a particular ethnicity.

A second reason why broadening tends to be more common than narrowing is related to the multi-ethnic nature of Singapore society: its multilingual character. Most Singaporeans are multilingual, speaking Singapore English as well as Malay, Mandarin, or Hokkien with varying degrees of fluency. A less obvious kind of multilinguality results from the exposure of Singaporeans, through the media and contact with expatriates and tourists, to different varieties of English. Singaporeans, then, are in continuing contact with different languages as well as different varieties of English. This kind of contact means that, whatever linguistic innovations are made in Singapore English, continued exposure to other Englishes, particularly Standard British English and Standard American English, will act as a constraint on the nature of the innovations. Thus, the resulting meaning of a given word will tend not to be narrower than its original sense because it will include the original meaning as well.

In other words, broadening will tend to be more common than narrowing because it is a process which ensures that the change in meaning accommodates the original meaning. Narrowing, on the other hand, does not allow for such accommodation because its effect is to exclude aspects of the original meaning. For example, Ho (1992) notes that the use of the word *fetch* in British English is sensitive to role relationships, if humans are involved. The fetcher is generally of a higher status than the person being fetched, and where relevant, both are of lower status than the person who initiates the fetching event. She gives the following examples:

(10)   a.   Go and fetch little Aggie for me.
        b.   Boss to a junior clerk: Go to the second floor and fetch
              Mr Smith (the accountant) for me.

In the first example, the fetcher is presumably an adult, and the person being fetched, little Aggie, is probably a child. In the second example, while the junior clerk may be of lower status than Mr Smith, the point is that the fetching is initiated by the boss, who is clearly of higher status than either the clerk or the accountant.

But in comparing the Standard British English *fetch* with its use in Singapore English, Ho notes that role relationship is not important in the latter variety so that anybody can fetch anybody else. This indicates that in Singapore English, the requirement that the fetcher be of a higher status than the person being fetched has been lost. Note that it is unlikely that Singapore English would have added a feature requiring the fetcher and the person being fetched to be of equal status, nor is it likely that Singapore English would have reversed the relative status of the persons involved. Continued contact with Standard British English would have made Singapore English speakers aware of the British usage. Because of this, any innovation made in Singapore English would most likely also accommodate the usage in the source language. This kind of consideration is more likely to promote broadening rather than narrowing of meaning.

Motivating Changes

While it is relatively easy to see when a change in meaning has taken place, it is far more difficult to decide why the change occurred. Lass (1980; cited in Hopper and Traugott, 1993: 63) concludes that 'the phenomena that give rise to language change are so complex that they will perhaps never be understood in enough detail for us to state precisely why a specific change occurred in the past or to predict when one will occur and if it does what it will be.' Because of this difficulty, Hopper and Traugott (1993: 63) suggest that '(r)ather than referring to "causes" or "explanations", we speak more cautiously of motivations or enabling factors, understanding always that we are referring to potential not absolute factors.'

In this section, we will briefly discuss some possible motivations for changes in meaning. We group the motivations into two sets:

(i) those that are general, and thus can apply to other aspects of language change, as well as semantic change
(ii) those that are specifically semantic in nature

General Motivations

Hopper and Traugott (1993) divide general motivations for language change into three broad categories:

I.   Changes due to child language acquisition

This assumes that changes in language result from a child's attempts to acquire the language of the parents. When the child tries to do so, the resulting language will differ in some ways from the original. The analogy often used is that of a person making a copy. There will inevitably be some kind of variation between the copy and the original. As each subsequent generation attempts to acquire the language of the previous generation, more and more changes accrue, effectively leading to greater variation.

This view of language change was perhaps most directly summed up by Henry Sweet in 1899 (Aitchison, 1981: 175):

> If languages were learnt perfectly by the children of each generation, then languages would not change...The changes in languages are simply slight mistakes, which in the course of generations completely alter the character of the language.

II.   Changes due to community interaction

Typically, a contact situation involves speakers of different dialects or languages. A whole community of speakers is put into a situation where there is prolonged interaction with another community, and often the languages involved are mutually unintelligible. The need to communicate can give rise to a lingua franca that mixes elements from the various languages, creating first, a pidgin, and with subsequent nativization, a creole.

For example, when Europeans settled in New Guinea, there were situations in which communication between the Europeans and the original inhabitants was essential. The need to communicate caused the European settlers and the native New Guineans to put together a working language, with words taken from the local New Guinean languages as well as various European languages such as Dutch, English and German. The working language that arose under these conditions was a pidgin, which allowed for limited communication. As New Guineans and Europeans mixed, and married, this often resulted in couples who had no common language other than the pidgin. This pidgin was taught to the children as a first language, causing the language to become even more elaborate in its grammar, and richer in its vocabulary. The result was a creole.

III. Changes due to communicative situations

In a communicative situation, the hearer and speaker are constantly in the process of negotiating meanings. Most of these meanings may not have been part of the original meaning of a word, but because the communicative situation allows them to be treated as such, they become conventionalized as part of the meaning. For example, Traugott and König (1991; see also Hopper and Traugott, 1993: 84) discuss how a word like *while*, which originally indicated simultaneity, came to indicate concessivity or surprise. In Old English, *while* was used as part of a phrase meaning 'at the time that', in sentences like the one below:

(11)   And camped there at the time that/while the fortress was worked on and built...

Later, in the early seventeenth century, *while* was interpreted to indicate surprise:

(12)   While others aim at greatness that is bought with blood, you strive to be not great but good.

This interpretation of surprise was reinforced by the belief, at the time, that it was unusual not to be bloodthirsty. In Modern English, we find examples like the one below where *while* indicates a contrast between two propositions:

(13)   While you like peaches, I like nectarines.

Traugott and König suggest that the changes that *while* underwent can be understood by postulating a set of inferences that accompany the communicative situations where *while* was used. Roughly, speakers and hearers understand that, at any given time, many things are happening. Therefore to assert the simultaneity of two events A and B (using *while*) is for the speaker to indicate to the hearer that this is in some way remarkable or surprising. And furthermore, to indicate that something is surprising is to contrast an event with some other (more expected) event. These inferences, over a period of time, motivate the changes in *while* from indicating simultaneity to indicating surprise, and finally, to signalling contrast.

Specifically Semantic Motivations

We shall consider three kinds of semantic motivations:

I.   Euphemism

Sometimes a word is called on to act as a substitute, being used so that speakers may avoid using some other word which is considered vulgar or taboo. In such cases, the substitute is known as a euphemism. The euphemism may then undergo changes in meaning precisely because it needs to cover some of the meanings associated with the taboo. For example, Crowley (1992: 151) notes that in colonial Papua New Guinea, Europeans often described the Melanesians as *natives*. As used by the Europeans, the word had a negative connotation, implying that the people so described were backward. As Papua New Guineans became aware of this, the term *native* was avoided. Instead, the word *national* was used to replace *native*. So, instead of saying that someone is a *native*, it is more polite to say that s/he is a *national*. Thus, in being used as a euphemism for *native*, the word *national* has undergone a change of meaning to describe someone who is a native, though without any negative connotations.

II.   Metaphor

A metaphor results when we use one concept to describe or understand another, different, concept. Typically, the concept used has a relatively more concrete sense while the concept to be understood or described is somewhat more abstract. For example, a word like *see* can be used non-metaphorically to describe a visual experience:

(14)   I saw the cat in the kitchen.

But it can also be used metaphorically to describe a mental experience of comprehension:

(15)   I see what you mean. (= I understand what you're saying)

Via metaphor, a word like *see* can then be used to mean 'understand'. Metaphor is an extremely common process because we are often trying to describe abstract ideas and experiences such as time, life and love. For example, consider whether there is an actual container in a sentence like *I'm **in** pain*, or whether there is actual possession in *I **have** a headache*. Because of the pervasiveness of metaphor, it is a highly productive process where many words come to acquire new meanings.

III. Metonymy

Metonymy is the process whereby a word acquires a new sense by virtue of association or contiguity. One of the most common examples of metonymy concerns the Old English word *gebed*, which is related to our Modern English word *bead*. In Old English, *gebed* originally meant 'prayer'. At the time, a series of prayers was typically counted by making use of the beads of a rosary. Because of this close association between the things said (the prayers) and the objects used to count them (the beads of a rosary), the word *gebed* came to mean 'beads for prayers'. Later on, *gebed* underwent a process of broadening and came to be used for beads of any kind, not just the beads of a rosary.

Singapore English Particles

In this section we will focus on the meanings of exclamations and particles. These convey attitudes and emotions, and are often seen as lexical items which are most uniquely Singaporean. These particles also tend to be used in CSE rather than SSE (Gupta, 1992). Although not as commonly found in SSE, it is clear that the particles are 'important and useful communicative devices to meet the linguistic and sociolinguistic needs of their speakers in informal domains, within a Singaporean culture and context, in Singapore or elsewhere' (Wong, 1994: 8). With this in mind, we will now look at the work of Wong (1994), which represents one of the most recent and sophisticated analyses to date.

Wong discusses three particles: *what, ma* and *me*, and aims to show that the particles have a systematic and invariant meaning, despite appearances that their meanings are highly variable or not uniform. (He uses slightly different orthographic representations for the particles because he is also interested in their phonological and phonetic properties, which we will not be concerned with here.)

According to Wong, the particles are used to indicate the status that a proposition has in a discourse context. For example, in a discourse, a speaker may be unsure that a particular proposition is actually true. To indicate this uncertainty about the truthfulness of the proposition, a specific particle is usually added at the end of the proposition.

It is also possible that a speaker may wish to assert a particular proposition because the proposition contradicts a belief held by the hearer. Adding one of the particles at the end of the proposition will then signal to the hearer that this proposition is intended as a contradiction.

In the next few sections, we will examine specific examples of the particles being used.

The Particle *what*

The following are some examples of the use of *what* in Singapore English (Wong, 1994: 58ff).

(16) a. Student A: Can I have some pins ah?
            Student B: Notice board got pins what.

      b. X: Why didn't you come in?
           Y: You told me to wait here what!

In (a), the particle *what* is attached at the end of the proposition *Notice board got pins*, while in (b) it is attached at the end of the proposition *You told me to wait here*. As we will see below, Wong's analysis claims that by appending the *what* particle to these propositions, the speaker essentially signals to the addressee that these propositions are intended to contradict some assumption that the former attributes to the latter.

It is unclear if the *what* particle is in anyway related to the English word *what*. Platt and Ho (1989) suggest that it is transferred from an earlier British usage, hence suggesting that the source language for *what* is English. On the other hand, Kwan-Terry (1978) prefers to treat *what* as having been borrowed from emotive particles in Chinese, thus making one of the background languages the source language. Whatever the actual source of the *what* particle, it is not always clear what kind of meaning the particle serves to convey.

The following is a simplified characterization of the meaning of *what*, adapted from Wong (1994: 57). P, R and Q represent propositions.

what

Condition: Someone says P to me.

I think: P is said because this person assumes R.
But I don't think R is true.
I think of Q, which will show that R is not true.

I want to make known Q because I want to show that R is not true.

So I say 'Q what', thus signalling that Q is intended to contradict R.

Essentially, Wong is claiming that *what* serves to contradict the reason for a given proposition. To perform this contradiction, the speaker can say Q (the contradiction) and attach the *what* particle to the end of it, signalling to the hearer that Q is a contradiction.

To see Wong's analysis at work, consider how the analysis can be applied to understand the use of *what* in the first example, (16a). The condition here is that someone, namely student A, says P. This gives us the following:

P = There is a request for pins.

On hearing P, student B thinks that the reason P is said is because no pins are available. This gives us:

R = There are no pins to be found.

Student B goes on to think that R cannot be true because there are pins on the notice board, giving the following equation:

Q = There are pins on the notice board.

Q therefore serves to contradict R. Student B then utters Q in order to contradict student A's belief in R. Thus, student B says: 'Q what' which appears as 'Notice board got pins what.'

The Particle *ma*

Here are some examples of the use of *ma*.

(17) a. Context: A pages for B but has forgotten he has done
                   so when B returns his call.
          A: How come you call me?
          B: You page for me ma.

      b. Context: C teases D about a potential romance.
          C: Why don't you go for him?
          D: Not the right one ma.

Unlike the *what* particle, which has raised some controversy as to the nature of its source language, most researchers agree that the *ma* particle is a borrowing from Chinese, though the precise dialect involved is still unclear. For example, Wong (1994) sees a similarity in tone between *ma* and Cantonese, while Smith (1985) finds that *ma* shares certain functions with the Hokkien usage.

In Wong's analysis of *ma* the particle is attached to a proposition to indicate that the proposition serves as a justification:

ma

   Condition: The speaker wants to justify a proposition P.

The speaker thinks: The justification for P is R, and R should be made known.

So, the speaker says 'R ma'.

Consider now how Wong's characterization of *ma* applies to example (17a). Here, there is a proposition P which the speaker B feels needs justification.

P = B calls A.

B sees that A needs to know the reason R for P. That is, there is a need to justify why B called A. This is made clear by A's question: 'How come you call me?'. B provides the justification R, and signals that R is intended as a justification by adding the *ma* particle to it.

R = A has paged for B.

This gives rise to B's utterance, 'You page for me ma'. The use of *ma* indicates to A that B is providing a justification for why B called A.

The Particle *me*

The *me* particle is relatively less common than the other two particles. Wong (1994: 80) goes on to suggest that it may be used only by Chinese Singaporeans, and not Singaporeans belonging to other ethnic groups. And even among the Chinese, this particle is not as common as the particle *what*.

The following examples illustrate the use of *me* in Singapore English:

(18)   a.   Context: G asks H where the colour pencil is twice. H uses the *me* particle to show surprise.
               H: You don't know me?
               G: No, I don't know. Didn't see.

        b.   Context: M wants to help N but N turns down the offer. It is likely that M is indignant at his offer of help being refused and challenges the proposition.
               M: I want to help you. Cannot me?
               N: Don't want.

According to Wong, when the *me* particle is attached to a proposition, it indicates that the speaker is seeking to confirm the truth of the proposition. Below is a simplification of the meaning of *me*.

me

> Condition: There is a proposition P.
>
> Something or someone makes me think that P might be true.
>
> But I find it difficult to accept that P is true because, previously, I had thought P was false.
>
> I want to confirm that P is indeed true.
>
> I say: P me?

Let us now see how Wong's analysis of *me* can shed light on (18a). The given proposition P is that 'G does not know (where the colour pencil is).' We can state this as:

P = G does not know.

G's ignorance becomes clear only after repeated questioning by H. Prior to that, H assumed that G knew the location of the colour pencil, which is why H asked G where it was.

When it becomes clear to H that G does not know the location of the pencil, H is surprised, and wants to now confirm P. That is, H wants to know if G really does not know. This is the reason for H's question, 'You don't know me?'. The use of the *me* particle indicates that H previously believed that G knew where the colour pencil was, but now has come to suspect that G might actually not know. Thus, H wants G to confirm the truth of P.

Controlling the Vocabulary of Singapore English?

Thus far, we have looked at the meanings of a variety of lexical items in Singapore English. Some of these items are recognizably English words such as *hawker, batch* and *fellow*. These words, while recognizably English, have meanings which depart in subtle ways from how they are used in other varieties such as Standard British English or Standard American English. Other items we have looked at are words originating from non-English languages, such as *amah, samseng* and *towkay*; these words are not found in Standard British English or Standard American English.

An important issue raised by the lexicon of Singapore English is the extent to which changes in the meanings of English words or the presence of words borrowed from non-English languages affect the intelligibility of Singapore English. Khoo (1993: 67) argues that, from a pedagogical perspective, it is both necessary and desirable that standards be provided 'to control the proliferation of vocabulary' so as 'to ensure that Singapore English does not lose its international intelligibility.' Khoo's focus is on a specific variety of Singapore English, SSE. She is particularly concerned with trying to decide what lexical items are suitable for inclusion into the vocabulary of SSE.

In this section, we will discuss some of Khoo's suggestions for 'controlling the vocabulary' of SSE, as she puts it. Khoo is quick to admit that her suggestions are exploratory and tentative, and our discussion should therefore bear this in mind.

Khoo proposes a general classification of words in Singapore English, dividing them into five different categories. These categories are ordered according to a scale of controversiality, so that as one moves down the list, the items in each category become more controversial with regard to their acceptability in SSE. The categories are as follows.

1. *Words which are borrowings from the local languages but are used and understood in the English-speaking world and appear as entries in the larger dictionaries of English.*

Examples of words in this category include *haji* 'a Muslim who has been to Mecca on a pilgrimage' (from Malay) and *towkay* 'a Chinese wealthy businessman' (from Chinese). According to Khoo (1993: 71-72), '(w)ords in this category are accepted widely in General English usage as attested to by the fact that they are codified in dictionaries.'

2. *Words which depict local customs and practices and are peculiar to the Singapore way of life.*

Words in this category are supposed to reflect aspects of the Singapore lifestyle and its values (1993: 72). Some examples are *tontine, graduate mother* and *void deck*. Khoo notes that although these lexical items 'may appear strange or deviant to native speakers of English' (1993: 72), their meanings are clear to individuals familiar with the Singapore lifestyle.

3. *Words used in General English but which have a different meaning in Singapore English.*

The English verbs *open* and *close* are often used in Singapore English to describe the operation of various appliances so that instead of saying, 'Switch on/off the radio/fan/tap', Singapore English speakers say, 'Open/close the radio/fan/tap'. And it is even possible in Singapore English to use prepositions as verbs so that one can say 'On/off the radio/fan/tap'. Singapore English speakers also tend to use the verb *cut* for *overtake*, giving rise to utterances such as 'His car cut mine'.

According to Khoo, words in this category, and the next two as well, require 'a stringent screening process…' (1993: 73). This is because speakers of other Englishes are quite naturally not going to expect these words to have different meanings. Therefore, when used differently by speakers of Singapore English, the words in this category are very likely to cause confusion.

4.   *Words used in Singapore English but which are not part of the English outside Singapore or outside Singapore and Malaysia.*

Khoo treats this category as essentially a collection of slang items and idiomatic expressions such as *shiok* 'delicious or enjoyable', *boleh tahan* 'that which can be tolerated or endured' and *no head no tail* 'meaningless or incoherent'.

5.   *Exclamations and particles which convey attitudes and emotions.*

These include particles such as *alamak*, an exclamation of Malay origin which can be used to express surprise or annoyance, and *aiyoh*, borrowed from Chinese, which expresses distress. There are some other particles such as *what*, *ma* and *me*, whose meanings are more difficult to pin down. In the previous section, we already saw one recent attempt to pinpoint the meanings associated with these other particles.

At this point, all Khoo has provided is a list of categories, with the assumption that items in the last three categories are the ones which need special scrutiny. As mentioned before, items in the third category are likely to cause confusion because they are English words which are used differently in Singapore English. Items in the fourth and fifth categories are words and phrases which are not found outside of Singapore and Malaysia, and thus have limited usage. Speakers of other Englishes will probably be unfamiliar with these items and, once again, confusion is likely to result.

There are a number of problems with Khoo's approach. One problem arises from her assumption that General English must serve as a reference point by which suitability or intelligibility is assessed. This can be seen from her suggestion that a word is more suitable to the extent that it follows the rules of English word formation. Implicit in this is the assumption that a

Singapore English word should follow the rules of General English word formation. This bias becomes clear when, in discussing the second category of Singapore English word classification, she says that certain Singapore English words may appear strange or deviant to native speakers of English. The implication is that Singapore English speakers are not native speakers. But as discussed in Chapter 3, we need to recognize that Singapore English has its own rules of word formation (among other rules), and that there is absolutely no reason why the rules of grammar found in Singapore English should be considered any less valid than the rules of grammar found in General English. And it surely is the case that Singapore English speakers are native speakers of Singapore English, the same way British speakers are native speakers of British English and American speakers are native speakers of American English.

This raises another problem with Khoo's approach: her assumption that there is indeed such a thing as General English. We need to ask ourselves if the notion of General English is really as unproblematic as Khoo seems to think. If General English is whatever (and notice that 'whatever' is extremely vague) all Englishes have in common, then by definition, Singapore English speakers should also be considered native speakers since there are undoubtedly some common properties between Singapore English and other Englishes. But surely, one might reply, no one can be really said to speak General English. One always speaks a specific variety of English; General English is just an abstraction over all varieties of English. If this is correct, then General English has no native speakers at all; only specific varieties of English have native speakers. So, unless Khoo is clearer about what she means by 'General English', she appears committed to either claiming that Singapore English speakers are native speakers of General English (and by implication, so is every speaker of any variety of English), or no one is.

This problem with the concept of General English leads to the final problem. Khoo's approach crucially depends on using General English as a reference. It is by using General English as a basis for comparison that Khoo decides which words are more (or less) problematic with respect to the issue of international intelligibility. But in the preceding paragraph, we noted that Khoo is committed to two possible positions. If General English is an abstraction that has no native speakers, then what does it mean to say that Singapore English needs to be monitored so that it will be more intelligible? Is not the problem of intelligibility now more democratically a problem for all speakers of English, not just Singapore English speakers? If, on the other hand, everybody is a speaker of General English, then the problem of intelligibilty does not or should not arise in the first place.

Towards the end of her paper, Khoo suggests some criteria that might be used in deciding whether or not particular items deserve to be included in the vocabulary of SSE.

The first criterion is frequency. How frequently is the word used by educated Singapore speakers? In what kinds of contexts is it used? Formal? Colloquial?

The next criterion is usefulness. Here, Khoo asks if there exists another word in General English with the same meaning. If so, is it possible to discard the Singapore English lexical item?

The next two criteria, grammaticalness and whether a word follows the rules of English word formation, are essentially the same. The more a word obeys English word formation rules, the more acceptable it becomes. For example, the adjective *kiasu* 'afraid of losing' easily takes on the suffix *-ism* to give rise to *kiasuism*. Presumably, this enhances its suitability for SSE.

Khoo's final criterion, intrinsic value, is extremely vague. She suggests that the intrinsic value of a lexical item can be based on qualities such as 'local colour and its general evocativeness' (1993: 77). Precisely what constitutes 'local colour' or 'general evocativeness' is unclear. Also, it is entirely possible that a lexical item possesses local colour precisely because it fails to conform to the rules of English word formation, in which case there is a conflict between the criterion of word formation rules and the criterion of local colour. Khoo does not address the possibility of a conflict between different criteria, and what to do in the case of such a conflict.

In summary, while Khoo's is a pioneering attempt to deal with an important issue, it is marred by unjustified and vague assumptions which, unfortunately, still continue to occasionally influence the study of Singapore English.

Conclusion

In this chapter, we looked at some of the semantic processes that the meanings of words undergo as they change. These may be classified into two types: broadening and narrowing. We then focussed briefly on the much more difficult question of why the changes in meaning take place. We divided the factors involved into those which are generally applicable to various aspects of language change, and those which are specifically concerned with semantic change.

Towards the end, we discussed Khoo's attempt to impose some control over the vocabulary of Singapore English, and asked if the attempt was based on legitimate assumptions concerning the grammar rules of Singapore English, as well as the status of Singapore English speakers as native/non-native speakers of English.

We closed with a discussion of the meanings of Singapore English particles and saw that the kinds of meanings associated with the particles are much more context-dependent, where the context typically specifies a kind of condition for the use and interpretation of the particles. This chapter has only skimmed the surface of word meanings in Singapore English. The study of word meanings in Singapore English is still fairly new, and much remains to be done before we can claim to truly understand the semantics of Singapore English.

Chapter 8

English as the Common Language in Multicultural Singapore

Ho Chee Lick and
Lubna Alsagoff

Introduction

This chapter examines the use of English as the common language in Singapore, a multi-ethnic (multiracial, multilingual and multicultural) post-colonial city-state. The chapter is in three parts. The first concerns the ideology of linguistic pragmatism, which leads to the belief that Singapore depends upon English for survival in the global marketplace. It also deals with the worry that embracing English might bring about the 'Westernization' of Singapore society. The second part addresses the belief that English is an 'ethnically neutral' language in Singapore — another major reason why it is considered the logical choice as the common language. The final part of the chapter investigates the role of English, as the common language, in Singapore's nation-building. Three conceptual paradigms of ethnicity-nationhood relationship are distinguished, which have distinct implications for the role of English: to homogenize, or to contain, ethnic differences, or to enable the diverse ethnic communities to learn and benefit from their differences.

Linguistic Pragmatism

English: The Language of the Global Marketplace

In Singapore, the choice of English as the common language is standardly rationalized in terms of 'practicalness' and 'necessity'. This must be understood within the context of linguistic pragmatism.

Pragmatism, one of the core ideologies by which much of governmental thinking and decision-making is motivated and justified, can be characterized as economic instrumental rationality (Chua, 1995). The leadership has repeatedly thematized 'national survival', with the following external and internal factors perceived as threats:

- physical limitations: a tiny island of only 226 square miles with virtually no natural resources;
- geopolitical environment: a nation with an overwhelming Chinese majority in a predominantly Malay region;

- domestic racial, religious and political extremism;
- fierce regional and global economic competition.

To ensure national survival, two major strategic goals must be achieved: political stability and economic success. While these are interdependent, economy is taken as the ultimate determinant: only through economic success, translated into high living standards of the people, can political stability be substantively guaranteed. Hence the essence of the ideology of pragmatism: Do whatever is necessary for economic success.

Linguistic pragmatism is a logical extension of pragmatism: just as the forces of the marketplace dictate economic issues and choices, so do they determine the worth and fate of languages as economic instruments. English, the language of the global marketplace, is crucial to Singapore's survival and success in the global economy — hence its dominant, common-language position *vis-à-vis* the other languages used on the island. The consequent increase in enrolment in English-medium schools at the expense of the Malay-, Indian- and Chinese-medium schools from the 60s through to the 80s, and the large-scale language shift in the household (school languages becoming home languages) over the past two decades are thus rationalized: people are pragmatic; following the linguistic marketplace principle, they just go for the language necessary for earning a living, achieving upward mobility, and so on.

Let us return to the belief in the vital importance of English to national survival. This is based on a conscious awareness of Singapore's smallness in the world, and the global dominance of English. It is believed that English can link Singapore to the rest of the world, allowing it to plug into the international grid of business and finance, giving it access to the knowledge and technology of the advanced industrialized nations of the West, and making it attractive to foreign investors — all deemed critical to the country's competitiveness in the global marketplace. And, English is seen as having served Singapore well, helping it to become one of the fastest-growing economies in the world, bringing phenomenal changes in the fortunes of the people. The supremacy of English in Singapore is thus legitimized: the needs of economic success call specially for English (and not any other language) and English has proven itself to be capable of perfectly satisfying these needs.

This must of course be taken in context. Firstly, it is premised on the nation's political ideology of the hegemony of economics over all other spheres of life (Chua, 1995). Secondly, it is determined by the character of Singapore's economic order, viz. an industrial-based capitalist economy reliant on international capital. Thirdly, it is dependent upon the power of English in the world today, and the economic, political, cultural and military might behind it. The 'necessity' and 'naturalness' of the choice of English as Singapore's common language are, after all, matters of domestic and international economics and politics.

'Westernization': The Problem

Ironically, while English is seen as necessary for Singapore's survival, it is also seen as bringing harm to the nation. Since the late 1970s, the government has been gravely concerned about Singapore's 'vulnerability' to 'undesirable Western influences' because of its heavy dependence on English and the West. This worry is clearly expressed in the following words of former President Wee Kim Wee:

> Singapore is wide open to external influences. Millions of foreign visitors pass through each year. Books, magazines, tapes, and television programmes pour into Singapore every day. Most are from the developed countries of the West. The over-whelming bulk is in English. Because of universal English education, a new generation of Singaporeans absorbs their contents immediately, without translation or filtering. This openness has made us a cosmopolitan people, and put us in close touch with new ideas and technologies from abroad. But it has also exposed us to alien lifestyles and values. Under this pressure, in less than a generation, attitudes and outlooks of Singaporeans, especially younger Singaporeans, have shifted. Traditional Asian ideas of morality, duty and society which have sustained and guided us in the past are giving way to a more Westernised, individualistic, and self-centred outlook on life...The speed and extent of the changes to Singapore society is worrying. We cannot tell what dangers lie ahead, as we rapidly grow more Westernised. (cited in Shared Values, 1991)

'Westernization', which refers to the perceived shift in the society's dominant values from Asian to Western, in particular from communitarianism to individualism (Lodge and Vogel, 1987), has been assiduously thematized by the country's leadership as being a serious threat to national survival. Politically, the undesirable Western influences are seen as encouraging disrespect for the government, and fanning public desire for Western-type liberal, pluralist politics. Excessive individualism is perceived as detrimental to the country's economic performance and competitiveness. Culturally, Westernization is thought to undermine the country's Asian heritage, rendering its people morally weak and directionless. To counter Westernization, the government has held firmly to the policy of bilingualism: the promotion, alongside the common language English, of ethnic mother tongues (Malay, Tamil and Mandarin) as the agents for the transmission of Asian moral values and cultural traditions. This will be further discussed in a later section.

It is worth pointing out at this juncture that this advocacy of East-is-good-and-West-is-bad has met with serious public challenges. Woon, at that time a nominated member of parliament, for example, remarks: 'The Eastern versus Western values debate is sterile. It is worse than sterile; it is dangerously simple-minded.' (Walter Woon, *The Straits Times* [henceforth ST], 13 September 1992). He explicitly debunks the conception that 'English-speaking' equals 'Westernized' and 'Westernized' equals 'bad'. Implicitly, he therefore also rejects the official formula which links ethnic mother tongues to virtuous Asian values. Woon's position can be summarized as:

- There are both good and bad things in every culture.
- The real question is how to promote good values while suppressing bad ones.
- Singapore, being a cosmopolitan society, is in a position to pick the best from both East and West; indeed, from every culture on the globe.
- Any good value in any culture can be acquired via any language.

We will come back to these ideas in the third part of this chapter when we discuss the notion of 'pick-the-best'.

✑ *English: An 'Ethnically Neutral' Language in Singapore*

Besides economics, another major justification for the common-language status of English has been its 'neutrality' — not belonging to the Malays, Indians or Chinese, and therefore not favouring any of the major ethnic communities in Singapore. Recall, though, that in the late 50s and early 60s, when Singapore's decision-makers saw a viable economic and political survival for the island only within the larger framework of a union with the Federation of Malaya, they claimed that 'moral, political, and practical considerations make Malay, rather than English, the obvious choice' as the common language (People's Action Party, 1959). Malay, an ethnic language, was seen then as being able to help 'remove communal barriers' (Ong Pang Boon, ST, 24 November 1964). Anyway, English, as an 'ethnically neutral' language, is ideally to serve two main purposes: (a) providing equal opportunities for everyone regardless of their ethnic background and (b) promoting racial harmony and national unity, and fostering a national (Singaporean) identity. We look at the 'equalizing' function of English here, and its 'unifying' function in the final part of the chapter.

Is English a social equalizer in Singapore? The answer is both yes and no. In view of racial relations, where national dominance of a racial language entails hegemony of the racial community to which it belongs, yes, English should function as a social equalizer. In the words of Prime Minister Goh, it provides 'an open level playing field' for all Singaporeans to compete equally (Goh Chok Tong, ST, 5 January 1997). However, from the perspective that it does favour the English-speaking over the non-English-speaking (Pendley, 1983; Pennycook, 1994), English's role as a social equalizer is questionable.

Historically, there has always been an asymmetry in power between the English-speaking and the non-English-speaking in Singapore. During the 140 years of British colonial rule (1819—1959), English, the language of the master, was the language in power. English-ness meant loyalty at that time. English education was favoured by colonial policies and restricted to a select few. It opened doors to political and economic opportunities as well as social prestige. Vernacular education, in contrast, was not regarded in official circles as relevant to Singapore, and was viewed negatively (Hill and Lian, 1995: 72). In short, under British colonialism, English was not meant to be a social equalizer. After independence, English remained as the language of government, law and commerce, thus retaining its power and prestige. Its continued dominance has since been rationalized in terms of necessity for national survival, as we have outlined above. At the individual level, its supremacy has been reinforced by its privileged association with employment opportunity, career advancement, material achievement and its premier place in the education system, especially in higher education. As Gupta (1994) remarks, while (Standard) English is ethnically neutral, ability in it is a class marker. Such a view has been supported statistically by the positive correlation between the use of English as a predominant household language and the level of household income (Kuo, 1985; Kwan-Terry, 1993; Tham, 1996). Incidentally, this socioeconomic inequality is taken by many in a way that substantiates the belief in the necessity of English for one's (and one's family's) economic and social survival and success, hence reinforcing the dominance of English.

When we look at the matter of language attitudes, we see certain signs of linguistic and cultural discrimination. Because English has a great deal more status and prestige than any of the vernaculars in Singapore, it is not uncommon for members of the English-speaking elite to show a negative attitude towards the vernaculars and their users. A case in point is their prejudice against Chinese languages (Mandarin and other Chinese dialects) and their speakers, which has been encoded in the Singapore English expression *cheena*. In a newspaper article entitled 'Confession of a Born-Again Chinese' (Sumiko Tan, ST, 17 July 1994), a Chinese ethnic English-speaking journalist tells her stories of the *cheena* syndrome. She candidly reveals her long-felt embarrassment about Chinese-ness, shared by many growing up with the derogatory notion *cheena* in the 1970s and 1980s. Meaning 'very Chinese', *cheena* has the distinct connotation of being 'un-hip' and 'backward'. The term refers to anything connected with the 'Chinese world', including Chinese languages, Chinese-medium schools, Chinese tear-jerkers, and even the colour red. What is not *cheena*? Basically, anything unconnected with China, especially Western music, books and fashion trends. She says: 'The books I read fed my appetite for all things Western. I grew up dreaming of green meadows, boarding schools, midnight feasts, brownies and elves.'

It is the perception of the superiority of English language and culture, admits Ho Kwon Ping, an influential English-speaking Chinese Singaporean, that underlies such a negative attitude towards Chinese-ness. He comments: 'The English-educated elite or intelligentsia tends to see Mandarin as something like a second-class language which they speak only at hawker stalls' (ST, 17 April 1994). A non-Chinese journalist, Cherian George, points out that this is a matter of prejudice and discrimination based on linguistic, rather than racial, division. Recalling his experience as a minority student in the country's most *cheena* junior college (Hwa Chong Junior College), he writes:

> It was not the minorities, but the English-educated Chinese outside the junior college that mocked it as 'so *cheena*'. Years later, when the divide [the English-educated vs. the Chinese-educated (Chinese Singaporeans)] was publicly discussed, and Chinese community leaders bristled at the condescension that they sensed from English-educated Chinese, I knew instantly where they were coming from. (ST, 10 December 1995)

That leads us to another Singapore English expression, *the silent majority*, used by the nation's political leaders (ST, 17 February 1996). This term refers to the estimated 770 000 low-income 'uncomplaining Chinese-speaking Singaporeans', more than half of whom are Chinese monolinguals (according to the 1990 census). They constitute a sizeable percentage of Singapore's population of 2.6 million. Their main grouse is that they have suffered for years a combination of 'economic disadvantage, socio-political alienation and cultural dislocation' because of their language handicap — they are Chinese-speaking in an environment dominated by the English-speaking. But they are uncomplaining ('silent') because they have difficulty in communicating with the ruling English-speaking elite — again, due to their language handicap.

What is reflected in the expressions *cheena* and *the silent majority* is social inequality, which needs to be earnestly and appropriately dealt with, rather than explained away in the name of the 'neutrality' of English. The liberating function of English must be wholeheartedly endorsed; its oppressing function should not be condoned.

The Role of English in Singapore's Nation-building

It is generally accepted in Singapore that English, rather than any of the vernaculars, is the language for the construction and expression of the Singaporean (i.e. national) identity. This stems from the consensus that Singapore should be a Singaporean nation, instead of a Malay, Indian or Chinese nation, and that the evolving national culture should be a Singaporean, rather than Malay, Indian or Chinese, culture. English, the common language to bring citizens of diverse ethnic origins together and to provide them with opportunities for interaction and mutual understanding, is therefore the ideal language to unify the nation in the building of a common Singaporean-ness. In this regard, the unrivalled role of English in Singapore's nation-building, *vis-à-vis* all the vernaculars, seems uncontroversial. However, as will be argued below, a reasonable understanding of how English plays this role must include understanding the different definitions of Singaporean-ness. Essentially, questions like the following must be raised. How is the Singaporean nation to be built out of the diverse ethnic communities? What place do ethnic cultures have in the construction of the national culture — should they be weakened or strengthened?

What is this Singaporean-ness that Singapore's nation-building aims to achieve, on the basis of its multi-ethnic-ness? A wide spectrum of ideological positions can be expected. We identify three of these below, which we call the fusion, mosaic and symbiosis paradigms of ethnicity-nationhood relationship. We argue that the distinctions among them have implications for the way in which the role of English in nation-building is perceived. Before examining them in turn, we want to point out that these three paradigms are not absolutely demarcated, and that it is most likely that a person (politician, academic, etc.) embraces some elements selectively from each, rather than subscribing exclusively and wholeheartedly to any single one of them.

The Fusion Paradigm

In the fusion paradigm, nation-building is understood as a long process of de-ethnicizing the population: gradually 'blurring' racial, linguistic and cultural differences and eventually 'destroying' ethnic distinctiveness (Chiew, 1990). In more concrete terms, this is a process in which the Malays, Indians and Chinese in Singapore gradually become Malay-, Indian- and Chinese-

Singaporeans respectively, and all ethnic-Singaporeans eventually become 'just Singaporeans'. The following statements depict what the ideal result is and how things can go 'wrong':

> If the pace of change is sustained by political will, a point will be reached when it becomes very difficult to revert back since so much has already been *lost and forgotten*, and when it becomes very easy just to move ahead towards the ultimate assimilation or integration...The ultimate outcome will be a new, *homogeneous* culture and society. (Chiew, 1990: 11; emphasis mine)

> The arduous task of building a Singaporean nation becomes more difficult when each ethnic group is made even more conscious of its racial identity and when the cleavages among the various ethnic groups are highlighted and reinforced instead of being minimised. (Quah, 1990: 45-6)

> At this critical [intermediate] stage now, reversion to a plural society is still plausible...If [citizens] actually identify more closely with their cultures, ethnic identities will be enhanced. As a consequence, the major ethnic groups will become more distinct, and national integration will be made more difficult. (Chiew, 1990: 17)

In the fusion view of nation-building, ethnicity and nationhood constitute a 'fundamental contradiction'. At the heart of this contradiction are 'competing loyalties'. Ethnicity is taken as synonymous with 'outpost nationalism' (the Malays oriented towards Malaysia and Indonesia, the Indians towards India and the Chinese towards China), as against Singapore-centred loyalty. Such a perception of ethnicity-nationhood relationship is premised on the assumption of the scarcity of identity. That is, identity or loyalty is taken to be finite: the more with an ethnic community, the less with the nation, and vice versa (see Tamney's critique, 1973). Thus nation-building is talked about in terms of 'the nurturing of the growth of a Singaporean national identity among the population, which will surmount all the chauvinistic and particularistic pulls of the Chinese, Malay, or Indian identities of the various ethnic groups' (Quah, 1990: 45), and in terms of 'making Singaporeans feel *more* Singaporean and *less* specifically Chinese, Malay and Indian' (Zainul and Mahizhnan, 1990: 85; emphasis mine). It is also important to point out that under the fusion view, difference is perceived as essentially centrifugal, undermining the common bonds, and hence as destructive. In short, ethnicity is associated with divisiveness, exclusivity, ethnocentrism, parochialism and chauvinism.

In the fusion paradigm, English, the 'non-ethnic' common language, therefore has a vital role to play in combatting ethnic (racial, linguistic and cultural) allegiances, in destroying ethnic distinctiveness, and in eliminating the population's ethnic consciousness. This function of English is understood as overcoming that of the vernaculars, which allegedly tends to bring about interethnic prejudice and animosity. We can see that point in the following remarks:

> The younger Chinese Singaporeans now habitually speak Singlish [the colloquial variety of Singapore English] and...are quite at home with their Malay, Indian, Eurasian or European colleagues or friends. However, their 'very Chinese' parents or grandparents...tend to be more prejudiced, less knowledgeable about non-Chinese cultures and have less in common with them. (Chiew, 1990: 17)

> The English-speaking Chinese probably has more in common with the English-speaking Malay and the English-speaking Indian than he has with the Chinese-speaking Chinese...Many (if not most) English-speaking Singaporeans are colour-blind when it comes to matters of race. (Walter Woon, ST, 13 September 1992)

In summary, in the fusion paradigm, English is regarded as an ideal tool for de-ethnicizing the population: it enables multi-ethnic Singaporeans to progressively distance themselves from, and eventually rid themselves of, their diverse ethnic-ness — towards a uniform Singaporean-ness.

The Mosaic Paradigm

Distinct from the fusion (i.e. de-ethnicization) paradigm of nation-building, the second position, which we refer to as the mosaic paradigm, emphasizes that ethnic communities are the building blocks of the nation, and that ethnic cultures are sources to draw from in the construction of a national culture. Such a position has been variously articulated: e.g. building a national identity while preserving the cultural traditions and identity of each ethnic community, or, anchoring the identity of Singaporeans in their ethnic and cultural origins. But what exactly is meant by the ethnic communities being the building blocks of the nation? And what is meant by drawing from the sources of the ethnic cultures: what to draw, how, by whom, why...? There appear to be received answers to these questions, expressed in the form of the official four-race model and the pick-the-best approach to nation-building.

Let us first consider the four-race classification of Singapore's citizenry. The guiding principle in the government's policy on ethnicity is multiracialism (covering multilingualism and multiculturalism), which means equal status and treatment of all races, their languages and cultures. Administratively, through language and culture planning, the entire population is officially constituted into four units of equal status, viz. Chinese, Malays, Indians and 'Others' (Eurasians, etc.), each with a designated mother tongue and heritage culture. This, it should be pointed out, entails reconceptualizing the internally heterogeneous communities as each definable in terms of one single language, paired with one associated culture. For instance, the Indian community is represented by Tamil, the official mother tongue, in spite of the use of Malayalam, Punjabi, Bengali, Gujerati, Hindustani, Hindi, Urdu, Telugu, etc. among its members; correspondingly, the diverse South Asian cultures are represented as having one monolithic 'Indian' identity: stereotypically a Dravidian South Indian Hindu culture (Siddique and Purushotam, 1982). Within one culture, there is further reduction. Chua (1995) calls it the selective reinvention of 'traditional' values and attitudes, those necessary to capitalist economic development, good citizenship, social discipline and allegiance to the country. Thus Chinese culture is largely taken as synonymous with Confucian ethics, containing the virtues of hard work, thrift, emphasis on education, filial piety, collectivism, loyalty, etc.

This reductionistic four-race configuration constitutes a standard model to interpret and express 'ethnic building blocks' and 'cultural diversity' in Singapore. It is archetypically displayed through institutionalized cultural festivals, and in National Day parades as an array of Chinese lion dance, Malay kompang, Indian bhangra and Eurasian folk dance. Essentially, the concept of ethnic building blocks is understood within the context of the ideology of multiracialism which, simultaneously, reassures the charter communities that their languages and cultures will be safeguarded, proclaims the nation's determination to preserve its various 'Asian roots' (to inoculate the population against 'Westernization'), and condemns racial chauvinism and ethnic politics. In other words, ethnicity is taken as something of specific practical use in nation-building, and something to be contained at the same time. Particular elements in the ethnic cultural heritages are utilized to the extent that they serve to enhance the nation's economic competitiveness, political stability, racial harmony and social cohesion, and to insulate the populace from the influx of 'undesirable Western influences'; on the other hand, promotion of ethnic languages and cultures is regarded as 'communal', 'parochial', potentially 'divisive' and 'disruptive', its limits to be policed through the elastic idea of 'racial chauvinism' (Chua, 1995).

Correspondent with the utilization-cum-containment conception of ethnicity is the pick-the-best approach to ethnic culture mainten-ance and national culture construction. Recall Woon's ideas presented in the earlier section on Westernization: that there are both good and bad things in every culture; that the real question is how to promote good values while suppressing bad ones; and that Singapore, being a cosmopolitan society, is in a position to pick the best from both East and West; indeed, from every culture on the globe. A few crucial questions pose themselves. How is goodness/badness defined? Are there any universal, objective criteria? Put another way, is there a culture-neutral or noncultural position from which to interpret and assess different cultures? Who should do the judging and picking? How should possible discrepancies be settled between the opinions of the ordinary folk and those of the elite, those of the insiders and those of the outsiders? What do promoting and suppressing mean? There are of course no ready answers to these questions. Certain established views can nonetheless be inferred from the Shared Values project (1988—91), a government initiative to institutionalize selected core values as a national ideology around which to develop a Singaporean identity.

In the White Paper on Shared Values (1991), the concept of pick-the-best is articulated in terms of 'incorporating the relevant parts of our varied cultural heritages, and the attitudes and values which have helped us to survive and succeed as a nation' (p. 1). Survival and success are further paraphrased as 'to prosper and live in peace among [our]selves and with [our] neighbours in the region' (p. 2) — in response to the perceived external and internal threats to the nation. The crucial notion here is 'relevance', which presupposes particular economic, political, cultural and ideological interests. As Hill and Lian (1995) observe, the underlying basis of the selected core values is pragmatism, and the rationale for them is set very firmly against a background of the problem of Westernization. The following is stated in the White Paper as an example of a Confucian ideal which is 'relevant to Singapore':

> The concept of government by honourable men (junzi), who have a duty to do right for the people, and who have the trust and respect of the population, fits us better than the Western idea that a government should be given as limited powers as possible, and should always be treated with suspicion unless proven otherwise. (Shared Values, 1991: 8)

Next, it is worth noting that the pick-the-best approach to the search for national shared values is top-down in nature. The project was initiated by the First Deputy Prime Minister, Goh Chok Tong (who became the Prime Minister two years later). A government committee was then set up to formulate a set of 'national' values. Ways of making these values 'common' or 'shared' by the citizenry, or of reconciling these with those of the different ethnic communities, were issues to be addressed next (Chiew, 1990; Hill and Lian, 1995). The subsequent task would be to weave them into the Singaporean way of life and instil them into all citizens, through teaching them in schools, workplaces and homes. As is common in Singapore, promotion of values means inculcation. There is the assumption that selective elements of a (national or ethnic) culture can be put in some 'software' and 'programmed' into people's minds.

In sum, unlike the fusion (de-ethnicization) paradigm, the mosaic paradigm (utilization-cum-containment of ethnicity) acknowledges the constructive role of ethnicity in nation-building. The model of ethnic building blocks embodies the ideal of pluralistic cultural democracy (Fishman, 1991): equal cultural and linguistic rights for all ethnic groups. The pick-the-best approach is conducive to adherence to tested traditions, those which 'have served our forefathers well over the cycles of history and enabled them to survive despite war, flood and famine' (George Yeo, ST, 12 November 1993), *vis-à-vis* all sorts of untested cultural, ideological and political fashions, wherever they come from.

Let us now consider the implications of the mosaic paradigm for the perception of the roles of English and the vernaculars. Bear in mind that on this view ethnicity is regarded as something to be both utilized and contained — against the ideological backdrop of 'crisis of survival', in which the nation faces, simultaneously and paradoxically, the dangers of 'deculturation/ Westernization' and 'racial chauvinism' (Clammer, 1981). The role of language is consequently variedly perceived, depending on which danger is being spotlighted. Where the threat of Westernization is the primary concern, the use of English is regarded as making Singapore 'vulnerable to alien lifestyles and values'; thus, the ethnic mother tongues, presumably encapsulating Asian moral values and cultural traditions, are needed for the purpose of 'immunization'. Conversely, where the threat of racial chauvinism is the primary concern, the role of ethnic languages is considered potentially 'divisive' and 'destructive'; the use of English as a 'neutral' and 'unifying' language is supposed to help prevent ethnic polarization and confrontation.

To sum up, in the mosaic paradigm, English and the vernaculars, like the building-block cultures they are associated with, are to be both utilized and contained. The languages are in a relationship of mutual containment. Their utility is prescribed largely thus: English for economic success and national unity, the vernaculars for cultural ballast.

The Symbiosis Paradigm

We turn now to the third position on ethnicity-nationhood relationship, which we propose and call the symbiosis paradigm. Like the mosaic paradigm (and unlike the fusion paradigm), the symbiosis view acknowledges ethnicity as contributive to nationhood. However, it goes beyond the utilization-cum-containment model, and espouses a self-creation concept of culture (Turner, 1994) and an ideal of interethnic relationship as mutual liberation. In what follows, we outline the symbiosis paradigm through critiquing some key assumptions that underlie the mosaic paradigm.

Consider the utilitarian notion of ethnicity. The presumption that a culture (ethnic or national) could/should be authoritatively delineated — with the 'good' and 'bad' things categorically determined — and inscribed on people, is particularly debatable. For one thing, the definition of such a culture and the criteria of value are open to ideological manipulation. Under pragmatism, for instance, a culture could be represented in such a way as to serve mainly as a handmaiden to economics. Thus in Singapore, at the national level, economy-dictated 'cultural' values such as discipline, competitiveness and meritocracy preponderate, over and above other cultural sentiments (Chua, 1995). And, at the ethnic level, the significance of heritage languages and cultures is popularly perceived as giving Singapore entrepreneurs an extra edge in penetrating the fast-growing Asian markets.

For another thing, cultural prescription breeds static dualistic thinking: in terms of good-bad, Asian-Western, traditional-modern, national-ethnic, common-unique, consensual-dissensual, and so forth. The cleavage between English-ness (/Singaporean-ness) and Malay-/Indian-/Chinese-ness, with the functional divide between English and the vernaculars, is often conceptualized in such dichotomous terms.

Most importantly, cultural inculcation lends itself to manufacturing followers, rather than nurturing critics and creators. This, in our opinion, is a major limitation of the mosaic view. Admittedly, the pick-the-best ideal embraces valuable elements of scepticism and criticalness, in the dynamic process of picking. Yet, in actuality the focus tends to be on the product ('the best') as something definitive, to be inculcated into the people. In this connection, we would espouse the praxis view of culture — as capacity and empowerment (Turner, 1994). In this view, a culture is a particular historical realization of the human capacity for collective self-creation and transformation. It constitutes most crucially the continual attempts of a community of people to interpret, through contestation and negotiation, their myriad significant experiences (both successes and failures), and to construct and debate models of realities of their past, present and future. From constant critical self-examinations and deliberations of disagreements, opposing viewpoints, conflicting beliefs and contradictory values necessarily arise, forming the source of vitality and originality. Reduc-tionism of culture to a clean book of teachings about only 'good' things, though necessary (perhaps) for certain administrative and educational purposes, essentially constrains the human capacity for culture.

Hence, what to promote in a culture, from the symbiosis perspective, cannot be limited to a body of confirmed encyclopedic knowledge, customs and rites. Most crucially, what ought to be cultivated is the spirit of interrogation and reasoned argument, and the ability, courage, willingness and sense of duty to be self-critical — to resolve one's own problems, surmount one's own weaknesses, and right one's own wrongs. The cultural rights that should be safeguarded are not merely the rights to inherit and preserve a culture, but fundamentally the rights to collective self-definition, self-production, self-assertion and self-transformation. From this vantage point, language is not so much an instrument of cultural transmission as an instrument of cultural criticism and creation. The connection between use of English and Westernization, and between use of ethnic mother tongues and Asian heritages, is therefore not seen as automatic and inevitable. The vital role of language, English and the vernaculars alike, in cultural self-creation will be to enable free and open inquiry, intellectual dialogue and constructive criticism.

Let us now consider the containment aspect of the mosaic paradigm. The underpinning ideology of this paradigm, namely multiracialism (or multiculturalism), rightly accentuates national unity, equality, commonality, harmony, sensitivity, moderation, restraint, compromise and tolerance, as constituting the foundation for the preservation and development of individual ethnic building blocks, and for their co-existence and cooperation. It requires that the 'thin line' between ethnic distinction and ethnic strife be closely watched, and that ethnocentrism, exclusivism, chauvinism and racism be unhesitatingly denounced. In a nutshell, these *-isms* mean: We are superior to all others, hence we should dominate; everything must be judged by our definitions and standards, and must serve our purposes. Needless to say, views, attitudes and behaviours of that nature are unjust and harmful. The whole nation should unite and fight against them resolutely and unceasingly. And, since the Chinese make up the majority of Singapore's population, Chinese chauvinism in particular should be severely exposed and fought. The demand that Mandarin be the common language in multiracial Singapore, for example, must be firmly rejected. It is precisely in this context that English, the non-racial language, has a containing role to play.

Yet, the 'neutrality' of English and English-ness should not be assumed a prior. It is naive to think that in Singapore English-ness is simply 'national-ness' — devoid of sectional interests, outside of relations of power and free of ideological biases. It is naive to see it as the invisible norm against which others are defined as 'ethnic' and hence to be contained (MacCannell, 1992; McLaren, 1994). Given its hegemony in the world (Phillipson and Skutnabb-Kangas, 1997) and its dominance on the island, English-ness is by no means neutral, nor innocent. As noted in the second part of this chapter, there has been a sense of linguistic and cultural superiority felt by some of the English-speaking elite who see the vernaculars as something like second-class languages used only at hawker stalls or among less educated, lower income people (Saravanan, 1993; Ho Kwon Ping, ST, 17 April 1994). Hence, while the nation guards vigilantly against ethnocentrism and chauvinism coming from Malay-ness, Indian-ness and Chinese-ness, it should not lose sight of the possibility of their coming from English-ness. While using English, the common language, to remove ethnic barriers and battle ethnocentrism and chauvinism, the nation should not allow these to take form via English. Here, it is important to point out that the *-isms* under discussion do not inhere in language and culture. As Baker (1993) insightfully reflects, while colour of skin, creed and language often become the symbols and badges of racism, the roots of racism tend to lie in fear and misunderstanding, and in the unequal distribution of power and economic rewards. The extent to which the nation succeeds in combatting ethnic chauvinism and racism is contingent upon the extent to which it succeeds in cultivating and safeguarding fundamental social justice and equality, as well as in fostering interethnic understanding and trust.

The myth of the non-existence of English-ness as a form of ethnicity in Singapore is, ironically, also implicit in the assumed connection between use of English and 'Westernization' (to counter which the nation's own 'ethnic' heritages are to be preserved and strengthened via the use of the 'ethnic' mother tongues; see the earlier section on Westernization). In that connection, English-ness is perceived as a foreign threat to national survival, rather than a local participant in nation-building. Within the symbiosis perspective, however, English-ness in Singapore is seen as an invaluable cultural tradition alongside Malay-ness, Indian-ness, Chinese-ness, etc. That it does not belong hereditarily to the three major racial communities does not make it a lesser form of ethnicity. Ignorantly and arrogantly dismissing it, from an 'ethnic' standpoint, as rootless, superficial, decadent or imperialistic is sheer ethnocentrism and chauvinism. Instead, English-ness should be acknowledged as a site of critical introspection, rigorous moral argumentation and vigorous self-creation for those who choose it as their culture. One of the major roles of English in Singapore's nation-building is therefore to promote and reinforce the self-criticalness and self-creativeness of English-ness — as a contributing ethnic building block.

As mentioned earlier, a symbiotic interethnic relationship is characterized not by mutual containment, but mutual liberation. In this regard, the symbiosis position calls for an ideology of multiculturalism with the following commitments (besides its commitments to unity, equality and tolerance). The first is a commitment to the cultivation and protection of self-confidence and self-respect in each ethnic group. This is grounded on the conviction that an ethnic group's self-esteem is a precondition of its self-recognition, to its self-creation and self-transformation discussed above, and that due recognition of self is in turn a prerequisite for a healthy relation of reciprocal recognition and respect among equals (Taylor, 1992). Cultivation of legitimate ethnic cultural-linguistic loyalty and pride is therefore to be carefully distinguished from political exploitation of them — to be reinforced rather than contained under multiculturalism.

From the viewpoint of symbiosis, multiracialism must also commit itself to the promotion of mutual trust and support. In this connection, irrational mistrust of others is seen as symptomatic of ethnocentrism. Lack of 'sympathetic interest in the needs and struggles of others' (Rockefeller, 1992) is considered a sign of exclusivism. Excessive wariness and tit-for-tat mentality are deemed destructive. Contrastingly, a true spirit of unity, trust and altruism is valued in which one ethnic group wholeheartedly supports the strengthening of another, seeing that as beneficial to the other, to oneself and to the whole nation. It is this spirit that ought to be nurtured in multi-ethnic Singapore through the sharing and use of English, the common language.

Above all, the ideal of symbiosis requires an ideology of multiculturalism committed to fostering interculturality, or intercultural consciousness (Gadamer, 1975; Anzaldua, 1987; Mohanty, 1991; Taylor, 1992; Caws, 1994; Giroux, 1994; McLaren, 1994; Kandiah, forthcoming). The essence of interculturality is an openness to the richness of differences, to the variety of human possibilities, and to opportunities for experience and understanding. Intercultural consciousness is liberating because it enables each culture to see its own limits, to interrogate and challenge its own perspectives and ways, and to expand its horizons through learning from cross-cultural differences. For all the cultures involved, an interrelationship based upon this consciousness is mutually liberating in nature, in the sense that it creates sites of crossing, dialogue, negotiation, reasoned argumentation and, most importantly, voluntary and open-minded mutual learning. In all these respects, English, the common language, certainly has a crucial role to play.

In summary, in the symbiosis paradigm which we have formulated, Singaporean-ness is essentially intercultural-ness: the diverse participating ethnic cultures — individually self-critical and creative, mutually trusting and respecting — learn and benefit from their differences, support and complement one another. This is antithetical to the fusion (de-ethnicization) paradigm of nation-building. It transcends the mosaic paradigm (utilizing-cum-containing ethnicity): it goes beyond equal treatment of groups, ornamental display of diversity, inculcation of values, institutionalization of commonalities, and condemnation of chauvinism.

In the symbiosis paradigm, English, on a par with Malay, Indian and Chinese languages on the island, is a powerful instrument for ethnic self-creation and transformation, in the spirit of self-confidence and self-criticalness. As the common language, its constructive role in nation-building is essentially to cultivate interethnic trust and understanding, to promote open-minded intercultural dialogue and mutual learning.

᎒᠕ *Summary*

This chapter investigated some aspects of the historical, social, political and cultural situatedness of English as the common language in multicultural Singapore, in an effort to denaturalize the 'necessity' and 'neutrality' of the language, and to evaluate the 'benefits' and 'dangers' it brings to society. It argued that the role of English in Singapore's nation-building cannot be simply assumed, but needs to be critically assessed against the background of different understandings of ethnicity, culture, multiculturalism and Singaporean-ness. It examined three conceptual paradigms of ethnicity-nationhood relationship, namely fusion (de-ethnicization), mosaic (utilization-cum-containment of ethnicity) and symbiosis (cultural self-creation and interculturality), and argued strongly for the symbiosis paradigm.

Chapter 9

The New Englishes:
Language in the Home

Joseph A. Foley

ଛ *The Beginnings of Child Language Development*

The general issue we will be addressing in this chapter and the one that follows concerns the relationship between development in language(s) and development in thinking. Since the late seventies, research (see Trevarthan,1987 for a summary) into neonatal behaviour has suggested that human beings are in fact born with a motivation to come to know the world around them. With specific reference to language development Halliday (1975; 1979), Oldenburg (1990) and Painter (1984; 1989) have shown how what Halliday called the 'protolanguage' develops as a means of facilitating this learning about the world. This is done by allowing the infant to use other persons to act as mediators in their engagement with the environment. The infant develops symbols which construct meanings such as ' you give me that', 'you do that again', 'look at this with me' and so on. In other words the protolanguage has a phonology and a semantic element but no grammatical or lexical element.

This protolanguage is eventually abandoned because of this limitation in its role as a resource for learning. The fact that there is no lexico-grammatical system in the protolanguage is a hindrance in categorizing the phenomena of existence. A child at this stage of development may have a symbol which embodies the meaning *Na-ge bu-shi Auntie T-shirt ma?* (Isn't that Auntie's T-shirt?), but none of these protolinguistic symbols would allow for the meaning 'T-shirt' to be constructed as a separable, identifiable meaning from 'Auntie'. The protolanguage is therefore abandoned because the formal properties of the symbol system (in this case the limited range of sounds uttered by the child and understood by those in contact with the child) act as a constraint on the meanings that can be construed. In fact it is the child's own impetus to learn, together with the experience of making meaning with others, which encourages the child to adopt a language system with the formal properties of a language (a phonology and a lexico-grammatical basis). Language proper is developed precisely because it is an optimal resource for learning (Painter, 1996). Children who develop their language(s) in an environment where a new variety of English is one of the language choices will, it is argued here, absorb that new variety to become an added resource for learning.

As soon as linguistic symbols become a medium of learning, then learning can only be understood as an interactive, interpersonal process. That is, the learning process occurs through the medium of others, through talk. It also follows that the environment being revealed to the child for knowing is mainly constructed through language (Painter, 1996). From instances of language in use, children gain experience in the functions and structures of the language. On any occasion of language in use, a language learner is making sense of the particular way in which language works and the particular context; and it is from the countless instances of this working of language in context that the linguistic and social systems are construed (Halliday, 1975).

In this chapter we would like to illustrate the relationship between new linguistic developments and how children can use these as part of their thinking skills. Equally important is the understanding of how developments in the preschool period are crucial in enabling a child to embark on the move from 'common-sense', everyday knowledge to the 'educational knowledge' of school learning. Common-sense knowledge is learned by doing, mediated by spoken language, while educational knowledge is more an institutionalized knowledge learned through instruction, mediated largely by written language. The argument put forward here is that in a multilingual and multicultural society such as Singapore and Malaysia, the ability to use a local variety of English together with one or more of the regional languages is an important tool for the child in the learning process. All conversational interaction between the child and the caregiver or peer reveals to the child not only information about the structures and uses of language but also is essential in developing the growing learning skills. Consequently, the strategies or processes of learning — classifying, comparing, generalizing, making cause-effect links, hypothesizing, inferring and so on — are all most usefully seen as above all strategies for meaning.

The Sociolinguistic Background

In countries where the new varieties of English have become established, they are by definition used in conjunction with other regional languages, at societal level if not at the individual level. Obviously, the ability to use more than one language is an important factor for the individual in the learning process. This is most clearly seen in the developing language of the young child. From what we have already said, conversational interaction between the child and the caregiver or peer reveals to the child not only information about language(s) (its structures and uses, which enables the child to construe its systems), but also information about the world in which this 'working of language' is occurring. The sociolinguistic context in which these new varieties of English emerge would probably have the following three factors (Gupta, 1994; although she was actually making reference only to Singapore):

(1) extensive contact between speakers with different language repertoires, including close domestic contact;

(2) an almost total absence of people who are monolingual in any of the languages;

(3) widespread learning of English, both formally and informally.
(Gupta, 1994: 5)

This 'formal' and 'informal' use of English results in a diglossic variation of English (a point discussed in earlier chapters) which is not dissimilar to what is found in many of the older varieties of English. So for example in Singapore and Malaysia, there is what Gupta terms a 'High' variety of Standard English and a 'Low' variety referred to as Singapore Colloquial English. Gupta has argued that nearly all children who have learnt English from birth will have this colloquial variety, rather than Standard Singapore English, as their first language. This, of course, is also true of most languages in the world where a diglossic situation exists in that informal and formal situations can demand a shift from colloquial to standard forms of the language. However, in contexts where the new varieties of English have developed, the English spoken often covers the full range of ability, upwards from individuals who have extremely limited use of English, to speakers who can use both the standard and colloquial varieties. Young children in these contexts are generally speakers of the colloquial variety and learners of the standard variety once they enter formal education (Gupta, 1994).

As has been indicated in earlier chapters, English has had the central role of enabling multilingual members of a community to be the social brokers in bridging the communicative gaps in cross-cultural communication. This very often means extensive code-switching. Singapore's multilingual model fits the nation's population into the four main ethnic blocs of Chinese, Malay, Indian and Others. Such a model is therefore seen to grant linguistic and cultural recognition to the multi-ethnic population by giving their 'corresponding associated languages' equal official status and legitimacy. The model also consolidates the respective official ethnic blocs by bringing together diverse ethnic subcommunities on the basis of a common ethnic origin, language and culture (Tan, 1995).

English is Singapore's official working language and the official perspective is that the 'utilitarian' purpose of this language functionally sets it apart from Mandarin, Malay or Tamil. The latter three are termed 'mother tongue languages' and their roles are perceived to be paramount in the transmission of ethnic values and cultures. Table 1 shows the changes in dominant languages used in households from the 1980 to the 1990 census.

	1980	1990
English	11.6	20.8
Mandarin	10.2	23.7
Chinese Dialects	59.5	38.2
Malay	13.9	13.6
Tamil	3.1	3.0
Others	1.7	0.7

(Lau, 1993: 6)

Table 1. Dominant Languages in Households (figures in percentages)

As can be seen from the table, the proportion of households using English as the predominant household language rose from 12% to 21%. This was due in part to the younger section of the population receiving their education in English. Among the Chinese households, there was a significant shift away from the use of Chinese 'dialects' towards English or Mandarin. The greater usage of Mandarin instead of 'dialects' among Chinese households reflects the success of the 'Speak Mandarin Campaign' and the emphasis on Mandarin as the second language among Chinese students (see Chapter 12). It is also interesting to note that the other census figures given indicate that the use of English has increased in Malay households from 2% to 6% and in Indian households from 24% to 34%.

In the formal education system, however, English is termed the 'First Language' as it is compulsory, while the mother tongue officially designated for one's particular ethnicity is called the 'Second Language'. The multilingual model predetermines that the Chinese should learn Mandarin, the Malays the Malay language and the Indians, Tamil. The only exceptions allowed are for children of mixed marriages and five of the Non-Tamil Indian groups. In the case of the former, the child's ethnicity is officially categorized as that of the father's and the 'choice' of the Second Language is accordingly determined. As for the Non-Tamil Indians (the Bengali, Gujerati, Hindi, Punjabi and Urdu speakers), until the recent change in the education policy allowing them to take their respective ethnic languages in school, the children were given the option of learning either Malay, Mandarin or Tamil (Tan, 1995).

Given the prominent role of English in Singapore, there has emerged a linguistic differentiation which marks stratification by social class. The 1990 Census of Population, for example, confirmed that the use of English as the principle household language is indicative of socioeconomic status. In households with incomes of less than $1000 per month, only 7.6% reported using English, whereas in households with incomes of $4000 and over, 33.5% reported using English (Lau, 1992). What this clearly indicates is that those who use English frequently and with proficiency are those in the higher socioeconomic and educational bracket. These language users are linguistically empowered, capable of using both the Standard (SSE) and Colloquial forms of Singapore English (CSE) and are therefore able to move with fluidity along the whole formality cline, ranging from the more 'formal styles' to 'intimate speech'. Individuals with lower levels of proficiency (usually, but not always, those from a lower socioeconomic background; there is still a section of the population who were not English-medium but Chinese-medium educated) have restricted movement along the formality cline.

The pressures of change in the various structures of society have determined that English now be made accessible to a wider circle of people. However, only the educated, highly socioeconomically positioned English users can achieve downward accommodation when interacting with members of the lower class. This switch from SSE to CSE and vice versa functions as an important indicator of class membership (Pakir, 1991: 6). For children who are growing up in Singapore, entry into this 'class membership' is primarily achieved through schooling. However, the home environment can also give the child a 'headstart' by creating a linguistically enriched context for the learning of more than one language as illustrated in the figure on the next page.

The sociolinguistic situation in Malaysia is slightly different. The Malays, being the indigenous people, form 53.3% of the population and have a native language called Bahasa Malaysia. There are a number of mutually intelligible dialects and the Chinese community, known as Babas, and the Indians, called Malacca Chetty, also use Malay. The impact of British rule encouraged large-scale immigration of Chinese and Indian labour in the second half of the nineteenth century. The Chinese came mainly from southern China and brought their own languages: Mandarin, Cantonese, Teochew, Hokkien, Hakka and Hainanese. The Indians brought with them several mutually unintelligible languages like Tamil, Hindi, Punjabi, Malayalam, Telegu and Singhalese. By 1975 the population census figures listed the Chinese as making up 35.3% of the population and the Indians, 10.6%. There are other indigenous languages in the East Malaysian states of Sabah and Sarawak, such as Iban and Land Dayak, among others. English, however, as in Singapore, cuts across these ethnic boundaries. The main difference between

SINGAPORE

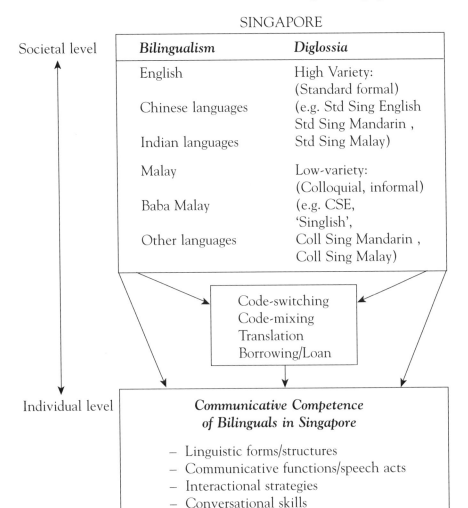

Figure 1. *Societal and Individual Bilingualism and Diglossia in Singapore*

the development of a local variety of English in Malaysia and Singapore is that after independence in 1957 the Malaysian government made Malay the national and official language of the country. So in Malaysia, Bahasa Malaysia is the medium of instruction at all levels, from primary to tertiary. English is taught as a second language in primary and secondary schools and is used at tertiary level in certain subject areas.

One factor which has greatly influenced the linguistic picture in Malaysia is the fact that many of the people in positions of influence today are those who went through the English-medium schools of the British colonial period. These people have set up English-speaking homes in which their children get exposure to English even before they go to school. For such children, especially non-Malays, whose own mother tongues are not seen to be a valuable asset in the country, English soon becomes their dominant language, to the extent that it practically replaces their vernaculars. Augustin (1982: 251) gives the following figures which point to the importance of English in the present Malaysian way of life. From a total of 1.1 million who completed secondary education between the years 1956 and 1970, 69.8% attended English-medium schools. Since the number of English-speaking families is greater in the urban centres, they form a large enough demand for English and provide their own English-speaking environment for themselves, so that English need not be restricted to the home and school but can be used among friends in social intercourse and also in transactions both official and non-official, among government bodies (Wong and Thambyrajah, 1991). A more recent study of how young Malaysian students perceive the role of English in their lives shows a dominance of needing English in academic and work environments but not necessarily for social needs (Kaur, 1995). This is summarized in the following table:

Theme	Rank	Function
Personal Advancement	1	prepare for future studies abroad
	2	improve my knowledge by reading English
	4	help me get a job in Malaysia
	5	help me get a job overseas
National Progress	3	use for diplomatic relations with other countries
	6	use for economic progress of Malaysia
Cross-cultural Communication	7	speak with tourists and foreigners in Malaysia
	8	speak when I travel overseas
	9	speak with my family and friends

(adapted from Kaur, 1995: 226)

Table 2. Functions related to English

As shown in the table, functions related to the students' personal advancement, primarily in terms of academic pursuits and for widening their knowledge, received the greatest priority over other functions. Students' need for English to help them in utilitarian functions such as employment received medium priority. However, English for diplomatic relations was considered to be of greater priority than English for economic progress. English within the family had the lowest ranking of all.

The present situation in Malaysia is marked by increasing efforts to elevate the status and standard of English instruction at the school level but this is not felt necessary for societal needs in the home. We could thus summarize the sociolinguistic situation in Singapore and Malaysia as follows: probably the political divergence since independence from colonial rule has resulted in Singapore using English as the dominant language of government, commerce and education and Malaysia using English as a second language in society but with a much more restricted role because of the importance of Bahasa Malaysia and Bahasa Indonesia, which cover much of the population in the Malaysian/Indonesian Archipelago. We find it more than likely, therefore, that English as a new variety will become more dynamic within the context of Singapore than Malaysia. As a consequence it is to Singapore that we would look for the development of English as a dominant language in the home.

The Acquisition of a New Variety of English

The question is, how do you determine in these contexts whether a child is a dominant speaker of English? As Gupta (1994) has pointed out, population census figures can give some indication but it does depend on how the data was collected. Self-reporting of home language use can be indicative but can also reflect parental aspirations rather than reality. Observation of the functional use of language in the more formal setting of the kindergarten (normally the child's first formal contact with the larger community apart from religious occasions) can also give some indication of the child's ability to interact functionally in English in a teacher-pupil setting. But what constitutes functional adequacy for a three-year-old is based on a generally vague notion of what is considered as adequate. If assessment was based on the English of children acquiring Standard English in the UK, US, Australia or New Zealand, children in countries where the New Englishes are found would probably not be seen as having appropriate English for their age. The criterion for assessing a child's command of English has to be with reference to the local situation. The level demanded by the more standard form of the local variety of English will of course have to have a wider concept of adequacy (Gupta, 1994).

Studies of the acquisition of language and, in particular, English have been dominated by two major paradigms — one derived from rhetoric and ethnography which emphasizes the developing functions or uses to which children put their language system and one with its roots in logic and philosophy which describes development in terms of the acquisition of grammatical structures (Campbell and Wales, 1970). While both approaches are equally concerned with the acquisition of a system, they differ in their interpretation of the relationship between system and behaviour, and in their conception of the degree and kind of idealization involved. The paradigm based on logical analysis, in the extreme case, idealizes language to the point where it becomes maximally reduced to an artificial logical language. Ethnographic/descriptive grammars, on the other hand, tend to minimize the gap between the ideal and the actual, drawing on language-in-use for their data (Halliday, 1984). We will suggest in this chapter that in order to understand the acquisition of the new varieties of English, it is most important to take an ethnographic approach. It is from the constant exchanges in specific contexts of family and peer group life that the child's understanding and use of language arise (Halliday, 1975). The immediate contexts in which the child participates are constantly providing linguistic challenges for the developing child. The child needs to gain control over an ever-expanding range of domains: from the home, neighbourhood and preschool to, eventually, school itself. In each domain the child is confronted with new phenomena which need to be named in order to share the experience, with new connections between phenomena which extend and modify the child's developing taxonomies, with enriched understanding of how phenomena work, with new social roles to take on and assign to others and with new insights into the nature and function of language. In the early stages, much of what a child hears is related to observable features of the environment, allowing the child to make ready connections between what is said and the significance of the utterance (Halliday, 1978). The constantly evolving context, however, is not to be seen simply in terms of the objects and events of the external world — the 'props' and conditions surrounding the ongoing activity (Halliday, 1975). Rather, it is a configuration of languages and other semiotic patterns concerned with the negotiation of roles and relationships, and the channel of communication. The child learns language as a system of meanings by engaging with language in functional contexts. It is through the deconstruction of these instances of language experienced in numerous contexts of situation that the child learns to construe the system. Thus language is the primary medium of socialization (Halliday, 1978; 1987).

On the other hand, linguists who stress the 'logic' of language have tended to describe language as a system or code in isolation from behaviour, use or context. Research studies drawing on such grammars are therefore concerned with the acquisition of particular grammatical structures. From the early sixties studies in early language development tended to be concerned with the acquisition of structure, word order and morphemes. Because children start to combine words at about eighteen months, this was generally taken as a natural starting-point for studies of language development (Lock and Fisher, 1984). Also a commonly held assumption was that the bulk of syntactic structures were acquired between the ages of two and five (McNeill, 1970) and that later development consisted mainly of the addition of a sophisticated lexicon. More recently, however, it was acknowledged that development did continue into later childhood and adolescence in a number of areas, in particular those of phonology, morphology/word class and syntax (Cruttenden, 1979; Romaine, 1984).

We would argue then, that if we attempt to look at the acquisition of new varieties of English in isolation from their cultural context, a number of problems arise. Firstly, these systems or codes found in the new varieties can only make sense with reference to an endonormative grammar of acquisition rather than some exonormative one. For example, the more informal code seems to have little inflectional morphology, yet studies looking at language as a code in isolation from behaviour all refer to a point at which features such as tense marking or plurality become categorical (children begin to speak without tense marking, then begin to use the past tense sometimes, until finally the use of the past tense becomes obligatory). In many of the new varieties of English in the colloquial form, tense reference is never categorical. That is to say, the model presented to the child may not have the degree of inflectional endings as found in some of the older varieties of English. Secondly, studies of language acquisition of the new varieties of English do not make any sense outside their natural sociolinguistic context. So, if the variety of English the child is acquiring does not, for example, use an inflected third-person singular present tense verb, the child may not learn it at all (or at least not until formal schooling) and certainly not at the same age as a child exposed to a variety in which it is the norm. The order of acquisition of a given form, therefore, may be related to the frequency of usage in the linguistic environment of the child (Gupta, 1994). Thirdly, differences in patterns of child-rearing and of expectations of interaction with children have been found to affect language development. There are both cultural and individual differences in the ways in which children are treated as conversational partners and studies in early development can trace such cultural traits to the amount of direct speech directed at the child and the degree of semantic contingency in adult speech developing out of children's utterances (Hasan, 1986). Thus the acquisition of new varieties of English has to be placed in an atmosphere of extreme linguistic tolerance, where many languages are used in the process of communication (Gupta, 1994). Fourthly, code differentiation where the child is exposed in a more formal setting to the standard variety of English such as Standard Singapore/

Malaysian English often occurs, as we indicated earlier, when the child begins formal preschool education. Parental awareness of approaching formal education may lead to the child being read to, and this results in an increase in the use of a more formal variety of English in the home. The sources of the standard local variety are various: television, radio and especially pedagogically oriented speech directed to the child in the standard form. All this presupposes a dominant English-speaking household where by the time a child reaches primary school (age 5 or 6) the use of the formal features of the colloquial variety and most of the features of the standard variety would approach the adult model. However, children who come from homes where English is not used as a dominant language — indeed, may be used very little — will often learn their colloquial variety of English in school and in general will have a much later acquisition of the standard variety.

It is sometimes assumed that children acquiring a non-standard variety of a language are educationally disadvantaged, as when they enter school they must learn the standard variety and this becomes an added burden. As Gupta (1994) indicates, it is difficult to make generalizations about this but if the example of Singapore and Malaysia can be used as an indicator, any disadvantage experienced by speakers of non-standard varieties comes from economic and social factors. The earlier a child enters into formal preschool education where exposure to both the colloquial and formal varieties of English is possible, the better prepared the child will be for a formal system of education where English plays a dominant role.

The Data

In the next section of this chapter we will illustrate some of the points made by looking at data collected in informal situations within the context of Singapore (Foley, forthcoming). However, it must be remembered that the concept of 'family' is much larger than that of the nuclear family and the degree of linguistic diversity very extreme indeed. Tan (1988) showed this in her study on code-mixing and code-switching in a Singapore household. The table on the next page gives some indication of language use in Tan's own household.

Tan found in her study that although participants shared the same background and certain context-bound expressions as in a closed network situation, their switching strategies also varied with their own personal habitual use of a language or languages. Accordingly, they showed different language use patterns although they shared the same family and neighbourhood background. In other words, within the closed network system, there are many smaller intersecting or non-intersecting network systems. This must be kept in mind as we examine the data that follows.

In general, it is probably true to say that children in the multilingual context of Singapore normally start off with a chronologically 'first' language before other languages are introduced, depending on the caregivers involved. 'Naming' is often a first strategy used in the introduction of a new language into the child's repertoire. The first two examples are illustrative of this learning strategy.

Languages Used

Household members	English W	S	Mandarin W	S	Hokkien W	S	Cantonese W	S	Malay W	S
Father	–	–	2	3	–	1	–	3	–	2
Mother	–	–	–	3	–	1	–	–	–	2
Brother	–	3	2	2	–	1	–	3	–	–
1 Sister	–	3	1	1	–	1	–	1	–	2
2 Sister	2	1	1	1	–	1	–	1	–	–
3 Sister	1	1	2	1	–	1	–	2	–	–
4 Sister	1	1	2	1	–	1	–	2	–	–
Self	1	1	2	1	–	1	–	2	–	–
Half Sister	2	1	2	1	–	1	–	2	–	–
Bro-in-law1	–	3	2	1	–	1	–	2	–	2
Bro-in-law2	–	3	2	1	–	1	–	2	–	2
Bro-in-law3	1	1	2	1	–	1	–	3	–	–
Sis-in-law	3	3	1	1	–	1	–	1	–	2
Bro Child 1	–	3	–	1	–	1	–	–	–	–
Bro Child 2*	–	–	–	–	–	–	–	–	–	–
1 Sis Child 1	–	3	–	1	–	1	–	2	–	–
1 Sis Child 2	–	3	–	1	–	2	–	–	–	–
1 Sis Child 3*	–	–	–	–	–	–	–	–	–	–
2 Sis Child 1	–	–	–	1	–	3	–	–	–	–
2 Sis Child 2	–	–	–	1	3		–	–	–	–

Key
W = written   1: Proficient
S = spoken   2: Quite proficient
           3: Not proficient
           –: No/Negligible knowledge
           * not yet learnt to speak at the time of the study

(adapted from Tan, 1988: 97)

Table 3. Languages used by Household Members

Example 1

Ping, (f) 4 yrs; 8 mths
Linguistic background: Ping spends most of her time with her mother who speaks only English to her and with her paternal grandmother who speaks Baba Malay (a mixture of Malay and Chinese). Ping at this stage is using Baba Malay in 'naming' with her paternal grandmother.

- Something hanging on the *puntat* [bottom (body term)].
- Pants must make *baik-baik* first [properly, well].
- Do you want to change her *baju* [clothing]?
- Mummy got *baju* to swim.
- Her *baju* is cute.
- *bengkak* eyes [swollen].
- It (= umbrella) closed — when you put inside your head become *bengkak*.
- Because didn't *kenna* the eye [get].
- No she wants to go *kai-kai* [out for a walk].
- She run and run then she *jatuh* [fall down].
- Because my daddy say, don't let *meh-meh* take ah [younger sister].

(Chionh, 1987)

Example 2

Sharon, (f) 4 yrs; 1 mth
Linguistic background: Parents speak mainly English and some Tamil to her. She spends two hours a day at an English-medium nursery. Sharon (S) and Mother (M) are talking in the kitchen.

M: You want to wash or not?
S: Yeah.
M: OK.
S: *** put the soap.
M: Don't waste the soap ah.
S: OK.
   This one ah? Why put on the big *panay* ['container' in Tamil]?
M: Better, then you don't spill it, *Intha* [here].
S: Open the *thani* [water].
M: No, no, *Thani vaenda* [don't want water]. You just wash it.
S: I like *puttu* (the red powder that Indians put on their forehead — Sharon has mispronounced it)
M: *Puttu?* Water *puttu.*
S: *Puttu* to put on my —
M: *Pottu da.* Not *puttu* *** *Kudi* [drink].
S: Who use at their head?

M: Quickly drink up your milk. Don't spill it ma.
S: Who put *puttu?*
M: Oh, some people use *pottu.*

                    (DELL Language Development Data, 1985)

In this second example, apart from the fact that the caregiver and child are using two languages to explain a cultural phenomenon within a particular community, the scaffolding of the language by the caregiver comes about in quite a 'natural' conversational dialogue in that it follows the sequential constraints. Thus we see English being used as the main medium of communication and a means to learning lexical items in Tamil and how they are pronounced.

The next set of examples give some indication of how more than one language can be used quite normally in the natural process of developing the common-sense knowledge of the home. In the first case English and Cantonese are being used and in the second, English and Malay.

Example 3

Eliza, (f) 3 yrs; 1 mth
Linguistic background: English and Cantonese are used at home where the child spends most of her time. In this present context Eliza (E) and the Adult (A) are looking at a picture book.

A: What is this?
E: *{ dEs   } (dress).
A: What about this?
E: *fu* [trousers in Cantonese].
A: *fu?*
E: Yes.
A: Are you sure?
E: *fu* so (also) - [f] - [f] so ***
A: Are they the same?
E: No.
A: Why are not the same? Tell me.
E: This one cannot — this one can.
A: Cannot what?
E: Cannot to *jiok fu* — then so hard to *jiok* [to wear].
A: This one hard to *jiok?*
E: Mm.
A: This one is easy to wear? What about this one?
E: This one can wear.

                    (DELL Language Development Data, 1983)

Following the argument that the new varieties of English normally develop in contexts where more than one language is in use, we see in this extract the child using the two languages in her present repertoire as a resource for naming. So for example, the Cantonese word for trousers *fu* gives the distinctive characteristic of the sort of trousers that Chinese ladies wear. At this stage of learning, to use more than one language in naming utterances is typical in that the child can enquire about or tell how to categorize some observed phenomenon. We also find a development of construing things into taxonomies. In this case it is a type of trousers. Naming as indicated is one of the early uses made of language, and the building up of a taxonomy that relates individual items to larger groupings is an essential stage in the learning process.

Example 4

Saffiya, (f) 5 yrs; 0 mth
This following extract is of an English-Malay-speaking girl (S), playing with play-dough and talking to her mother (M) and Norwita (the researcher) (N).

S: I'm playing with the bun.
N: Huh?
S: Playing with the bun.
N: What bun?
S: This one lah.
N: What's that actually?
S: Dough.
N: What is dough?
S: Mama tell something...dough dough dough dough flour lah flour flour.
N: Then what are you making the flour into?
S: Make people.
M: *Saffiya tengah buat apa?* [Saffiah, what are you making?]
S: *Er...buat orang* [make person].
M: *Buat orang? Tengah main dangan apa itu?* [What are you playing with?]
S: Dough.
M: Dough *dalam Bahasa Melayu apa?* [What is dough in Malay?]
S: *Tak tau* [Don't know].
(S is encouraged by M to describe what she is doing)
S: *Sekarang buat rambut* [Making the hair now].
    Sekarang buat buat rambut
    Panjang rambut [long hair].
M: *Taruh rambut atas kepala* [Put the hair on the head].
S: Oh huh.

N: The hair no need to be black?

S: No need.

N: The hair black what?

S: Then the dough white.

N: Then cannot do anything?

S: Don't have black flour.

M: *Rambut Saffiya warna apa?* [What is the colour of your hair?]

S: *Hitam* [Black].

M: *Habis kenapa tak buat rambut hitam?* [Then why don't you make black hair?]

(Extract continues)

.

N: *Saffiya nak kasi cikgu bunga tak?* [Do you want to give your teachers flowers?]

S: *Kita nak* [I want].

N: *Habis kenapa tak cakap dengan mama?* [Then why didn't you tell Mama?]

S: *Tak* [not].

N: What flowers that they give?

S: Hm rose all lah.

(Extract continues)

.

N: *Saffiya nak kasi bunga tak?* [Do you want to give flowers?]

S: *Kita nak tapi mama tak beli* [I want but Mama didn't buy any].

N: *OK mama belikan nak?* [OK shall Mama buy them?]

(Extract continues)

.

S: *Kita beli?* [I buy?]

N: *Kenapa tak boleh?* [Why cannot?]

S: *Dia beli lah kasi kita kasi cikgu* [You buy for me to give to the teachers].

(Extract continues)

.

S: Because I want to give to my English teacher and my *cikgu* [teacher].

(Extract continues)

.

S: *Satu cikgu satu er...teacher Cina satu* one teacher English *satu* teacher *Melayu* [one teacher er for the Chinese teacher, one for the English teacher and one for the Malay teacher].

(Extract continues)

.

S: Now I only want to buy two because I want to give *cikgu* [teacher].

(Norwita, 1987)

This is a good example of how children and adults calibrate their language and behaviour according to subtle cues about their changing roles in different contexts. For instance, the adult may unconsciously adopt a pedagogical role while the child takes on the role of responder. In other contexts, the adult becomes the 'companion' and the inequality status between the child and the adult is reduced. Very often the conversation is scaffolded by direct or indirect questioning, especially if it is a child-adult situation.

M: *Macam mana buat badan?* [How do you make the body?]
S: *Tak tau* [Don't know].
   Ah, ini press press [Ah, this].
   Badan kan round? [Isn't the body round?]
(Extract continues)

.

M: *Nanti boleh angkat beg angkat payung semua sekali. Nak?* [Then you can carry your bag and umbrella]
S: *Tak nak lah* [Don't want, lah].
   Nanti orang semua cakap eh empat tangan dia ada [Then people will say I have four hands].

Saffiya resorts to loaning words from English when speaking in Malay, as in the following instances:

M: *Tengah main dengan apa tu?* [What are you playing with?]
S: Dough.
M: Dough *dalam Bahasa Melayu apa?* [What is dough in Malay?]
S: *Tak tau* [Don't know].

.

S: *Habis tak ada* colour *hitam* [Then there isn't any black colour].

.

S: *Dah tu taruk* body? [After that put the body on?]

.

S: *Ah, ini* press press [Ah, this press press].
S: *Badan kan* round? [Isn't the body round?]

.

S: OK, *sekarang* shoe [OK, now shoe].

However, when speaking English she only uses one Malay word in the transcript:

S: Wait become *gila* [mad].

But Saffiya does attach a Malay suffix to an English adjective to make a verb:

S: *Kita* long-*kan* [let me lengthen it].

In the following exchange Saffiya learns the Malay word for 'body', *badan*, and makes it part of her usage later on. Children learn from this form of overt question-and-answer as a part of learning the common-sense knowledge of their environment.

M: *Dah itu?* [After that?]
S: *Dah tu taruh body* [After that put the body on].
M: Body *apa?* [What body?]
S: (No verbal response)
M: *Badan.*
S: *Badan.*
.
S: *Badan kan* round? [Isn't the body round?]
.
N: After the head is what? What are you doing now?
S: *Taruh badan* [Put (the) head (on)].

She also makes enquiries when she does not know a word:

N: Got toes or not to make after the legs?
S: I don't know how to make toes.
M: *Ada jari tak?* [Are there fingers?]
S: *Apa jari?* [What (is) jari?]
M: *Jari kaki* [Toes].
S: *Kita tak tau buat* [I don't know how to make].

Saffiya is aware of and can employ conversational strategies such as backchannelling to maintain the conversation:

M: *Taruh rambut atas kepala* [Put the hair on the head].
S: Uh huh.
.
N: Now are you putting on the legs, is it?
S: Uh huh.
.
M: *Kenapa kaki pendak sangat?* [Why are the legs so short?]
S: Uh huh lah.

She also shows cognitive development in her ability to categorize the parts of the body in terms of a relationship of meronymy:

(Superordinate)   orang (people)

(Meronymy)   badan   tangan   rambut   kaki
                [body]   [hand]   [hair]   [legs]

and seems to have a grasp of causal enhancement in Malay:

S: *Tak nak lah* [Don't want lah].
   Nanti orang semua cakap eh dia empat tangan ada [Then people will say that I have four hands].

What Saffiya is saying here is that if she makes a dough doll with four hands, then people will say that she has four hands. In this way Saffiya displays her ability to reason based on her knowledge of the world. It is also worthwhile noting that Saffiya, in order to argue her point, has to use a clause complex in Malay.

Saffiya, as with other children's language in the data, uses CSE as her target language in her conversation, as does Norwita because this is an informal situation. Examples would be the pragmatic particle 'lah' which is common in informal situations as a marker of intimacy. The subject noun phrase is also missing from many utterances such as:

S: Make people.

S: But what for? Wait become *gila* [mad].

And finally, some other features of CSE that can be found in Saffiya's speech are the missing copula, subject and verb, as in the following examples:

S: This one lah.

S: Yeah lah.

S: Playing with bun.

S: Make people.

S: Then the dough white.

S: No need.

The next example was collected from a preschool environment where children of different ages interact quite naturally, using English and Mandarin. So here the children are outside of the immediate environment of the home and for many it may be their first exposure to English.

Example 5

Michelle, 4 yrs; 2 mths (M). Sally, 4 yrs; 2 mths (S). Barbara, 2 yrs; 9 mths (B).

This example shows children playing among themselves. They use the colloquial variety of English as that is their target language, but also, they code-mix and eventually code-switch in Mandarin because of the communicative needs involved in the context. The activity is one that takes place in a play group. The three children are playing with Lego bricks. M has just made a 'birthday cake' for S. B is another child in the play group.

S: Wah. My birthday so nice. My birthday nice (Stands up).
M: Baby you like it?
S: (nods)
M: Like it ho?
S: Ah. No. I sister.
M: OK. Mummy put flower first. Flower, OK. OK. Little bit put here.
S: Ah. I don't want put there. I want put here (does so). So funny ah.
M: You like it or not?
S: Wait first ah mummy (goes off).
M: OK you mummy wait.
B: *Wo yao qu* [I want to go to the toilet] (goes off).
M: Comes back the birthday.
S: You say what's the number? (walks back to M)
M: Five dollar.
S: Yah. Five dollar.
M: (to S) Ten...six dollar then can go.
   You must give me six dollar money.
B: (runs back) Sally, you got to wear shirt only.
S: Must wear uniform shirt (runs off).
B: You see, this wore shirt only. (to M) Michelle wore shirt.
M: (to S) *Nimen kan shenme?* [What are you looking at?]
S: (whispers) Uniform shirt wear.
M: (nods knowingly) Ooh.
B: Wore shirt only.
M: *Na-ge bu-shi Auntie T-shirt ma?* [Isn't that Auntie's T-shirt?]
S: Hah?

M: *Wo shi you kan mama kan meimei dai* [I've seen mummy and younger sister wear it]. Birthday *yao-bu-yao?* [Do you want birthday or not?] *Yao ni jiu guaiguai* [If you want, be good].

S: *Wo chuan nide qian* [I wear your money]. *Kan wo, wo chuan hen mei hç.* [Look at me, I look very beautiful wearing it, right?]

M: *Jiejie hen mei* [Elder-sister looks very beautiful].

B: *Wo mai xin-de* [I buy a new one].

M: Mm. *Wo yao gei* Auntie May [I want to give it to Auntie May].
   (holds up the cake) Wah. So *zhong* ah [So heavy ah].

S: I help you hold.

M: Hold ah, *kuai-dian* [quickly].

(Both M and S get ready to walk off)

(Khoo, 1987)

This example, we would suggest, is typical of the multilingual situations in which we find the new varieties of English being used. There is obviously a richer range of discourse options available and accommodation is made in order to achieve effective communication given the nature of the situation and the participants. Also, the children are using a number of learning strategies: contradicting (Ah. I don't want put there), taxonomising (shirt, uniform shirt, T-shirt), linking cause and effect (if you want, be good), observation (*Jiejie hen mei*). There is a movement from the CSE into Mandarin. The main reason for this code-switching would seem to be that M is the dominant figure in the conversation and she frames the language to be used: *Nimen kan shenme?* [What are you looking at?] Gradually the code is switched following the rule of adjacency pairs where the first speaker establishes the relevant expectations of the subsequent speaker.

The preschool setting of kindergarten is probably the first formal environment where the child has to effectively communicate over long periods of the day and the languages at the child's disposal are essentially CSE and other language(s) that the child may be familiar with. This 'linguistic' experience, therefore, becomes a crucial stage in the preparation for formal schooling as the child no longer has the immediate support of the family and has to accommodate to the outside world in order to communicate effectively.

A final example comes from a situation where three languages are being used by a child to clarify a situation where communication is in danger of breaking down.

Example 6

Chonghui, (m) 7 yrs; 6 mths
The father is an officer in the army and the mother a graduate teacher. Chonghui

(CH) has one younger brother aged 5; 5. The languages used within the family are English, Mandarin (M) and Hokkien (H). At the time of this recording CH and his grandmother (GM) are talking about travelling to Johor Bahru, Malaysia.

CH: *Wo baba shuo ta yao mingtian yao qu* (M) [My father said that he might want to go to J.B. tomorrow].

GM: J.B.?

CH: Johor Bahru.

GM: Johor Bahru *ai ki, abbna ai ki lo* (H) [Grandma would like to come along].

CH: *Ai ki?* (H) [Want to go?]

GM: *Ha nah.* (H) *Shi lo,* (M) *hao-bbo?* (H) [Yes. Is it alright with you?]

CH: *Bu-dong, bu-dong* (M) [I'm not sure].

GM: Bus *ko-yi zo bbo?* (H) [Can the bus take all of us?]

CH: *Ni you* passport *ma?* (M) [Do you have a passport?]

GM: *Wu, abbna wu* passport (H) [Yes, Grandma has a passport].

CH: Expire-*le ma?* (M) [Is it expired yet?]

GM: Huh?

CH: *Bbo-liao.* (H) A, *hai zai...* (M) [It means 'no more'].

GM: *Sim-bbnih* expire? (H) [What is the meaning of expire?]

CH: (looks at researcher) How do you say 'expire' in Hokkien?

(Wee, 1992)

Again, this example shows clearly that new varieties of English can only be fully understood in the multilingual environment out of which they have developed. In this interaction the seven-year-old child uses three languages, Mandarin, Hokkien and English, to maintain the conversation. Indeed it is interesting how he uses the resources of all three languages, for example: the use of the defining clause *Bbo-liao* (It means) in Hokkien. This shows the child using the appropriate language as the Grandmother mainly understands Hokkien, but the word 'expire' he can only express in Mandarin (*hai zai*) or English — thus the appeal to the researcher for help. The child's dominant languages, English and Mandarin, are used to support a third language, Hokkien, which is necessary in this context to maintain the conversation structure so that it does not break down.

Conclusion

What we can see from these examples is that much of what a child hears is related to observable features of the environment, allowing the child to make ready connections between what is said and the significance of the utterance. Indeed, what the child hears will be incidental as members of his or her meaning group go about the business of everyday life. Social reality is learned indirectly through the accumulated experience of numerous small events (Halliday, 1978). The child is surrounded by sustained modelling of language in a variety of contexts. Older language users unconsciously make visible to the child the functions and forms of language. At certain points, the child will choose to engage in this ongoing linguistic enterprise, or the adult will attempt to engage the child at a level which he or she can manage (Painter, 1984). The primary caregivers, because they have shared the contexts of growth of the child's meaning system and unconsciously tracked its progress, are able to gauge what the child is capable of comprehending and, more importantly, what would constitute a reasonable challenge for the child. The ability to switch language in order to cope with this challenge is an important asset in the learning process. In the course of interaction, the caregiver will employ in one or more languages such strategies as supplying the child with appropriate words or 'chunks', elaborating on these chunks, extending the child's offering in various ways, prompting and guiding by asking questions and jointly reconstructing shared experiences. Because such modelling is usually based on the child's initial attempt at meaning, the child is more likely to be perceptive to the adult's intervention. Through this guided interaction, the adult is providing a 'scaffold' which will be gradually withdrawn as the child becomes more competent in that area (Bruner, 1983; 1986). But the learner, too, develops various strategies to facilitate learning. Halliday (1992) has outlined a number of these strategies.

- *Moving into new domains*
  The child will venture into new semantic domains when confronted with new contextual demands. Typical of this would be our last example, where the child tries to find the equivalent term in Hokkien for 'expire'.
- *Refining distinctions*
  The child constantly elaborates the system networks by refining distinctions that have already been made and developing increasingly delicate options both in terms of grammar and the lexis. In Example 4 we saw some of this happening with Saffiya when she says: *Nanti orang semua cakap eh dia empat tangan ada* [Then people will say that I have four hands]. Not only is Saffiya trying to reason something out but in order to do this, she uses clause complexing.
- *Deconstructing linked variables*
  The system is in a constant state of construction, deconstruction and reconstruction as each new perturbation leads the child to make new connections, often forcing the adjustment or relinquishing of previous 'knowledge'. In Example 3 the conversation shows the child having to readjust her thinking process to accommodate new knowledge.

Example 3

A: What about this?
E: *fu* [trousers in Cantonese].
A: *fu?*
E: Yes.
A: Are you sure?
E: *fu* so (also)- [f] - [f] so ***
A: Are they the same?
E: No.
A: Why are not the same? Tell me.
E: This one cannot — this one can.
A: Cannot what?
E: Cannot to *jiok fu* — then so hard to *jiok* [to wear].

- *Chunking*
  In addition to revealing the probabilities of the system, the learning of large stretches of 'wording' as uninterrupted wholes plays an important part in language development. Example 5 illustrates this with Michelle switching over to Mandarin and although Barbara initially replies in English, Michelle continues in Mandarin until the whole exchange shifts to Mandarin for several utterances.

- *Repetition*
  The repetition of 'chunks' of language allows the child to 'model the language as a probabilistic system' (Halliday, 1988: 13). In learning which options occur most frequently, the child is able to sequence the learning of grammar. Exemplification of this point would need a much more extensive database than the examples used here, but as an indication of what happens, we can see Saffiya interacting with Norwita (the researcher) and using a lexical verb in various grammatical structures.

Example 4

N: *Saffiya nak kasi bunga tak?* [Do you want to give flowers?]
S: *Kita nak tapi mama tak beli* [I want but Mama didn't buy any].
N: *OK mama belikan nak?* [OK shall Mama buy them?]
.

.
S: *Kita beli?* [I buy?]
N: *Kenapa tak boleh?* [Why cannot?]
S: *Dia beli lah kasi kita kasi cikgu* [You buy for me to give to the teachers].

Halliday (1994) describes language as a 'dynamic open system' in that such a system persists only through constantly changing in interaction with the environment. As the child engages in particular contexts of situation, certain demands are made upon his or her linguistic resources. The child's language develops in response to the current challenge. On the basis of these encounters, the child constructs transitional mini-paradigms which are specific to the contexts of situation in which he or she is engaging (Halliday, 1975). With each new change in context, the child may need to renovate these mini-paradigms by processes of addition, modification or complete reconstruction.

The expansion of the child's meaning potential, then, is not simply a matter of constantly adding new options to existing subsystems, but rather involves the constant reconstrual of the system in the light of new linguistic experiences. Painter (1992) points out that developments within the child's meaning potential enable new ways of thinking and learning, and that in the course of using the enriched language system, the learner may be alerted to new possibilities for meaning. Language development is thus seen as a series of implication sequences — certain options need to be available within the system before further development can take place. The argument put forward here is that in contexts where the new varieties of English exist, there is often a multilingual situation such that the child can increase the options available by being able to use more than one language to further development not only in linguistic skills but also thinking skills.

However, there is a major dilemma facing societies like Singapore. We have indicated that in the home the dominant form of English that is used will be Colloquial Singapore English. The question is how Singapore children can develop the ability to use not just the colloquial variety but also a standard variety. For children to learn the standard variety, it is important for them to be exposed to this standard variety and in Singapore this only seems possible through education, the mass media and reading. Kwan-Terry's (1991) study, for instance, indicates an increase in the use of English and Chinese (meaning Mandarin) in the home, which she also suggests might be due to the large number of people in the younger generation receiving English-medium education and to parental awareness of the importance of English in Singapore. This is supported, as we have seen earlier, by the 1990 census figures. However, what Kwan-Terry's study also shows is that as a result of the awareness among parents of the importance of English, a sizeable proportion of them who do not use English in speaking with their spouse but who have a fair command of the language, choose to introduce it through interaction with their children. In most of the cases cited in the study, the parents do not restrict themselves to the predominant use of English in speaking with their children but resort to code-switching between Chinese and English. It is often the father, probably because of his better command of English, rather than the mother, who uses both Chinese and English. As for the youngest generation, interaction among siblings is marked by an even greater increase in the use of English and Chinese. This can be accounted for partly by the encouragement the children have from their parents to use English and partly because they are all attending English-medium schools. Also, Kwan-Terry supports Gupta's claim that the variety of English used in these interactions, especially among children, is the colloquial variety rather than Standard Singapore English, as it is the colloquial variety that is used in non-formal situations. Kwan-Terry further argues that parents who speak English with their children in the home are mostly those who have had an English-medium education or who have had a Chinese-medium education at secondary level or above, and they too use the colloquial variety. Consequently, exposure to the more formal variety of English has to come mainly through television, radio and reading (newspapers and popular magazines). Evidence from Kwan-Terry's study shows that in the case of children from homes where English is used as the dominant language, the reading habit is acquired early. But about 40% of the children from other language backgrounds do not develop a regular reading habit and do not read any books outside their school texts. Effectively what this means is that entry into the formal school system is for most of these children the most likely occasion for any extensive exposure to a standard form of English. This is the topic we have to address in the next chapter.

Chapter 10

Language in the School

Joseph A. Foley

❧ The Background

Formal education is a superimposed second-order culture which consists of schemes of conceptual organization and behaviour designed to supplement the first-order processes of the primary socialization of family upbringing. The language of the classroom (both spoken and written) which gives access to educational knowledge is, therefore, both a tool for learning and learning itself. Education engenders special varieties, patterns of language that are specific to learning in school — including not only teacher-talk but also the language of the textbooks and other learning materials. So when children go to school, their language is recast into a new form, namely, as written language. As adults, we often tend to think of writing and reading as just a new channel, a new medium: children already know the fundamentals of language; they are now going to learn to process language visually. If we think of literacy as in any way changing children's language, we usually mean this — changing from the colloquial variety to the standard form of the language. We do not think of it as changing the way they mean (Halliday, 1995). In multilingual societies it can often happen that the language that the child becomes literate in may not be the dominant language of the home. Normally it is government policy that determines what languages are to be used in the formal education system.

This is the case in Singapore where literacy in the official languages reflects the government's campaigns to promote literacy, particularly in English and Chinese (Mandarin):

Language	1970	1980	1990
English	46.7	56.0	65.0
Chinese	49.4	59.6	61.5
Malay		16.6	16.0
Tamil		3.3	3.4

(Gopinathan, 1995: 68)

Table 1. Literacy in Official Languages: 1970, 1980, 1990
(expressed in percentages of the population)

The general literacy in Singapore went up from 52.3% in 1957 to 90% in 1990; those who were biliterate made up 46% of the population. These figures would change considerably if the age factor was considered, in that the section of the population under forty is more likely to be biliterate (English plus another language) than those over forty. In other words, in terms of language development more and more children are entering the formal education system with some degree of literacy in more than one language.

Following from what was said in Chapter 9 on early language development, the acquisition of a level of literacy begins to take on a central role around the age of five or six because children are just reaching the stage in their languages of socialization when they can handle meanings that are abstract: they can construe entities that have no perceptual correlate, like honour, duty, *tu-tsao* (creativity) and such like. This has two important consequences. First, it means that they can cope with abstract symbols, like letters or characters, and the abstract concepts that go with them (including the critical distinction between writing and drawing); so they can now master this new medium. Second, it means that they can cope with abstract categories, and so are ready to explore new forms of knowledge. In other words, they are ready for a reshaping of their previous experience.

However, in the social context where the new varieties of English have developed, the language used in the educational process has played a dominant role. The influence of pedagogical theories from the mainstream of educational practice and research has inevitably come from the countries where the 'old varieties' of English dominate. The indigenization of 'received' forms of a language, in particular, although not exclusively English, have often sat uncomfortably with the pedagogical theories. This stems from the problem of whether or not certain theoretical frameworks formulated in a particular society carry with them the normative values and dominant ideologies of that society. If we look at the indigenization process of the new varieties of English within the context of the school, a major consideration is the exogenous influences on the language curriculum. There is, of course the intended (as distinct from the implemented and achieved) curriculum as reflected in the English Language syllabuses and prescribed textbooks. There is an implicit assumption that since teachers follow the syllabuses, textbooks and instructional materials rather closely, the concepts and theories that have influenced the thinking in these materials are likely to have the greatest impact on practice in the classroom.

The Historical Background

Howatt (as quoted in Ho, 1994) noted that there was largely an unquestioned assumption that English should be taught in colonial schools in essentially the same way as in the mother country. The basic educational aim was the assimilation of British culture through the medium of 'English literature' (the same can be said for the USA). There was little or no provision for language work specially designed to help the non-native learner, and school grammars such as *Nesfield* were originally written to help children succeed in passing the Oxford and Cambridge Local Examinations. So in many of the colonized countries controlled by Britain, the sort of textbooks that could be found would be *The Beacon Readers*, *Janet and John Basic Readers* and the *Oxford English Course* (Ho, 1994).

Historically, then, the new varieties of English developed mainly in areas that were connected to British colonial rule and although Britain has few colonies left, its sphere of influence is still very great. In Commonwealth countries where English had a significant role to play in society, the influence of the British-regulated examination boards was such that they set the syllabuses, and the British model of teacher training unconsciously promoted the view that what was right for Britain as far as the English language was concerned would also be of value overseas. Also, in many of the countries in which the new varieties developed, English-stream schools became the elite schools and taught English with grammatical norms set by educated native speakers in Britain and codified for teaching purposes in terms of a grammar which was originally based on Latin. The textbooks used, imported from Britain and written by writers from Britain, had a curricular orientation and principles of teaching that were more relevant to English-speaking children in Britain. It is true that from the mid-sixties onwards publishers in Britain did encourage 'local' writers to use their expertise to write or adapt textbooks and we can see this as a first stage in the process of indigenization in textbook provision. However, most of the language study in schools was a preparation for the School Certificate examinations still controlled directly or indirectly by outside agencies such as the Overseas Cambridge Examination system. This meant that the syllabus for the School Certificate inevitably determined the content of the secondary school language syllabus as a whole and the methodology of teaching (Ho, 1994).

However, parallel to the elite schools in most of the colonial administered territories, there were the non-English medium schools using local languages. The language syllabuses of these schools used different reference points — a maintaining of the local (at least dominant) languages and yet at the same time a willingness to learn from the colonial authorities. The sources for textbooks and other teaching materials could be varied. But in colonial territories where Chinese was a dominant language, such as Hongkong, Singapore and certain parts of Malaysia, Chinese language textbooks were often sourced from mainland China or later, Taiwan. Thus there was a lack of fit between the western orientation of parts of the curriculum and a language syllabus that was based on other cultural traditions (Ho, 1994).

In the early sixties the English language as a subject in the non-English medium schools was coming more and more under the influence of new theories on teaching English as a foreign language. From the very early days of the introduction of English as a subject in the school curriculum, the methodology had been characterized mainly by the grammar translation approach. English was seen as simply another subject area aimed at providing students with a reading knowledge of English through the study of English grammar. Selected texts were studied and basic grammatical principles were applied together with the necessary vocabulary in order to understand the texts. The purpose of language study was essentially mastery of the language structure, with little attempt at genuine communication in English. The post-independence period for many of the former colonies saw an increase in scholars being sent abroad to Britain, the USA, Australia, New Zealand and Canada for training. This was particularly true of English. The majority of these scholars were trained as Teachers of English as a Foreign or Second Language (TEFL/TESL). Such methodology drew selectively on the principles of educational psychology which favoured discrete point and habituation in language learning. New technologies developed through the sixties could be grouped under the general heading of audio-visual approaches. Another important factor was that entry into many English-medium universities depended upon reaching a certain standard on the TOEFL examination (Test of English as a Foreign Language) which itself had been developed around discrete language item recognition and where repetition as a pedagogic technique seemed the most fruitful way of preparing for the examination. Such exam preparation had a washback effect on the pedagogical approaches taken by the teacher.

In addition, access to education for an ever-growing section of the population in the former colonial territories and the ever-widening internationalization of English meant that English was being used in other subject areas in the curriculum as well. Teachers trained in Britain, the USA, Australia and so on, brought with them a methodology that was English as a foreign language. Elitist schooling had to give way to programmes that embraced education-for-all and this meant many children who had little or no background using English at home. The elitist schools had to absorb the new English syllabuses which were revised and redesigned along the lines of the structural approach to English Language teaching. This is not to say that the old British grammar school tradition in literature teaching disappeared completely; it still had a powerful influence in the elitist schools but it was definitely on the wane.

The syllabuses for English were now designed mainly from the descriptive-structural grammar advocated by Fries (1952) and Hornby (1966). So language instruction consisted of sentence drills, substitution tables, transformations and guided compositions. The reading material was based on graded structure patterns with a limited vocabulary. Also, this view of the descriptive-structural grammarians led to a general interest in contrastive analysis for the explanation of students' errors. Examinations mainly built around multiple-choice questions became the norm and these used as distractors 'errors' that students might be expected to make (Ho, 1994).

It is probably true, even today to say that the dominant paradigm for English language teaching in those countries where the New Englishes have developed is based on methodologies which are more appropriate for the teaching of English as a foreign language. Yet it would be incorrect to label all learners in these countries as foreign-language learners; they would at least be second-language learners because English is used as a functional language in their own cultural context. The degree of functional use will depend to a greater or lesser extent on the contextual variations, which can be extremely complex. It might therefore be more useful to consider countries where these new varieties have developed in terms of a cline depending on whether English has an official or semi-official status, whether English is one of the main mediums of education and how functional English is in the community at large.

However, in countries where there is a perceived new variety of English, most syllabuses tend to be eclectic in that they consist of a combination of structural, situational, skills-based and task-based features. Only in a few countries has there been a conscious effort to teach English as the dominant language. That is to say that the methods of English teaching from primary school onwards presuppose a dominance of English in the home environment. As we have indicated in the previous chapter, in the context of Singapore and Malaysia there has been a clear separation in the paths taken. Malaysia sees English as very much in the role of a second language while Singapore has moved slowly but quite markedly into using the methodologies of English as the dominant language of education — using a first-language approach to teaching. This was clearly discernible in Singapore with the introduction in the early eighties of language-based projects in lower primary schools that were based on English as the L1. Two programmes had particularly significant impact on English language teaching. Both REAP (Reading and English Acquisition Programme) and LEAP (Language Activity Programme) were based on 'real language and real situations and a reliance on the pupil himself to set some of the parameters of his own learning' (Somerville-Ryan, 1985: 15). The objectives of these programmes were to move away from rather structured teaching strategies towards methods which stressed language as a 'tool' for communication within society. The new English syllabus introduced in 1991 was built around the same objectives of 'real language in real situations', with the emphasis on English as the dominant language of the child.

In principle, the variety of English taught in school is that of a standard form of English. Whether that be Standard Singapore English or a standard form of English based on British English is very much open to debate. There is no doubt that in the context of many countries where a new variety of English is developing, exonormative standards are still considered the models for the syllabus, for curriculum materials and, indeed, examinations. For example, *A University Grammar of English* (Quirk and Greenbaum, 1973) and dictionaries such as the *Longman Dictionary of Contemporary English* (1978) are standard reference books in the preparation of local textbooks or materials by the teachers. Yet in reality the model of English in the classroom will often show indigenization. A good example of this was shown in research done by Saravanan and Gupta (1997) on trainee teachers in Singapore. They looked at trainees' journals during their teaching practice which indicated certain syntactic structures that differed from the exonormative standard officially sanctioned in Singapore (pronunciation and lexis also differed, but this was not the focus of their study). An examination of the data showed that the differences in syntactic structures could be grouped into three categories.

In the first category there was variation in syntactic constructions such as concord and control over tenses. The trainees were able to identify such constructions because they occurred in simple clause structures and consequently labelled them as 'errors'. However, identical constructions existed in the trainees' writing and they did not seem to be able to identify them in the more complex clause structures found in extended discourse. If these were simply 'slips of the pen', they would be occasional rather than systematic. What was found in the trainee teachers' writings was fairly consistent as indicated by the following examples:

Infinitive Form
A trainee provided the following sentence in which she thought the faulty construction had appeared:

I have *to helped* him even if he is not my friend.

And yet trainees would write in their journals:

...and this concern must be manifested clearly to the students as it will serve *to motivated* them further.

Subject-verb agreement
Example from a student: *We doesn't know.*
Example from a teacher: Students may not gain much from pair-conferencing when you have a situation whereby one student *dominate* the other.

A second category consisted of syntactic constructions that might be considered as developmentally too complex for secondary school students to produce at this stage but which trainees used in their writing. The particular focus was on subject-verb agreement in subordinate clauses and number agreement within the noun phrase.
Examples from the teachers' own writing:

> Other *mistakes* that *reflects* inconsistencies in sentences include...
> *One of the story* involved visitors in the wax museum being chased after by two dinosaurs.

Crewe (1977) pointed out that in Singapore English adjectives and verbs are commonly formed by the addition of *-ed*. This can generate forms, such as *curioused, anxioused, understanded*, that the trainees commented upon in their pupils' work. The trainees themselves produced forms such as:

> In conclusion, the learners displayed *diversed* learning attitudes and interest levels.
> He *feedbacked* that...

Constructions in the third category that differ from the exonormative standards can be considered as already well-established in Singapore English. These include the use of *when/while*, *wh-questions* and the use of *modals*. There is evidence from classroom teaching notes and journal entries that these forms are being explicitly taught in English language grammar lessons as the norm, and trainees are not aware that these differ from exonormative standards.

According to the syllabus, there is a difference between the uses of *when* and *while*, based on exonormative standards; however, the lack of emphasis on these differences may not be obvious either to teachers or to learners. In fact, it turned out that the trainees did not distinguish between the two words; in their formal writing, they used the word *when* at times when Standard English would use the word *while*.
For example:

> *When* being interviewed he protested...
> *While* instruction was given to the students to begin reading...

One of the trainees was teaching the following in the grammar class:

The chauffeur says he was playing billiards *when* the criminal's wife,
Lily, was performing her act on stage at the Savoy.

In a discussion between the researchers and the trainee held prior to the
lesson, it became clear that she did not know that there was a difference
between the two words, *when* and *while*.

Of course, teacher use alone does not lead to the establishment of forms.
Teachers' awareness of an exonormative standard enables them to identify
'deviations' from this norm in their pupils' work in order to make it conform
to exonormative standards. However, when teachers are not aware of such
a standard, they transmit syntactic knowledge that can lead to the
establishment of indigenized forms, thereby helping to institutionalize an
indigenized variety of English. It could, of course, be said that such an
argument would depend upon the level of the trainees' English but some of
the syntactic patterns were found to be so pervasive and systematic that
they were used by trainees who had studied for four years in British universities
and spoke with an RP accent. The point is that certain syntactic
constructions (and this is even more clearly discernable in phonological
and lexical features) can become established because they are transmitted
unconsciously by teachers who think that these are the norm (Saravanan
and Gupta, 1997).

Pedagogical Frameworks and the Functional Use of Language

This leads us to one of the major topics treated in this present volume:
What framework can one use if one believes that a new variety of English
is developing? Three approaches have been suggested for such an analysis
(Gupta, 1994): one, that the new varieties are imperfectly learnt Standard
English and that therefore their features are errors; two, that the new varieties
are not to be considered deficient but are most usefully analysed in terms of
their differences from better-known varieties such as Standard British English;
three, that these new varieties are dialects of English and best analysed on
their own terms within a given community.

The following extract from a class discussion on 'errors' gives some
indication of the insecurity teachers and students feel when discussing what
is acceptable and what is not, particularly in the written mode.

Example 1

*The teacher (T) is using an overhead projector (OHP) on which is listed a number
of sentences with 'errors' found in the students'(SS) compositions.*

T: OK, what's wrong with thirteen?

S: Beehoon and satay?

T: Because beehoon and satay?...OK, OK. Bala, what's wrong with thirteen?

S: Fry?

T: Satay you fry? You know how to cook or not?

SS: [?]

T: OK, wait. I'm asking Bala.

SS: [?]

S: Satay you barbecue.

T: Alright, enough. I'm — I'm asking Bala, OK? Yes, Bala?

S: My mother cooked.

T: My mother cooked.

S: Beehoon and satay.

T: But what's wrong with cooked? Nothing wrong with cooked, what.

(Pause)

.

.

T: No, cooked is OK. Cooked OK. Nothing wrong with cooked.

S: [?]

T: He's feeling very bored already.

S: Oh, beehoon you have to separate.

S: Teacher, my grandmother cooked.

T: What is wrong with number thirteen?

S: [?] and cooked not specific

T: No, not necessarily.

SS: No just my.

T: Satay is a Malay word...So — OK, yes, satay is a Malay word...

S: So that thing.

T: OK, what is that thing?

S: How I know?

SS: The line.

SS: [?]

T: Very good. OK. Yes. So, satay is a Malay word. So you have to put it in inverted commas. What about beehoon? English word?

SS: Chinese.

SS: Chinese word.

T: OK. When — Now remember this OK. When you use, erm —

S: Kiasu.

T: A word that is not — OK, I'm coming to kiasu. When you come — When you use a word that is not — that is not an English word in an Eng — When you write in English and you use a word that is not English, you must put it in inverted commas. OK? Now, but kiasu — I don't know whether it's this class or another class. I don't allow kiasu in the — in the composition, OK? What is the difference?

S: Singlish.

T: Singlish. OK, but why beehoon and satay is OK?

S: [? Because of the satay]

S: Because there is another word for it.

T: OK, there — Very good. OK, she got it. Kiasu, there's an — there's — You can use English words to replace kiasu. OK? So, therefore it is not acceptable. Alright, if I use the word makan, is it acceptable?

S: No.

T: Not acceptable because —

SS: [?]

T: There is an English equivalent. Alright, but beehoon and satay, can you translate into English?

SS: Yes.

SS: No.

T: Well, maybe you can but it'll be too difficult, too complicated. So, therefore...

S: [?]

T: OK, well, speaking of that, some — somewhere — I read — I heard somewhere that satay actually comes from a word — from, er, erm, what is it. A Hokkien word meaning three pieces...

SS: Satay.

SS: [?]

T: OK, but of course the — the — this is not for sure. OK, never mind.

SS: [?]

T: Because satay does come in three pieces, right? Alright, anyway, never mind about the origins. OK, word like satay and beehoon, there's no direct translation into English. OK, no direct translation into English. Therefore, it is acceptable, but — Are you all listening?

SS: Yes.

T: It is acceptable but if you use it, you must put it within inverted commas, OK? And words that are not in English but you can find English translation, do not use it, OK?...OK, let me give you examples. OK, kampong. Can you use kampong, Amin?

S: Yes.

S: No.

S: Cannot.

S: Village.

T: Alright, it is because you can use village. Unless the kampong comes in a name. Kampong Glam. Of course you cannot say Glam Village.

SS: (Laughing)

T: Alright, if it's a name. In certain cases, I think — We leave this to your common sense in a way, OK? Sometimes you have to decide whether the word is acceptable or not. Alright, kiasu is definitely out...Alright, erm...Now, number fourteen shows a serious mistake.

(Tan, 1997)

Tolerance within the formal education system is, of course, a problem as it is this very system which is supposed to be the chief purveyor of a standard model. But as we have indicated earlier, this is not as straightforward as it may appear. Most teachers want guidelines and models and are happy to place into the system a chosen model of standard language. At the same time, the general public can exert considerable pressure. This can be illustrated by the following letter written to the major English language newspaper in Singapore:

TCS (Television Corporation of Singapore) should watch grammar

I am sure the latest TCS sitcom "Can I Help You?" will be well-received. Kudos to the show's producers for the splendid effort.

But it is unfortunate that a show with such a large target audience has grammatical errors. Take the show's title, "Can I Help You?". The word "can" expresses the doer's ability and power to execute a task. The correct word to use is "may". "May I help you?" correctly expresses an employee seeking a customer's permission to render him assistance. There was also a "Pantry room" in the show. "Room" is redundant, as "pantry" means a room for storing food or utensils.

It is heartening to note that the producers have gone through great lengths to inject local flavour into the sitcom. But such fundamental errors cannot go unchecked, especially when a large proportion of viewers are impressionable students who might pick the errors up and use them.

(*The Straits Times*, Saturday, 14 September 1996)

However, the passing on of normative values is only one aspect of an education system which uses English as the medium of instruction in the context of a developing new variety. Indeed it may be even more crucial to consider whether the pedagogical approach is suitable. That is to say, can the linguistic and pedagogical environment lead to the scaffolding necessary for the development of educational knowledge?

The major determining factor in deciding what sort of pedagogical approach should be taken is to consider how much English is used functionally in society. In Singapore, English is clearly used very widely. But if we take another society, similar in a number of ways to Singapore — for example, Mauritius — we may have a different sort of picture. Mauritius is a multilingual and multicultural island where English is the medium of instruction in education, and used in the judiciary and government. Yet Mauritius is unlikely to develop a new variety of English because English has little or no function outside of the domains indicated above. French creole is the lingua franca across the population while French is the main language used in the mass media (Foley, 1995). What effect this can have in the classroom and on the amount of control the students have in English can be seen from the following example.

Example 2

This is a Primary 6 English composition class, considered as above average in that the extract was recorded in one of the better schools in Mauritius. The teacher is outlining a guided composition based on a series of pictures from the textbook.

T: Premièrement, what is maybe the title...?
   A cyclone or the cyclone?
   Look at the first picture.
   What can you see in the first picture?
   Yes...? The cyclone.
   What about the house?
   The family in the house? How are they?
   They are worried right?
(Later)
   How is the house? Look at the roof?
   How do we say?
   Couler.
   How do we say in English?
S: Leak.
T: Where have they taken refuge?
   Quand ça? When?
   On vient de passer dans un cyclone.
   Quand?
   Comment on peut commencer.
   Allez, Last Friday. Last weekend ou bien last Sunday.
   On peut commencer?
   Allez qui peut répondre à cette question là?

                                                    (Foley, 1995: 215)

There is obviously considerable code-mixing and code-switching going on mainly because the teacher realizes that the children are not sufficiently familiar with English to use it effectively in writing. Even after five years of English in primary school, the students cannot use the language functionally simply because there is little opportunity to practise outside of the classroom. There would seem to be little possibility of any real educational scaffolding, at least through the medium of English in this particular context. Thus it is also highly improbable that the school system can lay the foundation for the development of a new variety of English as we suggest may be happening in Singapore.

If we turn to an English lesson in a Singapore school with a similar age group (Primary 5) and contrast the use of English in this classroom we will see that the children are using English effectively as their dominant language.

Example 3

T: We shall begin our English Lesson today with Silent Reading. Now for today, you will not read your own book. I want you to read this [?] article.

(T distributes handouts to SS. SS do Silent Reading: Approx. 2 mins.)

.

T: Alright, I think all of you have finished reading the passage. Put the passage away. I gave you an assignment last week and I asked you to create your own fantastic machine. Now, I have looked through all the drawings that you have done and I am very satisfied that some of you have come up with very imaginative inventions. I would like to show you a few of them. (T shows on OHT) So, this is one of them...A diamond-making machine. Who did this?

(S puts up hand)

And we have here another one. A machine that can bring us to space. Let's look at this one...a machine that can help me. Who did this? (S puts up hand) Can you tell us why you want fire here. Yes? Rosman.

S1: Tell lah.

T: Why do you want fire — here? What's the fire for?

R: To [?]

T: To?

R: To burn [?]

T: To burn animals?

(class laughs)

S2: Enemies.

T: Enemies? To burn enemies. And what about this box here? What's this box for?

R: For [?]

T: [?] For studying? To give you light for studying?

(R nods head in agreement)

T: Now, I would like you to look at this very fantastic machine.

(T shows on OHT)

SS: Waaaaahh!

T: Who drew this? (S puts up hand) Can you tell me what you have in your mind, what you have in your mind when you drew this?

SS: [?] (laughter)

T: Yes?

S3: Can help me do the housework.

T: To help you do the housework?

S3: Yes.

T: Do you have to do all the housework at home?

S3: Yes, little bit.

T: Little bit?

S4: Can help her mother what.

T: Oh, because she can help her mother do the housework. Alright, that's good. ... Now, I would like to tell you about somebody, Professor Thomas. He had invented a fantastic machine that could travel in space. So, one fine morning, he set off on a mission to visit Mars with three other astronauts. Suddenly, their machine broke down and they were forced to land on an unknown planet. Alright, let me show you.

(T shows pix on OHT)

Who do you think this person is? (T points to figure of an astronaut) Who is this person?

S5: The professor.

T: Yes?

S5: The professor.

T: Yes, the professor. What about this person? (T points to another astronaut) Yes?

S5: Another astronaut.

T: Another astronaut. Do you see this part? (T points to a section of OHT) Who can tell me something about this? Who are these people here?

S6: Astronauts.

T: Yes?

S6: Astronauts.

T: Another two astronauts. What about this one? What do you call this?

S7: Spaceship.

T: You can call this a spaceship. Now, do you have other terms to describe it? Yes?

S8: Spacecraft.

T: Yes?

S8:   Spacecraft.

T: Spacecraft. Any other words? Yes?

S9:   Rocket.

T: Rocket. You can call it a rocket. Any other words? Yes?

S10: [?]

T: Pardon?

S10: Time-machine.

T: Time-machine. Perhaps it's a time-machine. Any other words? Yes?

S11: [?]

T: Pardon?

S11: Saucer.

T: Saucer. Any other words? Alright, let me show you who they met.

(T shows on OHT)

SS: Aiyoohh!

T: Can you give me words to describe this?

S12: Space-creatures.

T: Space-creatures. What other words? Yes?

S13: Aliens.

T: Aliens. What other words? Yes?

S14: Space-creatures.

T: Space-creatures. OK. Yes?

S15: Monsters.

T: Monsters. Alright, somebody says monsters. Alright, look at their building.

SS: Waahh!

T: Look at the building. Alright. Now, I have a task for you and I want you to do it in a group. I'll give you sections of the scene here. And you will get a transparency and I want each group to write as many sentences as possible. You are to write the sentences in the past tense, based on the picture. So, I want the group leaders to come out now.

(Leaders collect materials from T)

(DELL Classroom Data CP1P5, 26 January 1994)

    This class carried on with the 'scaffolding' of their composition by group discussions and eventually produced outcomes which were shared with the whole class. This sort of interaction comes from the teaching methods (as indicated earlier) introduced in the mid-eighties in Singapore based on the teaching of reading and writing as a first language. It is clear that these children were comfortable with English at that stage of their educational career although the sample was taken from a school that was considered very average, that is to say, the population would be mainly from families where English was not the dominant language of the household.

There is, of course, the question of whether these new varieties of English can be effective conveyors of 'educational knowledge', which we would argue is more a question of the pedagogical approaches taken rather than the ability of a new variety to be an effective conveyor of such knowledge. In the next set of examples taken at a ten-year interval we can see how different pedagogical theories can influence the sort of scaffolding through which educational knowledge is built. In the first case, a structural/behaviourist framework was dominant in the language pedagogy in the language classroom at that time.

Example 4

Primary 6 classroom: Preparing to write a composition entitled 'Visiting a Sick Friend'. The teacher has outlined the main points of the composition on the blackboard.

T: You may use the following points:
   Why your friend was ill.
   Where your friend was.
   The visit or visits you paid him or her.
   What you did to help your friend in his or her work.
   How you cheer him up.
   And what happen in the end.
T: (addressing a particular pupil, S1).
T: And did he see a doctor?
S1: Yes.
T: And what did the doctor advise him?
S1: The doctor advised him to go to a...(unclear).
T: Was he badly hurt?
S1: Yes.
T: Was it that serious that he had to be hospitalized?
S1: Yes, it was that serious that he had to be hospitalized.
T: Did he see a doctor?
S1: Yes.
T: And now we come to the second point.
   See whether you know where your friend was at the moment.
   What about you Chai-How?
S2: I think he is at home.
T: And what is he doing at home?
S2: ...er...resting.
T: Did he see a doctor?
S2: Yes.
T: What about you Sheriffa?

S3: She had a bad injury and was to be hospitalized.

T: Did you find how many days she would be in hospital?

S3: ...er...a few days.

T: You can talk about which hospital your friend has been hospitalized. Do you know?
So which hospital?

S3: Tan Tock Seng.

T: Do you plan to visit her?

S3: Once in...once in two days.

T: If your friend is resting at home do you make a point to visit him?

S4: Yes, I make a point to visit him.

T: And what do you do when you visit your friend?

S4: I cheer him up.

T: Anything else to make his life more comfortable?

S4: Yes.

T: For example?

S4: Bring story books for him and tell jokes.

T: Since your friends or your friend will be away for quite some time, he'll be resting at home or he will be in hospital recuperating. Don't you think he will miss his lessons?

S5: Yes.

T: And what would you plan to do?

S5: I plan to help him in his work.

T: How would you plan to help him in his work?

S5: I would tell him all I learn about class.

T: Besides the help you are giving your friend what else would you do to cheer her up?

S6: Well, I would tell her...er...that the things that happen in the class and ...er...I would tell her, the important things that the teacher told us.

T: What else would you cheer your friend up in hospital?

S7: I would cheer him by playing games with him, like chess, scrabbles and computer games.

T: You are all had good friends. I wish I had such good friends like you. But after all your visits how does your friend feel?

S8: Maybe my friend will be very happy and she hope that...er...she hope that I visit her more often.

T: Does she feel better after your visit?

S8: Yes, she does.

T: Finally what happened in the end?

S9: After a few days in hospital she will have...[?]...and return home.

T: What about you Ivan?

S10: After a week he was...has strong enough to go back to school.

He was very grateful to me for helping him during his illness.

T: Now you have some suggestions for you to write your composition. I want you to write about 150 words on this topic.

(Saffiah bte M. Amin, 1984)

This sample of classroom discourse was recorded in 1984; the English syllabus was extremely structuralist and the textbooks followed the syllabus very closely. In fact Yap (1987) showed how clearly the syllabus followed various 'Grade Reader Schemes' mainly designed for adult EFL students in Europe. Although there were different instructional packages developed out of the syllabus: *New English Series for Primary Education* (NESPE) and the *Primary English Programme* (PEP) and at secondary level, *Course in Learning and Using English* (CLUE) and *Correct Use of English* (CUE), the teaching in the classroom reflected a structuralist/behaviourist approach. If we take this as a fairly typical example, it is questionable whether there is any real 'interaction' going on here in the sense of the scaffolding that can lead to educational knowledge. It is more like 'compliance' to 'direction' from the teacher as discussed by Allwright (1984). Allwright would claim that effective interaction to build up educational knowledge comes about when there is 'negotiation' and/or 'navigation' in the classroom. There seems to be little 'negotiation' in this sample of classroom discourse. In fact in many countries where the new varieties of English are developing, it would seem that classroom 'negotiation' occurs rarely as it involves a level of initiative-taking that many learners would find unacceptably 'risky' and many teachers unacceptably challenging. This could be accounted for by a number of reasons within a cultural context but there is little doubt that 'formal language teaching' such as demanded by the structural/behaviourist approach played its part.

'Navigation', on the other hand, should be more frequent: it very often involves a minor diversion from the main lesson topic to something of more direct and immediate interest to at least one of the learners. These diversions, if channelled purposefully by the teacher, can build up a sizeable contribution to the lesson from the individual learners and thus help in the construction of educational knowledge. In the language lesson, it may be simply using genuine communication in the target language. In the science classroom, it may be not only extending the child's knowledge of science, but at the same time his/her network of choices in the target language relevant to the particular register of science.

Also in this example, we have an easily recognizable 'guided composition' class. The type of question and answer paradigm involved in this 'exchange' underlines the effect that language, seen in behaviourist terms, can have on discourse in the classroom. The most obvious characteristics would be the polar-type replies and the repetition of the full utterance which would be highly unusual in real discourse. There is also the change from the recount of a past incident (fictional) to 'What would you do if...', and then back to 'Finally what happened?' There is a 'fuzziness' of the generic structures of the language which inevitably has consequences for the children's written discourse. Therefore, there is no real 'interaction' and it is hard to see how educational knowledge could be developed in this sort of situation.

The next example is from another primary classroom but ten years later. Again the school is considered as average and most of these children would not use English as a dominant language at home.

Example 5

T: I have made a copy of a few compositions [?] the other day. And we are going to do a critic. Right, we are going to do a critic. Before we do that, I want you to pay attention to this worksheet here: What do you think of your partner's essay. Alright? Afterwards you will be checking your partner's essay. And this is what I want you to do. Alright. Read your partner's composition. Right. You read your partner's composition first. Do you find any interesting words or phrases? If you find, you mark it, alright? If you do not, then you mark No. Alright? If Yes, now if you find interesting phrases, underline the most interesting words, phrases or sentence in your friend's composition. Alright? So, afterwards, when we go through some of these compositions, we will think of all these interesting words or sentences and we will underline it. Now when you do that, you use your pencil. Alright? The last time you used a pencil. Have your friend arranged the ideas in a clear manner? Right, for today's composition, the ideas must come from you. Right? [?]

(A few minutes later)

Now let's do one together. I've made a few (photocopied transparencies) which I've picked at random. (T places a composition on OHP) How the giraffe got its long neck. Right. [?] Just look through it first. Can somebody read? Somebody like to get up and read? Ridwan, can you see very clearly? Read that. Edwin, can you read? I'm sure you can see very clearly. Can you read for everybody to hear. I can't see because I've [?] my glasses. OK?

E: Once upon a time, all the giraffes had short necks and their legs were short. Because of their legs, they could not run very fast. At that time, there were many trees but the giraffes could not reach the trees. The greatest problem was when they were eating the grass on the ground, they could not see when something attacks. So when the giraffes were eating, the meat eaters would attack them. The giraffes held a meeting in the forest. The oldest giraffe said, we are getting fewer and fewer. We must think of a clever plan to prevent the meat eaters from attacking us. A young giraffe said, why don't we try to grow — our — [?]

T: [?] Necks. Necks. Grow our necks. Grow our necks.

E: Make our legs longer so that when the meat eaters attack us, we can run faster. All the giraffes think that this was a good idea. So all the giraffes went home and think of how to grow taller.

T: That's not the end huh. (T places page 2 on OHP)

E: The next day every giraffe was trying to grow. But pull each — some pulled each other and some try to make some — make some magic potions. The oldest giraffe had an old book about how to grow legs. The book says that — use a tail of a snake, wings of a bat, shell of the snail, eggs of a turtle, legs of the frog, and last of all the — poison of the — scorpion. The oldest giraffe added all the — things and stir. After stirring for forty minutes he — took a teaspoon of the medicine. An incredibly thing happened. The oldest giraffe's neck grew and the legs grew longer. Every giraffe took a spoonful and soon all the giraffes had grown taller. Till this day, the giraffes will not grow anymore.

T: OK. What have you got to say about this composition? Yes? Sochian?...(?)...Alright, if you were checking or if you were editing this composition, what have you got to say?...(?)...Now first let's think of the arrangement of ideas. Are the arrangement of ideas good?

(SS nod heads)

OK. Right? Yes, right? Because the story is in sequence. The arrangement is in sequence. When you read it, you know what the story is all about. All arranged properly. Section of arrangement of ideas is OK. Now, do you think any details are left out? Do you think there are enough details? Are there enough details? Are there?

SS: Yes.

T: Yes, [?] enough details there to tell a very — complete story. The arrangement of ideas is good. Alright. Clear. So all [?] arranged properly. How about interesting words or phrases? Are there interesting words or phrases? As we go along we will look at some of the interesting words and phrases. [?] Alright? Now how about the grammar? How about the tenses? Do you see a lot of spelling mistakes?

SS: Yes.

T: Right. Now we are going to check for spelling and the tense. Alright? Look out for spelling and tense. Alright? Spelling we will check with an S. [?] Alright? Spelling and tense. And of course arrangement of ideas, you will see WW. What does WW means?

SS: Wrong word.

T: Wrong word. Alright. Any — what about the tense? Is it correct? Is it in the correct tense?

SS: No.

T: Is it correct? [?] Correct? Any idea? Yes, Ridwan?

R: [?]

T: We are talking about generally, some parts of the tenses are wrong. Right? We have to go through it section by section. Alright? Some parts of the tenses are wrong. How about punctuation? How about punctuation? Is the punctuation good?

SS: No.

T: No? Why is it no good? Why is it no good? Why is it no good?

S1: [?]

T: Sentences are too long. Sometimes [?] full stops, but there should not be a full stop. Sometimes [?] commas, and there should not be commas. OK? Let's — let's go through it together, alright ? OK. Keep in mind, ah, we are going to think of — look out for spelling error, tense, wrong word, punctuation. And if you see any interesting word or phrases, you put a pass on top of that word. OK? These are the five things you are going to look out for. Number 1. Let's read the first essay.

(T reads)

(DELL Classroom Data CP2P6 (a follow-up of lesson on 25 January 1994), recorded 27 January 1994)

There is clearly much more interaction and group work than in the previous example. The teacher wants the pupils to work together to compose the texts and only then will they write an individual account. This is much more in line with the 'process' and 'genre' approach more commonly seen in L1 classrooms in Britain, the USA, Australia, etc. It would seem that not only is English being used as an effective tool for communication but it is creating the sort of discourse that allows educational knowledge to be transmitted. The pupils are being exposed to a standard form of English and it would be hard to identify features of the language that were specifically Singaporean. Only in the features of the oral language would this be marked.

If a new variety of English is to become an effective tool for communication not just at the local level but also as a means of international communication, the argument would be that a new variety of English cannot develop unless it can play a full role in the educational process. Therefore it becomes equally important to see how English is used in other subject areas in the curriculum and not just in the officially designated 'English class'. The following extract is taken from a science class at Secondary 2 level (age 13) in Singapore. Once more the sample is from a class where most children would not use English as their dominant language at home but have now had eight years of school through the medium of English.

Example 6

T: Class, listen. Last week, we did heat. What aspect...what did we do?

SS: Expansion and contraction.

T: Yes, what happens when we heat objects, when we heat solids. Today, we will do heat again. This time, how the heat travels through solids, liquids and gases. How does it travel? Three ways...Have you heard...can you see? Right. Heat can travel by means of conduction, convection and radiation. Three ways in which heat can travel from one place to another. We will know [?] about how heat is conducted. (T prepares transparency) Heat. Now, how does the fish in the pan becomes hot? Once you put it in a hot plate, then the pan, then the fish. The bottom of the pan receives heat from the hot plate and eventually the fish gets hot. Now, during this time, when the fish was heated, did you see any movement?

SS: No.

T: OK. The fish there, hot plate, pan. No movement. Right or wrong?

SS: Yes.

T: So the transfer takes place without the matter moving. Did the matter move?

SS: No.

T: This is called conduction. [?] When heat is transferred to heat energy without the matter moving, it's called conduction. Alright, can you give me some examples of everyday experience of conduction taking place? Jefferson?

SS: [?]

T: OK. What happens?

SS: [?]

T: Now you have a hot cup of coffee, right ? You have a spoon. You stir the coffee. What happens?...Alright, Karim? [?] What do you experience? What do you experience?...Alright, I will ask you a few more questions. You hold the spoon and stir. Now before you put the spoon into the hot coffee [?] do you hold the spoon? Do you hold the spoon?

SS: Yes.

T: Now you put the spoon into the coffee and stir. What happens?

SS: It becomes hot.

T: Yes, the other end of the spoon becomes hot after some time. Right? This is something you experience everyday. Good. What else has taken place?

SS: [?]

T: And what do you call this when heat travels through a solid? Mumtaz?

SS: Expansion.

T: He calls this expansion? (class laugh) Yes, Sudiman, what do you call this?

SS: Conduction.

T: Yes, we call this conduction. Now you would have observed also that heat travels from a region where it is very, very hot to a region that is less hot as in the case of the spoon. Alright? One end of the spoon was in hot liquid, right?

SS: Yes.

T: Then later, the other end became hot too, right?

SS: Yes.

T: What happened was the heat from the hotter region travels and went to the other end. This heat transfer is called conduction. Now, we come to good and bad conductors. This, you've already done in Primary Six, right? You've already done in Primary Six?

SS: Yes.

T: So you know what I'm talking about? Good and bad conductors. Let's look at good conductors. Now, what materials are good conductors of heat?

SS: Metals.

T: Metals, yes. Metals are usually good conductors of heat. In general. In general, metals are good conductors of heat and non-metals are poor conductors of heat. Now there's another word for poor conductors.

SS: Insulators.

T: Insulators. So you call them, the poor conductors, insulators. (T prepares transparency) Now this diagram shows conductors starting off with silver, here. The best conductor, of course, is silver. The next, copper. So it goes like this. First, (T points to silver) lead, iron, aluminum, gold, copper, silver. Silver is the best conductor of heat. So is gold or iron useful matters. Sorry, copper and iron. Which one is a better conductor of heat?

SS: Copper.

T: Copper. [?] The best insulator will be?

SS: Mercury.

T: [?] Now we now know two things we've done so far, that heat travels through solids, conduction. And we defined what conduction is. And also, we know that during conduction, heat travels from a region which is very hot to another region that is less hot and we know that things of metal are generally better conductors of heat. Correct?

SS: Yes.

T: Do you have any questions so far?

SS: No.

T: (T prepares another transparency) Right. Pots and pans are usually made of metals. Pots and pans are usually made of metals, example, stainless steel or aluminium, because metals will conduct heat from the fire quickly to the food. This is making use of conduction. Alright? (T prepares another transparency) However, the handles of these utensils are usually...however, the handles of these utensils are usually made of wood or plastic. What is the purpose of this? Why? You know...the spoon. One end [?] the other end is [?] What is the purpose of this? Of course you should know. It is to prevent much heat from reaching our hands when we hold the utensils. (T shows another transparency) Why is food sometimes kept in styrofoam containers? Why? Can anyone tell me? Why? Banu?

SS: To retain the heat.

T: To retain the heat. Alright...to retain the heat. That is correct. Alright. Why is styrofoam a good insulator? It will help keep the food warm for a longer time than if it is kept in other types of containers. Can a styrofoam container keep ice-cream or similar types of food cold?

SS: No.

T: Try to keep ice-cream in a styrofoam container to see how long it takes to melt. What do you think? Anyone? Daniel, your answer? Will it melt?

SS: Yes.

T: Yes, it does. Good. (T shows picture on transparency) Now, electric soldering iron. Now I think you have it in the workshop, right?

SS: Yes.

T: You have it in the workshop. Now, the picture shows an electric soldering iron. In a soldering iron, electric energy is changed to heat energy [?] which is then used to join wires. Suggest suitable materials for the handles. I think you have no problems. The answer is provided, right? You've got them. (on transparency) Plastic or wood or copper. All of you have used the soldering iron?

SS: No.

T: Kulprit, you have?

SS: No.

T: In the workshop?

SS: No.

T: Workshop? You've not done it? OK. Any questions, class?

SS: No.

(T shows another transparency)

(DELL Classroom Data SCS2, 10 July 1995)

There is a considerable proportion of teacher-talk in this lesson and it is mainly explanatory, given the nature of the lesson. The teacher is a science teacher and not directly an English subject teacher. But there is basically very little difference between the language used in this classroom and what you might find in, let us say, in a classroom in the UK. This example would reinforce the argument that in the development of a new variety of English, the new variety must be capable of giving access to educational knowledge and that would require a standard form which is capable of both local and international use.

Conclusion

As we indicated at the beginning of this chapter, most if not all the new varieties of English have developed in multilingual and multicultural environments. The establishment of a standard form of the local variety is not something that can be decreed by some norm-giving body; it must be something that comes out of the community itself. What would appear to be more important is the effective use of English in the developing new varieties as a means of moving from 'common-sense' knowledge to 'educational knowledge'; the former will most often be developed through a colloquial variety of English together with one or other languages of the community. Thus common-sense knowledge acts as the bridge to educational knowledge as children enter into the formal education system. The development of educational knowledge will mainly be through English and this is where the 'standard' variety is established. The new varieties of English should be a medium which is sufficiently rich to allow the empowering of the learner in society because, as has been argued, this is what educational knowledge is about. However, it has also been argued that the pedagogical barriers of poor teaching or inappropriate methodologies can arrest this development. That is to say that having a syllabus which is designed as if the students were studying English as a foreign language when the context demands a syllabus which treats English as a dominant working language of society, might well produce users of English that do not meet the demands of society at the local or international level. The argument for 'a local variety of English for local consumption' can only lead to a policy of disempowerment where one section of the population lacks access to the avenues of power, while another gains all the advantages provided by their ability to use a more widely acceptable variety. International frontiers are widening all the time. English, because of historical reasons, has a major role to play in this widening process, and society has a duty to see that all its citizens have an opportunity to participate.

The dominant role allocated to English, after Singapore's independence, in all spheres of national and international activity, was only partly motivated by the need to sustain equilibrium across the ethnic/linguistic groups that made up the population. The main reason was economic: the government realized that Singapore had to plug into the international grid in order to survive. Multinational investment and technology had to be attracted to Singapore and one major attraction was a workforce that could communicate in English. The investment in English seems to have paid off, and individuals have not been slow to recognize the opportunities that proficiency in English can provide. In order to have an effective English-speaking workforce, Singapore created an adult education programme under the responsibility of the Institute of Technical Education (ITE). Although ITE caters mainly to vocational and industrial training, it also conducts the Continuing Education and Training programme. The establishment of an Open University degree programme in English Language and Literature has created a link between the workplace and the use of English such that the opportunities that open learning systems provide be made available to a larger cross-section of the population (Das, 1994).

In multilingual Singapore, language diversity has been seen as an obstacle to nation-building in that language loyalty could lead to interethnic conflict when the functional status or sentimental value of one's own ethnic language is at stake. The pragmatic approach has characterized Singapore society's attitude towards language policy and language management and has allowed for flexible responses to changing social, economic and political conditions, such that language planning in Singapore represents a case of centralized planning without a central language planning agency (Kuo and Jernuud, 1994). Further discussion of this point will be taken up in Chapter 12. The argument put forward in this chapter has been that English as a new variety has the basis for development in Singapore because it is well-anchored in the home and in the school. However, the long-term success of the development of a new variety of English (which because of geographical and cultural proximity will affect Malaysia as well) will require management of the internal linguistic diversification into the colloquial and standard varieties and into usages that rely on developing indigenous norms. The establishment of such norms is one of the essential roles of language in the school system.

Chapter 11

Singapore Literature in English

Ismail S. Talib

☙ *Introduction: The Colonial Background*

The writing of literature in English in Singapore was not uncontroversial, especially when one looks at the early stage of the country's history (Talib, 1994a). The majority of Singaporeans are of Asian descent, and English was certainly not the mother tongue of the vast majority of the population. As such, the cultural usage of English as in its use for the writing of literature, was not readily accepted (Talib, 1994b: 155-7). Another problem was the association of the language with the British colonial masters. Even if one may argue, quite legitimately, that language as such is 'neutral' and should not be too closely associated with its main or original users, some of the appalling aspects of colonialism were somehow bound with the language and its use. In this respect, it was unquestionably not apropos for one to extol the virtues of the use of the English language and the writing of literature in the language shortly after independence from the British. The Japanese occupation of Singapore also helped to diminish the significance of the language, quite apart from its related contribution to the political awakening of the population with regard to the view of the British and other colonial political powers as invincible forces (Talib, 1994a: 420-1).

In spite of decolonization, there was the realization at the same time that English was an important language in the sense that it had enormous practical value. It was, and is, the language of commerce, and business dealings could definitely be enhanced through the use of the language. It was also the language of science and technology. As such, there was no question about the retention of English due to its significance for modernization and economic development. In this light, the colonization of Singapore by the British, and the legacy of English-language education that it left, should also be viewed as a fortuitous historical accident, instead of something which should entirely be viewed negatively. Nevertheless, as mentioned earlier, the use of the English language for the writing of literary works meant that one was using the language for cultural purposes; as such, the desirability of using English for the writing of literary works could be put to question. There is a conflict here between language as it is used for instrumental aims —

when it is used, for example, for business and for the learning of science and technology — and its use as a means of cultural expression (for a related distinction in the context of language education, see Talib, 1992b). This conflict, although much less intense than it was shortly after independence from the British, is still with us in Singapore today. However, the nature of the conflict has shifted away from the question of whether English should be used for the writing of literary works (Thumboo, 1985: 9), to the values that one may imbibe when one uses the language (Talib, 1994b: 158-9).

There were several factors which hindered the development of an indigenous local literature in the English language until after independence. In addition to the political and cultural problems associated with the use of the language for the writing of literary works, the fact that the English literature taught in schools was almost entirely British-based did not help in the development of an indigenous local literature in the language. The nature of literature education in English schools meant that potential writers did not have the appropriate local — or at least, locally relevant — literary role models to emulate in writing in the language. Granted, the writing of literature in English by non-British (or non-American) writers at that time was not as extensive as it is today. But a consequence of this unavoidable fact was that potential authors tried to imitate British writers in writing their works. The imitations were also limited to British writers of earlier eras, as there was a general avoidance of twentieth-century or recent works in the teaching of literature in schools (Yeo, 1991: 345). It could have helped the development of literature in English during British colonial rule if more modern literature had been taught, as there was more awareness of non-British or non-European cultures — some of which was positive — in the modernist works of authors such as Conrad, T. S. Eliot and Pound. It was only later, at the University, that students were exposed to modern literary works in English (Thumboo, 1982: 3). Thankfully, many of the works written in imitation of earlier British authors are now left forgotten in school magazines and college publications which are no longer readily available on the open shelves of libraries in Singapore and elsewhere.

The Malaysian Connection

One needs to mention here that Singapore was once part of Malaysia, and during much of British rule, the island was not regarded as separate from parts of Malaya or what is known today as Peninsular or West Malaysia. During pre-colonial times, the indigenous language of this area was Malay. The British recognized this themselves and apart from the English language itself, certainly placed a higher estimation of the language in the educational system when compared to the other languages spoken by the local population.

This is not the place for me to discuss the development of literature in the Malay language, but there was clearly a movement towards the promotion of Malay literature at the expense of literature written in English in the early years of the history of post-colonial Singapore (Talib, 1994b: 155-6; Thumboo, 1976: xxxiv-xxxv). One prominent poet who studied in the University of Malaya in Singapore, and who was a close associate of such prominent local poets in the university as Edwin Thumboo and Lee Tzu Pheng, was Muhammad Haji Salleh, who eventually abandoned English to write entirely in Malay.

As Muhammad Haji Salleh returned to Malaysia, he should be considered a Malaysian poet, but one major problem with Singaporean literature in English is the difficulty of separation between the two geopolitical entities. Indeed, in Edwin Thumboo's collection *The Second Tongue*, which was published eleven years after Singapore's separation from Malaysia, Thumboo did not perceive a need to separate Singapore poetry in English from Malaysian poetry written in the language (Thumboo, 1976). In the case of Muhammad Haji Salleh's place in Thumboo's collection, he was prominently featured, due to the quality of his poetry written in English. In Muhammad's English-language poetry, one could sense the immense power of his use of the language, as seen for example, in the lines below from the poem 'the meeting' (Thumboo, 1976: 61):

> your heart in your hand
> you offered me a palmful of water.
> you, giver, close-fingered catcher
> of desert rain, let drip
> part of the palm-pool you save.
> so I, the droughted traveller
> on my way to a pool
> stopped to wet the lining of my mouth,
> where the heart has come to stay.

The neologism 'droughted', used as an adjective or prequalifying noun here, is not clumsily used, but in fact adds to the intensity of his language (see comments on neologism in the context of lexicography in Talib, 1992a: 190). Muhammad has twenty-one poems in *The Second Tongue*. In this regard, he has more poems than other poets who are more closely associated with poetry in English today, such as Ee Tiang Hong, Lee Tzu Pheng, Arthur Yap, Robert Yeo, Kirpal Singh, Shirley Lim, Hillary Tham, Wong Phui Nam and Thumboo himself (who was perhaps exercising editorial modesty by not including too many of his own poems — only eight — in the collection).

Muhammad Haji Salleh is really part of Malaysian literature — more in the Malay language now than in English. In the same vein, Wong Phui Nam is really part of Malaysian literature in English. But one hesitates to mention Ee Tiang Hong, Shirley Lim and Hillary Tham. With them, one reaches another problem in the delineation of literatures in English when viewed from a geopolitical perspective, that is, the fact of migration. The problems of nationality and migration become very real issues when one compiles a bibliography of Singaporean literature in English. I commented in 1992 that: 'Even today, the Journal of Commonwealth Literature still discusses Singaporean and Malaysian literatures together in their annual review of studies on the literatures of the two countries' (Talib, 1992a: 193). More than thirty years of separation should have allowed us to separate them, but at the same time, one has to say that there is a sense of artificiality in this. Nevertheless, if one were to continue to treat the literature in English of the two countries together, one would be beset by two increasingly artificial situations. One is the progressively unfeasible political and literary alliance, and the other is the increasingly inexplicable separation of Singapore from countries other than Malaysia. One reason for the latter factor has to do with migration which, with more specific reference to the idea of a national literature of Singapore, has been discussed more extensively in another study (Talib, 1997c).

Migration and Problems of Classification: The American Connection

One may think that Singapore is quite free from the classificatory problems caused by migration — as seen in the case of Malaysian-born writers such as Ee Tiang Hong, Shirley Lim and Hillary Tham mentioned above — but this is not the case. After all, even Thumboo and Catherine Lim were born in what is now called Malaysia, although, for various reasons, there is no problem with calling them Singaporean writers today. But how about Wong May? Is her volume of poetry, *Superstitions* — published by Harcourt Brace and Jovanovich in New York in 1978 — more American than Singaporean? In a related vein, her poetry has been described by Leong Liew Geok as located 'within a Western consciousness' and written 'primarily for a Western audience' (Leong, 1995: 439). Or, should one regard her, as she was born in China, more Chinese than either Singaporean or American? One mentions Wong May not only because she seems to be a test case, but because she is also a remarkable and original poet in the language who was at one time associated with Singapore. She has recently been described by Robert Yeo, for example, as a 'distinguished poet' who crucially acted in an advisorial capacity in the publication of some of his early poems (Yeo, 1996: 36). Another hint of the quality and influence of her poetry is suggested by Lucy

Tan (*nom de plume* of the newspaper columnist Tan Sai Siong). Tan mentions that her 'Fragment 94', one of the poems in her collection *108 Fragments*, 'is an attempt to pay tribute to the literatures that have inspired me, in particular, the writings of Singapore's finest but probably its least acknowledged literary greats — Arthur Yap and Wong May' (Ong, 1997).

What may emerge from the problem of migration is the contrast between what can best be described as a migratory sensibility and physical migration itself; in other words, the contrast between symbolic and corporeal migration. The two are of course connected, especially when one begins with corporeal migration, and one should not talk of a contrast *per se*. Before looking at symbolic migration, let us look at the simpler fact of corporeal migration. One may think that apart from Wong May, who is, arguably, always a problematic case to begin with, there are no other instances of note in Singaporean literature in English (if, indeed, it could continue to be described as 'Singaporean literature in English'), but this is not the case. Apart from Wong May, there are two recent instances: the novelist Fiona Cheong and the playwright Chay Yew, both of whom were born and received a good part of their education in Singapore. As an indication of the importance of Chay Yew in American letters today, he has been described, for instance, as 'an acclaimed playwright', as someone who has a 'rising-star status', and as 'one of the most cutting-edge and critically acclaimed young Asian playwrights of the '90s' in *The Los Angeles Daily News* (Weeks, 1996). The artistic director of the East West Players, Tim Dang, has even predicted that 'Chay is going to be the next big Asian-American writer' (Weeks, 1996; Finkle, 1995). One notes here that he is now regarded as an 'Asian-American' and not quite a 'Singaporean' writer, but a firm distinction, surely, is not something easy to maintain.

One may think that these writers, stationed as they are in the United States, might present a positive image of Singapore which may act as a counterbalance to the usually negative image portrayed in the Western press, but this is not always the case. *The Los Angeles Times*, for example, begins with the observation that 'Chay Yew's first work — an AIDS drama — was summarily banned in his native Singapore by government conservatives offended by its positive portrayal of a strong, handsome, hard-working gay man' (Finkle, 1995). Indeed, the reason for emigration for Singapore writers, unlike many other Asian immigrants in the United States, is seldom economic, but can usually be better described as educational or broadly political, and this factor may be reflected in their work.

Fiona Cheong's first novel, *The Scent of the Gods* (1991), has also been well-received in the United States. Generally positive reviews of the novel have appeared in *The San Francisco Chronicle*, *The San Diego Union-Tribune*, *The Washington Times*, *The Seattle Times*, *The Los Angeles Times* and the

New York Times, among others. It does seem to be the case that if one were to reside in the United States, one would get more publicity than if one were to remain in Singapore. But the same negative image of Singapore that one finds in the American response to Chay Yew's AIDS play is also found in the American response to her work (for a general review of the attitude of the Western press to Singapore and its literary authors, see Talib, 1997b). For example, *The Los Angeles Times* reviewer notes that the main character, Su Yen, 'watches the rise of Singapore's squeaky-clean police state, and learns a bitter lesson in politics when her favorite uncle and older cousin are destroyed by the growing power of the central government' (Solomon, 1993). One is not sure if this is an entirely correct reading of the novel. Perhaps the reviewer reads what he wants to read in the novel. Indeed, one of the weaknesses of *The Scent of the Gods* is its difficulty with the representation of a reality as seen through the eyes of a child, and many of the social and political suggestions in the work remain as suggestions, and not statements. Technically, Cheong has not quite achieved the dual adult-child perspective found, for example, in Henry James' *What Maisie Knew* or the film *Badlands*, directed by Terence Mallick.

A 'Boundaryless' World: Towards Cross-cultural Understanding?

It has become more recognized in the increasingly 'boundaryless' world we are living in, that one of the pedagogical functions achieved in the study of world literature or post-colonial literature is the strengthening of cross-cultural understanding (see, for example, Talib, 1996; and the other studies in Carroll, 1996). The term cross-cultural here should be understood in terms of the understanding between East and West, or, between North and South in the case of post-colonial literature. These recent Singapore-born literary representatives in the West have so far not acted as catalysts for a more sympathetic cross-cultural response in the way that some authors from India, Africa and the Caribbean have done in the West. However, at least some attempt was made to achieve this sympathetic response by the *New York Times* reviewer of Cheong's novel. The reviewer notes that a somewhat different picture from the popular image of Singapore as a country with a 'seemingly robotic citizenry, smiling and marching as if in an Asian version of "Nineteen Eighty-four" ' has emerged from his reading of the novel (Coale, 1991).

Hybridity

Migration often results in the creation of a mixed identity: someone is neither one nor the other, neither *here* nor *there*. It is interesting to note, for example, that *The Los Angeles Times* describes Chay Yew as *both* an Asian-American writer *and* a native of Singapore. This mixed identity however is more than just a dual identity; it is more than a simple mixture of two elements. It could be suggested that the word *hybridity* is more appropriate here, as one is really talking of a heterogeneous mixture (see, for example, Talib, forthcoming). Also, the author need not be a migrant in the physical sense to write about migration in the symbolic sense; in the same vein, one need not be a genetic hybrid to be a *cultural hybrid*. The latter type of *hybridity* is in fact a prevalent psychosocial phenomenon in the contemporary world. Indeed, as will be argued shortly, the *migrant* with a heterogeneous identity is a symbolic presence in literary works which have created an impact in recent years. Arguably, the symbolic migrant is in all of us as we approach the end of the millenium, even if we are, physically speaking — to borrow Yeats' words — 'rooted in one dear perpetual place'.

Migration as Theme

As our bridge between the two types of *migrancy*, we have to return to Wong May again. With regard to her symbolic migrancy, Leong Liew Geok has described Wong's poetry as creating 'the impression of the poet...as [a] perennial itinerant...[who is] relatively independent of any sense of cultural or ethnic self' (Leong, 1995: 438). Leong is describing the content of Wong's poetry here, not the fact that she is a migrant. In Wong, we have a combination of the two. However, even with writers who cannot be described as migrants, transnational movements do act as a positive stimulus to creative writing. Stella Kon (1991: 305), for example, notes that:

> Most of my work has been done while I was living away from Singapore. My writing was, perhaps, an exile's effort to re-create in words the feelings of being in Singapore, being a Singaporean.

Not only does physical displacement from what the writer regards as home act as a stimulus to creative writing, but the migratory theme or theme of exile itself does seem to be prominent, at least among writers who are taken note of seriously in the contemporary critical milieu. This may not be physical exile that one is talking of, as it touches, even if one remains in what should have been one's home, on the basic question of identity: who am I, and where do I belong? This question underlies the beginning of what is perhaps the most famous poem by a Singaporean writer in English, 'My Country and My People' by Lee Tzu Pheng (1980: 51):

My country and my people
are neither here nor there, nor
in the comfort of my preferences,
if I could even choose.

These lines certainly touch on national issues, on states of being, and not merely on the movements of itinerants who do not permanently 'belong' to any physical place. Although one wonders what the persona means by 'the comfort of [her] preferences' with regard to her country and her people, we can say here that many of us have forcibly homogeneous mental projections of what we are and what we should be. The persona of the poem here is clearly not free from these projections. The theme of migration or exile is very dominant in what is described as the *post-modern* character of contemporary reality. In this regard, literary works which try to avoid it in the attempt to create a sense of national belonging, or to promote the conception of a national literature, may end up as technical and not merely as ideological failures. It has been argued elsewhere that this was the case with Rex Shelley's *The Shrimp People* (Talib, 1997c), which is one of the best novels in English to have been written by a Singaporean. Ultimately, Shelley's novel fails to sustain the technical and stylistic brilliance at the beginning, as a result of his artificial attempt, later in the novel, to circumvent the narrative's natural inclination towards the theme of migration and exile.

❧ *A 'National' Literature?: Post-modern Obstacles*

The theme of migration is prominent in the poetry of Boey Kim Cheng, who has been described by Shirley Lim as '[t]he best post-1965 English-language poet in the Republic today' (Lim, 1996). Many of Boey's poems were written in relation to his travels as a hitchhiker. It has been rightly said that in his poetry, 'the evolution of a national literature [that] is often seen as essential in forging a Singaporean identity does not seem to be one of his preoccupations' (Tan, 1996). Hence he does not face the technical and ideological difficulties that beset Shelley's novel. As in Wong May, there is the combination of the physical and symbolic migrant in Boey's poetry, but in the apt words of Lee Tzu Pheng, it is, ultimately and more importantly, 'in the country of the spirit that the poet finds himself wandering' (1989: 7). The spiritual nomad in him proves to be domineering in his wanderings across the physical landscape, and his occasional failure to reach his intended concrete destination appears, by contrast, to be an accidental accompaniment (Boey, 1992: 23):

A masterstroke of oversight has landed me

in the middle of nowhere, an interim
of lost connections, an unplanned pause
between journeys, the cold desert air
gripping the old bones of the mind.

Indeed, one senses that the persona *wants* to be lost. He is lost in the material
sense due to an 'oversight', which is a word with an ambiguous meaning: it
can either mean supervision and control (as in the related word 'overseer'),
or, failure to see what should have been seen. Paradoxically, it is through
being lost that one may come closer to discovering and understanding oneself,
and hence the situation is not entirely undesirable.

Boey's poetry is not a symbolic enactment of an arcane mystical quest,
but touches on an aspect of the post-modern sensibility that is of immense
relevance to contemporary Singapore. In this relation, Shirley Lim (1996)
has noted that:

> The experience of having had a life "elsewhere", even of being
> someone else elsewhere, is increasingly common among post-1965
> generation-Singaporeans who have lived abroad for years of tertiary
> education or who travel frequently. The telos of "Singaporeanness",
> under the pressures of globalisation and a borderless information
> age, is transforming to include an outside-Singapore subject-
> formation. How is this generation to ground itself on a little island
> when the whole world beckons?

The whole quest for a 'national literature' or a 'Singapore classic' (Singh,
1980) is left behind. Coming back to the concept of hybridity, one is talking
here not only of mixtures available within Singapore, but also from outside
Singapore. Granted, transnational cross-cultural influences have been with
mankind for several hundred if not several thousand years. However, the
pace of contemporary cultural transformation is much faster than it was
before, so that the resting point where one says that something is culturally
'Singaporean' — difficult as it was to locate with regard to post-independence
Singapore, given the country's short history — is becoming even more
difficult to locate.

In this light, it is surprising that one of Singapore's most cosmopolitan
theatre directors, Ong Keng Sen, has said that '[u]nlike many Singaporean
directors, I am very preoccupied with looking for a Singaporean form and
structure' (1996: 31). Equally surprising is the interviewer's description of
Ong's sensibility as *post-modern*, when a statement of this kind has the odour
of a modernist or even pre-modern Romantic desire to define oneself in
relation to one's community or *tribe* (for another view of Ong's supposed

post-modernity, see Talib, 1997a). It does not quite relate to the post-modern tendency towards globalization and cross-cultural and transnational hybridity. But Ong's statement should be viewed dialectically: as, really, a desire to home in after an intensive period outside the ambit of what can be described as 'Singaporean'. It is interesting that Ong should want to look for the Singaporean in form and structure, and not in content, when we do not quite have a stable history of a technically developed Singaporean theatre in English which he can rely on to define his terms. The undertow of his statement does seem to point to his desire to be identified as Singaporean, even if what he does is too original to be considered as part of any Singapore *tradition* in the dramatic and performing arts. In this regard, Singapore tradition in the dramatic and performing arts is, to begin with, merely embryonic if it exists at all. After all, identity is quite often associated with what one wants to be considered as, and not quite what one *is* or *should be*, the latter of which is often based on other's yardsticks, which can easily be questioned.

Generic Hybridity in Dramatic Works

With Ong Keng Sen, one reaches another hybrid element, that is, the ambivalent status of drama as literature. In Ong, we have a figure who is more a theatre director than a playwright. Indeed, there was an initial reluctance to include drama in this chapter because of its ambivalent status. In drama, one is dealing not only with the *literate* aspects of an art form, but with the *orate* and *visual* aspects as well. In fact, one has to look more at the *orate* and *visual* elements of a theatre director's art, and less at the *literate*, as this is really the preserve of the playwright. It can even be said that with Ong, one has to look even more at the non-literate aspects. One of his productions, *Broken Birds*, is a case in point. The play, which was written by Ong and Robin Loon, deals with Japanese prostitutes in Singapore. Ong's production has been described as a *docudrama*, in the sense that there is a mixture of the non-fictional (hence the *docu-* prefix) and fictional (in the sense that *drama* as an art form is quite often assumed to be fictional, or, it has to incorporate factually questionable elements for it to be effective). The *docudrama* conceived by Ong also has music, dance, photographic slides and film, in a way similar but not identical to opera (at least the operatic traditions we know of).

The ambivalent generic status of drama as *literature* is also exploited by Kuo Pao Kun in his play *Mama Looking for Her Cat*. There are a number of different languages used in Kuo's play. The different languages may allegorize the difficulties of communication between the various language communities, but as has been argued elsewhere, an equally important but less apparent aspect of the play has to do with the clash between the *orate* and *literate* traditions (Talib, forthcoming). This is seen in the work in terms of intergenerational discord. In mentioning Kuo's work, it is important to note that he is not only a theatre director but a playwright as well. His plays are written with a keen awareness of their limitations as *literary* works, leaving more space than usual for theatrical possibilities which the director can exploit. These possibilities extend beyond what can be conveyed through the written word.

🐚 *Linguistic Hybridity: 'Pronunciation' in the Written Text*

Other languages may not only be represented as such in literary works, by embodying them wholesale in the text, as in Kuo's *Mama*, but they may also *interfere*, in various ways, in the way the language is used. The portrayal of the interference of non-English languages is a very important way through which language is represented in literatures in English outside Britain, and Singaporean literature in English is certainly not an exception. Due to its importance, the rest of this chapter will deal with some of the problems encountered in the analysis of linguistic representation.

Arguably, the interference of other languages is another aspect of *hybridity*, although it may not be discussed as such by most linguists. In my view, the introduction of the concept of *hybridity* may be useful, as it emphasizes the social nature of such linguistic mixtures, which should not be seen entirely as technical non-interactive features of language.

One way one shows the interference of another language is through the representation of the way the local dialect of English is spoken. In literature in English, this can be done by altering the spelling of certain words. Here are two examples from a single page of *The Shrimp People*:

"Come on, Ethel...there's a place nex to me...here, dis one."

"Doan fergait de *chinchalok*!"

In the examples above, one notices the missing final consonant in a word-end consonant cluster, or rather, what would have been a consonant cluster in Standard British and American English: 'nex[t]' and 'Doan' (instead of 'Don't'). There is also the tendency to change the 'th' sound in 'this' and 'the' to 'dis' and 'de'. Both these tendencies are familiar in the pronunciation of varieties of English outside Britain and the United States, as will be shown shortly. What is also evident in the examples from Shelley's novel is the attempt to imitate the pronunciation of certain vowels in Singapore English by changing the spelling of some words. This is clear in 'Doan fergait'. But what we notice is the fact that such attempts at changing the spelling of certain words may not always be unambiguous, especially when it comes to the pronunciation of vowels or vowel groups. 'Doan fergait' may seem to indicate that diphthongs are involved in 'Doan' and '-gait'. However, anyone who knows Singapore English will probably guess that monophthongs (or something closer to monophthongs than in Standard British or American English) are intended: 'Doan' is probably closer to the monophthongal pronunciation of 'loan' in Singapore English and '-gait' to the relatively monophthongal pronunciation of 'bait' or 'wait'.

'Foreign' Loan Words

Another way a writer may represent other varieties of English is through the introduction of foreign loan words in the text. We have already seen the example of *chinchalok* from Rex Shelley's work above. Arguably, a word like *chinchalok* — which can unsatisfactorily be described as a sauce made from tiny shrimps — may not have an equivalent in English, and therefore, the 'foreign' Malay word, in this instance, is borrowed unaltered. The following are two extracts from the novel *Rice Bowl* by Suchen Christine Lim, where loan words could have been avoided, but there are very good reasons why they remain in the extract:

'Aaah, here is Sister Beatrice. Hello, sister, mana pergi?'
'Aye, aye, mana Marie-Therese? She not here, she not there. Hujan sa-kali! I look everywhere for her; dia belum makan,' the old sister complained as she hobbled into the chapel looking for her lost lamb. (1991: 198)

'You always angry with me and Ang Mo; you now go and dance with this Ang Mo. Got meaning or not? Where got meaning I ask you? I cheap; I say you the cheap one! I go out I get paid, you go out you got nothing, you give him free service. I go to bring back money for you!' (1991: 70)

In the first extract above, Marie-Therese uses the words 'mana pergi?', which are Malay words meaning 'where are you going?'. Likewise, 'mana Marie-Therese?' means 'where is Marie-Therese?'. The phrase 'dia belum makan,' means 'she hasn't eaten [yet]'. However, the translation of phrases in another language is not always straightforward. The meaning of 'Hujan sa-kali!' for example, is not entirely clear. On the surface it means 'it rains once', but what is probably intended here is 'it rains once again', which should have been, in Malay, 'hujan sekali lagi!'. In the second extract, the lexical item 'Ang Mo' means 'red-haired' in Hokkien.

ба *Importance of Other Languages and Grammatical Interference*

The presence of other languages, whether overtly or in the undercurrent of the language used, is important in literature of this kind. The overt use of other languages is seen in the actual use of lexical items or even in whole phrases or sentences, as seen in the quotations in the paragraph above. This is known as *code-mixing* or code-switching in sociolinguistics. (*Code-mixing* refers to the use of lexical items in another language, whereas *code-switching* refers to the use of phrases, whole sentences or several sentences; some linguists, however, feel that the distinction may not always be clear). The less direct presence of another language occurs when the grammar of the other language appears to have an influence on the syntactic arrangement of words, but the words themselves are in English, and not in the the the other language. This other language can be described as the *base* that determines the *surface* syntactic arrangement of the English words used in the poem.

The interference of another language's grammar or usage on the surface construction of English is also seen in the two extracts from the Suchen Christine Lim novel above. In the first extract, we have the missing copula (indicated in square brackets) in the sentence 'She [is] not here, she [is] not there'. The missing copula is also a feature of the second extract: 'You [are] always angry with me and Ang Mo'; 'I [am] cheap; I say you [are] the cheap one!'. Another prominent feature of the second extract is the pervasive use of the word 'get' or 'got', even in instances where it would have been avoided in Standard British or American English: 'Got meaning or not? Where *got* meaning I ask you?' 'I go out I *get* paid, you go out you *got* nothing, you give him free service'. Like the missing copula, this is a feature which is frequently encountered in spoken Singapore English.

ба *Aesthetic Evaluation of Language Use*

An important consideration in the analysis of language in literature is aesthetic evaluation. One can contrast this to the non-literary uses of language, where aesthetic evaluation is less important. In reading and analysing literature, we do not merely analyse a work based on whether or how a certain language or dialect is used. Arguably, aesthetic evaluation is not always based on whether the language or dialect is used accurately. However, this is a moot point, as the failure to reflect the language as it is actually used may also have some effect on aesthetic evaluation, as we will see shortly. However, it can also be argued that the impact may be, for some works, only slight. When a Singaporean takes a look at the first four paragraphs of 'The Taximan's Story' by Catherine Lim (1978: 76), he or she will note that the language here is not exactly how Singaporeans speak. More precisely, the language used in the story is not quite the language that one expects from a Singaporean taxi driver (see my discussion in Talib, 1992b). Specifically, there is a problem here with the consistency of usage, and the *level* or *variety* of English which the taxi driver uses. In this respect, this is really a consideration of CSE, which the character uses at certain points in the story, and the surprisingly more 'standard' variety elsewhere.

For an example of the uncertain *level* of language use in the taxi driver's language — or more precisely, the uncertainty between his usage of CSE and SSE — the word 'madam' is used rather frequently in the story. However, this word does not sit well with the use of English elsewhere in the text. The problem here is that the taxi driver's use of English appears to switch between the colloquial and standard varieties at various parts of the text. His occasionally more elegant use of English is thus suspect, as there is no reason why he should resort to such a variety of language use when the more colloquial variety seems to be more consistent.

If one confines oneself to the first four paragraphs of the story, one has doubts on the appropriateness, in terms of the taxi-driver's language use, of the word 'sure': 'Sure, will take you there'. The same can be said of the phrases 'plenty good time', 'not to worry', 'make a living' and 'no education, no capital or business'. Furthermore, the final 's' plural indicator in 'jams' and 'twenty years' seems to be out of keeping with the norm of language use in the passage. So does the presence of the copula in 'What is it you say, madam?', and 'Today is much better' (note the absent copula in the extract from Christine Lim above). There does seem to be quite a lot that is inappropriate if one confines oneself to only the first four paragraphs.

What is suggested above is that even CSE has some kind of grammar (for a more detailed discussion, see Chapter 5 of this book). Any inconsistencies as regards the grammar of this variety of English — even if they rise up to the more 'acceptable' language of the standard variety which may be described, in layman's terms, as 'grammatical' English — are suspicious to a person familiar with the colloquial variety. On the other hand, it is also the case that some purported instances of language use in the colloquial variety may be suspicious, because they simply do not follow, as far as one knows, the grammar or usage patterns of this variety of English. This is the case with the phrases 'Must work hard if wants to success in Singapore' and 'one childs'. In the former, the use of the verb 'wants' appears elegant, but looks awkward if the subject is missing, and one is not sure about the usage of 'to success' as a verb in the level of English which the author tries to imitate. In the latter, the addition of the 's' after child, considering that the 's' is deleted even for plural nouns in the grammar of the colloquial variety, does not seem to be right.

There are clear problems with the level of language use in the Catherine Lim story. But this, to many of us, may not affect our aesthetic appreciation of the story. In this light, let us see if the situation applies to the reading of poetry.

❧ *Analysing* **Poetry**

As we shall see shortly, there are similar problems when one compares the linguistic analysis and aesthetic appreciation of Catherine Lim's story with Arthur Yap's '2 Mothers In a HDB Playground' (1980: 54-5; Yap's poem is analysed in another context in Talib, 1996). An analysis of Yap's work may give you an idea of how to approach poetry.

One of the problems with Yap's poem is the use of the copula. In the Lim story, the use of the copula is occasional, but its use still does seem, to someone familiar with CSE, to be unnatural. In Yap's poem, however, it is persistently present. Here are some examples, with all instances of the copula in italics:

> ah beng *is* so smart, . . .
> your kim cheong *is* also quite smart, . . .
> what boy *is* he in the exam? . . .
> this playground *is* not too bad, but i'*m* always . . .
>   at exam time, it'*s* worse. . . .
> my ah beng *was* like that, / now he's different. . . .
> if you give him anything / he's sure to finish it all up. . . .
> maybe they *are* better. . . .
>   money'*s* no problem. it'*s* not that . . .
>   throwing money / into the jamban *is* the same. . . .
> the sofa *is* so soft, i dare not sit. . . .
>   after 6 months, it *is* already spoilt. . . .

There is also the rather frequent use of the [s] or [z] consonant, as represented by the letter 's', when it is likely to be avoided in the CSE which Yap tries to imitate. The consonant may appear in relation to the copula, as in 'at exam time, it's worse', 'now he's different', 'he's sure to finish it all up', 'money's no problem', and 'it's not that'. It also appears in the plural form of a noun: 'vitamins'; and in the possessive: 'cheong's father' and 'ah beng's father'. Most frequent is the use of the [s] or [z] consonant, as represented by the letter 's', in relation to the singular present tense verb. In this relation, we can note that the singular present tense verb form is not commonly found in the colloquial variety which the poem tries to make use of. However, it is found abundantly in the poem:

kim cheong eats so little',

… cheong's father buys him
vitamins but he keeps it inside his mouth
& later gives it to the cat',

ah beng's father spends so much,
takes out the mosaic floor & wants to make terazzo or what

ah pah wants to take you chya-hong in new motor-car

The Successful Representation of Language Use

Arguably, the successful representation of language use in literary works is not easy, but this does not mean that it is beyond the writer's reach. In Rex Shelley's *The Shrimp People*, for example, the author controls the shifts between CSE and a more standard variety of Singapore English subtly and naturally. Shelley is capable of shifting from language that is not widely divergent from the standard variety towards a more colloquial style. This can be seen in his shift, within a single paragraph, from 'In the kitchen, they swore and cursed because the devil curry was not ready, the onions not sliced thin enough … quick!' to italicized lexical items from Malay and Hokkien, such as *sambal lengkong*, *achar* and *tau-yu-bak*. The paragraph continues with a more colloquial variety of language: 'He was a one, this Padre'. 'He really was a one…'. An unmistakably colloquial level of Singapore English then intrudes 'Oh, you mean Dolly Paul's wedding? Yes lah!...whoa that was a one.' and 'You mean Millicent's daughter? Yes lah! The fight? Yeaaaaah...those Danker boys. Disgraceful!...Hey Millie, what ever happened to your old beau, that Dutch fellow? Please lah, Dulcie...let sleeping dogs lie.' In spite of the extensive shifts within a single paragraph, the transitions are managed very well by Shelley.

Conclusion

Generic hybridity has been mentioned earlier in this chapter. There may be more of such hybrid art forms emerging in Singapore in the future, with television, cinema and the Internet providing new avenues for works of a more widely defined conception of *literature*. What this may also mean is the emergence of more popular art forms in serious scholarship. Indeed, the songs of Dick Lee, for example, have been seriously studied (see, for example, Wee, 1996). This can also be said of television programmes, such as *Under One Roof*, and local movies, such as *Mee Pok Man*. In relation to local movies, there may be more local productions, some of which may be in English. The film *Army Daze*, based on the original dramatic script by Michael Chiang, has been produced, and at the time of writing, another film is being made, based on Ming Cher's novel *Spider Boys*. With Ming Cher, we have another notion of *hybridity* — that which hinges on migration: the author is now a New Zealand citizen, although his novel, like Fiona Cheong's *Scent of the Gods*, is about his earlier life in Singapore. With an increasingly 'borderless' world, it will be even more difficult to define what *Singapore literature* is, even, as we saw, in relation to writers who have remained in Singapore. This difficulty is by no means allayed by the emergence of more generically hybrid art forms which depend on our literate, orate and visual facilities. One consequence of this is that the successful analyst of literature needs to also be a successful analyst and critic of culture as a whole.

Chapter 12

Language Planning and Management in Singapore

Wendy Bokhorst-Heng

Introduction

In this chapter, we will consider language planning in Singapore, with a particular focus on the English language. An analysis of language planning in Singapore is fascinating for a number of reasons. The first is its linguistic complexity. Although the small island state has a population of just over 3 million, it has four official languages. In addition, at least thirty other languages and dialects are represented in the population. The second and related reason is that, in spite of such linguistic diversity and complexity, there is no official language-planning body. Instead, language planning is done at the very top levels of government. The former Prime Minister, Lee Kuan Yew, has especially shown a personal interest in the nation's language issues, and has set in place many of today's language policies. The direct involvement of government in language planning brings us to the third reason why the study of language planning in Singapore is so instructive, which is that it highlights and makes transparent the sociopolitical nature of language planning. It is this third reason which is perhaps the most significant. For, by noting the sociopolitical nature of language planning, we are required to look beyond merely the effects of language policy on language behaviour to a consideration of the ideological and discursive nature of language planning. As described by Blommaert, language planning 'carries implicit assumptions about what a "good" society is, about what is best for the people, about the way in which language and communication fit into that picture, and about how language planning can contribute to social and political progress' (1995: 18). This also means that language planning is time- and society-specific. As such, any inquiry into the practices of language planning requires an awareness of the peculiar and historical context in which language planning measures emerged and were implemented, and the sociopolitical effects of these policies. It is with this understanding of language planning that we turn to an analysis of the planning of English in Singapore.

ໄ༄ *Language Planning in Singapore*

Language planning in Singapore emerged out of its historical context of colonial domination. In the first place, Singapore's linguistic diversity can be traced to immigration trends that formed as a result of colonial commercial practices. When Singapore was founded in 1819 by Sir Stamford Raffles, there were only about 1000 people living on the small island. However, this was soon to change. Singapore's increased economic and trading activity attracted a rapid influx of merchants, entrepreneurs and indentured labourers from regions as diverse as the southern provinces of China, India, Malaya and other parts of Southeast Asia. The result was the development of a population group characterized by multiracialism, multiculturalism and multilingualism. At the time of the 1957 constitutional conference, in the twilight of the colonial era and the dawn of self-government, 33 mother tongue groups were present. Of these, 20 were spoken by more than a thousand speakers (Chua, 1962). The Chinese community, comprising 75.4% of the population, was the most heterogeneous group: 39% claimed Hokkien to be their mother tongue, 23% Teochew, 20% Cantonese, 7% Hainanese and the rest, one of seven other dialects. The Malay community, representing 13.6% of the population, was quite homogeneous: 85% held Malay to be their mother tongue and the rest, one of six other dialects. Of the Indian community, 8.8% of the population, 59% said Tamil was their mother tongue, 16% Malayalam and the rest, one of six other dialects. The rest of the population, 'Others' including Europeans, Eurasians, Arabs and other expatriates, mostly listed English as their mother tongue (71.6%). In addition to the complexity this pattern of language suggests, the census data shows that the four languages selected to be the official languages of the nation were in total mother tongue (although more could speak and understand these languages) for only 18.6% of the population: Mandarin 0.1%, Malay 11.5%, Tamil 5.2% and English 1.8%. As we will examine later in this chapter, why these languages were chosen to be the official languages had to do with the government's view of how they could contribute to the social and political progress of the nation.

However, the colonial legacy was about more than just linguistic diversity. It was also one of social inequality. Colonial education policy in Singapore was essentially one of non-interference: each community was free to establish their own form of education. And so, four separate educational systems emerged based on the different languages — Mandarin, Tamil, Malay and English — each modelled after education in their respective homelands. Colonial policy dictated that English was in no way to be taught *en masse*. The high cost of English education and the scarcity of qualified English teachers were the most common reasons given by the administration for the limited provision of English education. But it was more than that. The colonial administration had what Silcock (1964) called a 'pathological fear' of overeducating the natives and of producing unemployed clerks and intellectuals — lessons painfully learned in India. The argument was thus to limit English education. However, English schools received the bulk of government funding.[1] They also charged the highest fees that only the wealthy could afford, and were the only schools that led to higher education and ultimately to a career in the public sector. As a result, English education very quickly developed into elite education. Such policies inevitably resulted in a wide gulf between the Asian-language-educated, whose career choices were usually limited to unskilled labour, and the English-educated who formed the aristocratic elite and middle class.

After the Second World War, the colonial government changed its tactics. First of all, recognizing that the dismantling of colonialism was inevitable, they began to concentrate on increasing the provision of English education as a way to preparing Singapore for independence (Bokhorst-Heng, 1998). Furthermore, especially since the 1949 revolution in China, the Chinese middle schools in Singapore had become, in the eyes of the government, hotbeds of Chinese nationalism and revolutionary fervour. The middle-school students were also drawn into local labour disputes, strikes and riots organized by the trade union movement. These political activities were thus additional reason for the government to promote English education as the means by which national identity could emerge, and to wean students away from the Chinese-medium schools. In 1954, the number of students enrolled in English schools actually surpassed that in Chinese schools (Colony of Singapore, Annual Report of the Department of Education, 1954). This is not to say that there was no support for Chinese-medium education. Indeed, in 1954 there were still about 100 000 students enrolled in Chinese-medium schools (All-Party Report, 1955: 8), representing a sizeable portion of the Chinese population. And in 1956, the Chinese community founded the first Chinese-medium university, Nanyang University (also known as Nantah).

It was out of this historical context that language planning emerged in Singapore. At the time of independence, the newly formed government made two important decisions regarding language planning. First, Malay was designated as the national language, reflecting Singapore's political history as being part of Malaysia and reflecting its geographical location as

[1] In 1948, 75.3% of total education expenditure was allocated to English primary, secondary and higher education, 8.7% to Malay education, 5.6% to Chinese education and 0.5% to Tamil education. (Colony of Singapore, Annual Report of the Department of Education, 1948: 28).

being situated in a predominately Malay region. In practice, the role of Malay as the *national* language is primarily ceremonial, used only when singing the national anthem and for military drills. A little-known fact is that since 1979, the status of Malay as the national language is no longer even stated in the constitution. Second, Malay, Tamil, Mandarin and English were made official languages. While these languages were perhaps not their mother tongues, each ethnic group could at least claim official linguistic representation. The decision to make English, a residual language of colonialism, one of the official languages is perhaps more curious. Professor Jayakumar, then Minister of State (Law and Home Affairs), explained the position of English in Singapore this way:

> First, English is the major international language for trade, science and technology and proficiency in the language is essential as Singapore becomes a leading financial and banking centre. Second, education in English is the key to the productivity concept. With increasing modernisation, skilled workers who know English will be in greater demand. And third, when it is the common language here, it will enable all Singaporeans — regardless of race — to communicate with one another...English thus is key for both the individual and the nation. For the individual, it is the key to acquisition of skills and training and career advancement; for the nation, it is the key to a better educated and skilled workforce thereby ensuring higher productivity and economic growth.

> (*The Straits Times*, 19 August 1982)

As a so-called 'neutral' (non-ethnic) language, English thus plays a role at three levels. At the national level, English is the pragmatic choice to meet the government's larger economic objectives. This economic consideration is important as economic growth has always been perceived by the government as tantamount to the viability of nationhood. Virtually all policy action is considered in economic terms, including language. In 1972, Inche Rahim Ishak said: 'In Singapore, rapid industrialisation has been chosen as the key to progress, hence language and culture will have to fit in with this pattern of priorities' (*The Straits Times*, 27 March 1972). At the community level, English is seen to be the obvious choice for interethnic communication. And at the individual level, since all members of society would have access to English, the gap between the English and Asian-language-educated would narrow. All individuals would have equal access to the benefits that a knowledge of English offered.

As we mentioned earlier, there is no language planning agency in

Singapore, as there is in Malaysia and Indonesia. Instead, the official languages are guided by exoglossic norms, following the norms that are established at international centres of language development and management (Kuo and Jernudd, 1994), notably the UK, Malaysia, India and China. Language policies and objectives usually appear in ministerial statements. These are then passed on to the various ministries for implementation. We will focus here on some of the policies that have been milestones in language planning, focussing on the two major institutions responsible for the implementation of these policies: education and the mass media. Of course, policy is only one aspect of language planning. For a discussion on the pedagogical issues, for example, the reader is encouraged to look at work done by Kuo and Jernudd (1994), Ho (1994) and Foley in this volume.

Language Planning and Policy Implementation: In the Schools

> In a free and independent Malaya in which every Chinese, every Indian, every Malay, will no longer be Chinese, Malay or Indian but Malayan, what language or languages shall they speak? What language or languages shall the Government use? What language or languages will be acceptable to the people? What are the language or languages of an independent and democratic Malaya? They are thorny delicate problems.
>
> (Lee, Singapore Legislative Assembly Debates, 1955/56, Col.262-264).

The questions raised by Lee Kuan Yew in the Legislative Assembly were clearly not just about language. They were more about what an 'independent and democratic Malaya' would look like, and about how language would participate in that image. Given that, at this stage, independence was only considered viable through merger with Malaya, Lee Kuan Yew's questions were very crucial. A 'Malaysian Malaysia', the Malaysia that Lee Kuan Yew envisioned, could not easily dismiss the presence of multilingualism. Yet, the growing trend in Malaya of *Malay* nationalism threatened such a multilingual model. Against such a model, what would the different languages be able to contribute to the social and political process of independence? What would their position be in the new state? These questions were not only asked by Lee Kuan Yew; they were also the questions asked (although with different motives) by the militant Chinese nationalists in Singapore. The escalating unrest within the Chinese schools and the labour union movement demanded that such questions be addressed. So an All-Party Committee was appointed (of which Lee Kuan Yew was a member) to investigate the situation of the Chinese schools and to make recommendations for the improvement of Chinese education. However, it is very difficult to separate Chinese schools from the larger issues of Asian-language and English-medium schools. And so the committee was soon embroiled in the larger issues of language and education at a national level.

One of the key observations of the All-Party Committee was that linguistic diversity was problematic. Apart from a smattering of English and Bazaar Malay, there was no real common language in Singapore. It concluded that: 'Without one or more common languages officially encouraged in Singapore and fostered in the schools, the ideal of unifying the various races into one common people cannot be realised, and the links of common understanding, outlook and identity of interest cannot be speedily forged' (p. 9). Among the recommendations of the Committee in their 1955 Report of the All-Party Committee of the Legislative Assembly on Chinese Education (known as the All-Party Report) was that, while the system of separate language schools remain, all schools should offer English and Malay as common languages. The rationale for the emphasis on English was that: (a) it was already the common language among the various racial communities; (b) it carried commercial and industrial value; and (c) it was the language of the Commonwealth countries to which Singapore would belong (p. 9). The decision for English, as mentioned earlier, was also seen as a way to narrow the gap between the Asian-language schools and the English-medium schools. In fact, it stressed that all schools be treated equally. This meant increased funding for the Asian-language schools and the assurance that these schools would be cultivated rather than threatened with extinction. The rationale for Malay was linked to the desire for Singapore to gain independence through merger with Malaya.

The recommendations presented in the All-Party Report also need to be understood against the backdrop of developments in the Peninsula. In 1951, the government released an education report put forward by a committee led by L. J. Barnes (an Oxford don). Although its original focus was Malay education, the recommendations affected all aspects of education in the Federation. Most contentious was the recommendation that the separate Asian-language schools be phased out and replaced by a national school system. Only Malay and English would be the media of instruction (Wilson, 1978: 150). There was great anxiety on the part of the Singaporean Chinese that the government of the colony might follow suit. Another committee led by Dr. William Fen and Dr. Wu Teh Yao was set up at the request of the Singapore government to look into Chinese schools in the Federation. Their report at least acknowledged some of the concerns of the Chinese community.

However, the All-Party Report was more significant in that it was the first *Singaporean* committee with Singaporean members, which presented a *Singaporean* view. It proposed an educational model very different from that proposed by the Barnes committee. While the committee agreed that Malay should be taught as a common language, it nonetheless argued that education must operate within a multicultural and multilingual framework, and that the Asian-language schools remain.

The model of a Malaysian Malaysia, modelled on multiculturalism, ultimately clashed with the Malaysian government's desire for a Malay Malaysia (Bokhorst-Heng, 1998). And thus, Singapore's merger with Malaysia was brief: from 1963 to 1965. With independence in 1965, it was clear that Malay, although the national language, would have no significant place within either the education or economic sectors. Furthermore, unlike Malaysia, which has long struggled with the image of English being a vestige of colonial oppression, Singapore embraced English. Rather than championing one language to symbolize national unity and national identity, Singapore conceptualized its nation within a rubric of multiracialism and multilingualism, and deemed English as the neutral and pragmatic necessity for the nation's progress.

This view of multiracialism and multilingualism became the bedrock of the bilingual policy. One of the first policy actions of the independent government was to introduce bilingualism as a way to unify the education system and to align it with its national objectives. Its decisions were largely based on the recommendations made in the 1955 All-Party Report. Different language-medium schools were allowed to remain. However, those in the English-medium schools were to learn their 'mother tongue' as a second language, and those in Asian-language schools would learn English as a second language. Furthermore, Math and Science in Primary 1 in all non-English schools and all technical subjects in secondary schools were to be taught in English. Civics, and for a short time, History, were to be taught in the mother tongue in English schools. In effect, this policy of bilingualism made English the lingua franca of Singapore, giving the policy the name 'English-knowing bilingualism' (Kachru, 1993: 40-42): English plus one of the three ascribed mother tongues. In a curious twist, these 'mother tongues' are defined according to one's father's ethnicity (and thus may not be the language spoken in the home). Therefore it can be said that there is multilingualism at the national level, and bilingualism at the individual level in terms of official policy — although most Singaporeans speak a variety of languages to varying degrees of proficiency.

Changes also appeared in other areas of education. In 1975, the Chinese-medium Nanyang University began to use English as a medium of instruction, along with Mandarin. Three years later, in 1978, a 'Joint Campus' scheme was introduced. Under this scheme, courses common to both the University of Singapore and Nanyang University were combined and offered at the University of Singapore's Bukit Timah campus, in English. The purpose was to give Nanyang students greater exposure to English — although as Mary Tay, a prominent linguist in Singapore, noted, most students chose Hokkien for intercampus communication (personal communication, December 1994). Finally, in 1979, English was made the primary medium of instruction in all pre-university classes — including non-English-medium schools.

Although Lee Kuan Yew had expressed concern about the success of the bilingual policy throughout the 1970s, it was not until 1978 that the bilingual policy received its first formal evaluation. Under the leadership of the then Minister for Defence, Dr. Goh Keng Swee, the 'education team' responsible for this evaluation declared the policy a failure. They found that less than 40% of students had attained the minimum competency level in two languages. Furthermore, they identified the continued use of dialects in the home as being the key obstacle to the success of the bilingual policy. 'The majority of the pupils are taught in two languages, English and Mandarin,' the Committee explained. 'About 85 percent of these pupils do not speak these languages at home. When they are home, they speak dialects. As a result, most of what they have learned in school is not reinforced' (1979: 4). This was a significant reversal in thinking from only a few years earlier, when the writers of the 1956 All-Party Report saw dialects as *facilitating* the learning of Mandarin. However, it was an inevitable reversal, considering the apparent difficulty children from dialect-speaking homes were having in coping with learning both Mandarin and English.

The immediate effect of the Goh Report was that language was directly linked to educational progress under the New Education System (NES). The objective of the NES was 'to make students as bilingual as they can be' (*The Straits Times*, 31 March 1979). That is, it aimed to enable above average and average pupils to be proficient in English and at least literate in Malay/ Chinese/Tamil. Director of Education Chai Kai Yau told parents in no uncertain terms that they had to face the 'hard facts' that there would be 'children who cannot learn so many things' (*The Straits Times*, 5 July 1979). Only the bright pupils could be effectively bilingual. Following the Goh Committee's recommendation that the first three years of primary schooling concentrate primarily on language learning, about 50% of curriculum time was to be spent on language learning as opposed to factual knowledge. At the end of year three, primary students were to be streamed into either the *Normal bilingual* course (a 3-year programme) involving two languages, *Extended bilingual* (4 years) also involving two languages but at a slower pace, or the *Monolingual* course (5 years). The student allocation in these was to be about 60%, 20% and 20% respectively. At the end of Primary Six, students in the *Normal* and *Extended* courses would sit the Primary School Leaving Exam (PSLE), streaming them into either the *Special, Express,* or *Normal* secondary course. *Monolingual* students would sit the Primary School Proficiency Exam (PSPE) leading to vocational training. The *Special* bilingual stream (the top 10%) was to be reserved for 'those pupils who are ablest' to do two 'first' languages (English and Mandarin), and possibly a third language (like German). It would be offered only at the nine Chinese-medium Special Assistance Plan (SAP) schools. These SAP schools were selected by the government to be elite, 'effectively bilingual institutions', responsible for protecting the Chinese heritage and producing the next generation of 'social brokers'. The *Express* bilingual stream was for above-average pupils who would do a 'first' and 'second' language (e.g. English and Mandarin). The *Normal* bilingual stream was for average students who would also do two languages but at a basic level. The student allocation in these streams was to be about 31%, 41% and 20% respectively. In this structure, effective bilingualism thus became a key marker of an elite leadership, for only the brightest students were offered full opportunities to be effective bilingualists. They were the future decision makers, the keepers of the 'key to an internal stabiliser in the form of cultural heritage' (*The Straits Times,* 31 August 1989). According to Lee Kuan Yew, bilingual speakers 'have binocular vision, seeing the world in three dimensions' (*The Straits Times,* 26 February 1977) — a necessary feature of leadership.

The overall result of these policies, in the context of the socio-political-economic systems that supported it, was the further enhancement of the predominant position of English. Enrolment in the English-medium schools continued to soar, from 47% in 1959 to 91% in 1979 and 99% in 1983. As a 1978 survey by *The Straits Times* revealed (5 May 1978), as long as there were clear economic advantages to English-language proficiency, parents would continue to send their children to English-medium schools, rather than Asian-language schools. What Lee Kuan Yew said of the status of English during colonialism remained true in independent Singapore: 'There were no English-educated trishaw riders or rickshaw pullers, labourers or coolies, as they used to be called, because whoever became English-educated need not become a coolie or a trishaw rider. Other more profitable avenues of employment were open to them' (*The Straits Times,* 17 August 1959). Any objection parents may have had to English education was actually pre-empted by the government with the implementation of the bilingual policy. For, as Puru Shotam (1987) noted, English-knowing bilingualism actually made Chinese-medium education redundant. 'For why send your child to Chinese stream schools when the time table of an English-medium school ensured exposure to Chinese for up to forty percent of the time a child spent in school?' she queried (1987: 98). Parents thus had nothing to lose, but much to gain, in sending their children to English-medium schools.

Citing enrolment figures for 1984, Goh Kim Leong, Permanent Secretary (Education) noted that: 'Only 260 children had enrolled for Chinese-medium primary one classes next year (1984). This is out of a total of more than 38 000 children who will start school in January. This is the smallest number of children to enrol in Chinese schools. No parent has put his child in a Malay-medium school since 1976. And there has been no primary one pupil for Tamil schools since 1982' (*The Straits Times*, 22 and 24 December 1983). He recommended a national school system, with English as the medium of instruction in all schools and mother tongue taught as a subject.[2] Only the nine SAP schools and four primary schools selected to be 'Seed schools', where English and Chinese would continue to be offered at the first language level, would be exempt from this ruling. And so, in 1984 the progressive conversion to English began. By 1987, all schools had been converted to English-medium.

This short overview of language planning and policy in the schools shows the steady increase in the status and usage of English in Singapore. This emphasis on English has been very closely tied to human resource development in Singapore, and the dependence of Singapore on attracting foreign investment and operations in Singapore. Furthermore, it has been very closely tied to the basic needs of communication in a multilingual nation. In Singapore, the question of language diversity needed to be addressed. English was one of the answers.

Language Planning and Policy Implementation: In the Mass Media

One only needs to look at a newspaper stand in Singapore to see the practical implications of the country's policy of multilingualism. Newspapers, all published under the rubric of Singapore Press Holdings, are available in all four official languages. The 1994 circulation figures showed their relative distribution as in Table 1.

---

[2] It is worth noting that a common system of education with English as the medium of education for all was first proposed by the Malay Teachers' Union in 1970. They also proposed that, to preserve cultural-linguistic identity, the teaching of Chinese, Tamil and Malay and their respective literatures be made compulsory. However, at that time the government rejected their proposal for fear that it might upset supporters of Malay and Tamil education. (Tham, S. C. (1989) The Perception and Practice of Education. In K. Sandhu and P. Wheatley (Eds.), *Management of Success: The Moulding of Modern Singapore*. Singapore: Institute of Southeast Asian Studies, 477–502.)

Newspaper	Circulation
Berita Harian (Malay)	61 015
Business Times (English)	34 765
The New Paper (English)	128 346
The Straits Times (English)	364 377
Lianhe Wanbao (Chinese)	124 000
Lianhe Zaobao (Chinese)	204 000
Shin Min Daily (Chinese)	110 000
Tamil Murasu (Tamil)	4 900*

* Figure for 1993

Source: Media Directory, 1995; Singapore Facts and Pictures, 1994

Table 1. Circulation Rates for Singapore's Daily Newspapers (1994)

Television similarly provides a glimpse of Singapore's multilingual 'Instant Asia'. The Television Corporation of Singapore (TCS; formerly Singapore Broadcasting Corporation) has two channels: Channel 5, which offers primarily English programmes; and Channel 8, which is mostly in Mandarin. Singapore Television Twelve (STV) operates Prime 12, which is a mixture of Malay, Indian and foreign programmes; and Premiere 12, which is mostly in English. In 1990, Pennycook (1992) found about 63.8% of total SBC programming was in English, 27.7% in Mandarin, 4.0% in Malay and 4.5% in Tamil. However, the availability of Malaysia's TV1 and TV2 raised Malay viewing time considerably. TV1 and TV2 had 46.2% of their programming in English, 41.6% in Malay, 8.1% in Mandarin and 4.1% in Tamil. It is also worth noting that, as Kuo and Jernudd (1994) have pointed out, the scope of the languages on television is actually broader when subtitling is taken into consideration. Generally, non-English programmes have English subtitles, and English language programmes often have Mandarin or Malay subtitles. Radio also broadcasts in separate language channels, ranging from about 28% Mandarin to 22% for Tamil (Kuo and Jernudd, 1994: 35).

While all the four official languages are represented in the various forms of mass media, it is significant that in all, English makes up the majority. *The Straits Times* alone boasts the largest circulation figures, and English newspapers in total take up 52% of total circulation. On television, even if we combine Malaysian television with that of Singapore, English still makes up the majority: English 55.7%, Malay 21.2%, Chinese 18.7% and

Tamil 4.3%. As with education, English is clearly the dominant language of the mass media.

But the participation of the mass media in language planning is evident in ways other than just the implementation of the multilingual policy. Gonzalez *et al.* (1984: 69-71) summarized four key ways in which TCS is involved in implementing official language policies. These can be applied to the mass daily press as well. First, the mass media is involved in the *direct presentation and explanation of the policies to the public*. This includes reporting on ministerial statements in which the policies first appear as detailed in press releases, and often providing some background information. These same ministers will often participate in interviews, panel discussions and debates on the particular issue. From early April 1978 to January 1982, fifteen panel discussions, debates and documentaries involving issues of language policy were featured on television. Lee Kuan Yew was the keynote speaker in five of them, where he held discussions with journalists and other panellists as a way to explain the rationale of the bilingual policy (Bokhorst-Heng, 1998). Each of these programmes was detailed in the press, often with full transcripts reproduced over a few days. The press would also provide feature stories, editorials and background commentary to further explain the policy. Second, the mass media is involved in *control of the language medium and form of programming*. We have already noted the allocation of language on television and radio programming and in the press. But the mass media also has a role in the language used. For television and radio, this includes control of pronunciation (for example, newsreaders are trained to speak in British Received Pronunciation (RP)). For the press, it includes the decision to switch from Chinese classical to simplified characters. Language campaigns, such as the Speak Mandarin Campaign, have also been heavily featured both in the press and on television. Third, the mass media is involved in language planning through its *control of programme content*. In addition to direct government-sponsored programmes to educate the public concerning a particular policy, there are other public service programmes and features that function to similarly influence language behaviour. These include spot advertisements and mini-programmes on television. A regular column featuring Chinese legends is offered in both English and Mandarin in *The Straits Times*. The press is also involved in conducting numerous surveys to measure the success of the policy. These are just some of the ways the mass media supports the government's policy through programme content. Finally, the mass media participates in language planning through *direct language teaching*. Radio and television have always been a popular means of language teaching. Before the Speak Mandarin Campaign, English was the language most frequently taught over the air. Mandarin has now taken over as the most popular language. SBC launched a Conversational Mandarin Programme in late 1979, involving twenty-six 30-minute lessons. Also in conjunction with the campaign, *The Straits Times* has featured a bilingual page giving language instruction. Telephone 'Dial-a-Mandarin' lessons have also been used. And most recently, Mandarin lessons have been made available by the Ministry of Information and the Arts on the Internet in conjunction with the 1996 campaign.

So far we have discussed the role of education and the mass media in terms of their role in the implementation of government-led language planning. In the next section, we will turn our attention to some of the effects of the spread of English in Singapore, and how these effects can be understood.

English in Singapore: The Language of Wider Communication?

On the surface, the rising dominance of English appears to follow Fishman's (1968) notion of nation/nationism (as opposed to nationality/nationalism). Nationism, Fishman argues, involves a diglossic situation where indigenous languages co-exist with a 'language of wider communication' (LWC), with the latter functioning as the working language in society. They are recognized primarily on the basis of their functional utility in the domains of science and technology. In Singapore, it is certainly true that English has been accorded the status of LWC, a status which has been reinforced by a concurrent definition of 'mother tongue' as the language of culture. As S. Rajaratnam observed, 'I think Singapore is the only country which has made a foreign language, English, the working language' (*The Straits Times*, 12 July 1986). It is the language of government bureaucracy, the language of the courts, the language of international trade, the language of science and technology, the language of business. English is presented as available to all. In fact, as mentioned earlier, giving everyone access to English was a key strategy of the newly independent government to create a more equal society. Lee Kuan Yew explicitly stated in his 1970 Dillingham address:

> The deliberate stifling of a language which gives access to superior technology can be stifling beyond repair. Sometimes, this is done, not to elevate the status of the indigenous language, so much as to take away a supposed advantage a minority in the society is deemed to have, because that minority has already gained a greater competence in the foreign language. This can be most damaging. It is tantamount to blinding the next generation to the knowledge of the advanced countries.

English has been described as the 'dominant working language' (Kuo, 1980), as being the language of the 'emergent national culture' (Benjamin, 1976), as the language of a 'supra-ethnic national identity' (Tay, 1993), or as a 'link language', unifying the different races (*The Straits Times*, various). English-educated Singaporeans are seen as being potentially less ethnocentric and demonstrating greater loyalty to Singapore (Tan and Chew, 1970), and as 'social brokers' (Murray, 1971). In the earlier years of Singapore's development, such a view of English as equally available to all and as having the potential to function as a national language, was perhaps understandable. However, more recent developments with respect to the place of English in Singapore, and the emergence of different varieties of English, make it necessary to rethink such views.

Tan (1995) is one of a number of scholars who challenge the applicability of Fishman's LWC to English in Singapore. She argues that, when applied to the status and meanings of English in Singapore, Fishman's notion of nationism is fundamentally flawed. Her strongest criticism is that such a view projects English in apolitical terms as utilitarian and neutral. Nationism 'assumes uncritically an ideology of modernisation which fails to connect the spread of the language with an understanding of the dialectics inherent in its development' (1995: 18). The principal error in Fishman's notion of nationism and LWC is that it assumes a unitary meaning of language, when in fact, it carries a multiplicity of competing meanings in their various domains of usage. What particularly argues against this notion of unitary meanings in the English language is how the language is embedded in a system of meritocracy in Singapore. Recent work by Singapore scholars on the meanings of English in Singapore bear this out, showing how English has not only unifying, but also divisive, possibilities (Gupta, 1994; Kandiah, 1994; Pakir, 1991; 1994; Platt and Weber, 1980; Tan, 1995).

In the first place, while English has been presented as available to all, the 1990 census showed that literacy in English stood at 65% of the population (Census, 1991). Conversely, this meant that 35% of the population was not able to read English. In terms of actual language use, the figures were substantially lower: 20.3% of the population reported English as a predominant household language, compared to 26.0% for Mandarin and 36.7% for other Chinese languages. Thus a high percentage of literacy does not mean that English is widely used by all. Furthermore, those who use English frequently and with proficiency are those in the higher socioeconomic and educational bracket. The 1990 census showed that proficiency in English is directly associated with social mobility and socioeconomic status. According to census figures, 7.6% of households with incomes less than $1000 per month used English as their household language, compared to 33.5% of households earning over $4000 per month. Because educational streaming occurs very early in one's education (since 1992 at Primary 4), and because English is such a crucial feature of this process, students who come from homes where English is used extensively have a strong advantage over others.

In her study of students' use of extracurricular language lessons, Kwan-Terry (1991) noted that 60.5% of students in the 'gifted' stream at the primary level came from such backgrounds. In contrast, only 2.3% came from backgrounds where Chinese dialects were used. In the monolingual stream, the reverse was true. Children from English-speaking homes were not represented at all, while 60.6% came from dialect-speaking homes. She further found that more than half of all primary students hired tutors for extracurricular language lessons. English lessons were the most common, and were largely taken by those from middle-income homes. Those from the higher-income bracket tended to take mother tongue lessons. For obvious financial reasons, those from the lower-income bracket were largely unable to send their children for extra tuition. As such, Kwan-Terry concludes, 'children from English-speaking homes where the father has a university education commanding a high income stand a much higher chance of getting into the top academic group where they are assured of a good future, as they are advantaged both on account of their language background and the financial resources available to them to help them cope with the language demands of the education system. Children from disadvantaged homes, on the other hand...are devoid of the necessary financial resources to avail themselves of help when help for the learning of languages is needed' (1991: 88). And thus the social stratification system is perpetuated.

The socioeconomic and educational link with English language proficiency is also evident in the educational background of the cabinet ministers. All of the 1996 cabinet ministers, except for BG Lee Hsien Loong (who received his primary and secondary education in Mandarin), are English-educated and all received their higher education in Australia, the UK, USA, or Canada. Of parliament as a whole, only 17 MPs, or 21% of the 81-seat House, have at least a secondary-school education in the Chinese stream. Only 8 are fully Chinese-educated, meaning they also received their tertiary education at Chinese-medium Nanyang (Bokhorst-Heng, 1998).

In this challenge to the notion of English as the LWC in Singapore, we also need to consider the distinction between Standard Singapore English (SSE) and Colloquial Singapore English (CSE) (see also Alsagoff and Ho in this volume). Pakir's (1991) model of the 'Expanding Triangle of English Expression' (Figure 1) shows how these two varieties of Singapore English negate any notion of there being a single 'English' language that can stand as the Language of Wider Communication in Singapore.

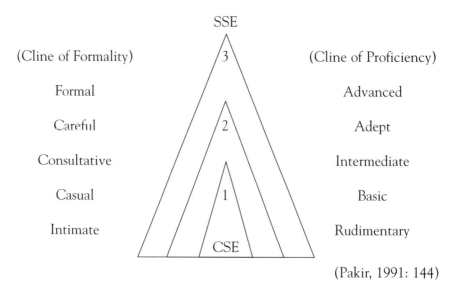

(Pakir, 1991: 144)

Figure 1. Expanding Triangle of English Expression by English-knowing Bilinguals in Singapore

According to Pakir, those users of English with higher education are located at the top ends of both the cline of formality and of proficiency. They are capable of both the Standard (SSE) and the Colloquial (CSE) forms of Singapore English, and are therefore able to move with fluidity along the whole range of the formality cline. Those with lower levels of proficiency, most often coming from a lower socioeconomic background and having lower education, are found at the base of the triangle. They are typically restricted in their movement along the formality cline, usually restricted to colloquial forms of Singapore English. The model is somewhat limited in that it remains unclear how one might place an individual speaker on this triangle (what is the difference between basic and rudimentary?). It also remains to be seen whether all speakers of SSE are indeed able to move all the way down the proficiency cline to speak CSE at the lowest level. However, what the model does show is that clearly one cannot speak of there being a single 'English' language in Singapore that can stand as the LWC. It shows that the English language carries a complex array of meanings, and is steeped in Singapore's socioeconomic and power relations.

In this section, we have considered some of the effects of the spread of English. Most notably, we have argued that, while perhaps English has provided Singaporeans a common medium of communication, it has at the same time created a new gap based on socioeconomic status. Furthermore, recent trends are showing that this language-based social hierarchy is beginning to reproduce itself. Finally, we have seen how English itself is multiple. There is a continuum of English in Singapore, ranging from a more standard form to a more colloquial form.

✤ *The Management of English and of the Effects of English*

We have called this section the 'management' of English, as opposed to 'planning', deliberately. While the spread of English in Singapore can be seen largely as a result of deliberate government planning and policy, it cannot be said that all of the effects of this spread, while perhaps anticipated, were planned. And so, what we see here is the management of these effects. This management has come about in two ways. One is more direct language policy measures in respect to the Singlish-English debate. The other has to do with language meanings, largely through specific policies and discourses about the 'mother tongues' and, more specifically, Mandarin. We are focussing on Mandarin here, not to slight the position of Tamil and Malay, but rather, because of the government's view that the effects of English have been most evident in the Chinese community. Our attention here will be on the bilingual policy in general, and the Speak Mandarin Campaign in particular, as being part of the management of English.

'Singlish Why Cannot?'

Others in this volume have provided a comprehensive discussion of the features and definitions of CSE and Singlish in contrast to SSE. As such, the focus here will be on the way these two varieties of English have been managed by the government, and on the way these forms of English have been understood by both the government and the people. Already in 1977, the government showed concern about the emergence of Singlish. One of the cabinet ministers noted at a seminar on the teaching of English: 'Whichever way English evolves, we have to ensure that the English spoken by our pupils is internationally intelligible' (*The Straits Times*, 18 August 1977). The concern expressed here of course reflected the government's view of English as a prerequisite for modernization and economic development. Such concerns led to the recruitment of native English speakers to teach in schools and to train local teachers and to the organization of regular in-service courses and seminars to upgrade the level of English in various companies and in the civil service. The British Council and the Regional Language Centre (RELC) have been active in teaching English and in making recommendations regarding the learning and standard of English in Singapore.

However, a more recent debate concerns the notion of what kind of English is appropriate for identity. Such discussions first appeared in *The*

Straits Times in 1982 in response to some comments made by a cabinet minister who viewed the language negatively (7 August 1982). His remarks sparked a brief but significant discussion in the press. What is most interesting is the clear diglossic distinction the readers made between high (H) SSE and low (L) CSE. Consider the comments of one reader:

> It is about time the arbiters of our Singapore life style realise that while good writing requires a certain amount of formality and literary convention, the charm and vitality of colloquial speech depends completely on spontaneity and a total lack of self consciousness. What a pompous, boring and insufferable society we will be if all Singaporeans were to speak as though they were writing a prize winning essay.
>
> (*The Straits Times*, 13 August 1982)

This argument for a diglossic use of SSE and CSE appeared again in the press the following year. Responding to a negative account of two nurses speaking in Singlish with each other, one reader argued there was nothing objectionable about this conversation. 'Given the context and presumably,' he wrote, 'the tacit understanding between the nurses, any other way of saying the same thing would sound most affected and ridiculous.' The reader went on to use Platt's Singapore English speech continuum to further the argument: '...the basilect is distinctively and delightfully Singaporean. We don't have to apologise for it and we should be free to use it — unblushingly — when the occasion arises...Let the basilect stay, but let's also have a wide enough repertoire to "switch" to higher "lect" if need be' (*The Straits Times*, 26 April 1983). The *Business Times* noted that the use of Singlish was even becoming trendy among young professionals (25 June 1992), as a familiarity marker and an act of identity. The use of Singlish for group identity was stressed by the fact that they did not use Singlish when there was a foreigner or expatriate in the group. However, not all Singaporeans speak so fondly of Singlish. Some have called it a brand of 'mongrel-lingualism' (*The Straits Times*, Forum Page, 24 January 1985), and others, a pollution of English.

But what made the debate over the usage and meanings of Singlish particularly poignant was when the domains assigned to SSE(H) and CSE(L) were challenged. The most clear example is the debate around the use of Singlish on television, which some felt was a domain where the high variety of English was more appropriate. The debate was most active in 1993 when several popular English television entertainment programs, such as 'The Ra Ra Show', 'Gotcha!' and 'Mum's Not Cooking', had some of their characters liberally speaking Singlish. One reader wrote to *The Straits Times* that 'Singlish is Singaporean slang which may be comfortable to use, but it has its limits and proper contexts of use. For instance, it would be improper to use Singlish in a court of law or in Parliament.' Because 'the power of the media to influence the masses is great,' the reader argued, 'unless the Government wishes to encourage the use of Singlish, it should step in, via Singapore Broadcasting Corporation (SBC), to regulate if not eradicate altogether its use in commercials and programs' (*The Straits Times*, 11 May 1993). Those arguing for the high SSE to be used on television declared Singlish to be 'a perversion of the English language,' a 'grotesque form of English.' They expressed concern over the kind of influence the use of Singlish on television would have on the younger generation, and the impression tourists and other foreigners would have of Singaporeans. Those arguing that television is an appropriate domain for Singlish argued that television was meant for entertainment, not for education, and that Singaporeans had a right to hear their own voice. The headline in *The Straits Times* captures their view: 'Singlish: What's so dem long about laughing at ourselves?'

Whether it was in response to public pressure as the press claimed, or whether in response to a directive from the government over real concerns about the effect that the language used on television may have on their audience (no studies have been done to verify or refute this claim), the SBC announced in July 1993 that Singlish would no longer be allowed on television (*The Straits Times*, 1 July 1993). As the SBC was largely controlled by the government, we can assume that this decision was in line with government policy. The SBC produced 'clear guidelines' on the use of English in its programmes. It defined Standard English as 'grammatically correct and pronounced in the correct way'. Local English was defined as 'grammatically correct but spoken in a recognisably Singaporean accent'. And Singlish was defined as 'ungrammatical English spoken by those with a poor command of English' (*The Straits Times*, 10 July 1993). The assumption was that what is 'correct' pronunciation is British Received Pronunciation. The definitions given by SBC were rather curious, for as we have already seen, Singlish is not spoken by only those with a 'poor command of English'. Furthermore, for some Singaporeans anyway, there is the notion of domain and the ability to code-switch where appropriate.

Mother Tongue and the Management of English

As we noted earlier, one of the first policies of the government at the time of independence was to institute the bilingual policy. Essentially, the bilingual policy has been premised on what Pendley (1983) calls the 'functional polarisation' of language, and Kuo and Jernudd call the 'division of labour between languages' (1994: 30). Lee Kuan Yew's 1972 speech at the Singapore Teachers' Union Dinner describes this polarization:

...when I speak of bilingualism, I do not mean just the facility of speaking two languages. It is more basic than that. First we understand ourselves...then the facility of the English language gives us access to the science and technology of the West. It also provides a convenient common ground on which...everybody competes in a neutral medium.

With the language [mother tongue] go the fables and proverbs. It is the learning of a whole value system, a whole philosophy of life, that can maintain the fabric of our society intact, in spite of exposure to all the current madnesses around the world.

On the one hand, English needs to be spoken for instrumental and pragmatic reasons — for employment and the transfer of technology and information with the broader global community. In this view, the English language is seen as neutral and cultureless. On the other hand, mother tongue is a demarcation and embodiment of culture, acting as a cultural ballast and anchor for the Singaporean. English is for *new knowledge*, to keep the nation abreast with its economic and development objectives; mother tongue is for *old knowledge*, to keep the people anchored and focussed amidst the changes around them (Lee, *The Straits Times*, 24 November 1979). While the lines within this polarization appear well-defined, in practice, tensions often arise. As discussed earlier, can English, which is not a mother tongue, develop a 'Singaporean' identity? What effect would this potential indigenization of English have on the other languages in Singapore? In more recent years, Mandarin is increasingly valued not for its cultural appeal but for its growing economic currency with the opening of China's markets. Will the lines between commerce and culture, English and mother tongue, be challenged?

Perhaps even more problematic from the perspective of the government is that, in practice, it is nearly impossible to compartmentalize language in such a manner. In fact, to assume English can be merely the neutral language of commerce (which itself is not neutral) is to deny the true nature of language. The words of Lloyd Fernando on the use of English in Southeast Asia will suggest what is meant here: 'It is not British culture which should be feared in South East Asia...It is rather certain Western habits of thinking which are now deeply infused into the language to which we must be much more alert' (1986: 89-90). Using Saville-Troike's terminology, Pakir (1989) calls Singapore a 'soft-shelled' community, meaning that the spread of English has made Singapore vulnerable to outside (Western) influences. The Malay and Indian communities, it is felt, are mostly protected against such influences, largely due to the strength of their religions and customs. However, with no common religion or culture uniting them, the Chinese community is seen to be more vulnerable (*The Straits Times*, 30 August 1988).

The multiplicity of dialects has been seen as a major hindrance to the development of a common culture. And so, in order to protect the Chinese community against the undesirable effects of the English language and to provide them with a cultural ballast, in 1979 the government launched what has become an annual Speak Mandarin Campaign. The Campaign is not just about language, but very much about culture, Confucianism and Asian values. It is an attempt to facilitate the emergence of a culture, an effort to manage the negative influences of the dominance of the English language.

Three official reasons have been given for the Campaign. First of all, there is the *educational argument*. The Campaign began as a response to the findings of the Goh Report in 1979. The continued use of dialects in the home was identified by the Goh committee as being the primary reason for the failure of the bilingual policy. Children were forced to learn two languages in school — English and Mandarin. Thus, to reduce their learning burden, parents were encouraged to sacrifice their dialect for the sake of their children's education. If children spoke Mandarin at home, they would have only one language to learn in school.

The second reason was the *communicative argument*. Although Hokkien and Bazaar Malay had historically served as the media of interdialect communication within the Chinese community, it was felt that this practice should be discouraged. In the first place, to support the children in learning and speaking Mandarin, the use of dialects in all spheres should be avoided. And second, Mandarin was a better form of interdialect group communication as it was also more useful outside of Singapore, whereas Hokkien was more limited. Thus, the communicative argument was directly linked to the need to strengthen the bonds between the different dialect groups.

Finally, the campaign put forward the *cultural argument*. As mentioned above, the dominance of English, while desired by the government, also created a quandary for the government. Dr. Chan Seow Phun presented the problem this way:

> Our universal English education has served us well in producing a workforce which is better educated and relevant to the economy. However, it has also produced a new generation of Singaporeans who are more and more westernised because of their constant exposure to and absorption of western values. Some of these values, such as their concept of individual rights and freedom cannot, in my opinion, be the principles on which we should build our nation.

(Parliamentary Debates, 17 January 1989, Vol. 52, prt 1, Col 67-68)

Chinese Singaporeans were dangerously vulnerable to Westernization and the negative effects of English dominance. They needed to be reminded of their cultural identity and roots; to know and understand where they came from. And they needed a cultural ballast to protect their identity. Mandarin was seen to be the key to that identity, and to be capable of being such a ballast. In his televised speech on 21 February 1978, 'Mandarin: lingua franca for Chinese Singaporeans', Lee Kuan Yew argued:

> We must keep the core of our value systems and social mores. To do that, we must have our children literate in Chinese and English. To be literate, they must be Mandarin-speaking, able to read the books, the proverbs, the parables, and the stories of heroes and villains, so that they know what a good upright man should do and be. Hence the Mandarin part of our bilingual policy must succeed.

> (*The Straits Times*, 22 February 1978)

In the campaigning for Mandarin, English was no longer presented as neutral, but rather, as a carrier of Western and undesirable values, as a threat to the identity and *Asian-ness* of Singapore. Speaking at the Singapore Teachers' Union Anniversary Dinner (5 November 1972), Lee Kuan Yew referred to the Caribbean society to portray what Singapore might well become. He saw the Caribbean society as being 'deculturalised' and as being a 'calypso-type society...speaking pidgin English, mindlessly aping the Americans or British with no basic values or cultures' of their own, and leading a 'steel-beating and rum-brewing-and-drinking, happy-go-lucky life.' Frankly, he declared: 'I do not believe this [kind of society] is worth the building...worth the preserving.' Without effective language skills, Singapore would become a deculturalized society, which would impede the emergence of a national identity and ultimately threaten the survival of the nation. It was to prevent such a scenario that Chinese Singaporeans were encouraged to embrace Mandarin.

Within the framework of the Campaign, there has also been an emphasis on Asian values and on Confucianism. In his address at the opening of the 7th Parliament on 9 January 1989, President Wee Kim Wee introduced the idea of a National Ideology/Shared Values as Singapore's response to the threat that Westernization and Western liberalism posed for Singapore:

> ...the speed and extent of the changes in Singapore society is worrying. We cannot tell what dangers lie ahead, as we rapidly grow more westernised.

> What sort of society will we become in another generation? What sort of people do we want our children to become? Do we really

want to abandon our own cultures and national identity? Can we build a nation of Singaporeans, in Southeast Asia, on the basis of values and concepts native to other peoples, living in other environments? How we answer these questions will determine our future.

If we are not to lose our bearings, we should preserve the cultural heritage of each of our communities, and uphold certain common values which capture the essence of being a Singaporean...We need to enshrine these fundamental ideas in a National Ideology. Such a formal statement will bond us together as Singaporeans, with our own distinct identity and destiny. We need to inculcate this National Ideology in all Singaporeans, especially the young.

(Parliamentary Debates, 9 January 1989, Vol. 52, Col.13-14)

On 2 January 1991, the 'White Paper on Shared Values' was accepted by Parliament. Taking most of the President's recommendations, the White Paper states the following as being the core principles to guide the imagining of the nation: nation before community, and society before self; family as the basic unit of society; regard and community support for the individual; resolving major issues through consensus, not conflict; and racial and religious harmony. Prime Minister Goh Chok Tong saw the 'Shared Values' as 'moral anchors [to] buttress Singapore's Asian value system against over-Westernisation and deculturalisation' (*The Straits Times*, 6 January 1991).

Taken as a whole, then, the bilingual policy, the Speak Mandarin Campaign, and the discourse on Asian and core values, can be seen as a strategy used by the government in the management of English, and the management of the effects of English in Singapore.

Conclusion

In this chapter, we have considered language planning in Singapore. While the focus has been on the English language, it is apparent that language meanings and policies involving the different languages are completely interdependent. The planning of the different languages works towards what is seen to be a 'good' society, towards what is seen to be best for Singapore and Singaporeans, and towards how the different languages can contribute to social and political progress. Out of its colonial past with linguistic diversity, ethnic complexity, social inequality, and with the marriage of language to this inequality, language planning emerged. And as Singapore modernizes and attempts to manage its changing social and political circumstances, language planning continues.

Bibliography

Adamson, L. and N. Smith (1995) Sranan. In J. Arends, P. Muysken and N. Smith (Eds.) (1995).

Afendras, E. A. and E. C. Y. Kuo (Eds.) (1980) *Language and Society in Singapore*. Singapore: Singapore University Press.

Afendras, E. A., S. Millar, E. Mac Aogáin, A. Bamgbose, Y. Kachru, A. P. Saleemi, B. Preisler, P. Trudgill, F. Coulmas and P. Dasgupta (1995) On 'new/non-native' Englishes: A gamelan. *Journal of Pragmatics, 24*, 295-321.

Agnihotri, R. K. and A. Saghal (1985) Is Indian English retroflexed and r-full? *IJOAL, XI*, 97-108.

Aitchison, J. (1981) *Language Change: Progress or Decay?* London: Fontana.

Allwright, R. (1984) The importance of interaction in classroom language learning. *Applied Linguistics, 5*, 156-71.

Association of Accredited Advertising Agents Singapore (1995) *Media Directory*. Singapore: Integrated Information Pte Ltd.

Alsagoff, L. (1995) Colloquial Singapore English: The relative clause construction. In A. Pakir (Ed.) (1995).

Anzaldua, G. (1987) *Borderlands/La Frontera*. San Francisco: Spinsters/Aunt Lute.

Arends, J., P. Muysken and N. Smith (Eds.) (1995) *Pidgins and Creoles: An Introduction*. Amsterdam, John Benjamins.

Augustin, J. (1982) Regional standards of English in Peninsular Malaysia. In J. B. Pride (Ed.), *New Englishes*. Rowley, Mass.: Newbury House.

Baker, C. (1993) *Foundations of Bilingual Education and Bilingualism*. Clevedon: Multilingual Matters.

Bamgbose, A. (1971) The English Language in Nigeria. In John Spencer (Ed.) (1971).

Bao, Z. M. (1995) 'Already' in Singapore English. *World Englishes, 14.2*, 181-88.

Baugh, A. C. and T. Cable (1993) *A History of the English Language. Fourth Edition.* Englewood Cliffs, New Jersey: Prentice Hall International.

Bautista, M. L. S. (1986) English-Pilipino contact: A case study of reciprocal borrowing. In W. Viereck and W-D. Bald (Eds.), *English in Contact with Other Languages: Studies in Honour of Broder Carstensen on the Occasion of His 60th Birthday.* Budapest: Akademiai Kiado.

Benjamin, G. (1976) The cultural logic of Singapore's 'multiracialism'. In R. Hassan (Ed.), *Singapore: A Society in Transition.* Kuala Lumpur: Oxford University Press.

Bickerton, D. (1980) Decreolisation and the creole continuum. In A. Valdman and A. Highfield (Eds.), *Theoretical Orientations in Creole Studies.* New York, Academic Press.

Bickerton, D. (1981) *Roots of Language.* Ann Arbor, Mich.: Karoma Publishers.

Bickerton, D. (1984) The language bioprogram hypothesis. *The Behavioral and Brain Sciences, 7,* 173-221.

Bickerton, D. (1986) Creoles and West African languages: A case of mistaken identity?. In P. Muysken and N. Smith (Eds.) (1986).

Blommaert, J. (1995) The politics of multilingualism and language planning: Introductory remarks. Proceedings of the Language Planning Workshop: The Politics of Multilingualism and Language Planning. Political Linguistics Conference, Antwerp, December 1995.

Bloom, D. (1986) The English language and Singapore: A critical survey. In B. K. Kapur (Ed.), *Singapore Studies.* Singapore: Singapore University Press.

Boey, K. C. (1992) Déjà vu. In K. C. Boey, *Another Place.* Singapore: Times Books International.

Bokhorst-Heng, W. D. (1998) Language, Mass Media and the Nationalist Agenda. Ph.D dissertation. Toronto: Ontario Institute for Studies in Education, University of Toronto.

Brown, A. (1988) Vowel differences between received pronunciation and the English of Malaysia and Singapore: Which ones really matter? In J. Foley (1988).

Brown, A. (1991) *Pronunciation Models.* Singapore: Singapore University Press.

Brown, A. (1992) *Making Sense of Singapore English.* Singapore: Federal Publications.

Bruner, J. S. (1983) *Child's Talk: Learning to Use Language.* New York: W. W. Norton.

Bruner, J. S. (1986) *Actual Minds Possible Worlds.* Mass.: Harvard University Press.

Buckley, C. B. (1902). *An Anecdotal History of Old Times in Singapore.* Fraser &

Neave: Singapore. [Reference to the reprint of 1965. Kuala Lumpur: University of Malaya Press.]

Butler, S. (Chair) (1992) Panel discussion: A dictionary for Singapore and its practical implications. In A. Pakir (Ed.) (1992).

Campbell, R. and R. Wales (1970) The study of language acquisition. In J. Lyons (Ed.), *New Horizons in Linguistics*. Harmondsworth: Penguin.

Carroll, M. (Ed.) (1996) *No Small World: Visions and Revisions of World Literature*. Urbana, Illinois: National Council of Teachers of English.

Caws, P. (1994) Identity: Cultural, transcultural, and multicultural. In D. Goldberg (Ed.) (1994).

Chafe, W. (1976) Givenness, contrastiveness, definiteness, subjects, topics, and point of view. In C. Li (Ed.), *Subject and Topic*. New York: Academic Press.

Chaudenson, R. (1979) *Les Créoles Françaises*. Fernand Nathan: Paris.

Cheong, F. (1991) *The Scent of the Gods: A Novel*. New York: Norton.

Cheshire, J. (Ed.) (1991) *English around the World: Sociolinguistic Perspectives*. Cambridge: Cambridge University Press.

Chiew, S. K. (1980) Bilingualism and national identity: A Singapore case study. In E. A. Afendras and E. C. Y. Kuo (1980).

Chiew, S. K. (1990) Nation-building in Singapore: An historical perspective. In J. Quah (Ed.) (1990).

Chionh, K. (1987) Multiculturalism in the Curriculum. MA dissertation. Department of English Language and Literature, National University of Singapore.

Chomsky, N. (1986) *Knowledge of Language: Its Nature, Origin, and Use*. New York: Praeger.

Chomsky, N. and M. Halle (1968) *The Sound Pattern of English*. New York: Harper and Row.

Chua, B-H. (1995) *Communitarian Ideology and Democracy in Singapore*. London: Routledge.

Chua, S. C. (1962) State of Singapore: Report on the Census of Population, 1957. Singapore, Department of Statistics: Government Printing Office.

Chua, S. C. (1990) A study of the 'What' Particle in Singapore Colloquial English. Academic Exercise. Department of English Language and Literature, National University of Singapore.

Clammer, J. (1981) Chinese ethnicity and political culture in Singapore. In L. A. Gosling *et al.* (Eds.), *The Chinese in Southeast Asia. Vol. 2.* Singapore: Maruzen Asia.

Clarke, L. (1992) Within a stone's throw. Eurasian enclaves. In M. Braga-Blake (Ed.) (Co-researcher A. Ebert-Oehlers), *Singapore Eurasians.* Singapore: Eurasian Association/Times Editions.

Collier, J. (1947) *Indians of the Americas: The Long Hope.* New York: Mentor.

Colony of Singapore (1948) Department of Education Annual Reports. Singapore: Government Printing Office.

Colony of Singapore (1954) Department of Education Annual Reports. Singapore: Government Printing Office.

Conrad, A. W. and J. A. Fishman (1977) English as a world language: The evidence. In J. A. Fishman, R. L. Cooper and A. W. Conrad, *The Spread of English: The Sociology of English an an Additional Language.* Rowley, Mass.: Newbury House Publishers.

Crewe, W. J. (1977) *Singapore English and Standard English: Exercises in Awareness.* Singapore: Eastern Universities Press.

Crewe, W. J. (Ed.) (1977) *The English Language in Singapore.* Singapore: Eastern Universities Press.

Crowley, T. (1992) *An Introduction to Historical Linguistics.* Auckland: Oxford.

Cruttenden, A. (1979) *Language in Infancy and Childhood.* Manchester: Manchester University Press.

Crystal, D. (1987) *Cambridge Encyclopedia of Language.* Cambridge: Cambridge University Press.

Crystal, D. (1995) *The Cambridge Encyclopaedia of the English Language.* Cambridge: Cambridge University Press.

Das, B. (1994) Language education and the working adult: The experience in Singapore. In S. Gopinathan, A. Pakir, W. K. Ho and V. Saravanan (Eds.) (1994).

de Souza, D. (1960) The changing place of English in the educational system of Ceylon. In J. Sledd, A Report on the Conference of Teachers of English Held at the University of Ceylon, Peradeniya, 3-8 January 1960. Department of English, University of Peradeniya.

de Souza, D. (1969) The teaching of English. *The Ceylon Observer,* 18-28 April 1969.

De Souza, D. (1977) *Language Status and Corpus Planning in Post-Independent Singapore.* Singapore: RELC.

Department of English Language and Literature [DELL] (1981-1995) Language Development, Data Collection. Department of English Language and Literature, National University of Singapore.

Dictionary of Contemporary English (1978) London: Longman.

Doraisamy, T. R. (1985/1986) *Forever Beginning: One Hundred Years of Methodism in Singapore.* (Two volumes) Singapore: Methodist Church in Singapore.

Edwards, J. (1994) *Multilingualism.* London: Routledge.

Ferguson, C. (1959) Diglossia. *Word, 15,* 325-340.

Fernando, L. (1986) *Cultures in Conflict: Essays on Literature and the English Language in South East Asia.* Singapore: Graham Brash.

Finegan, E. (1994) *Language: Its Structure and Use.* New York: Harcourt Brace College Publishers.

Finkle, D. (1995) Going on: The post-aids-play play. *The Village Voice,* 29 August.

Firth, J. R. (1957) *Papers in Linguistics 1934-1951.* London: Oxford University Press.

Fishman, J. A. (1968) Nationality-nationalism and nation-nationism. In J. A. Fishman, C. A. Ferguson and J. Das Gupta (Eds.) (1968).

Fishman, J. A. (1991) *Reversing Language Shift.* Clevedon: Multilingual Matters.

Fishman, J. A., C. A. Ferguson and J. Das Gupta (Eds.) (1968) *Language Problems of Developing Nations.* New York: John Wiley.

Foley, J. A. (1995) English in Mauritius. *World Englishes, 14.2,* 205-223.

Foley, J. A. (forthcoming) Code-switching and learning among young children in Singapore. *The International Journal of the Sociology of Language* (1998).

Foley, J. (Ed.) (1988) *New Englishes: The Case of Singapore.* Singapore: Singapore University Press.

Fries, C. C. (1952) *The Structure of English.* London: Longman.

Fries, P. (1983) On the status of theme in English: arguments from discourse. In J. S. Petofi and E. Sozer (Eds.), *In Micro and Macro Connexivity of Text.* Hamburg: Buske.

Fromkin, V. and R. Rodman (1993) *An Introduction to Language.* New York: Harcourt Brace College Publishers.

Gadamer, H-G. (1975) *Wahrheit und Methode.* Tubingen: Mohr.

Garvin, P. and M. Mathiot (1970) The urbanization of the Guarani language: A problem in language and culture. In J. A. Fishman (Ed.), *Readings in the Sociology of Language*. The Hague: Morton.

Giroux, H. (1994) Insurgent multiculturalism and the promise of pedagogy. In D. Goldberg (Ed.) (1994).

Givon, T. (1983) *Topic Continuity in Discourse: A Quantitative Cross-Language Study*. Amsterdam: John Benjamins.

Goldberg, D. (1994) *Multiculturalism: A Critical Reader*. Oxford: Blackwell.

Gonzalez, A., A. Halim and A. Palakornkul (1984) An Overview of Language Issues in South-East Asia 1950-1980. In Richard B. Noss (Ed.), Singapore: Oxford University Press.

Gooneratne, Y. (1968) *English Literature in Ceylon 1815-1878*. Dehiwela: Tisara Prakasakayo.

Gopinathan, S. (1974) *Towards a National System of Education in Singapore 1945-1973*. Singapore: Oxford University Press.

Gopinathan, S. (1994) Language policy changes 1979-1992: Politics and pedagogy. In S. Gopinathan, A. Pakir, W. K. Ho and V. Saravanan (Eds.) (1994).

Gopinathan, S., A. Pakir, W. K. Ho and V. Saravanan (Eds.) (1994) *Language, Society and Education in Singapore: Issues and Trends*. Singapore: Times Academic Press.

Görlach, M. (1988) Varietas Delectat: Forms and functions of English around the world. In G. Nixon and J. Honey (Eds.), *An Historic Tongue: Studies in English Linguistics in Memory of Barbara Strang*. London: Routledge.

Graddol, D., D. Leith and J. Swann (Eds.) (1996) *English: History, Diversity and Change*. London: Routledge.

Gunatilleke, G.(1954) A language without metaphor. *Community*, 1.2.

Gupta, A. F. (1992a) Contact features of Singapore Colloquial English. In K. Bolton and H. Kwok (Eds.), *Sociolinguistics Today: International Perspectives*. London: Routledge.

Gupta, A. F. (1992b) The pragmatic particles of Singapore Colloquial English. *Journal of Pragmatics*, 18, 31-57.

Gupta, A. F. (1994a) A framework for the analysis of Singapore English. In S. Gopinathan, A. Pakir, W. K. Ho and V. Saravanan (Eds.) (1994).

Gupta, A. F. (1994b) *The Step-tongue: Children's English in Singapore*. Clevedon: Multilingual Matters.

Gupta, A. F. (1996) English and empire: Teaching English in nineteenth-century

India. In N. M. Mercer and J. Swann (Eds.), *Learning English: Development and Diversity*. London/New York: Routledge/Open University.

Gupta, A. F. and P. Y. Siew (1995) Language shift in a Singapore family. *Journal of Multilingual and Multicultural Development, 16.4*, 301-314.

Gutmann, A. (Ed.) (1992) *Multiculturalism and 'The Politics of Recognition'*. Princeton: Princeton University Press.

Hall, R. (1966) *Pidgins and Creole Languages*. Ithaca: Cornell University Press.

Hall, R. A. (1944) Chinese pidgin English grammar and texts. *Journal of the American Oriental Society, 64*, 95-113.

Hall, R. A. (1962) The life-cycle of pidgin languages. *Lingua, 11*, 151-156.

Halliday, M. A. K. (1975) *Learning How to Mean: Explorations in the Development of Language*. London: Edward Arnold.

Halliday, M. A. K. (1978) *Language as Social Semiotic*. London, Edward Arnold.

Halliday, M. A. K. (1979) One child's protolanguage. In M. Bullowa (Ed.), *Before Speech: The Beginning of Interpersonal Communication*. Cambridge: Cambridge University Press.

Halliday, M. A. K. (1984) Language as a code and language as behaviour: A systemic functional interpretation of the nature and ontogenesis of dialogue. In R. P. Fawcett, M. A. K. Halliday, S. M. Lamb and A. Makkai (Eds.), *The Semiotics of Culture and Language, Volume 1: Language as a Social Semiotic*. London: Frances Pinter.

Halliday, M. A. K. (1985) *An Introduction to Functional Grammar*. London: Edward Arnold.

Halliday, M. A. K. (1987) Spoken and written modes of meaning. In R. Horowitz and S. J. Samuels (Eds.), *Comprehending Spoken and Written Language*. Califonia: Academic Press.

Halliday, M. A. K. (1988) On the ineffability of grammatical categories. In J. D. Benson, M. J. Cummins and W. S. Greaves (Eds.), *Linguistics in a Systemic Perspective: Current Issues in Linguistic Theory 39*. Amsterdam: Benjamins.

Halliday, M. A. K. (1992) Towards a language based theory of learning. In *Symposium on Language Acquisition*. Tokyo: Phonetics Society of Japan.

Halliday, M. A. K. (1994) The place of dialogue in children's construction of meaning. In R. B. Ruddell *et al.* (Eds.), *Theoretical Models and Processes of Reading. Fourth Edition*. Newark, Delaware: IRA.

Halliday, M. A. K. (1995) Language and the reshaping of human experience. In B.

Dendrinos (Ed.), Proceedings of the Fourth International Symposium on Critical Discourse Analysis. Greece: University of Athens.

Halliday, M. A. K. and R. Hasan (1976) *Cohesion in English*. London: Longman.

Hancock, I. F. (1971) West Africa and the Atlantic Creoles. In J. Spencer (Ed.)

Hasan, R. (1986) The ontogenesis of ideology: An interpretation of mother-child talk. In T. Threadgold, E. A. Grosz, G. Kress and M. A. K. Halliday (Eds.), *Semiotics, Ideology and Language*. Sydney: Sydney Association for Studies in Society and Culture.

Hill, A. H. (Ed.) (1969) *The Hikayat Abdullah by Abdullah bin Abdul Kadir: An Annotated Translation*. Kuala Lumpur: Oxford University Press.

Hill, M. and Lian, K. (1995) *The Politics of Nation Building and Citizenship in Singapore*. London: Routledge.

Ho, C. L. (1995) Two different notions of grammaticality: Correctness vs. systematicity. In A. Pakir (Ed.) (1995).

Ho, M. L. (1992a) The language bioprogram hypothesis and Singaporean English. *RELC Journal, 23.1*, 1-14.

Ho, M. L. (1992b) The semantics of some verbs of movement in Singaporean English: Bring/take, send, follow, and fetch. In A. Pakir (Ed.) (1992).

Ho, M. L. (1995) The acquisition of a linguistic variable. In A. Pakir (Ed.) (1992).

Ho, S. O. (1964) *Methodist Schools in Malaysia: Their Record and History*. Petaling Jaya: Board of Education, Malaya Annual Conference.

Ho, J. H. M. (1997) Relative Clauses in Singapore Colloquial English. Unpublished Honours thesis. Department of English Language and Literature, National University of Singapore.

Ho, W. K. (1994) The English Language curriculum in perspective: Exogenous influences and indigenization. In S. Gopinathan, A. Pakir, W. K. Ho and V. Saravanan (Eds.) (1994).

Holm, J. A. (1988) *Pidgins and Creoles. Volume 1*. Cambridge: Cambridge University Press.

Hopper, P. J. and E. C. Traugott (1993) *Grammaticalization*. Cambridge: Cambridge University Press.

Hornby, A. S. (1966) *The Teaching of Structural Words and Sentence Patterns*. London: Oxford University Press.

Hung, T. T. N. (1996) Towards a phonology of Singapore English. In Pan-Asiatic

Linguistics: Proceedings of the Fourth International Symposium on Languages and Linguistics. Mahidol University, Bangkok, Thailand.

Janson, T. (1984) Articles and plural formation in creoles: Change and universals. *Lingua*, 64, 291-323.

Jespersen, O. (1923) *Growth and Structure of the English Language*. New York: D. Appleton-Century Company.

Kachru, B. B. (1966) Indian English: A study in contextualization. In C. E. Bazell, J. C. Catford, M. A. K. Halliday and R. H. Robins (Eds.), *In Memory of J. R. Firth*. London: Longman.

Kachru, B. B. (1981) The pragmatics of non-native varieties of English. In L. E. Smith (Ed.), *English for Cross-Cultural Communication*. Hong Kong: MacMillan.

Kachru, B. B. (1982) Models for non-native Englishes. In B. B. Kachru (Ed.) (1982).

Kachru, B. B. (1983) *The Indianization of English: The Indian Language in India*. Delhi: Oxford University Press.

Kachru, B. B. (1985) Standards, codification and sociolinguistic realism: The English language in the outer circle. In R. Quirk and H. G. Widowson (Eds.) (1985).

Kachru, B. B. (1986) *The Alchemy of English: The Spread, Functions and Models of Non-native Englishes*. Oxford: Pergamon Institute of English.

Kachru, B. B. (1992) World Englishes: Approaches, issues and resources (state of the art article). *Language Teaching*, January 1992, 1-14.

Kachru, B. B. (1994) Englishization and contact linguistics. *World Englishes*, 13.2, 135-54.

Kachru, B. B. and R. Quirk (1981) Introduction. In L. E. Smith (Ed.), *English for Cross-Cultural Communication*. Hong Kong: MacMillan.

Kachru, B. B. (Ed.) (1982) *The Other Tongue: English Across Cultures*. Urbana: University of Illinois Press.

Kandiah, T. (1971) New Ceylon English (review article). *New Ceylon Writing, 1971*, 90-94.

Kandiah, T. (1981a) Disinherited Englishes: The case of Lankan English. Sections III.2-V. *Navasilu*, 4, 92-113.

Kandiah, T. (1981b) Lankan English schizoglossia. *English World-Wide*, 2.1, 63-81.

Kandiah, T. (1987) New varieties of English: The creation of the paradigm and its radicalization. Sections I-III.2. *Navasilu*, 9, 31-41.

Kandiah, T. (1990) New varieties of English: The creation of the paradigm and its radicalization. Sections III.3-V.1. *Navasilu, 10,* 126-39.

Kandiah, T. (1994a) English and Southeast Asian language planning practice extracting regional patterns and theoretical principles. In T. Kandiah and J. Kwan-Terry (Eds.) (1994).

Kandiah, T. (1994b) New varieties of English: The creation of the paradigm and its radicalization. Sections V.2-VI. *Navasilu, 11 & 12,* 153-63.

Kandiah, T. (1995) Centering the periphery: Towards participatory communities of discourse (foreword). In A. Parakrama, *De-hegemonizing Language Standards: Learning from (Post)Colonial Englishes about English.* London: Macmillan & New York: St. Martin's Press.

Kandiah, T. (1996) Syntactic 'deletion' in Lankan English: Learning from a new variety of English about——. In R. J. Baumgardner (Ed.), *South Asian English: Structure, Use, and Users.* Urbana: University of Illinois Press.

Kandiah, T. (1998) Epiphanies of the deathless native user's manifold avatars: A post-colonial perspective on the native speaker. In R. Singh (Ed.), *The Native Speaker: Multilingual Perspectives.* New Delhi/Thousand Oaks/London: Sage, pp. 79-110.

Kandiah, T. (forthcoming b) The threshold as entrance(?)/ deferment(?)/ non-arrival(?)/ plight(?)/ vogue(?)/....(?). In K. K. Seet (Ed.), *Liminality: States of Transition in Singapore Theatre.* Singapore: University of Singapore Press.

Kandiah, T. and J. Kwan-Terry (Eds.) (1994) *English and Language Planning: A Southeast Asian Contribution.* Singapore: Times Academic Press.

Kaur, K. (1995) Why they need English in Malaysia: A survey. *World Englishes, 14.2,* 223-230.

Khoo, C. K. (1981) Demographic Characteristics: Census of Population, 1980. Release No. 2. Singapore: Department of Statistics.

Khoo, R. (1993) Controlling Pandora's Box: Standards for the vocabulary of Singapore English. In A. Pakir (Ed.), *The English Language in Singapore: Standards and Norms.* Singapore: Unipress.

Khoo, T. (1987) Children's Play: An Exploratory Study. Academic Exercise. Department of English Language and Literature, National University of Singapore.

Kon, S. (1991) Cross cultural influences in the work of a Singapore writer. In E. Thumboo (Ed.) (1991).

Krapp, G. P. (1925) *The English Language in America.* New York: Century.

Kress, G. and R. Hodge (1979) *Language as Ideology*. London: Routledge and Kegan Paul.

Kuo, E. (1985) Language and social mobility in Singapore. In N. Wolfson *et al.*, *Language of Inequality*. Berlin: Mouton.

Kuo, E. C. Y. (1980) The sociolinguistic situation in Singapore: Unity in diversity. In E. A. Afendras and E. C. Y. Kuo (Eds.) (1980).

Kuo, E. C. Y. and B. H. Jernudd (1994) Balancing macro- and micro-sociolinguistic perspectives in language management: The case of Singapore. In S. Gopinathan, A. Pakir, W. K. Ho and V. Saravanan (Eds.) (1994).

Kwan-Terry, A. (1978) The meaning and the source of the 'la' and the 'what' particles in Singapore English. *RELC Journal*, 9.2, 22-36.

Kwan-Terry, A. (1989) The specification of stage by a child learning English and Cantonese simultaneously: A study of acquisitional processes. In H. W. Dechert and M. Raupach (Eds.), *Interlingual Processes*. Tübingen: Gunter Narr Verlag.

Kwan-Terry, A. (1991a) The economics of language in Singapore: Students' use of extracurricular language lessons. *Journal of Asian Pacific Communication, 2.1 (1991)*, 69-89.

Kwan-Terry, A. (1991b) Home language and school language: A study of children's language use in Singapore. In A. Kwan-Terry (Ed.) (1991).

Kwan-Terry, A. (1993) Cross-currents in teaching English in Singapore. *World Englishes, 12.1*, 75-84.

Kwan-Terry, A. (Ed.) (1991) *Child Language Development in Singapore and Malaysia*. Singapore: Singapore University Press.

Labov, W. (1966) *The Social Stratification of English in New York*. Washington: Center for Applied Linguistics.

Ladefoged, P. (1993) *A Course in Phonetics*. New York: Harcourt Brace College Publishers.

Lass, R. (1980) *On Explaining Language Change*. Cambridge: Cambridge University Press.

Lau, K. E. (1992) Singapore Census of Population, 1990: Statistical Release 1. Singapore: SNP Publishers.

Lau, K. E. (1993) Singapore Census of Population, 1990: Statistical release 3. Singapore: SNP Publishers.

Le Page, R. B. and A. Tabouret-Keller (1985) *Acts of Identity: Creole-Based Approaches to Language and Ethnicity*. Cambridge: Cambridge University Press.

Lee, K. Y. (1970) The Twain Have Met. The Dillingham Lecture, Hawaii, USA, 11 November 1970. Prime Minister's Speeches, Interviews, Statements, Etc., 1970.

Lee, K. Y. (1972) Traditional Values and National Identity. Speech presented at the Singapore Teachers Union's 26th Anniversary Dinner, Shangri-La Hotel, 5 November 1972. *The Mirror*, 20 November 1972, Vol.8, No.47.

Lee, T. P. (1989) Foreword. In K. C. Boey, *Somewhere-Bound*. Singapore: Times Books International.

Lee T. P. (1980) *Prospects of a Drowning*. Singapore: Heinemann Educational Books.

Lees, R. B. (1965) Two views of linguistic research. *Linguistics*, *11*, 21-29.

Lefebvre, C. and J. S. Lumsden (1989) 'Les langues créoles et la théorie linguistique.' *Canadian Journal of Linguistics*, *34.3*, 249-72.

Leith, D. (1996) English — Colonial and postcolonial. In D. Graddol, D. Leith and J. Swann (Eds.) (1996).

Leong, L. G. (1995) The poetics of history: Three women's perspectives. In E. Thumboo and T. Kandiah (Eds.), *The Writer as Historical Witness*. Singapore: UniPress.

Lewis, D. R. (1994) *Neither Wolf nor Dog: American Indians, Environment and Agrarian Change*. New York: Oxford University Press.

Li, C. and S. Thompson (1981) *Mandarin Chinese: A Functional Reference Grammar*. Berkeley: University of California Press.

Lim, C. (1978) *Little Ironies*. Singapore: Heinemann Asia.

Lim, S. (1996) Singapore: Too much presence for young. *The Straits Times*, 2 November.

Lim, S. C. (1991) *Rice Bowl*. Singapore: Times Books International.

Lock, A. and E. Fisher (Eds.) (1984) *Language Development*. London: Croom Helm.

Lodge, G. and E. Vogel (1987) *Ideology and National Competitiveness: An Analysis of Nine Countries*. Boston: Harvard Business School Press.

MacCannell, D. (1992) *Empty Meeting Grounds: The Tourist Papers*. London: Routledge.

Marckwardt, A. H. (1980) *American English. Second Edition*. Revised by J. L. Dillard. New York: Oxford University Press.

McNeill, D. (1970) *The Acquisition of Language*. New York: Harper and Row.

McCrum, R., W. Cran and R. MacNeil (1986) *The Story of English*. London: Faber and Faber.

McLaren, P. (1994) White terror and oppositional agency: Towards a critical multiculturalism. In D. Goldberg (Ed.) (1994).

Mohanan, K. P. (1992) Describing the phonology of non-native varieties of a language. *World Englishes, 11*, 111-28.

Mohanty, C. T. (1991) Introduction. Cartographies of struggle: Third world women and the politics of feminism. In C. T. Mohanty *et al.* (Ed.), *Third World Women and the Politics of Feminism*. Bloomington: Indiana University Press.

Morgan, J. L. (1973) Sentence fragments and the notion 'sentence'. In B. B. Kachru, R. B. Lees, Y. Malkiel, A. Pietrangeli and S. Saporta (Eds.), *Issues in Linguistics: Papers in Honour of Renée Kahane*. Urbana: University of Illinois Press.

Mufwene, S. S. (1986) The universalist and substrate hypotheses complement one another. In P. Muysken and N. Smith (Eds.) (1986).

Mufwene, S. S. (1990) Transfer and the substrate hypothesis in creolistics. *Studies in Second Language Acquisition, 12.1*, 1-23.

Mufwene, S. S. (1994) New Englishes and criteria for naming them. *World Englishes, 13.1*, 21-31.

Mühlhäusler, P. (1986) *Pidgin & Creole Linguistics*. Oxford: Blackwell.

Murray, D. P. (1971) Multilanguage Education and Bilingualism: The Formation of Social Brokers in Singapore. Ph.D dissertation. Stanford University, 1971.

Muysken, P. and N. Smith (Eds.) (1986) *Substrata Versus Universals in Creole Genesis*. Amsterdam: John Benjamins.

Muysken, P. and T. Veenstra (1995) Universalist approaches. In J. Arends, P. Muysken and N. Smith (Ed.) (1995).

Nathan, E. (1986). *The History of the Jews in Singapore (1830-1945)*. Singapore: Herbilu.

Nathan, J. E. (1922) *The Census of British Malaya, 1921*. London: Dunstable and Watford.

Norwita Binte Mohamed Ariff (1987) The Communicative Competence of a Bilingual Child. Academic Exercise. Department of English Language and Literature, National University of Singapore.

O'Donnell, W. R. and L. Todd (1980) *Variety in Contemporary English*. London, Allen and Unwin.

Oldenburg, J. (1990) Learning language and learning through language in early childhood. In M. A. K. Halliday, J. Gibbons and H. Nicholas (Eds.), *Learning, Keeping and Using Language*. Amsterdam: John Benjamins.

Ong, S. F. (1997) Modern Verse by Straits Times Columnist. *The Straits Times*, 4 January.

Othman, Sulaiman (1990) *Malay for Everyone: Mastering Malay through English*. Petaling Jaya: Pelanduk Publications.

Painter, C. (1992) The Development of Language as a Resource for Thinking: A Linguistic View of Learning. Paper presented at the 19th International Systemic Functional Congress, Macquarie University, Sydney, Australia.

Painter, C. (1984) *Into the Mothertongue: A Case Study in Early Language Development*. London: Frances Pinter.

Painter, C. (1989) Learning language: A functional view of language development. In R. Hasan and J. Martin (Eds.), *Language Development: Learning Language, Learning Culture: Meaning and Choice in Language: Studies for Michael Halliday*. Norwood, N. J.: Ablex.

Painter, C. (1996) The development of language as a resource for thinking: A linguistic view of learning. In R. Hasan and G. Williams (Eds.), *Literacy in Society*. London: Longman.

Pakir, A. (1989) The Role of Language Planning in Education in Singapore. Paper presented at the Third Tun Abdul Razak Conference, Ohio University, 1-2 April 1989.

Pakir, A. (1991a) The range and depth of English-knowing bilinguals in Singapore. *World Englishes*, 10.2, 167-79.

Pakir, A. (1991b) The status of English and the question of 'standard'. In M. L. Tickoo (Ed.), *Language and Standards: Issues, Attitudes, Case Studies*. Singapore: SEAMEO/RELC.

Pakir, A. (1994) Educational linguistics: Looking to the East. In J. Alatis (Ed.), *Georgetown University Round Table on Languages and Linguistics 1994*. Washington, D.C.: Georgetown University Press.

Pakir, A. (1994) Education and invisible language planning: The case of English in Singapore. In T. Kandiah and J. Kwan-Terry (Eds.) (1994).

Pakir, A. (Ed.) (1992) *Words in a Cultural Context*. Singapore: UniPress.

Pakir, A. (Ed.) (1995) *The English Language in Singapore: Implications for Teaching*. Singapore: Singapore Association for Applied Linguists.

Parakrama, A. (1995) De-hegemonizing Language Standards: Learning from

(Post)Colonial Englishes about English. London: Macmillan and New York: St. Martin's Press.

Pearce, R. H. (1965) *The Savages of America: A Study of the Indian and the Idea of Civilization. Revised Edition.* Baltimore: The John Hopkins Press. [Originally published 1953].

Pendley, C. (1983) Language policy and social transformation in contemporary Singapore. *Southeast Asian Journal of Social Sciences, 11.2 (1983)*, 46-58.

Pennycook, A. (1994) *The Cultural Politics of English as an International Language.* London: Longman.

People's Action Party (1959) *The Tasks Ahead: The People's Action Party's Five-Year Plan, 1959-1964.* Singapore: People's Action Party.

Phillipson, R. and T. Skutnabb-Kangas (1997) Linguistic human rights and English in Europe. *World Englishes, 16.1*, 27-43.

Platt, J. (1975) The Singapore English speech continuum and its basilect "Singlish" as a creoloid. *Anthropological Linguistics, 17.7*, 363-74.

Platt, J. (1977) The sub-varieties of English: their sociolectal and functional status. In W. J. Crewe (Ed.) (1977).

Platt, J. (1987) Communicative functions of particles in Singapore English. In R. Steele and T. Threadgold (Eds.) (1987).

Platt, J. (1980) Multilingualism, polyglossia, and code selection in Singapore. In E. Afendras and E.C.Y. Kuo (Eds.) (1980).

Platt, J. T. and H. Weber (1980) *English in Singapore and Malaysia: Status, Features, Functions.* Kuala Lumpur: Oxford University Press.

Prator, C. H. (1968) The British heresy in TESOL. In J. A. Fishman, C. A. Ferguson and J. Das Gupta (Eds.) (1968).

Puru Shotam, N. (1987) The Social Negotiation of Language in the Singaporean Everyday Life World. Ph.D dissertation. Singapore: National University of Singapore.

Quah, J. (1990) Government policies and nation-building. In J. Quah (Ed.) (1990).

Quah, J. (Ed.) (1990) *In Search of Singapore's National Values.* Singapore: Times Academic.

Quirk, R. (1972) *The English Language and Images of Matter.* London: Oxford University Press.

Quirk, R. (1985) The English language in a global context. In R. Quirk and H. G. Widdowson (Eds.) (1985).

Quirk, R. and S. Greenbaum (1973) A *University Grammar of English*. London: Longman.

Quirk, R., S. Greenbaum, G. Leech and J. Svartvik (1972) A *Grammar of Contemporary English*. London: Longman.

Quirk, R. and H. G. Widowson (Eds.) (1985) *English in the World: Teaching and Learning the Language and Literatures*. Cambridge: Cambridge University Press.

Report on the Administration of the Straits Settlements: Report on Education (various authors). 1855-1864, 1874, 1884, 1886-1938.

Richards, J. C. (1977) *Variation in Singapore English*. In W. J. Crewe (Ed.) (1977).

Roach, P. (1991) *English Phonetics and Phonology: A Practical Course*. Cambridge: Cambridge University Press.

Rockefeller, S. (1992). Comment. In A. Gutmann (Ed.) (1992).

Romaine, S. (1984) *The Language of Children and Adolescents*. Oxford: Basil Blackwell.

Romaine, S. (1988) *Pidgin and Creole Languages*. London: Longman.

Rubin, J. and B. H. Jernudd (1971) Introduction: Language planning as an element in modernization. In. J. Rubin and B. H. Jernudd (Eds.), *Can Language Be Planned? Sociolinguistic Theory and Practice for Developing Nations*. Honolulu: The University Press of Hawaii.

Saffiah bte. Mohammed Amin (1984) The Teaching of Writing in Primary Six and the First Year of Secondary School. Unpublished Honours thesis. Department of English Language and Literature, National University of Singapore.

Saravanan, V. (1993) Language and social identity amongst Tamil-English bilinguals in Singapore. In R. Khoo *et al.*, *Languages in Contact in a Multilingual Society: Implications for Language Learning and Teaching*. Singapore: SEAMEO Regional Language Centre.

Saravanan, V and R. Gupta (1997) Teacher input in Singapore English classrooms. *RELC Journal, 28.1*, 144-160.

Shared Values. (1991) Singapore, White Paper, Cmd. 1 of 1991.

Siddique, S. and Purushotam, N. (1982) *Singapore's Little India: Past, Present and Future*. Singapore: Institute of Southeast Asian Studies.

Siddique, S. and Purushotam, N. (1993) Spouse selection patterns in the Singapore Indian community. In K. S. Sandhu *et al.*, *Indian Communities in Southeast Asia*. Singapore: Times Academic.

Siegel, J. (1996) Bislama pronouns. In D. Graddol, D. Leith and J. Swann (Eds.) (1996).

Simpson, D. (1986) *The Politics of American English, 1776-1850*. New York: Oxford University Press.

Singapore Ministry of Information and the Arts (1994) *Singapore Facts and Pictures, 1994*. Singapore: MITA.

Singapore Yearbook of Statistics, 1990 (1991) Singapore, Department of Statistics: Singapore National Printers.

Singh, K. (1980) Towards a Singapore classic: Edwin Thumboo's 'Ulysses by the Merlion'. *The Literary Criterion, 15.2*, 74-87.

Singh, R. (1994) Indian English: Some conceptual issues (afterword). In R. K. Agnihotri and A. L. Khanna (Eds.), *Second Language Acquisition: Socio-cultural and Linguistic Aspects of English in India*. New Delhi: Thousand Oaks and London: Sage Publications.

Singh, R. (1995a) 'Initiation' and 'Conclusion'. In R. Singh, J. D'souza, K. P. Mohanan and N. S. Prabhu, On 'new/non-native' Englishes: A quartet. *Journal of Pragmatics, 24*, 283-94.

Singh, R. (1995b) 'New/non-native' Englishes revisited: A reply to my colleagues. *Journal of Pragmatics, 24*, 323-33.

Singh, R. (1997) *Lectures against Sociolinguistics*. New York: Peter Lang.

Singh R., J. D'souza, K. P. Mohanan and N. S. Prabhu (1995) On 'new/non-native' Englishes: A quartet. *Journal of Pragmatics, 24*, 283-94.

Solomon, C. (1993) Review of *The Scent of the Gods*. *Los Angeles Times*, 18 July.

Spencer, J. (Ed.) (1971) *The English Language in West Africa*. London: Longman.

Steele, R. and T. Threadgold (Eds.) (1987) *Language Topics: Essays in Honour of Michael Halliday*. Amsterdam: John Benjamins.

Talib, I. S. (1992a) Singaporean literature in English and a dictionary of Singaporean English. In A. Pakir (Ed.) (1992).

Talib, I. S. (1992b) Why not teach non-native English literature? *The English Language Teaching Journal, 46*, 51-55.

Talib, I. S. (1994a) The development of Singaporean literature in English. *Journal of Multilingual and Multicultural Development, 15*, 419-29.

Talib, I. S. (1994b) Responses to the language of Singaporean literature in English. In S. Gopinathan, A. Pakir, W. K. Ho and V. Saravanan (Eds.) (1994).

Talib, I. S. (1996) Nonnative English literature and the world literature syllabus. In M. Carroll (Ed.) (1996).

Talib, I. S. (1997a) The child, the masochist and the actor: Use and abuse of history in theatre at the recent Asian Festival of Arts. *The Arts Magazine*, September-October, 68-9.

Talib, I. S. (1997b) Eastern criticisms, western perceptions: The Singaporean writer, the western press, and the image of Singapore. *Harvard Asia Pacific Review, 1.2*, 78-81.

Talib, I. S. (1997c) Emigration as a resistant factor in the creation of a national literature: Rex Shelley's *The Shrimp People*. In G. Kain (Ed.), *Ideas of Home: Literature of Asian Migration*. East Lansing, Michigan: Michigan State University Press, 101-14.

Talib, I. S. (forthcoming) Problems of translation and communication in cultural hybridity: Kuo's 'Mama Looking for Her Cat'. In K. K. Seet (Ed.), *Liminality: States of Transition in Singapore Theatre*. Singapore: University of Singapore Press.

Tamney, J. B. (1973) The scarcity of identity: The relation between religious identity and national identity. In H. D. Evers, *Modernization in Southeast Asia*. Singapore: Oxford University Press.

Tan, K. L. (1996) A Poet Bound To Go Somewhere. *The New Straits Times*, 28 August.

Tan, P. T. (1988) A description of patterns of code-mixing and code-switching in a multilingual household. In J. Foley (Ed.) (1988).

Tan, R. and S. F. Chew (1970) An Analysis of the Attitudes of Pupils in Chinese Medium, English Medium and Integrated Schools on Selected Variables. Unpublished academic exercise. Department of Sociology, University of Singapore.

Tan, S. B. (1997) Approaches to Language Teaching in the Express and Normal (Academic) Streams. Unpublished Honours thesis. Department of English Language and Literature, National University of Singapore.

Tan, S. H. (1995) The Manufacturing of Social Consent — The Dynamics of Language Planning in Singapore. Working Papers on Language, Literature and Theatre. Department of English Language and Literature, National University of Singapore.

Tang, F. K. (1996) Towards a postmodern sensibility: An interview with Ong Keng Sen. *The Arts, 3*, 31.

Tauli, V. (1974) The theory of language planning. In J. A. Fishman (Ed.), *Advances in Language Planning*. The Hague: Mouton.

Tay, M. W. J. (1979). The uses, users and features of English in Singapore. In J. C. Richards (Ed.), *New Varieties of English: Issues and Approaches*. Singapore: SEAMEO Regional Language Centre. [Repr. in Tay, 1993].

Tay, M. W. J. (1982) Phonology of educated Singapore English. *English World-wide*, 3, 135-45.

Tay, M. W. J. (1985) Comments and replies. *World Englishes*, 4.3, 387-88.

Tay, M. W. J. (1986) Lects and institutionalized varieties of English: The case of Singapore. *Issues and Developments in English and Applied Linguistics*, 1, 93-97.

Tay, M. W. J. (1993) *The English Language in Singapore: Issues and Development.* Singapore: Unipress.

Tay, M. W. J. and A. F. Gupta (1983) Towards a description of Standard Singapore English. In R. Noss (Ed.), *Varieties of English in Southeast Asia*. Singapore: RELC Anthology Series, No. 11.

Taylor, C. (1992) The politics of recognition. In A. Gutmann (Ed.) (1992).

Taylor, D. (1971) Grammatical and lexical affinities in Creoles. In D. Hymes (Ed.), *Pidginization and Creolization of Languages*. Cambridge: Cambridge University Press.

Taylor, D. (1977) *Languages of the West Indies*. Baltimore: Johns Hopkins University Press.

Tham, S. C. (1989) The perception and practice of education. In K. Sandhu and P. Wheatley (Eds.), *Management of Success: The Moulding of Modern Singapore*. Singapore: Institute of Southeast Asian Studies.

Tham, S. C. (1990) *A Study of the Evolution of the Malay Language: Social Change and Cognitive Development.* Singapore: Singapore University Press.

Tham, S. C. (1996) Multi-lingualism in Singapore: Two Decades of Development. Census of Population, 1990, Monograph No. 6, Singapore.

Thomas, E. and A. Fam (1984) Cross-cultural methodological problems in the study of children's cognitive development. *Singapore Journal of Education*, 6(1), 30-35.

Thomas, L. (1966) Variation in English grammar. In D. Graddol, D. Leith and J. Swann (Eds.) (1996).

Thomason, S. G. and T. Kaufman (1988) *Language Contact, Creolization, and Genetic Linguistics*. Berkeley: University of California Press.

Thumboo, E. (1976) Introduction. In E. Thumboo (Ed.), *The Second Tongue: An Anthology of Poetry from Malaysia and Singapore*. Singapore: Heinemann Educational Books.

Thumboo, E. (1982) The search for style and theme: A personal account. In B. Bennett *et al.* (Eds.), *The Writer's Sense of the Contemporary*. Nedlands: The Centre for Studies in Australian Literature.

Thumboo, E. (1985) General Introduction. In E. Thumboo *et al.* (Eds.), *The Poetry of Singapore*. Singapore: The ASEAN Committee on Culture and Information.

Thumboo, E. (Ed.) (1991) *Perceiving Other Worlds*. Singapore: Times Academic.

Todd, L. (1984) *Modern Englishes*. Oxford: Basil Blackwell.

Todd, L. (1984) *Modern Englishes: Pidgins and Creoles*. Oxford: Blackwell.

Tongue, R. K. (1979) *The English of Singapore and Malaysia. Second Edition.* Singapore: Eastern University Press.

Traugott, E. C. and E. König (1991) The semantics-pragmatics of grammaticalization revisited. In E. C. Traugott and B. Heine (Eds.), *Approaches to Grammaticalization.* Amsterdam: Benjamins.

Trevarthan, C. (1987) Sharing makes sense: Intersubjectivity and the making of an infant's meaning. In R. Steele and T. Threadgold (Eds.) (1987).

Turnbull, C. M. (1980) *A Short History of Malaysia, Singapore and Brunei.* Singapore: Graham Brash.

Turner, T. (1994) Anthropology and multiculturalism: What is anthropology that multiculturalists should be mindful of it? In D. Goldberg (1994).

Warren, J. F. (1993). *Ah Ku and Karayuki-San: Prostitution in Singapore (1870-1940).* Singapore: Oxford University Press.

Wee, C. J. W.-J. (1996) Staging the new Asia: Singapore's Dick Lee, pop music, and a counter-modernity. *Public Culture, 20,* 489-510.

Wee, T. T. (1992) A Study of Code-switching in Two Multilingual Children in Singapore. Academic Exercise. Department of English Language and Literature, National University of Singapore.

Weeks, J. (1996) Curtain rising for Chay Yew: Trilogy speaks volumes about acclaimed playwright. *Los Angeles Daily News,* 14 March.

Wierzbicka, A. (1991) *Cross-Cultural Pragmatics.* Berlin: Mouton de Gruyter.

Williamson, J. A. (1952) *The Evolution of England. Second Edition.* London: Oxford University Press. (First published 1931)

Wilson, H. E. (1978) *Social Engineering in Singapore: Educational Policies and Social Change, 1819-1972.* Singapore: Singapore University Press.

Wong, I. F. H. and H. Thambyrajah (1991) The Malaysian sociolinguistic situation: An overview. In A. Kwan-Terry (Ed.) (1991).

Wong, J. O. (1994) A Wierzbickan Approach to Singlish Particles. MA thesis. Department of English Language and Literature, National University of Singapore.

Yap, A. (1980) *Down the Line*. Singapore: Heinemann Asia.

Yap, F. C. (1987) A Comparison between the English Syllabus for the New Education System (Primary) and Other Graded Structure Lists. Unpublished Honours thesis. Department of English Language and Literature, National University of Singapore.

Yeo, R. (1991) Coming home: Perceiving others and finding self. In E. Thumboo (Ed.) (1991).

Yeo, R. (1996) Staying honest: Reflections on 25 years of writing. *The Arts*, 3, 36.

Zainul, A and A. Mahizhnan (1990) The new environment, the young Singaporeans and national values. In J. Quah (Ed.) (1990).

Index

fulguration 82, 85, 86
fusion 122, 197, 207–209, 212, 216, 217

G
grammar 11, 20, 34, 37, 41–45, 58–64,
   69, 73–77, 83, 87, 92, 104, 127–129,
   133–138, 148, 151, 189, 198, 199, 226,
   227, 240, 241, 246–250, 254, 263,
   282–284

H
High Variety 45, 98–102, 132, 223, 304
hybridity 275–280, 285, 286

I
indigenized variety 39, 251
inner circle 3, 6
institutionalized variety 78
intelligibility 80, 175, 196–198
interculturality 216, 217
interference 3, 11, 17, 77, 80–86, 89, 91,
   280, 282, 288
interrupted transmission 19, 20

J
jargon 43, 44, 58, 59, 63

L
Language Bioprogramme Hypothesis 20,
   39, 60–66, 69–73
language change 41, 71, 133, 187, 188,
   199
language contact 18, 19, 33, 41, 43, 73,
   74
language development 218, 226, 227,
   231, 241, 242, 245, 291
language genesis 14, 18–21, 35, 41, 43,
   73, 74
language repertoire 124, 220
lectal continuum 95–98, 122, 130–132
lexicon 20, 34, 87, 98, 175–183, 196,
   227
lexifier language 19, 20, 42–44, 47–49,
   177
life cycle 43, 44, 58

lingua franca 34, 41, 109, 186, 188, 255,
   293, 308
linguistic competence 81, 91, 92, 102
linguistic pragmatism 201, 202
Low Variety 45, 98–102, 132

M
mesolect 35, 44, 45, 95, 97, 130, 157
metaphor 14, 40, 85, 93, 190
metathesis 165, 166
metonymy 191
migration 25, 36, 222, 273–277, 286,
   288
monolingualism 13, 79–82, 104
mosaic 207, 209, 212–214, 216, 217, 285
mother tongue 3, 6, 34, 41, 63, 117, 203,
   204, 210, 212–215, 221, 224, 270, 288,
   290, 293, 296, 299–306
multiculturalism 13, 25, 28, 29, 81, 82,
   94, 210, 214–217, 288, 293
multilingualism 13, 25, 28, 29, 81, 82,
   94, 210

N
narrowing 182–187, 199
nation-building 201, 207–212, 215–217,
   269
national identity 208, 209, 289, 293,
   300, 308, 309
native speaker 42, 44, 58, 70, 78, 80, 103,
   107, 113–117, 122, 130, 131, 196, 198,
   199, 246
nativization 11, 12, 188
neutral language 201, 204, 214, 306
normal transmission 19, 24, 31, 32, 35–
   39, 81, 91, 96, 99
noun 14, 16, 42, 47, 48, 53, 57, 65, 66,
   85, 86, 99, 100, 132, 133, 136, 139,
   143–149, 156, 157, 163–170, 214,
   230, 231, 236, 250, 272, 284, 305
nucleus 159, 160

O
onset 56, 159–161
outer circle 3, 6, 8, 11, 12